GW01086864

1988

Maj Gen P E de la Billière CBE DSO MC and Bar- KCB
Lt Col R Holworthy- OBE
Lt Col J W Parker- OBE
Maj (QM) R Burnett- MBE
CSjt J W Downie- BEM
Sjt W R Taylor- BEM
Lt A K Arkell- MID
CSjt B Greensill- MID
LCpl P R Marshall- MID
LCpl R C Munro- MID
LCpl D Wood- MID

1989

Maj Gen J D G Pank- CB
Maj T A Matthews- MBE
WO2 B A Goodson- BEM
Sjt H Richardson- BEM
Lt Col M H Philp- MID
Maj R M J Rollo-Walker- MID
Maj M S R Vincent- MID
WO2 J Boote- MID
Pte P K Kharikhou- MID

1990

WO2 (RQMS) W P Thornton- MBE
CSjt F Leck- BEM

1991

General Sir Peter de la Billière KCB CBE DSO MC & Bar- KBE
Brig J W Parker OBE- CBE
Maj P Bradley- MBE
Maj D W Eustace- MBE
Maj T J Gregson- MBE
Capt J M Chapman- MBE
Capt D J Wood- MC
CSjt M Small- BEM
Sjt J M Langelier- BEM
Lt Col R P Cousens- MID
Maj R C Lloyd-Williams- MID
Maj K A Oliver- MID
Capt T P Evans- MID
Cpl N Hartshorne- MID
Cpl S C Smith- MID
Bandsman J Bennett- MID
Bandsman (A/LCpl) P D Lawson- MID
Bandsman I Mair- MID

1992

Maj Gen A Makepeace-Warne MBE- CB
Col R V Brims- OBE
Lt Col R P Cousens- OBE

Lt Col R N R Jenkins- OBE
Maj T J Martin- MBE
Maj J H H York- MBE
Capt D J Wood MC- MBE
WO2 G Jenkinson- MBE
Maj A Amber- MID
Maj M J C Payne- MID
Maj G Whitmore- MID
WO2 P A Richardson- MID
LCpl G P Robinson- MID
Pte A R Thompson- MID

1993

Col N A King- OBE
Lt Col C M G Elcomb- OBE
Lt Colonel J K Marsham- OBE
Maj A M W Mortimer- MBE
Capt T Manley- MBE
Lt N Ilic- QGM
Capt M E A Wilson- MID
Lt I J O'Bryan- MID
WO2 J Hall- MID
WO2 T F Walker- MID
Sjt A P Abson- MID
Cpl A Dickson- MID
LCpl M Jones- MID

1994

Maj A Amber- MBE
Maj J P F R Bendall- MBE
Maj P C Luxton- MBE
Maj T B Radford - MBE
Lt Col M J W Grubb- QCVS
Maj D Wroe- QCVS

1995

Col T G French - OBE
Lt Col T F L Weeks- OBE
Capt T Marsh- MBE
WO2 A D Carter- MBE
CSjt N J James- MBE
Lt Col T F L Weeks OBE- QCVS
Maj C C S Booth- QCVS
Capt E J R Chamberlain- QCVS

1996

Maj Gen M D Regan OBE- CB
Lt Col B W Barry- OBE
Maj J P de Vos- MID
Pte M G Mitchell- MID

1997

Lt M J Turnbull- QCVS

1998

Maj P Davies- MBE

1999

Lt Gen J F Deverell OBE- KCB
Brig R V Brims OBE- CBE
Lt Col T J Martin MBE- OBE
Lt Col L J C Anderson- MBE
Maj J W Hall- MBE
WO2 R Morris- QCVS

2000

Col D H R Stephenson- CBE
Lt Col (Retd) R G Woodhouse- MBE
Maj L J Collins- MBE
Maj E P Davies- MBE
Maj H E Shields- MBE
Capt J A D de Labillière- MBE
Capt D Wilson BEM- MBE
WO2 J W Legge- MBE
Cpl R B Finch- QCB
Major N Ilic QGM- QCVS
WO2 J Brum QGM- QCVS

2001

Lt Col A M W Mortimer- OBE
Lt Col T P Evans- MBE
Maj C Lawton- MBE
Maj T D McMurtrie- MBE
Capt P J Fox- MBE
Maj Gen R V Brims CBE- QCVS
Col T J Gregson MBE- QCVS
CSjt D M Sainsbury- QCVS
CSjt S P Wilkinson- QCVS

2002

Col R R Smith- OBE
Maj T D McMurtrie MBE- OBE
WO2 V J Williams- MBE
Maj T D McMurtrieMBE- QCVS

2003

Maj Gen R V Brims CBE- DSO
Lt Col P A Kellett- OBE
Maj M R Goldsack- MBE
Maj T J Roper- MBE
Maj M H L Whistler- MBE
Capt D Wroe- MBE
WO2 A Garner- MBE
Sjt A D Curson- MID
Cpl P J Helliker- MID
LCpl D T Ridley- MID
Maj R G Arundell- QCVS
Maj J H Bowron- QCVS
WO2 S Priddle- QVRM

2004

Col (Retd) D K W Farrant- MBE
Maj M Bonner- MBE
Maj K C Hickman- MID
WO2 J M Waite- MID
LCpl D M Dimmock- MID
LCpl S P Smith- MID
Sgt D M Budden- QCB
LCpl D A Jones- QCB
Lt ColG P Chambers- QCVS
Lt ColW J Pointing- QCVS
CSjt S S G Fenton- QCVS
Maj P D Griffiths- QVRM

2005

Maj J H Bowron- DSO
Lt ColA T D Lerwill- OBE
Maj R A Noble- MBE
Sgt A D Kuss- MID
Cpl A M Wilson- MID
Pte B T Ludbrook- MID
Lt ColH E Shields MBE- QCVS
Maj M E Thornton- QCVS
Brig R R Smith OBE- Bronze Star (US)

2006

The Light Infantry awarded:
Theatre Honour IRAQ 2003
Battle Honour AL BASRAH

Col P R Sharland- CBE
A/Col N Welch- OBE
Lt Col J H Bowron DSO- OBE
Lt Col M R Goldsack MBE- OBE
Maj N Ilic QGM- MBE
Maj H L Kennedy- MBE
Capt D Crook- MBE
Capt M J Dicks- MBE
Lt (A/Capt) T H Illingworth- CGC
Maj R A Head- MC
LCpl N A T Coleman- MC
Cpl S A Houston- QCB
Lt Gen R V Brims CBE DSO- LoM (US)

2007

Lt Gen R V Brims CBE DSO- CB
Col E P Davies MBE- CBE
Lt Col S C D Mills- OBE
Lt Col T B Radford MBE- OBE
Lt Col M E Thornton- OBE
Capt T H Wilson-Hutton-Stott- MBE

'Second to None'

A Portrait of The Light Infantry 1968–2007

Faithful

Cede Nullis

Auctore Splendore Resurgo

'Second to None'

A Portrait of The Light Infantry 1968–2007

GENERAL EDITOR
Colonel Mark Goldsack OBE

With a Preface by **HRH Princess Alexandra KG, GCVO**
Colonel-in-Chief of The Light Infantry 2002–2007,
Deputy Colonel-in-Chief 1968–2002

Foreword by **Lieutenant General Robin Brims CB, CBE, DSO**

THIRD MILLENNIUM
PUBLISHING, LONDON

Editor's Note

'There are nine and sixty ways of writing tribal lays and every single one of them is right'.

– Rudyard Kipling

The formation of The Rifles on 1 February 2007 marked the end of nearly four decades of exceptional service to the Nation by The Light Infantry. This was no ordinary Regiment and no ordinary story. It was a story that had to be told. It was clear that we were blessed with considerable resources for the task: Antony Makepeace-Warne's *Exceedingly Lucky* provides a detailed and thorough history of the period 1968–1993; there is the magnificent Photographic Archive that has been put together by Ron Berry; The *Silver Bugle* provides a rolling commentary of the activities of the Regiment through the whole life of The Light Infantry; John Wykeham's editorship of a variety of Regimental pamphlets, *The Light Infantry Handbook*, and *Leading Light* all captured much of our DNA; we also have an enormous resource in the various county museums and of course The Light Infantry Museum and Archive have now been established in Bodmin. On top of all this a vast number of Light Infantrymen of all ranks have contributed vignettes, tales, memorabilia, articles, memoirs and photographs. One day if anyone cares to write a more formal history of The Light Infantry an extensive stockpile of information will be found on which to draw.

The real question posed was how best to turn the contribution of The Light Infantry into an enduring monument. The Light Infantry Committee settled on two legacy projects – the Memorial at The National Arboretum and a book that covered the whole life of the Regiment. In 2009 I agreed to pull together the book, written by Light Infantrymen, which would attempt to capture something of the flavour of the Regiment. The result is this book. It is not a traditional history: rather, as its name suggests, it is a portrait of what it got up to. The end result has I hope captured the soul of the Regiment. Precisely because it is a portrait it is not definitive, and the major challenge has been not what to include but what to leave out – even accounting for those lively contributions that cruised, if not actually crossed, the boundaries of law, sound morals and good taste!

I am grateful to those, too numerous to mention by name, who have helped in all areas, from providing articles and photographs for insertion in the chapters, conducting research, proof-reading and corrections, to ensuring that The Light Infantry family has been kept fully abreast of progress via the various regimental websites that have proved an invaluable means of communication. Thanks are also due to many others who have given help and advice, including Trevor Stipling from the Archives and the Museum and Andy Foster from RHQ.

As editor I thank especially Ted Shields, Mike Thornton, Toby Evans, Ian Baker, James Hardy, Ben Barry, Andy Child and Dickie Head for all their help so freely given, not only in compiling chapters but also in taking on a myriad of tasks that meant, working together with Chris Fagg, Matt Wilson, Neil Burkey and Bonnie Murray from Third Millennium Publishing, we were able to assemble the book and meet our (revised) publication date. As General Editor I accept complete responsibility for any errors or omissions.

This then is the portrait of the Regiment. I hope it captures something of the ethos and spirit of The Light Infantry and describes something of what we bequeath to The Rifles, where all that was best in The Light Infantry is being melded with the best of the other joining regiments to forge in the heat of operations a Regiment that has established the finest of reputations in the British Army.

Contents

Preface: **HRH Princess Alexandra**   6

Foreword: **Robin Brims, Lieutenant General**   8

Part 1:   **FOUNDATION AND TIMELINE: 1670–1968**   10

From Light Companies to Light Infantry **12** / Timeline **14** /
The Light Infantry 1968–2007 **22**

Part 2:   **THE BATTALIONS**   26

The First Battalion **28** / The Second Battalion **50** / The Third
Battalion **72** / The Fourth Battalion **92** / The Volunteer
Battalions **96** / The First Battalion, The Royal Gloucestershire,
Berkshire and Wiltshire Light Infantry **110** / The First Battalion,
The Devonshire and Dorset Light Infantry **113**

Part 3:   **THE WIDER REGIMENT**   116

Training **118** / Regimental Headquarters **128** / The Bands and
Bugles **136** / The Regiment's Cadets **140**

Part 4:   **COMBAT OPERATIONS**   142

Mauritius **144** / Cyprus **147** / Northern Ireland **150**
Airmobility **154** / The Balkans **157** / Sierra Leone **161**
Iraq **164** / Afghanistan **169**

Part 5:   **THE WAY AHEAD**   172

Forming The Rifles **174**

Appendix   182
List of Subscribers   185
Index   188
Acknowledgements   192

I am pleased to learn that a Portrait of the Regiment has been written covering the period 1968-2007.

This book covers many significant national events surrounding the story of the The Light Infantry and touching the lives of all those who have served in every part of the Regiment.

I am proud to acknowledge the sacrifice of those who lost their lives while serving in The Light Infantry and of those who were wounded in the service of our Nation.

During its existence, The Light Infantry set a standard of service that was second to none and in setting that standard has bequeathed a magnificent inheritance to The Rifles.

Alexandra

HRH Princess Alexandra
Colonel-in-Chief (2002-2007)
Deputy Colonel-in-Chief (1968-2002)

Foreword

The need to innovate and adapt were made very clear by Sir John Moore. The Light Infantry adopted his principles from its formation in 1968 to the point of joining with others to create The Rifles in 2007. That The Light Infantry also placed such great importance on the individual and his freedom of thought and action sometimes makes change difficult to accept, but innovation and adaptation are the creators of change.

This portrait of The Light Infantry is as much about people and places as anything else. The success of The Light Infantry was based on our people and the deep roots in our home places: our Counties. It was these vital ingredients that sustained us through the long operation in Northern Ireland, the seemingly endless Cold War and its successor operations consequent on a new world order.

The four pillars of The Light Infantry – Regular, TA, Cadets and Association – also played a crucial role in helping us adapt as we grew at one stage to three Regular battalions, four TA battalions, 11 Army and 20 Combined Cadet Units, and 54 Association branches – all of which made us the largest General Service infantry regiment.

As someone who joined The Light Infantry in 1970 and was still serving when we amalgamated with others to become The Rifles it gives me great pleasure to write this Foreword. I trust that the readers will find in the book human accounts that will prompt memories and bring people together again in friendship. It will, I hope, also form a baseline for historians in the future – although the emphasis is on the stories about individuals and their service.

As we recall the happier memories and moments, we must never forget the sacrifice of the 46 Light Infantrymen who were killed in action. They and their families have paid the ultimate sacrifice. Others will need our help due to wounds, seen and unseen, that are the unhappy co-travellers of soldiers. We stuck together as individuals in action; so we stick together in retirement.

I commend this book about an Exceedingly Lucky Regiment. It was good – and great fun.

Robin Brims, Lieutenant General
Durham, August 2010

Opposite: Light Division Chapel windows, Sir John Moore Barracks, Winchester.

Below: HQ 1 UK Armoured Division during the invasion of Iraq, 2003 – The Light Infantry contingent! Left to right: Capt James Faux, Lt Col Tim Radford, Maj Gen Robin Brims, Maj Mark Goldsack, Capt Nick Cole and LCpl Poat.

IN MEMORY OF THOSE
MEMBERS OF THE
LIGHT INFANTRY
WHO DIED IN THE SERVICE
OF THEIR COUNTRY

ROLL OF HONOUR

The Roll of Honour records the names of all those members of The Light Infantry who have died whilst on operations since 1968. The names of all those who have died whilst serving are recorded in The Light Infantry Book of Remembrance held in The Light Division Chapel, Sir John Moore Barracks, Winchester.

Private B K KANNAN	11 August 1968	Cyprus
Private P K EASTAUGH	23 March 1971	Northern Ireland
Private J R RUDMAN	15 September 1971	Northern Ireland
Private R V JONES	18 August 1972	Northern Ireland
Serjeant A B WHITELOCK	24 August 1972	Northern Ireland
Private R ROWE	28 August 1972	Northern Ireland
Corporal I R MORRILL	28 August 1972	Northern Ireland
Private T A STOKER	19 September 1972	Northern Ireland
Private T RUDMAN	30 September 1972	Northern Ireland
Lance Corporal A KENNINGTON	28 February 1973	Northern Ireland
Corporal T P TAYLOR	13 May 1973	Northern Ireland
Private J GASKELL	14 May 1973	Northern Ireland
Private R B ROBERTS	1 July 1973	Northern Ireland
Lance Corporal R MILLER	18 September 1973	Northern Ireland
Private S R HALL	28 October 1973	Northern Ireland
Captain N C T LORING	6 January 1975	Oman
Private K B ROSS	24 March 1976	Cyprus
Private R D TURNBULL	29 June 1977	Northern Ireland
Private M E HARRISON	29 June 1977	Northern Ireland
Private L J HARRISON	9 August 1977	Northern Ireland
Private R J F McLAUGHLIN	3 February 1979	Cyprus
Private R STAFFORD	21 July 1979	Northern Ireland
Private P A BOWES	13 March 1982	Cyprus
Corporal D P SALTHOUSE	6 December 1982	Northern Ireland
Private G M CURTIS	10 June 1983	Northern Ireland
Private N I BLYTHE	12 November 1987	Northern Ireland
Private J J WILLBY	6 February 1988	Northern Ireland
Private B BISHOP	20 August 1988	Northern Ireland
Private P L BULLOCK	20 August 1988	Northern Ireland
Private J BURFITT	20 August 1988	Northern Ireland
Private R GREENER	20 August 1988	Northern Ireland
Private A S LEWIS	20 August 1988	Northern Ireland
Private M A NORSWORTHY	20 August 1988	Northern Ireland
Private S J WILKINSON	20 August 1988	Northern Ireland
Private J WINTER	20 August 1988	Northern Ireland
Private G SMITH	3 December 1988	Northern Ireland
Corporal S WRAY	22 July 1992	Belize
Private P TURNER	28 August 1992	Northern Ireland
Private S L FOX	28 February 1996	Bosnia
Private A J RICHARDSON	12 March 1997	Northern Ireland
Lance Corporal P D T THOMAS	17 August 2004	Iraq
LCpl S SHERWOOD	29 October 2005	Afghanistan
LCpl P CRADDOCK	27 March 2006	Afghanistan
Corporal J J COSBY	6 July 2006	Iraq
Corporal M CORNISH	1 August 2006	Iraq
Private M A TENCH	21 January 2007	Iraq

THE LIGHT INFANTRY COLLECT

O God, who requirest that thy servants be found faithful, grant to us of The Light Infantry the spirit of unity and brotherly love, so that we may ever be ready to give swift obedience to thy call, yielding to none in giving glory to thee, through Jesus Christ Our Lord.

PART 1

Foundation and Timeline: 1670–1968

From Light Companies to Light Infantry
The Story of The Bugle Horn

Armies have always had to adapt their methods of fighting and their equipment to the type of country in which they might be required to operate. On the plains and along the river valleys of Europe, where visibility could be measured at least in hundreds of yards, battles for several centuries after the introduction of firearms tended to be fought by infantry in close order.

When, however, the British Army found itself fighting against the French and their Native American allies in the wilderness of North America, conditions were very different. It was clearly necessary to meet and beat the enemy at his own game, and to this end one company in each regiment was organised on a lighter, more mobile scale than the rest. These 'light companies' were the first light infantry, and from 1770 onwards every foot regiment included one in its establishment.

Our forces in America included contingents of Hanoverian and Hessian troops, and some of them had adopted the Prussian practice of organising special units of *Jäeger*, consisting of men from the German and Austrian forests skilled in the arts of the chase. Their ancestors had succeeded in extracting huntsmanlike sounds from the horn of the bugle, the wild ox that at one time abounded in the forests of Europe. As time went on, 'bugle horns' were shaped from metal (those with silver in them gave the sweetest note), and the bugle horn also became a badge to identify those connected with hunting in its various forms. The British Army probably had its first experience of both horn and badge from the German troops sent out to North America during the Seven Years War.

The bugle horn, easily carried, and sonorous and penetrating in sound, was the ideal replacement for the drum, and it was unofficially adopted to an increasing extent in the light companies. By the end of the century a number of 'Field Sounds' were in use, among them 'March', 'Extend', 'Run', 'Lie Down', 'Arise', 'Form Indian File', 'Skirmish', 'Pursue the Enemy', and so on. Indeed there were so many Sounds that the unmusical must have been hard put to it to remember them all.

Thus the bugle horn became by degrees a distinctive feature of the light companies, and increasingly it was used as a sign or badge to distinguish them from the other companies in the regiment. This did not always make for harmony, because sometimes the members of the light company tended to give themselves airs. It is on record that when the 32nd Foot (later to become the 1st Battalion **The Duke of Cornwall's**

Previous pages:
Battle of Salamanca,
22 July 1812.

Left: The statue
of Sir John Moore,
during the early years
at Sir John Moore
Barracks, Winchester.

Light Infantry) landed at Lisbon in 1811 to come under the Duke of Wellington's command, some of the officers of the light company, sporting their bugle horn badge, were asked by the local inhabitants if they belonged to the band, a misapprehension that the remainder of the regiment did not allow the light company to forget in a hurry.

As the Army became more and more deeply committed in the struggle against Napoleon it became evident to the more farsighted that the time had come to establish a separate Corps of Light Infantry. The first regiment selected for this role was the 52nd Foot, of which Sir John Moore was Colonel, and in July 1803, the 52nd Light Infantry joined a brigade of troops, which also included the 95th (Rifle) Regiment, that was being assembled at Shorncliffe to receive light infantry training under the direction of Sir John Moore himself. The brigade was joined a year later by the 43rd, whose application to convert to light infantry had been approved by the Commander-in-Chief. It was these three regiments, the 43rd, the 52nd and the 95th, equipped with the Baker rifle, that formed the hard core of the Light Division that so distinguished itself during the Peninsular War under the Duke of Wellington. All were subsequently incorporated in The Royal Green Jackets, who themselves became incorporated into The Rifles in 2007.

Sir John Moore was a great trainer of troops, and that he set store by the use of the bugle is shown from an instruction that he issued when commanding troops in Ireland at an earlier date:

'The same sounds must be taught to the bugles of the three battalions – and the men made familiar with them – for tho' in common the voice is, I think, to be preferred, yet in many cases the bugle alone can be used.'

Below: It can be seen that although the wild ox or bugle may be extinct, his horn is very vigorously alive, and with the formation of The Rifles in 2007, a new chapter of its long and distinguished association with The Light Infantry has now been opened.

Five years later the 68th (later the 1st Battalion **The Durham Light Infantry**) and the 85th (later the 2nd Battalion **The King's Shropshire Light Infantry**) were converted.

Before the end of the Napoleonic Wars two more regiments had submitted requests to become light infantry: the 71st Highlanders and the 51st Foot. A letter from the Horse Guards stated that 'His Majesty had been pleased to approve of the

51st Regiment being immediately formed into a Light Infantry Corps upon the same plan as the 43rd, 52nd, 68th, 71st and 85th Regiments'. This was a particularly happy choice because it was in the 51st that Sir John Moore had obtained his first commission and from 1790 to 1796 he had commanded the Regiment as its Lieutenant-Colonel. Later it became the 1st Battalion, **The King's Own Yorkshire Light Infantry**.

In 1814 came official recognition of a practice by then well established 'by sufferance' if not 'by order':

'His Royal Highness the Prince Regent having been pleased to command that the Caps of the Rifle and Light Infantry Corps and the Rifle and Light Infantry Companies of Regiments shall have a Bugle Horn with the number of the Regiment below it instead of the Brass Plate worn by the rest of the Infantry.'

Be this as it may, the badges adopted by the 43rd, 52nd and 68th Light Infantry bore a striking resemblance to each other, and they evolved with little change into the badges of **The Oxfordshire and Buckinghamshire Light Infantry** and **The Durham Light Infantry**. The 85th Light Infantry followed suit, as can be seen in the later badge of **The King's Shropshire Light Infantry**. The leopard's face in the badge, the emblem of Shropshire, records the union, in 1881, of the 53rd (Shropshire) Regiment and the 85th (then The King's Light Infantry). The 71st and, a few years after their conversion to light infantry, the 51st, fell to the rival attractions of the French hunting horn, as is apparent from the badges of **The Highland Light Infantry** and **The King's Own Yorkshire Light Infantry**.

The Light Infantry family received several additions during the following century. In 1822 the 13th Foot applied to become light infantry and when, in 1842, they were authorised to bear on their colours and appointments 'a Mural Crown superscribed Jellalabad' the Bugle Horn and Crown were combined in one badge, afterwards that of **The Somerset Light Infantry**.

In 1859, the 32nd Foot was, by order of Her Majesty Queen Victoria, directed to be 'clothed, equipped and trained as a Light Infantry Regiment' in consideration 'of the enduring fortitude and persevering gallantry displayed in the defence of the Residency of Lucknow' during the Indian Mutiny. Their Bugle Horn found its way in due course into the badge of **The Duke of Cornwall's Light Infantry**, backed by the red patch which was carried forward in the cap badge of **The Light Infantry**, and about which there will be more to say later.

At its peak The Light Infantry numbered seven regiments, each of two regular battalions and numerous territorial ones, but in their existing form they could not all survive the reorganisation that was initiated in 1957. **The Somerset Light Infantry** amalgamated with **The Duke of Cornwall's Light Infantry** to form **The Somerset and Cornwall Light Infantry**, and this left four regiments to take their place in the new Light Infantry Brigade. It was these that merged in 1968 to become **The Light Infantry**, whose story is told in this book.

LIGHT INFANTRY BADGES

THE LIGHT INFANTRY
A Bugle Horn, stringed in silver.

**THE SOMERSET LIGHT INFANTRY
(PRINCE ALBERT'S)**

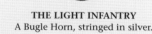

**THE DUKE OF CORNWALL'S
LIGHT INFANTRY**

THE SOMERSET AND CORNWALL LIGHT INFANTRY
A Bugle Horn, stringed, ensigned with a mural crown, all in silver.
Between the strings of the bugle horn a red patch.

**THE KING'S OWN YORKSHIRE
LIGHT INFANTRY**
within a French Hunting Horn,
a Pomme thereon the White Rose.
Motto: Cede Nullis (*Yield to none*)

**THE KING'S SHROPSHIRE
LIGHT INFANTRY**
within a Bugle Horn,
stringed, a leopard's face.
Motto: Aucto Splendore Resurgo
(*I rise again with increased splendour*)

THE DURHAM LIGHT INFANTRY
within a Bugle Horn, stringed, the letters 'DLI'.

Timeline

SOMERSET LIGHT INFANTRY (PRINCE ALBERT'S) 13TH	**1685** *EARL OF HUNTINGDON'S REGIMENT FORMED*	**1689** *Battle of Killiecrankie*	**1690** *Battle of the Boyne*	**1704** *Siege of Gibraltar*	**1743** *Battle of Dettingen Battle of Fontenoy*	**1746** *Battle of Culloden*

DUKE OF CORNWALL'S LIGHT INFANTRY 32ND AND 46TH				**1702** *REDESIGNATED AS 32ND (FOX'S MARINES)*	**1704** *Siege of Gibraltar*	**1741** *REDESIGNATED AS 57TH FOOT (PRICE'S REGIMENT)*	**1743** *Battle of Dettingen*

KING'S OWN YORKSHIRE LIGHT INFANTRY 51ST AND 105TH

Left: The Earl of Huntingdon.

Below: The Siege of Gibraltar.

KING'S SHROPSHIRE LIGHT INFANTRY 53RD AND 85TH

DURHAM LIGHT INFANTRY 68TH AND 106TH

1680

1751
*REDESIGNATED
AS 13TH (1ST
SOMERSETSHIRE)
REGIMENT OF
FOOT*

*Left: Uniforms of
the King's Shropshire
Light Infantry.*

1748
*46th (South
Devonshire) Foot in
North America*

1777
*Battle of Paoli. 2nd Light Infantry ambush an
American division. Red feathers worn by 42nd to
commemorate this, later incorporated as a red patch
behind The Light Infantry cap badge in 1968.*

1782
*32ND (THE
CORNWALL) FOOT*

1755
*RAISED AS 51ST
FOOT*

1756–63
Seven Years War

1759
Battle of Minden

1771–82
Battle of Minorca

1782
*51ST (2ND
YORKSHIRE, WEST
RIDING) FOOT*

1755
*RAISED AS 55TH
BY COLONEL
WILLIAM
WHATMORE*

1757
*RENUMBERED
53RD
(SHROPSHIRE)
FOOT*

1759
*85TH (BUCKS
VOLUNTEERS)
RAISED IN
SHREWSBURY*

1756–63
*In Europe during
Seven Years War;
disbanded following
sea disaster, 1763*

1773
*Raised again for duty
in the West Indies*

1775–83
*American War of
Independence*

1782
*RENAMED 53RD
(SHROPSHIRE)
REGIMENT*

1758
*68TH FOOT
RAISED*

1764
*Antigua and St
Vincent*

1770
*Company of Light
Infantry raised in
North America from
68th*

1782
*68TH (DURHAM)
FOOT*

Above: The Battle of Culloden, 1746.

1782

Left: Maj Gen Sir John Moore (1761–1809). Recognized as the father of Light Infantry training in the British Army, Moore commanded successively the 51st, the 56th and then the British Army in Spain against Napoleon. He died at the siege of Corunna, Spain, by French forces under Marshal Soult and in a simple ceremony was buried, wrapped in a military cloak, in the ramparts of the town. After British forces were evacuated by sea, Soult took care of Moore's grave and ordered a monument to be raised in his memory.

SOMERSET LIGHT INFANTRY (PRINCE ALBERT'S) 13TH

1801
Battle of Aboukir Bay

1808–9
West Indies and Canada

DUKE OF CORNWALL'S LIGHT INFANTRY 32ND AND 46TH

1808–15
Peninsula; France

KING'S OWN YORKSHIRE LIGHT INFANTRY 51ST AND 105TH

1790
Ireland; Gibraltar; Corsica; Sir John Moore Commanding Officer

1796
Sir John Moore promoted to Brigadier General

**1809
REDESIGNATED AS LIGHT INFANTRY CORPS**

Battle of Lugo; Siege of Corunna

1811
*Badajoz: Ensign Joseph Dyas (**above right**) twice leads the Forlorn Hope of the 51st to storm the breach at San Cristobel Fort.*

1812
Fuentes d'Onor, Salamanca, Vittona, Badajoz

KING'S SHROPSHIRE LIGHT INFANTRY 53RD AND 85TH

1783
Disbanded following sea disaster

1789
Returned from North America

1793
Re-raised

1793–7
War against French Republic; Nieuport; Tournay; Santa Lucia; 2nd Battalion formed

**1809
REDESIGNATED AS LIGHT INFANTRY IN PENINSULA**

1814
To North America, part of the force which captured and burnt Washington

DURHAM LIGHT INFANTRY 68TH AND 106TH

**1808
68TH DESIGNATED A LIGHT INFANTRY REGIMENT**

1811
In Portugal with Wellington

1812
Salamanca

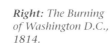

1813
Vittoria

Right: The Burning of Washington D.C., 1814.

Left: A Sergeant from the 68th Foot (Durham Light Infantry), 1815.

1783

1822
*REDESIGNATED
13TH LIGHT
INFANTRY*

1839–42
*First Afghan War;
Ghuznee; Jellalabad*

1851–5
Gibraltar

1853–6
Crimean War

1857–8
Indian Mutiny

1881
*PRINCE ALBERT'S
(SOMERSET) LIGHT
INFANTRY LATER
REDESIGNATED THE
SOMERSET LIGHT
INFANTRY (PRINCE
ALBERT'S)*

1815
Waterloo

1848–9
*32nd in India: Second
Sikh War*

1854
*Crimea: Alma
Balaclava
Inkerman*

1857
Indian Mutiny

1858
Siege of Lucknow

1881
*1ST AND 2ND
BATTALIONS DUKE
OF CORNWALL'S
LIGHT INFANTRY*

1882
2nd Battalion to Egypt

1815
Waterloo

**1821
RENAMED AS
KING'S OWN
LIGHT INFANTRY**

1852
*2nd Burmese War:
Battle of Pegu*

1870s
Second Afghan War

1878
*105th Foot from
Madras*

**1881
KING'S OWN
(SOUTH YORKSHIRE
REGIMENT) LIGHT
INFANTRY**

**105TH (MADRAS
LIGHT INFANTRY)
BECAME 2ND BN**

1885
1st Battalion in Burma

**1821
RENAMED AS THE
KING'S LIGHT
INFANTRY**

1878–9
Second Afghan War

**1881
THE KING'S
SHROPSHIRE
LIGHT INFANTRY
(53RD & 85TH)**

1885
1st Battalion in Sudan

1814
*Pyrenees; Nivelle;
Ortez*

1815–55
*Garrison duties;
Canada*

1853–56
Crimean War

1854
Battle of Inkerman

1864
New Zealand

**1881
REDESIGNATED
AS 1ST BATTALION
THE DURHAM
LIGHT INFANTRY**

**106TH (BOMBAY
LIGHT INFANTRY)
BECAME 2ND BN**

1887
*2nd Bn in India
where they dominated
the polo scene from
1890–99*

Left: *Men of the
68th Light Infantry
from the Crimean
War, 1855.*

1885

Left: An Irish Eviction, 1886. It was necessary to obtain the assistance of the Army in order to effect the eviction of one of Lord Clanricarde's tenants from his house at Woodford. Two hundred men from Prince Albert's Somersetshire Light Infantry, under Maj Kinloch, assist the civil authorities.

SOMERSET LIGHT INFANTRY (PRINCE ALBERT'S) 13TH

1914–18
19 Battalions raised; Marne, Aisne, Ypres, Hooge, Somme, Albert, Arras, Cambrai, Palestine, Tigris, Mesopotamia; 2nd Bn on North West Frontier

1919
Third Afghan War

DUKE OF CORNWALL'S LIGHT INFANTRY 32ND AND 46TH

1889
2nd Battalion to the Boer War

1900
Paardeberg

1914–18
15 Battalions raised; Mons, Marne, Ypres, Somme, Arras, Passchendaele, Cambrai, Sambre, Doiran, Gaza

KING'S OWN YORKSHIRE LIGHT INFANTRY 51ST AND 105TH

1899–1902
2nd Battalion to the Boer War

1914–18
13 Bns raised; Mons, Le Cateau, Messines, Ypres, Somme, Cambrai, Havrincourt, Sambre, Italy, Macedonia

1915
1st Bn in France, then Salonika

1918
1st Bn in France; 1st Bn in Mesopotamia; 1st Bn Germany

KING'S SHROPSHIRE LIGHT INFANTRY 53RD AND 85TH

1894
1st Bn in Hong Kong; 2nd Bn served in South Africa throughout the war reinforced by Rifle Volunteer Corps from Shropshire and Herefordshire

1908
Volunteer forces re-formed as 4th Bn The King's Shropshire Light Infantry and 1st Bn The Herefordshire Regiment

1914–18
15 Battalions raised, 9 in action; Armentières, Ypres, Frezenberg, Somme, Arras, Cambrai, Bligny, Epehy, Doiran, Jerusalem; Hong Kong, Singapore, Macedonia, Palestine, Egypt, Gallipoli

1918
1st/4th receive Croix de Guerre for action at Battle of Bligny

1918–39
1st/2nd Regular bns; Two TA bns: 4th Bn The King's Shropshire Light Infantry and 1st Bn The Herefordshire Regiment; 1st Bn in India; 2nd in England, Germany and West Indies

DURHAM LIGHT INFANTRY 68TH AND 106TH

1899–1902
1st Bn in India, England, Ireland, South Africa

1908
Volunteer Rifle Corps reformed as 5th, 6th, 7th, 8th, 9th Territorial Bns The Durham Light Infantry

1914–18
37 Battalions raised; Aisne, Ypres, Hooge, Loos, Somme, Arras, Messines, Lys, Hindenburg Line, Sambre; 1st Bn in India

1919
Third Afghan War

1918–39
1st Bn in India, Afghanistan, Germany, Silesia, England, Northern Ireland and China; 2nd Bn in Turkey, India, China, the Sudan and England

Left: The Durham Light Infantry Militia at the Cape, 1900.

1886

Left: Battle of Menin Road Ridge, digging out wounded from 13th Durham Light Infantry Regimental Aid Post blown up by shell. Near Zillebeke, 20 September 1917.

1939–45
Hill 112, Mont Pincon, Rhineland, Rhine, North West Europe 1944–5, Cassino II, Cosina Canal Crossing, Italy 1944–5, North Arakan, Ngakyedauk Pass; 2nd Bn in Gibraltar, 1st in India against Afghan tribesmen

1944
2nd Bn in Italy for final Battle of Cassino; 4th and 7th Bns (part of 43rd (Wessex) Division) fight from Normandy to Germany; 10th Bn converted to 7th (Light Infantry) Bn The Parachute Regiment in action on D-Day

1945
2nd Bn in Greece; 2nd Bn in Austria

1939–45
Hill 112, Mont Pincon, Nederrijn, Geilenkirchen, Rhineland, North West Europe 1944–5, Gazala, Medjez Plain, Cassino II, Incontro; 2nd Bn to France with BEF, Dunkirk, North Africa, Italy

1945
Greece

1924–35
England then 1935 Gibraltar

1922–47
2nd Bn to India; in Burma in 1942

1939–45
5 KOYLI and 8 KOYLI as Light AA Regiments; 7 KOYLI as Royal Armoured Corps regiment; 9 KOYLI formed from The Yorkshire Dragoons; 1st Bn in France, Norway, India, Iraq, Persia, Syria then Sicily and up through Italy with the 8th Army then Palestine; 1st/4th and 2nd/4th Bns in Norway, France, North Africa, Italy and Greece; Anzio, Fontenay le Pesnil, North West Europe 1944–5, Argoub Sellah, Sicily, Salerno, Minturno, Gemmano Ridge, Burma

1945
1st Bn in Europe

1939–45
1st Bn with BEF in France, part of rearguard covering withdrawal from Dunkirk, Normandy Landing, Antwerp, Venraij, Hochwald, Bremen, North West Europe 1944–5, Tunis, Anzio, Italy

1942
2nd Bn in England

1943
1st Bn in Tunisia, then Italy

1944
Anzio

1944
2nd Bn in Normandy on D-Day; followed by two TA Bns; all fought through to Germany

1936
7th converted to AA role; 7th to a searchlight regiment

1939–45
18 Bns raised; 1st Bn in Western Desert, Mediterranean and Italy; 2nd Bn at Dunkirk then Burma; Tilly sur Seulles, Defence of Rauray, Gheel, Tobruk, El Alamein, Mareth, Primosole Bridge, Salerno, Kohima

1944
Five bns in Normandy; Bns fought at Knightsbridge, El Alamein, Mareth, Mersa Matruh, Sicily, Primosole Bridge, Rauray, Salerno and Camino

Right: Men of 'A' Company, 6th Durham Light Infantry, 50th Division, in the village of Douet, 11 June 1944.

1945

Right: 1st Bn Somerset Light Infantry, the last British battalion to leave India, 1948.

SOMERSET LIGHT INFANTRY (PRINCE ALBERT'S) 13TH	1947 *TA Bn re-formed*	1948 *1st Bn leave India*	1950 *1st and 2nd amalgamated to 1st Battalion*	1950–9 *1st in Germany, Malaysia and Cyprus*		
DUKE OF CORNWALL'S LIGHT INFANTRY 32ND AND 46TH				1959 *AMALGAMATED WITH SOMERSET LI AS SOMERSET AND CORNWALL LI* *1st Bn (regular) in Osnabruck; two TA bns(4th/5th Bn The Somerset LI (TA); 4th/5th Bn The Duke of Cornwall's LI(TA). Regimental Depot at Bodmin, Regimental HQ at Taunton*		
KING'S OWN YORKSHIRE LIGHT INFANTRY 51ST AND 105TH	1946 *In Minden for Minden Day*	1947 *2nd Bn in Malaysia*	1948 *1st Bn suspended; 2nd Bn now 1st Bn The King's Own Yorkshire Light Infantry (51st and 105th)*	1951 *1st Bn in England then Germany*	1952–3 *Kenya against the Mau Mau*	1955 *Aden*
KING'S SHROPSHIRE LIGHT INFANTRY 53RD AND 85TH	1946–7 *1st and 2nd Bns in Middle East*	1947 *Herefordshire Regiment re-named The Herefordshire Light Infantry*	1948 *1st and 2nd amalgamated to form new 1st Bn; moved to Hong Kong*	1950–3 *1st Bn longest serving infantry bn in Korean War*		
DURHAM LIGHT INFANTRY 68TH AND 106TH	1946 *1st Bn in Greece; 2nd Bn in India then Malaysia*	1948 *1st and 2nd Bns amalgamated to a new 1st Bn*	1949 *In Germany, then Korea, Egypt, England,Aden, Cyprus, Berlin, Hong Kong, Borneo*	1952 *2nd Bn raised: disbanded 1955; 1st Bn with UN Forces in Cyprus*		

Right: Lt Curtis VC (DCLI) showed great gallantry in attempting to rush a strongly held hill-top position on the Imjin River. Being wounded and rescued by his men, he nevertheless tried again to rush the position but was eventually killed in the attempt. He was commanding a platoon in 1st Bn Gloucestershire Regt in Korea, 1951.

1946

Right: Somerset and Cornwall Light Infantry New Colours presented, Gibraltar, 1962.

1959
AMALGAMATED WITH DUKE OF CORNWALL'S LI AS SOMERSET AND CORNWALL LI

1962
1st Bn SCLI receives Colours in Gibraltar; In West Berlin, Gravesend and Aden

1968
FORMS THE LIGHT INFANTRY

1956
Cyprus

1961–4
Malaysia, also Sarawak and Indonesia

1964
Part of Strategic Reserve Division (3rd)

1965–6
Aden

1967
Berlin

1968
FORMS THE LIGHT INFANTRY

1955–7
1st Bn in Kenya against Mau Mau; Malaysia and Mauritius

1968
FORMS THE LIGHT INFANTRY

1968
FORMS THE LIGHT INFANTRY

Right: An officer of the 1st Battalion, King's Shropshire Light Infantry, leads soldiers on a patrol through the dense bamboo of the Kenya forest, 1955.

1968

The Light Infantry 1968–2007
A Thumbnail History

Genesis and Vesting Day

The title of The Light Infantry was approved in l967 by HM The Queen. The Light Infantry Vesting Day took place on 10 July 1968 amalgamating the four regular Light Infantry regiments of The Somerset and Cornwall Light Infantry, The King's Own Yorkshire Light Infantry, The King's Shropshire Light Infantry, The Durham Light Infantry and The Light Infantry Volunteers. The Shropshire Light Infantry Depot at Shrewsbury became The Light Infantry Depot and the Regiment was grouped with The Royal Green Jackets in The Light Division. The Light Infantry deliberately structured itself on Vesting Day in a manner that embodied equally all the traditions and customs of the former regiments in all battalions. The silver bugle cap badge, drill from the 'at ease' position, rapid marching pace and green beret bear testimony to the Regiment's ancestry. Key distinctions of dress were also carried forward: red backing for the cap badge from the DCLI, sashes tied to the right from the SCLI, The Inkerman

SPECIAL ORDER OF THE DAY
BY
GENERAL SIR GEOFFREY MUSSON, K.C.B., C.B.E., D.S.O.
COLONEL, THE LIGHT INFANTRY.

On this day, we form as The Light Infantry and combine into one Regiment the traditions of all the old Light Infantry Regiments.

I am confident that those now serving in The Light Infantry will give to the new Regiment the loyal service that they have given to their Regiments in the past and thus enhance still further the proud heritage and traditions which were begun by Sir John Moore some one hundred and sixty years ago.

To all Light Infantrymen in all parts of the world I send my very best wishes for their future and that of The Light Infantry.

Geoffrey Musson.

General,
Colonel, The Light Infantry

Left: Colonel-in-Chief HM Queen Elizabeth, The Queen Mother, as Duchess of York.

chain from the DLI and white roses on Minden Day from the KOYLI. The Regiment also had the distinction of being excused from drinking a Loyal Toast – a privilege inherited from both the KSLI and the DLI. The primary Regimental Day was 22 July, the anniversary of the Battle of Salamanca (1812), a battle in which all the former regiments fought. The Light Infantry was intensely proud to have as its first Colonel-in-Chief Her Majesty Queen Elizabeth The Queen Mother who was succeeded on her death by Her Royal Highness Princess Alexandra who had taken on the mantle of Deputy Colonel-in-Chief from Vesting Day. Vesting Day was the culmination of a series of events that had started in1934 when The Light Infantry Club was formed as a vehicle to develop a close association between all Light infantry Officers. This was followed in 1951 with the formation of The Light Infantry Brigade. In 1957 the Defence

Right: 4th Battalion The Light Infantry on Vesting Day in Cyprus, 10 July 1968.

White Paper started the process that would significantly reduce Britain's large conventional forces and end conscription. The outcome for The Light Infantry Brigade on 6 October 1959 was the reduction by one battalion. This was achieved by the amalgamation of The Somerset Light Infantry (Prince Albert's) and The Duke of Cornwall's Light Infantry, to form The Somerset and Cornwall Light Infantry. The Light Infantry Brigade was reduced by a further battalion in November 1958 when The Oxfordshire and Buckinghamshire Light Infantry joined The Green Jacket Brigade. In 1966 The Territorial Army was disbanded and reformed the following day as The Territorial Army and Volunteer Reserve. In July 1967 The Light Infantry Volunteers was formed. By 1967 it had become clear that national economic difficulties would require a further reduction in the Infantry. The Army Board settled on forming Divisions of Infantry. The Light Infantry Brigade would be grouped with The Green Jacket Brigade in The Light Division and in doing so The Light Infantry Brigade would be required to reduce by one battalion. The Council of Light Infantry Colonels accepted reluctantly that if required to reduce the mechanism would be to form a large regiment first and then reduce by one battalion.

The Early Years: 1968–78

On formation the 1st Battalion (1LI) was in Gravesend, the 2nd Battalion (2LI) was in Berlin – at that time a divided city – the 3rd Battalion (3LI) was based at Terendak Camp near Malacca in Malaysia as part of 28 Commonwealth Brigade, with companies detached on internal security duties in Mauritius, and the 4th Battalion (4LI) was in Cyprus as part of the United Nations Force in Cyprus (UNFICYP). The early years of The Light Infantry saw a constant draw on all battalions to deploy at short notice on emergency tours of Northern Ireland. 3LI was the first battalion deployed shortly

followed onto the streets by both 1LI and 2LI. Elements of all three battalions were involved in The Battle of the Shankill in Belfast in October 1969. Other operational commitments over the period saw 3LI in Mauritius, 2LI in the Far East and multiple deployments on UN duties as part of UNFICYP in Cyprus. Residential tours also saw the battalions as part of the British Army of the Rhine training in Kenya, Canada and the United States. Throughout the 1970s the entire Regiment was heavily committed to operations, either on planned tours or as emergency reinforcements, and an intense training programme in support of the British Army of the Rhine. The frequent separation arising from these commitments and the intensity of operations placed a great burden on the families and underlined the importance of the Regimental and Battalion 'family' in times of hardship. Colours were always a central part of the Regiment's Ceremonial life and the Colours of the former Regiments were laid up over this period by their successor battalions: 4LI laid up the 1DLI Colours in Durham Cathedral on 12 December 1968; 3LI took the opportunity to lay up the Colours of 1 KSLI in Bridgnorth on 16 April 1971; In January 1974 the Colours of 1 KOYLI were laid up in York Minster by 2LI. New Colours were required by the new Regiment, a process started on 7 May 1971 when Her Majesty Queen Elizabeth The Queen Mother, the Colonel-in-Chief, presented new Colours to 2LI, 3LI and LI(V) at Colchester. Her Royal Highness Princess Alexandra, the Deputy Colonel-in-Chief, then presented new Colours to 1LI on 25 May 1972 in Lemgo and on 14 July 1978 to 7LI(V) at Palace Green, Durham. Developments in the wider regiment over the period saw a significant expansion in the Volunteers. In 1970 many of the old Territorial Army and Yeomanry units which had been reduced to cadre form were expanded. By the summer of 1972 a new Light Infantry Volunteer battalion – 6LI(V)

COMMAND

After the Passing Out Parade and four weeks' leave I found myself in October 1968 on a plane back to the Far East to join the 3rd Light Infantry commanded by Lt Col JP St C Ballenden, 'Big John'. Big John was the only officer I would have followed anywhere, and the most popular officer I have ever come across! The troops believed that if taken in front of Big John for committing the smallest of crimes, he would give you 28 days jail. Every now and then Big John would gather the whole battalion together, usually in a gymnasium, and talk to us. There is a story I heard often. When the battalion was in Plymouth, prior to going to Malaysia, the Commanding Officer was concerned about fights between soldiers and members of the Royal Navy in Plymouth. He ordered that in future any soldier caught fighting with sailors would be severely punished. Big John, then a Major, being Field Officer of the week, went to the NAAFI Club. He saw seamen taking advantage of KSLI soldiers who simply refused to retaliate. But Big John did, he punched a sailor. He received a suitable punishment, but won the heart of the squaddies!

Cpl Jim Parker

had been raised in the West Country, and LI(V) became 5LI(V). In April 1975 a new Territorial Army battalion of the Regiment, 7LI(V), was formed in the North East, most of its companies being in County Durham. This busy period was not without its lighter and ironic moments. On return from Belize in February 1975, 1LI found themselves collecting refuse from the streets of Glasgow during a prolonged strike by dustmen, Battalion Tactical Headquarters being located at the Govan incinerator. On 7 July 1977 2LI was privileged to take part in a magnificent parade staged by the British Army of the Rhine to mark the Silver Jubilee of Her Majesty The Queen. In June 1977 3LI returned to West Belfast for another four-month tour at the end of which, almost without drawing breath, the Battalion deployed in a fire-fighting role in Tyne and Wear. The Battalion provided a skeleton fire service until industrial action by the firemen was resolved.

The Years of Consolidation: 1979–1989

Over this period the Regiment consolidated both its structure and its reputation on the basis set by the quality of the operations it had conducted over the first ten years of its existence. Continued Northern Ireland commitment placed a heavy burden on The Light Infantry over the period and dominated its operational deployments. That said, deployments to UNFICYP continued, complemented by further training in Jamaica, Canada, the United States and Kenya. Other overseas deployments included residential tours in Cyprus, Gibraltar, Hong Kong and the Falkland Islands. Domestic commitments included supporting the Fire Service,

the Prison Service, the Ambulance Service and deploying to Greenham Common. The period also saw the start of The Light Infantry involvement with Airmobility. This started in January 1983 when 1LI joined 6 Airmobile Brigade – a role for which The Light Infantry was particularly suited. The techniques of Airmobility were developed by 1LI – a role which was taken up by 2LI when, at the end of 1984, there was a straight swap, 1LI moving to Weeton Camp and 2LI moving to Peninsula Barracks, Deilinghofen.

A period of Public Duties in London, the second in the history of the Regiment, was undertaken by 3LI, in January and February 1984. However, ceremonial was not confined to 3LI. 1LI had the honour of finding the ceremonial guard of honour for Her Majesty The Queen at a ceremony held at Utah Beach, Normandy, to mark the anniversary of D Day. On 26 October 1979 Her Majesty Queen Elizabeth The Queen Mother presented new Colours to 6LI(V) in Bath and during 1978 a formal association was established between the Regiment and the carrier HMS *Invincible* which was to prove an enduring and rewarding friendship. On 28 June 1985 the Regiment celebrated its tercentenary, marking the three hundred years since the founding of the Earl of Huntingdon's Regiment. Festivities were centred largely on the West Country, Her Royal Highness Princess Alexandra attending a parade and service of thanksgiving at Wells.

The wider Regiment continued to develop at pace. In January 1983 adult recruit training was concentrated at the Rifle Depot, now retitled the 'Light Division Depot (Winchester)'. The Regimental flag was finally lowered at Sir John Moore Barracks, Shrewsbury, on 3 October 1986, to be raised again at the new Sir John Moore Barracks, the newly built Light Division Depot at Winchester. The new Depot was opened formally by Her Majesty The Queen and Her Royal

Below: 2LI patrolling out of Bessbrook Mill, South Armagh, 2005.

Above: 1LI returned to Iraq on Op TELIC 3 (Oct 2003–April 2004) and on Op TELIC 8 (April–Nov 2006).

one of the companies being from the Worcestershire and Sherwood Foresters Regiment (29th/45th). On 31 May 1991 Her Majesty Queen Elizabeth The Queen Mother presented new Colours to the three regular battalions at Tidworth. With the outcome of the 'Options' studies very much in mind, but yet to be announced, it was to be a particularly memorable regimental occasion, even though the 1LI presence was much reduced and 3LI could only spare a small party from operations in Northern Ireland. It was decided that the reduction by one regular battalion should be achieved by the merger of the three existing battalions; 1LI would occupy the barracks currently occupied by 2LI and 3LI would renumber as 2LI and remain in Germany. On 25 February 1993 the three regular battalions merged to become two, a major reorganization achieved with a smoothness and efficiency that does nothing but credit to the 'large regiment' concept.

Operationally the period saw the continuing provision of support in Northern Ireland by both regular battalions. In October 1990 the Salamanca Band deployed to the Gulf in their role as Medical Assistants. The Band remained in the Gulf throughout the war, three members being mentioned in dispatches for gallantry. The Regiment also deployed to the Balkans – Bosnia and Kosovo – Sierra Leone, Lebanon, Iraq and Afghanistan. This was alongside continued overseas residential tours in Germany and Cyprus (including Falkland Islands garrison commitments) and training worldwide in Kenya, Belize, West Indies, Canada and the United States. The Light Infantry went to war in Iraq in 2003. It was the first time that combat elements of the modern Regiment had been to war since it was formed in 1968. During the war with the regime of Saddam Hussain (in the Spring of 2003) 1LI deployed two Armoured Infantry Companies to Iraq as part of the Desert Rats, and fought with the 2 RTR Battle Group. Between October 2003 and April 2004, 1LI returned to Iraq on Ops TELIC 3 and 8. Throughout the War, 2LI was deployed in Cyprus, protecting the vital forward operating base for British Forces in the region. When in September 2003 the situation on the ground in the aftermath of the war became tense, the Battalion was deployed (from Cyprus) into Iraq to support existing operations on Op TELIC 2, returning to Cyprus in early November 2003. 2LI returned to Iraq on Ops TELIC 6 and 7. Both Battalions and those who joined The Light Infantry family in 2005 from the Devonshire and Dorset Regiment and The Royal Gloucestershire, Berkshire and Wiltshire Regiment, continued to play a role in the operational deployment cycle for both Iraq and Afghanistan. The Light Infantry was deployed on operations in Mauritius when it was formed and was deployed on operations in Afghanistan when it merged into The Rifles. Throughout its existence The Light Infantry served the Nation with distinction across the world in a wide variety of operational deployments. In doing so it established a reputation that was second to none in the British Army.

Highness Princess Alexandra on 27 November 1986, and was to be the centre for the training of all Light Division recruits. In January 1986 the 8th Battalion The Light Infantry (Volunteers) (8LI(V)) was formed in Yorkshire – the final link in the re-establishment of the Regiment in our counties.

On 20 August 1988 a coach carrying a party from A Company 1LI from Aldergrove to Omagh was blown up by a roadside bomb near Ballygawley. Eight men were killed and a further 27 wounded. In Germany 2LI rapidly assembled Salamanca Platoon, a reinforcement platoon of volunteers, to join 1LI in order that, in spite of the losses, the pace and scale of operations could be sustained. In February 1989 1LI moved to Berlin and had nearly a full year of duties in the allied garrison before the Berlin wall was breached on 9 November 1989. This momentous event was to signal the end of the Warsaw Pact as an effective military alliance and in turn the end of the Cold War.

'Options' and After: 1990–2007

1990–2007 was the period started by Options for Change that culminated with formation of The Rifles in 2007. The dramatic changes in the Soviet Union and Eastern Europe in 1989–90 provoked a search for a rapid and conspicuous 'peace dividend'. In February 1990 the Secretary of State for Defence, Tom King, announced 'Options for Change' studies to address the size, shape and role of Britain's post-Cold War defence forces. The outcome of these studies was a significant reduction in the Infantry, and both regiments of the Light Division were required to reduce by one regular battalion. It was with some relief that, on 10 December 1991, it was announced that all four Volunteer battalions would remain, albeit reduced to three companies and, in the case of 5LI(V),

PART 2
The Battalions

The First Battalion
1968–2007

On 6 July 1968 the 1st Battalion The Somerset and Cornwall Light Infantry marched off the parade ground at Milton Barracks, Gravesend, under the review of Field Marshal The Lord Harding of Petherton. After a brief pause to change collar badges and to insert red backing to their cap badges they returned to the parade ground as The First Battalion The Light Infantry. The year 1968 was one of great change: the Tet Offensive had been launched in Vietnam, the crew of Apollo 8 orbited the moon and became the first human beings to see the 'dark side' and, nearer to home, 5,000 Warsaw Pact tanks invaded Czechoslovakia. 1968 was also, astonishingly, the only year in the century when the British Army lost no soldiers in action.

In August 1968 1LI moved to Abercorn Barracks, Ballykinler, under Lieutenant Colonel Colin Frith. It was early days in 'The Troubles'. In August 1969 the Battalion had a welcome break on exercise in Kenya. Meanwhile violence erupted in Londonderry, and the British Government authorized the use of troops to contain sectarian violence and protect Catholic areas, and the Battalion returned to Belfast to patrol the peace line between Catholics and Protestants. 2LI and 3LI were also in the Province at the time. On Saturday 12 October Major David Hancock describes events on the Shankill Road: 'A riot squad from 2LI was holding the immediate area of Unity Flats... The radio told me that a policeman had been shot dead and another wounded. I went forward on foot to link up with 3LI. Two or three soldiers of 3LI were being treated ... for gunshot wounds in the legs. The crowd was roaring, violent and evil. The shooting continued. This was something new for soldiers in Belfast.' The novelty would soon wear off as Northern Ireland became familiar and dangerous territory to a generation of Light Infantrymen.

In March 1970 an advance party of more than 100 left for Lemgo, Germany, to prepare for the new role of mechanized infantry against a background of increased rioting in Belfast – stoning and petrol bombs were becoming commonplace.

Previous pages: The Baseline – the cornerstone of every good Light Infantry battalion's riot drills!

Left: *The aftermath of an IRA attack – Belfast in the 1970s was a dangerous place for soldiers and civilians alike.*

Opposite: *A cross-section of life in the First Battalion.*

of explosives discovered and 400 shooting incidents. The Battalion suffered four losses and a further 18 soldiers were wounded. In November the handover was to 3LI. On returning to Germany, at the request of the townspeople of Lemgo, the Battalion marched through the town behind the Band and Bugles before a period of well-deserved leave.

Less than four months later 1LI was brought to 24-hour notice to return to Northern Ireland. Mechanized Infantry and Internal Security training resumed prior to deployment to South Armagh, South Down and Newry, with two companies detached to Belfast from July to November 1973. Private Ian Jackson was critically injured by a bomb and Sergeant Bill Watt

Left: 1LI smoke break. Field Training at Soltau, Germany, 1972. Left to right: Ptes Burns, Sutton and Clarke.

When 1LI came together in Lemgo in May it was the first time for nine months that they had been as one. The Battalion worked hard to re-role including working on Saturdays and was surprised to learn that, in July, it was placed on 24-hour readiness to go 'somewhere in Northern Ireland'. Two companies were tasked with guarding nuclear ammunition locations, while the remainder of the Battalion prepared for a periodic REME examination (PRE). The Army trains extensively on focusing on the target and then regularly gives its soldiers, and especially the infantry, several all at once!

30 January 1972 became infamous as Bloody Sunday. Twenty-seven protesters were shot by the British Army during a civil rights march. Thirteen people, seven of whom were teenagers, died immediately, another died of his wounds some time later. Two protesters were injured when they were run down by Army vehicles. Five of those wounded were shot in the back. The Widgery Report on the incident was criticized by many as a whitewash and the subsequent report under Lord Saville was not concluded until 38 years after the event. Whatever happened that day may never be totally clear but it was plain that the British Army had been brought to the Province to protect Catholics, and the relationship gradually deteriorated until the damage of that single day rendered it irreparable for many years to come.

Lieutenant Colonel Barry Lane assumed command ten days before leaving for Ulster in July 1972. The Battalion was tasked as part of Operation MOTORMAN with removing barricades that had created no-go areas in Belfast and Londonderry. They were supported by a company from 42 Commando Royal Marines and a Commando Squadron of Royal Engineers. Operation MOTORMAN lasted several intense weeks as barricades were removed, military bases and observation posts established and a new intelligence base was created under the Intelligence Officer, Captain Gage Williams. The tour concluded with 89 arrests, 24,000 cars searched, 400lbs

1LI TOURS

Milton Barracks, Gravesend, July – August 1968 (Residential Tour)
Abercorn Barracks, Ballykinler, August 1968 – May 1970
Stornoway Barracks, Lemgo, May 1970 – March 1974
Belfast, March – July 1971 (Emergency Tour)
Op MOTORMAN, Belfast and Londonderry, July – November 1972
South Armagh, July – November 1973
Meanee Barracks, Colchester, March 1974 – January 1976
Belfast, May – June 1974
Belize, August 1974 – February 1975
South Armagh, July – September 1975
Stanley Barracks, Hong Kong, January 1976 – January 1978
Lucknow Barracks, Tidworth, January 1978 – March 1981
West Belfast, June – October 1978
UNFICYP, November 1979 – April 1980
Buller Barracks, Munster, March 1981 – December 1984
Belfast, May – September 1983
Weeton Barracks, Blackpool, November 1984 – November 1986
Falkland Islands, July – November 1985
Lisanelly Barracks, Omagh, November 1986 – January 1989
Brooke Barracks, Berlin, January 1989 – August 1991
Kiwi Barracks, Bulford, August 1991 – July 1993
Belize, April – November 1992

MERGER OF 1ST, 2ND AND 3RD BATTALIONS 26 FEBRUARY 1993

Lucknow Barracks, Tidworth, February 1993 – January 1994
Meanee Barracks, Colchester, January 1994 – April 1997
Fermanagh, May – December 1994
Fermanagh, South Armagh, June – December 1996
Episkopi Garrison, Cyprus, April 1997 – April 1999
Dreghorn Barracks, Edinburgh, April 1999 – April 2002
Northern Ireland, June – December 2000
Sierra Leone, Op SILKMAN, March – June 2001
Alanbrooke Barracks, Paderborn, April 2002 – January 2007
Iraq, Op TELIC 1, March – May 2003
Iraq, Op TELIC 3, October 2003 – April 2004
Iraq, Op TELIC 9, April – October 2006

FORMATION OF THE RIFLES 1 FEBRUARY 2007

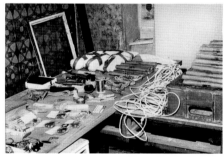

NORTHERN IRELAND 1969

(This is a verbatim copy of the actual letter received by the two LI Battalions named)

From the people of Omar St., Lesson St., Panton St., Milken St., Balacava St., Alma St., Colen St., Peel St.,Lemon St., Albert St., Milton St., Milan St., Feara St., Garnet St., Cape St., Raglan St. Balkan St., Plevna St.,

To The 1st Bt. of the Light Infantry

We the people of Omar St. have put our signatures on behalf of our people to ask you Sir to please give us back the 1st Infantry as we have put are trust and confidence in them. Sir we got to know them and since they gone the people of the Falls Rd. are very down hearted we can't understand why you keep changing them.

For the 1st Infantry we are very proud of You's we want you back for the Falls Rd. is miserable without you. The 3rd Infantry does not and will never measure up to your standards and you's were right when you's said you's where the best for we the people want you back. If not the people will have lost faith in you're Generals, Majors etc., for we always get promises well we the people only ask for one thing that is give us back The 1st Bt. of The Light Infantry. We the people welcome you with open arms well we close now as we want this to reach You's in time.
Please Please
Sir Give Us Back the
First Infantry.
The people Back them and put their trust in them as they well know. If you don't believe us ask them yourself.
God Bless You's all.
Falls Rd. *Omar* St. Back.1st Infantry.
Hoping to see you's all soon. Get Rested Quick
God love you's
Omar St.
To: Terry the Cook
After reading this and you's approve give it to your commanding officer.
From the People
of the Falls
(Omar St.)

Top: A fireteam from a multiple patrol approaches a crossroads, Belfast, 1970s.

Above: A makeshift bomb factory in Ardoyne.

Above right: A Riot Baseline in training.

of the Royal Army Medical Corps conducted an emergency tracheotomy using a clasp knife and a Bic pen case. Sergeant Watt was awarded the British Empire Medal and went on to become Jackson's best man at his wedding.

March 1974 saw 1LI arrive in Meanee Barracks, Colchester, as part of 19 Airportable Brigade and was a straight swap with 2LI who took over in Lemgo. Training for the new role began along with preparation for a six-month unaccompanied tour in Belize planned for August. This was disrupted in May by the Belfast Ulster Workers' Council strike which led to 1LI returning to the Province until early June.

A Company remained in Colchester, when the remainder of the Battalion deployed to Belize in August. Belize is roughly the size of Wales. Unlike Wales, however, it is bordered by Mexico to the north, Guatemala to the south and west, and the Caribbean to the east, and is generally sunny! Britain granted British Honduras self-government in 1964 and it was officially renamed Belize in 1973. Progress toward independence was hampered by a Guatemalan claim to sovereignty over the territory. When Belize finally attained full independence on 21 September 1981, Guatemala refused to recognize the new nation. About 1,500 British troops remained to protect Belize from the Guatemalan threat.

All platoons were planned to go through a two-week jungle training centre but Hurricane Fifi struck neighbouring Honduras with winds of 170mph, killing many people and causing considerable damage from flooding and landslides.

I SAY, DON'T YOU WEAR BELTS ROUND YOUR WAIST

Mr KEVIN BARRY (JUNIOR) ES
Alias Chris 'Dusty' Murphy.

1. An illegitimate descendant of the GREEN hero of the same name. A GRA company commander who made a name for himself by petrol bombing in the FALLS ROAD. Is reported to be a plausible liar and should not be allowed to talk if arrested. He is usually armed.

4. Photograph.

Far left: A young Ian Paisley with the Commanding Officer – Lt Col Barry Lane.

Below left: Lt Col Makepeace-Warner (L) – author of Exceedingly Lucky: A History of The Light Infantry 1968–1993.

Left: The Battalion scrapbook saw no end of entries.

A contingent was sent to support disaster-relief efforts rescuing refugees, providing supplies and medical support. Later on, training, including adventure training, continued apace and soldiers were encouraged to take leave outside Belize and explore Mexico, Nicaragua and beyond.

Shortly after the return to Colchester in February TAC HQ, C and Sp Company were deployed to Glasgow to cover for the Glasgow dustmen's strike, prompting unfavourable comparisons of the soldiers' salary with that of the striking dustmen. Canada in June 1975 was somewhat more exciting with Exercise 'Pond Jump West' at Camp Wainwright. Adventure training in the Rockies was followed by individual and tactical training.

The Battalion assumed 'Spearhead' duties on 28 August against a rapidly deteriorating background in Northern Ireland following a series of sectarian killings. Predictably 1LI was deployed to South Armagh in September for four weeks. On returning to Colchester training and preparations began for the forthcoming posting to Hong Kong after Christmas leave.

More than 300 families moved to high-rise flats near Gun Club Hill Barracks, Kowloon, in January 1976. The first Sino–Hong Kong border tour took place in April, tasked with securing the border, maintaining surveillance and apprehending illegal immigrants from China. Training continued in the New Territories – the mountainous area surrounding Hong Kong – and sub-units spent a month on rotation jungle training in Brunei. Typhoon Ellen killed 28 Chinese civilians in Hong Kong and the Battalion sent a detachment to assist in the emergency recovery. An earthquake in the Philippines also saw a party of six under Sergeant Derek Brennan fly to Manila with medical and emergency supplies. Twenty-eight soldiers commanded by Captain David Eliot flew to Korea in September for a two-month tour as part of the UN Honour Guard. Captain John Badgery would take a platoon the following year. In November, as a result of a reduction in the garrison strength, 1LI moved to Stanley Fort on Hong Kong island.

In January 1977 A Company took part in Exercise 'Kauri Pine' in New Zealand. Hong Kong celebrated the Queen's

Above: Media coverage of Battalion activity.

A WEEK AT MILLIONARIO

Belize, 1974

It was 0830 hours on Sunday morning (CSM was still in bed!) when a small party from 5 P1 and a sapper from the attached field section set off for a week's `hard labour' at Mr Littlejohn's ranch some 60 miles deep in the heart of the jungle. So that we wouldn't get lost, our OC navigator led the way (a bad mistake!) but eventually after four hours of gruelling muddy tracks and plenty of back seat navigation from Sgt Bob Dyer we arrived at the ranch. We were greeted by a furry-faced six-foot American and his wife and four daughters. After all the greetings, and once the previous party had departed, we settled into our new surroundings. The last party returned with the OC navigator. That evening, Mr Littlejohn invited us into his house to discuss our programme for the week. He ended up telling us war stories and showing us photos of jaguar hunts during the past years. On Monday morning we split into two groups. One went shooting jaguar with the dogs, but ended up catching an armadillo (hard-shelled anteater). The other group went riding with the two daughters and horses. The following day, the groups changed round and it was the turn of the rose riders to catch a wild pig. It was surrounded in a hole by the dogs. The two girls then killed it in a very unladylike manner with the shotguns and long knives (which they always carry). Wednesday was a lazy day; it poured with rain all day and it was the start of Hurricane Fifi. On Thursday it was still raining and we all helped get the horses in from the jungle, and to strap down the vehicles and buildings. At last Sunday morning came, and it was time to pack. By 1500 hours, the winds started getting stronger so Mr. Littlejohn decided to move us all with his family to a nearby cave which offered good protection. And so, by 1600 hours, the Army had all kit and food safely stowed away. We reckoned the civilians were disorganized, so we helped them too! We had one narrow escape when a falling tree tried to hammer Pte Ridgement into the ground. Luckily, his reflexes were quick which was surprising after two huge helpings of peaches for lunch and eighteen hard tack biscuits. At 1700 hours, the wind was very strong so we made for the cave and safety After a little organization by our 'Commander' Dyer, it was quite homely. Of course Mr. Littlejohn's two bottles of whisky came in handy, and I noticed they had NAAFI stamped all over the bottle. After a restless night thinking of vampire bats and creepy crawlies (and two wild girls with machetes), we emerged from our cave. There were broken branches everywhere and broken trees were littering the area. We set to work for most of that day clearing a large tree in the middle of Mr. Littlejohn's camp and then started to clear the main swamped track which leads out to civilisation. On Saturday, we all went riding to clear more trees from the tracks. Albert the mule took Sapper Thomas for a ride on his own. Thomas was later to be found hanging from a tree in the jungle calling A L B E R T. I think this was also the time when Jimmie Jewell and one of the girls, Cindy, suddenly vanished and came back 45 minutes later with an excuse that they had been hunting an armadillo: both looked flushed and out of breath!

Pte K. Bath

(Editorial Note: The centre of Hurricane Fifi passed within a few miles of Mr Littlejohn's farm at about 1800 hours on the Thursday. They were therefore the nearest soldiers to the centre of the hurricane, apart from the Recce Platoon, which had been posted on the coast.)

Silver Jubilee with a vast parade involving over 5,000 people and 1LI were honoured to lead the two-mile-long parade through the Central District. In late July 1LI were told that they would conduct an Operation BANNER tour in Northern Ireland in July 1978 and plans began to reduce the Battalion strength to a smaller establishment (the officially approved scale for a unit in a given role). Stanley Fort was handed over to 1 RGJ and the Battalion moved to Lucknow Barracks, Tidworth, in January 1978.

On 28 June 1LI took over West Belfast from 41 Commando Royal Marines. The emphasis was on police primacy, and joint RUC/military patrols took place on a regular basis. The tour was quieter than previous tours although there were 416 arrests and numerous finds of explosives, ammunition and equipment demonstrating the increasing sophistication of the provisional IRA. Proxy bombs were used to attack military bases and Second Lieutenant Andrew Trelawny was shot in the neck by a sniper but fortunately recovered quickly. October saw a welcome return to Tidworth. From May to June 1979 the Battalion took part in Exercise 'Pond Jump West' in Canada and returned to Tidworth to be placed on Spearhead commitments once again in July.

A six-month UN Tour of Cyprus began in November. In 1964 United Nations Peacekeeping Force in Cyprus (UNFICYP) was established in an attempt to preserve peace and security in the context of the confrontation between the Greek Cypriot and Turkish Cypriot communities. A coup d'état in Cyprus on 15 July 1974 by Greek Cypriot and Greek elements favouring union with Greece was followed by military intervention by Turkey, whose troops established Turkish Cypriot control over the northern part of the island. A de facto ceasefire came into effect on 16 August 1974. The ceasefire lines extend approximately 180 kilometres and the buffer zone varied in width from less than 20 metres to some seven kilometres. The Battalion was required to undertake patrols and maintain a reaction force but incidents between the Greeks and Turks were rare and were generally quickly resolved at local level. Once back to Tidworth the Battalion began preparations for its move in March 1981 to Buller Barracks, Munster, in Northern Germany under 3 Armoured Division.

The majority of the British Army's armoured might was based in Germany as a part of the British Army of the Rhine. As a result of the Cold War there were detailed deployment plans and strict controls on manning to maintain a high level of readiness. Ammunition out-loading exercises were common and 90 per cent of armoured vehicles had to be at four hours' notice to move – a significant challenge for colleagues in armoured units. Despite the painstaking plans for the defence of Western Europe however, the strategic policy of forward defence was based on political rather than military logic – the West Germans did not want World War Three to be fought in their back yard so there was no strength in depth and little planning

for manoeuvre warfare. This, along with the arms race, meant that a nuclear war was a real possibility and culminated in the appropriately named policy MAD: mutually assured destruction. Nuclear, biological and chemical (NBC) warfare became part of every exercise, and annual personal weapon tests and regular checks of equipment using CS gas were conducted. The debilitating effects of wearing full NBC protective clothing is

Above: Chinooks herald the arrival of 6 Airmobile Brigade.

Below left: 2Lt Cummings on street patrol in Belfast, 1981.

Below: Roger Hopkins attending to a casualty.

Above: A car bomb is neutralized in a controlled explosion.

difficult to imagine but coupled with sleep deprivation even the most basic tasks become almost impossible. Cries of 'Gas, Gas, Gas' on exercise signalled the donning of protective equipment, a prolonged period of discomfort and chaotic fumbling about that often bordered on farce.

The quality of life in Germany was generally good. A strong infrastructure of hospitals and schools had been developed, Local Overseas Allowance was a welcome boost to soldiers' income, and cars could be purchased tax free. Relations with the local population were good and marriages to the townswomen were not uncommon. Nonetheless, access to good-quality married quarters remained a problem, as it had been in Tidworth. Training opportunities were excellent, with occasional tasks such as inner German border patrols adding to the variety of life. Just before Christmas 1LI was warned for an Operation BANNER tour in Belfast from May to September 1983. In March 1982 companies went in turn to Portugal for exercise 'Night Echo' practising platoon- and section-level exercises.

Elsewhere, tensions were mounting in the South Atlantic as Argentina threatened the Falkland Islands. Many people in the UK had never heard of the islands and guessed that they were somewhere off the Scottish coast, or thought that a conflict of this nature was confined to the history books. The war lasted 74 days, and resulted in the deaths of 255 British and 649 Argentine soldiers, sailors and airmen, and three civilian Falklanders. It also led to a change in military doctrine towards mission command and manoeuvre warfare; the lessons of the Second World War had to be re-learned – that in contact the situation changes, commanders are killed and communication breaks down. Rigid orders and detailed plans would be the first casualties of contact. The new 'estimate process' of producing a plan was taught and tested at every level in the Army with the aim of allowing commanders at the lowest level to take the initiative when things did, inevitably, change in battle. It was a philosophy that sat well with The Light Infantry ethos.

Northern Ireland was never far away and in May 1983 1LI returned once again to West Belfast. July was traditionally a violent month, the 12th marking the Battle of the Boyne, fought in 1690 between the Catholic King James and the Protestant King William. It was won by William and ultimately helped ensure the continuation of Protestant supremacy in Ireland. It is difficult to understand why a battle in 1690 could have such importance, but the modern context was that the police force (RUC) and the local army (UDR) were more than 95 per cent Protestant, the best land, schools and employment opportunities were in Protestant areas, and the drums and noise of the marching bands that paraded on days like 12 July were intimidating to witness.

Internment began in August 1971 and involved arresting and imprisoning without trial people accused of being paramilitary members. It led to widespread rioting and protests. On the anniversary in 1983 a series of disturbances led to Thomas Reilly being shot dead by Private Iain Thain of 1LI

A LOOK BACK WITH PLEASURE
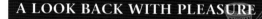

Hong Kong 1976–8

It would seem wrong to leave Hong Kong without a brief look back. Our two years in the Far East will be remembered with nostalgia by some and loathing by others. Members of the Battalion either enjoyed their time immensely or waited longingly for the end of our time here. Most of us quickly overcame the heat and the variety of smells and would have enjoyed a longer stay. The opportunities for water sports, the sun, and the high and low social life have been a great attraction. One of the most appealing aspects is the high rate of LOA and the accompanying high standard of living. We came down to earth with a bump when we landed at Brize Norton.

Soldiering in the Far East has had its moments. For those who joined the Army to see the world, our stay has given ample opportunity. Nearly everyone has experienced the jungles of Brunei. Luckier ones have been to New Zealand, and some have been to Korea and served with American, Philippine and Thai Troops as part of the UN Honor (sic) Guard. Hong Kong itself has provided Internal Security training when we have worked with The Royal Hong Kong Police, as well as more conventional training in a hot climate on the outlying islands and in the New Territories. We have built up considerable experience of helicopter- and sea-borne operations; no one can say it has been a rest camp or that we shall return untrained. Any soldier posted here for two years has had the opportunity of seeing the Far East at little personal expense. The Leave Scheme is equivalent in cash of a return trip to Singapore. Some have been to Australia; some to Bali and Indonesia; others to Thailand, Bangkok or Pattya. One of the most rewarding journeys was a fly-drive scheme to Malaysia which encompassed Penang, the Malaysian peninsula and Singapore. A number have also sampled the ski slopes of Japan and the bars in Manila.

Two stories hit the Chinese papers, both concerned with our barracks at Stanley Fort. The first dealt with the Stanley cobra hiding in the camp laundry. It was discovered by a visiting hygiene officer and the QM, Captain Robert Cox, who spotted the five-foot snake peeping back at him from a bucket. He reeled back muttering `Oh my God, it's a cobra.' Subsequent efforts to catch it proved unsuccessful.

The second concerned a visiting officer who was badly scared by the Officers' Mess ghost. This officer was gripped by absolute terror when he had gone upstairs to change. He is said to have been approached by a figure in uniform when he was experiencing unreasoning fear. Lts Mike Howard and David Nichols deny frightening him.

Now it's over, and it will be 98 years before we return. We have seen so much change in two years that to contemplate Hong Kong in a century is impossible.

MULTIPLE PATROLLING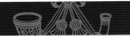

The 1st Battalion, stationed in Lemgo, was sent to Belfast in July 1972. No-go areas had been established and the advance party arrived on Bloody Friday. Within ten days the Battalion was going into the No-go areas in Operation MOTORMAN. We didn't really know how to patrol safely and shortly my platoon was caught in a three-sided ambush where one soldier was shot in the back. Next day I asked Captain Rex Rice if we could cease patrolling until we had worked something out better. I sat down with Sjt Reah and Cpl Vigus and we worked up the idea of having four four-man groups or patrols commanded by a corporal or lance corporal. Each patrol would be leapfrogging with the other covering. The two four-man patrols would work in parallel with the other two. As we put this into practice, I could tell immediately that the junior commanders loved it and were enthusiastic. It proved its worth and we had no further casualties whilst on patrol although many shootings took place.

When it was time to hand over to 3LI, my shadow platoon commander was Charlie Pack. He came out a number of times on patrol and saw the 16-man patrol technique being used. On our last night patrol, they were waiting for us and a crowd cut off two of my patrols in some alleyways. They were being stoned and would have been torn apart. We also heard high-velocity shots. We, however, were two streets away and I gave instructions for the two trapped patrols to come out one man at a time through the back alleys where we could provide cover. Mercifully all the soldiers got away and we leapfrogged our way out of the area safely. We left the Province, and on our return nine months later I discovered that the 16-man patrol technique had been adopted by the whole British Army in Ulster, presumably because of 3LI's adoption of it and writing it up.

Richard Beath

Above: House searches in West Belfast.

Left: Capturing Martin Meehan, the most wanted man in Ardoyne.

who was later convicted of murder. It was the first time that a British soldier serving in Northern Ireland had been convicted of murder while on duty. Normally soldiers convicted of a criminal offence are automatically discharged from the Army but, unusually and controversially, Thain was allowed to continue his service after his detention. In September the Battalion returned to Munster in preparation for a new role as part of 6 Airmobile Brigade. Training once again took priority and some exercises included the full-scale issue of wartime ammunition, the average carrying weight being nearly 100lbs. With such a burden neither normal walking nor running is possible, only a steady plod with several steps required to stop.

In December 1984 the Battalion left Germany for a newly built barracks at Weeton, near Blackpool. Field training was difficult due to the lack of nearby training areas, and companies had to travel to Catterick, Warcop and Otterburn to re-learn basic skills and conduct live firing. In early July the Battalion deployed to the Falkland Islands and South Georgia until November. In June of the following year the Battalion was once again back in Canada on Exercise 'Pond Jump West'. The training was up to company level but culminated in a tough inter-platoon competition won by 4 Platoon under Second Lieutenant Tom McMurtrie.

A sad goodbye to the nightclubs of Blackpool and the numerous 'night attacks' on the local talent as the Battalion headed for Lisanelly Barracks, Omagh, in November 1986 after an extensive and by now very well-developed training period in purpose-built complexes in Lydd, Hythe and elsewhere. For many members of the Battalion this was not the first visit to the Province – for a large number this was their third or fourth tour. Patrols, often of three to four days, were generally routine and without incident, always wet – if not from rain then seeping through boots from the sodden ground. Most patrols started by helicopter. The Navy pilots would arrive in all weathers, the Army in most conditions but the Air Force could not be relied upon if the wind disturbed their silk scarves on the way from the Mess to the cockpit! Occasionally civilianized

Clockwise beginning with right: The human fruit machine; Maj Dickie Head puts the Askold Cup to good use. The Askold Cup is a silver kovsh, a traditional 17th-century Russian drinking cup originally carved out of wood in the shape of a bird. It was presented by Officers of the Imperial Russian Navy following a herculean drinking effort from the Officers of the 2nd Battalion The Duke of Cornwall's Light Infantry in Aden Harbour on their return from Hong Kong; Capt Tom Hext and the Battalion Shooting Team.

patrol vehicles (CPVs) were used – essentially a minibus without windows designed to look like an ordinary shop van. The rifleman's boot was the ultimate means of transport.

Warning orders for deployments around the Province would frequently arrive from the formal chain of command sometime after the wives' club had already issued their own. Any mention of 'don't tell anyone' typically resulted in an express service. The Army spends millions in training and technology to improve communications but they remain amateurs compared to the wives' network!

James Bendall was the Adjutant and had joined us from the Royal Green Jackets. He was calm, composed and exuded an air of confidence. One evening in the Mess, his customary game of chess with a glass of claret was rudely interrupted by a phone call which he took outside. He returned a few moments later, took a deep drag of his cigar surveying the room, and said as if asking for a glass of water, 'Tom, apparently there is a bomb outside the main gate – can you go and sort it out please?' and then calmly returned to his chess match. Here was a demonstration of leadership – there was no point in everyone

Below: Maj Ben Barry OC A Company with US soldiers at the Urban Training Centre, Hammelburg.

panicking or rushing to the main gate to increase the risk or complicate matters – it simply needed someone, Lieutenant Tom Hext in this case, to review the situation and take charge. James put this into perspective with a few calm words of command. Soldiers look for leadership in times of danger, not panic or fear. Sadly James died in his sleep some years later, far too young.

Lieutenant Colonel Mitchell Philp assumed command in May 1987 and had a relatively calm first year. On 20 August 1988 soldiers of A Company were returning from leave in a civilian bus. A bus load of short-haired young men all wearing desert boots, jeans and T-shirts might as well have had 'British Army' written on the side of the coach. An IRA roadside bomb ripped the bus apart at Ballygawley. Seven men were killed and another died of his wounds in hospital, and a further 27 were injured. Sadly this was not to be the last time that a lack of expensive helicopter support would contribute to an increased risk of loss of life. The shock of the incident was exacerbated by the graffiti that appeared shortly afterwards in the hard republican areas: 'The Light Infantry are 8 lighter now'. A Company was planned to go to South Armagh and the difficult decision was taken to continue with the deployment and with professionalism and determination they began to dig in near the border with the Republic. Meanwhile the staff at Musgrave Park Hospital did a magnificent job of getting the injured back

Left: Children playing in front of a Loyalist marching band, 1972.

Below: Sjt Bob Pickford on Exercise 'Trumpet Dance'.

to fitness. The Battalion was reinforced by a platoon from 2LI under Lieutenant Mark Adams to help with our various operational commitments.

Equipment was upgraded as the 7.62mm SLR rifle was replaced with the SA80 and new improved webbing was issued. Twenty-six months is a long tour and the Battalion was looking forward to a change of role and environment in Berlin. They had patrolled in all corners of Northern Ireland and had become expert at crossing blackthorn hedges and electric cattle fences – getting caught up in either is not funny unless you are watching! Once again leadership skills and fieldcraft had been tested to the full but now the Soviet threat and Cold War skills had to be re-mastered.

The Battalion moved to Brooke Barracks, Berlin, in January 1989. Corporal Paul Wharton of the Durham Light Infantry was in Berlin to witness the barbed-wire construction of the Wall on 13 August 1961. Major Paul Wharton returned with 1LI to see it being torn down on 9 November 1989.

The Wall was more than 87 miles long and when it was completed consisted of reinforced concrete 12ft high. More concrete was used to prevent escapees driving through the barricades although at strategic points the construction was weaker to allow Warsaw Pact armoured vehicles to break through in the event of war. The top of the wall was lined with a smooth pipe to make scaling harder. It was reinforced by mesh fencing, anti-vehicle trenches, dogs on lines patrolling the 'death strip', over 116 watchtowers and 20 bunkers. More than 5,000 people escaped but over 100 perished in their attempts.

The city was divided into four sectors: French, British, American and Soviet. The Allies had diplomatic immunity to

THE BALLYGAWLEY BOMB

Pte (later LCpl) Peter Jackson was on the Ballygawley bus. He was wounded in the explosion, losing the sight of his left eye. His recollection is of a full bus, possibly one junior NCO and a soldier escort armed with a 9mm pistol. Having returned from UK from a long weekend they left Aldergrove Airport and he fell asleep! He was told later that the bus was diverted into the path of the bomb by diversion signs placed by the bombers. This is his story.

'After the bombed bus came to a rest the following events are still very vivid in my mind. I woke to a cool breeze blowing across my face and a clear night sky covered with stars. I sat there for a while looking at the stars, in a dream-like state, when I noticed the twisted metal framework hanging over me. I glanced around to my right at the window frame which had all its glass missing and to my left was a confused scene of crushed bodies and limbs amongst metal coach seating and baggage all in semi-darkness. "Bloody hell it's happened" were the first words I shouted on the realisation of my situation and then "Oh hell" on the possibility of the IRA pushing home their attack, knowing full well that we were unable to defend ourselves should these scumbags decide to follow up and finish off the survivors. I decided to get out of the bus and move to cover, to wait for the arrival of my Battalion QRF. Well that was the plan but carrying it out was not that straight-forward. I tried to help my mate Simon Lack on my left get out with me, but the only part of him visible was his foot, with the rest of him hanging downwards through the floor of the bus. He gave out the odd moan but my attempts proved fruitless, so I had to leave him. My legs for some reason wouldn't support my weight or allow me to stand so I rolled over and out through the side coach window to the ground outside, a fall of about 2 metres which caused me more discomfort because by now the pain of my injuries was really kicking in. God it was hard going but I managed to crawl to a bush nearby to hide; OK for now, but still too close for comfort. I paused there a while looking back towards the wreckage praying that the IRA would

"piss off" and not come down to finish us off, so I wouldn't have to witness the murder of my helpless surviving mates, still on the bus. God if only I had a weapon I could do something to help prevent that from happening. It was at this point, just before crawling off again, I heard the sound of a military helicopter and people started to appear from cars on the road, some helping, some laughing (but I had got used to that sort of behaviour during my NI Tour). The feeling of anger and the worry of another attack passed with the arrival of the military on the scene and now my thoughts turned from escaping the area to my own injuries particularly the left side of my face and the loss of vision in my left eye, for at that point I had no idea of my injuries, but it hurt like hell.'

Peter Jackson

(Editorial Note: Eight soldiers of 1LI were killed in this incident, many were wounded, including several severely who, like Peter Jackson, needed long-term hospital care before, in his case, being medically discharged from the Army having permanently lost the sight of his eye.)

Above: The Ballygawley Memorial Plaque from Sir John Moore Barracks, Winchester.

THESE TREES WERE PLANTED ON 25 APRIL 1989 BY HER MAJESTY, QUEEN ELIZABETH, THE QUEEN MOTHER IN MEMORY OF EIGHT SOLDIERS OF HER REGIMENT KILLED AT BALLYGAWLEY ON 20 AUGUST 1988 THE TREES WERE DONATED BY THE PEOPLE OF COUNTY TYRONE

Nº 378
MEMORIAL SERVICE
in Memory of those who died at Ballygawley on 20th August 1988
WEDNESDAY 28th SEPTEMBER 1988 2.30 p.m.
Light Division Depot Chapel, Winchester

travel to the East in service dress or mess kit in the evening but had to return via Checkpoint Charlie by midnight. One west Deutschmark bought ten Ostmarks so soldiers could afford the best restaurants, trips to the opera and almost anything in the shops if they could find one in the East with much to sell. The few Trabant cars that chugged along the streets intermittently were in stark contrast to the Mercedes, BMWs and Audis just over the Wall in the West.

Against this background the BBC filmed a documentary called *Inside Out* about life in the Army. It was not a PR success! With three months of unlimited access professional journalists could produce any story they wished and they focused on the one area that really differentiates military life from civilian in

peacetime: discipline. It was not truly reflective of life in the Battalion but it did make for fascinating television. It was also used at the Staff College and elsewhere to help train officers for working with the media – a skill that has become increasingly important in the modern world.

Training took place with the allies, including the mortar platoon abseiling from American Huey helicopters and FIBUA training in their excellent 'Doughboy City' complex. Some training took place in West Germany, in particular for Support Company who had been operating as a rifle company in Northern Ireland but now needed to bring their support weapons skills up to speed and (in the case of the anti-tank platoon) learn the antiquated Wombat. This required a convoy through the corridor in East Germany which was checked by Soviet officers (as was the Berlin train which travelled daily to Braunschweig and back – 1LI provided the final train guard on 7 February 1991).

There were regular 4am call-outs to ensure that the Brigade was operationally ready and a Quick Reaction Force Platoon spent three days' duty at a time fully armed in an underground cellar in case of any crisis. 1LI were, of course, in the middle of East Germany surrounded by Warsaw Pact troops and the reality was that if war did start Berlin would probably be bypassed and then cut off – the Army's presence was a show of force and determination but of limited military strategic impact.

Ceremonial duties were an important part of Berlin life and on one notable occasion the Battalion were on parade with the Irish Guards and their wolfhound mascot and the Royal Welch Fusiliers with their goat. Not to be outdone RQMS Martyn Bonner enlisted a small Lancashire Heeler, resplendent in rifle green coat with miniature medals, and proudly marched out onto the Maifeld!

The sudden collapse of the Wall meant a busy few weeks for the soldiers providing aid for refugees, setting up temporary accommodation and handing out countless cups of coffee and tea. On New Year's Eve a vast crowd gathered at the Brandenburg Gate. Thousands of Germans from both sides were joined by thousands of tourists from all over the world to witness a fantastic fireworks display in a huge celebration.

Training continued after the Wall fell and the Battalion made full use of the excellent facilities in Berlin, including the Olympic sports complex, until a Farewell Retreat marked the end of a memorable and historic period in the Battalion's life as it prepared for Bulford and Belize.

In 1990 the Secretary of State for Defence, Tom King, a former officer of The Somerset Light Infantry and one of a dwindling number of MPs with any military service, launched a wide-ranging review called 'Options for Change' which inevitably looked for a 'peace dividend' as the Warsaw Pact

threat collapsed. In 1991 Operation GRANBY was launched in the Gulf and covered both deployments in defence of Saudi Arabia (Operation DESERT SHIELD) and the liberation of Kuwait (Operation DESERT STORM). Operation GRANBY granted some respite to planned cuts but ultimately the Light Division was to lose two battalions, one from The Royal Green Jackets and the other from The Light Infantry. It was agreed that the best way to implement the cuts would be a merger and 'M Day' was set for 26 February 1993.

Against this background of uncertainty 1LI moved to Kiwi Barracks, Bulford, in August 1991. In September a reinforced company joined 7 Regiment Royal Horse Artillery for Exercise 'Pond Jump West' in Canada and training for Belize began after Christmas leave. All platoon commanders attended the jungle warfare instructors' course in Brunei and many others were sent on specialist training courses. Lieutenant Colonel Tim Weeks took command for the start of the tour in April. The Battalion was dispersed throughout the country in company-sized locations and would come together for Exercise 'Mayan Sword' and field firing at Baldy Beacon. Snakes, scorpions and other delights were always a risk but heat exhaustion was a constant danger. Carrying the necessary amount of water itself added to the problem and acclimatization was essential. Adventure training was a bonus and many benefited from diving around the Cayes – the world's second largest barrier reef. Captain Paul Taylor established the British Army's first QM's Department based on a commercial basis: he would happily furnish you with an underwater motor for scuba diving for a small, competitive fee! The tour provided an excellent opportunity to hone section-level skills – patrolling, map reading and basic fieldcraft were all tested to the full.

Above: On exercise in West Berlin in the Grunewald. Note the urban camouflage on the Chieftain Tank.

Left: LCpl Vickery directs fire on a GPMG(SF), BAOR.

THE FALL OF THE BERLIN WALL 1989

I had known Berlin as a child when my father (Major Simon Firbank – 1LI) served there from 1970 to 1972. My mother had lived there in the late '50s as well with her father (Lt Col John Howard MC – DCLI) and so I had known of and seen many parts of the city through their eyes. In so many ways nothing had changed when I arrived with 1LI in February 1989, in my own right. The buildings on the eastern side of the wall were just the same and just as pockmarked by bullets and shrapnel as they had been at the end of WW2.

Just before the Battalion arrived in Berlin, three students had tried to swim the River Spree near the Reichstag to gain freedom from the East. We were shown a video of their escape. The first, a man, made it to the west bank and got out, a second man made it to the bank but had to be helped out he was so exhausted. The third student, a girl, was struggling some way behind and we watched in horror as an East German patrol boat pulled alongside her, the soldiers cocked their weapons and dragged her from the water by her hair. I have no idea what fate awaited her. Nothing much looked like changing during our tour…

In October 1989 we learned from the civilian government, the Senat, that Berlin was considering bidding to hold the Olympic Games not too far into the future on the basis that travel between East and West Berlin would be sufficiently relaxed to hold it together. A week later I met a German businessman at a dinner party who reckoned that the wall would be down within five years; less than a month later it was.

On 9 November 1989 I was watching the Ten o'Clock News in the mess at Brooke Barracks with a (then) potential officer, Oliver Marsh, when we heard that travel restrictions across the wall for East Germans were to be relaxed. The preceding weeks had seen other momentous changes in nearby Eastern bloc countries and we sensed that this was a moment in history not to be missed. To our amazement we managed to drive through the huge crowds that were amassing near the wall, right into the small Allied car park at Checkpoint Charlie. Clearly the Berliners, East and West, thought that the border was to be completely opened and huge crowds gathered on both sides. In the West every time a car came across they thronged around thinking it was an East German, thrusting oranges, chocolate and bottles of Sekt through the windows, only to realise that these were Poles and Romanians and that no East Germans were getting through.

We sat on the painfully thin road sign pointing down Friederich Strasse and watched in amazement as a very drunk man riding near the wall, on a bicycle, suddenly veered right into the checkpoint, past the first line of guards and into the Russian sector. Whereas a few days and possibly a few hours earlier he would have been very severely treated, they

gently turned him round and sent him back West. At that moment I knew it could only be a matter of hours or days before the wall collapsed.

Later that night we moved to Staaken, a crossing point from West Berlin into East Germany rather than East Berlin. At one stage the crowd here just surged forward into the checkpoint and we were carried across the border with them and then just as quickly back again. Almost as if they were not sure that they really wanted to test the guards' patience to that extent. Scenes like this went on for many more hours but eventually the border guards gave up and began to let Germans cross from the East. I was never sure if an official order was given or if they just sensed that it was all over (it is now!!) and that they should let people through en masse.

The most moving spectacle of all was seeing families who had not seen each other for nearly 30 years until that morning, part again in the evening to go back to their houses in the east, having the confidence that they could come again tomorrow!

The Battalion set up beds for refugees in schools and gyms around the city as well as manning tea and coffee stalls in Falknsee Chausee and Potzdammer Platz. The Ostmark and the Deutschmark went to parity, ending our cheap nights out in the East and the assault pioneers were despatched to claim a sizeable chunk of the wall to place in The Light Infantry Museum in Winchester. Eventually, the Portacabin that was Allied Checkpoint Charlie, one of the icons of the Cold War, was winched away on 22 June 1990 and the famous Quadriga atop the Brandenburg gate that for so long had faced East was removed, repaired and replaced facing West.

Rupert Firbank

Returning to Bulford in November 1LI went into baulk in preparation for the merger, with a large part of the work landing on the Adjutant, Captain James Hardy's desk. Thirty officers and 154 Senior NCOs and soldiers left on redundancy in the reduction from three regular battalions to two. 1LI was established in Lucknow Barracks, Tidworth, in February 1993 after the merger and moved to Meeanee Barracks, Colchester, in January 1994 as part of 24 Airmobile Brigade, commanded by Brigadier Robin Brims. A smaller Army meant an increased workload and to give an example of how busy life was for the modern infantryman, the Colonel of the Regiment, Major General Michael Regan, listed some of the key events of their very busy schedule in 1993 in his annual report:

- Merger of battalions in February.
- Subsequent takeover and handover of three different barracks and a move from the Tidworth/Bulford area to Colchester.
- A major overseas exercise in the USA.
- Conversion to the airmobile role (in half the usually allotted time).
- Participation in a major multi-national airmobile exercise.
- Recruiting tours in Somerset and Yorkshire.
- Preparation for a period as the Spearhead battalion.
- Preparation for reinforcement of the police at Gatwick.
- Preparation for a firemen's strike which thankfully did not materialize.
- Support of training for Operation GRAPPLE (Bosnia) and for Northern Ireland.
- Sundry minor exercises and competitions.
- Initial training and preparation for a Northern Ireland tour in 1994.

The word 'busy' appeared in almost all *Silver Bugle* articles and other reports of the Battalion's activities, occasionally replaced by 'frenetic'. The Battalion's year was almost entirely dominated by an operational deployment to Fermanagh from May to December; the first major incident – a mortar attack – occurred just two hours after they assumed responsibility for their area of operations! Thankfully there were no casualties. During the Battalion's tour of duty the Northern Ireland 'ceasefire' was announced. 1LI had been stationed in Northern Ireland when the troubles had started 24 years earlier.

The Battalion was warned in June for service in Bosnia and part of the Brigade under command of Brigadier Robin Brims deployed in August. The preparation for Bosnia gave an unparalleled opportunity to train initially at low level and then at all levels of command, with priority use of areas and ammunition, which considerably enhanced their capabilities, cohesion and operational effectiveness.

1LI was warned for a move to Cyprus for a two-year tour from April 1997. After three and a half years in Colchester, a tour as the resident battalion in Episkopi would provide a somewhat more settled existence. Over the past year, the Battalion's tour in South Armagh, due to start in March, had been cancelled – only to be replaced promptly by one in Fermanagh beginning in June. This again gave way to a warning for duty as the stand-by Northern Ireland Rural Reinforcement Battalion. The Canary Wharf bomb in March 1996 precipitated the deployment of reinforcements and the Battalion moved to the Province in June, unfortunately missing out on their promised exercise in June and July in Canada. Fortunately, the duties in Northern Ireland were relatively peaceful and the majority of 1LI were back in Colchester at the beginning of October.

The Battalion moved to Cyprus in April 1997, assuming the role of the Western Sovereign Base resident battalion in Episkopi. Two days after assuming command, the Battalion deployed to counter public disorder and riots by elements of the local population around the Sovereign Base Area. A successful eviction of rioters from the Peel Park Police Station resulted in Commendations to two Senior NCOs and to two soldiers for their part in the action. Training included a deployment on exercise with 5 Royal Armoured Division of the Jordanian Army in Jordan, and a further multinational exercise in the desert with troops from Egypt, France, Italy, USA, UAE and UK.

Opposite left: Maj Ted Shield salutes the President of Sierra Leone, May 2001.

Opposite right: CSjt Chris Smart teaches the Sierra Leone Army how to give orders using a model.

Below: The Recce Platoon on exercise in 'The Zone'.

The Battalion fulfilled a number of duties, including four occasions when deployed on protection duties in support of the Sovereign Base Police. In March 1998 a company strength of 110 soldiers moved to the Falkland Islands for a roulement tour lasting four and a half months. Based at Mount Pleasant Airport, they had elements deployed island-wide with platoons on long-range settlement patrols, Quick Reaction Force, and in-depth infantry training across the Falklands.

Back in Cyprus, in August, as was widely reported in the national press, a major bush fire swept through one of the quarters areas. Fanned by a strong breeze, it took 48 hours of exhausting effort to bring under control, by which time 13 married quarters had been completely destroyed.

The Battalion conducted a six-week deployment to Jordan where they trained with 12 Mechanized Division of the Royal Jordanian Forces – a good respite from the guards and duties of Cyprus, as well as being a great training opportunity to get the Battalion together in a broad joint-operations scenario.

In April 1999 the Battalion moved to Dreghorn Barracks, Edinburgh, and this proved a highly popular posting, both with the single and married soldiers. The support given by the local community was excellent. The barracks had been recently modernized with excellent training and adventure opportunities. It was another busy year with a considerable variety of tasks ranging from the training in total of some 3,000 reservists and formed units for operations in Bosnia and Kosovo (whilst acting as the UK standby battalion) to the undertaking of Winter Public Duties at Edinburgh Castle. An intensive exercise period in the early summer provided an

excellent opportunity to develop the junior command element – both young officers and NCOs. Special attention was also paid to the preparation and performance of all NCOs for their career courses at Brecon. Fitness was emphasized – eight-mile marches with 35–50lbs of equipment and weaponry became the weekly norm.

The First Battalion's year was dominated by training for and deployment yet again to Northern Ireland where they undertook the duties of the Rural Reserve Battalion. They moved to Portadown in late June 2000 and were at the heart of the public-order operations in response to the Loyalist Drumcree marches, and the nightly violence at Drumcree Bridge. The deployment did not stop an extensive programme of individual course and qualification training. Companies exercised in Gibraltar, USA and Kenya and an adventurous training expedition was mounted in Canada in conjunction with the Canadian Army. Making life fun and providing the financial resources for soldiers and officers to be able to take up opportunities offered by service in the Army was an important part of the retention battle which, despite the Army's smaller scale, was becoming an increasingly important part of Regimental priorities.

1LI went early in 2001 to Kenya for six weeks, where a series of company-level training packages was completed. These comprised jungle operations, live firing, and a battalion-level all-arms exercise, but within the period there were extensive opportunities for everyone to enjoy adventure-training pursuits not possible in Scotland. Some 350 of the Battalion then moved on to Sierra Leone on the west coast of Africa on Operation SILKMAN. Sierra Leone had gained its independence from Britain in 1961. A civil war broke out in 1991 and UN troops established an unstable ceasefire until the war was finally declared over in 2002. The country is rich in minerals including diamonds but is the third-lowest-ranked country on the UN's Human Development Index and seventh-lowest on the Human Poverty Index, suffering from endemic corruption. 1LI was deployed as the Short-Term Training Team tasked to provide protection for British personnel and provide training for the Sierra Leone Army (SLA). The Battalion lived in a rundown SLA camp called Benguema, some 20km inland from the capital, Freetown. The Battalion arrived at the end of the dry season with temperatures routinely in the high 30s and then the rainy season turned the dusty camp into a sea of mud.

SLA discipline was 'unusual' and absentees averaged 70 to 100 a day from a force of 1,000. Basic skills were lacking – aiming before firing appeared to be a novelty! At the end of the tour 1LI were relieved by 2LI and then returned to Edinburgh to start their own training for conversion to the Armoured Infantry role in Germany. Edinburgh was no particular respite as duties connected with the foot and mouth outbreak, a firemen's strike in Liverpool, the UK Standby Battalion and the Edinburgh Tattoo all created their own differing pressures.

However, April 2002 saw a return to Germany and Alanbrooke Barracks, Paderborn. Much of the year was spent changing over to the role of Armoured Infantry. Under the guidance of the Armoured Infantry Training and Advisory Team, the Battalion converted into a unit ready to fulfil the demanding operational role it held within 20 Armoured Brigade. This conversion process focused on three distinct core areas. The first was the training of the 220 individuals of all ranks who occupied a turret position in either Warrior Armoured Fighting

Above: Maj Edward Chamberlain gives orders for the assault into Iraq.

Below left: The Assembly Area fills up!

Below: Ad hoc mapping was produced by the Divisional Geographic Cell.

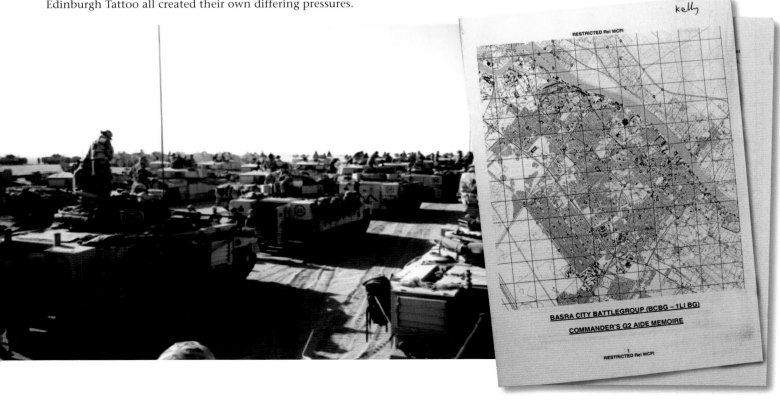

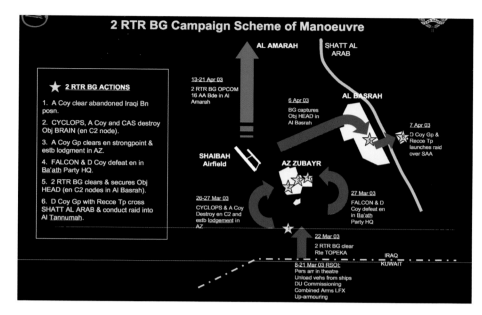

Top: Op TELIC 1 – the 2 Royal Tank Regiment Battle Group actions.

Above: Oil wells burning during the capture of Basra.

sanctions by the UN Security Council, enforcement of no-fly zones and ongoing inspections to prevent Iraqi development of nuclear, chemical or biological weapons. Numerous failures to comply led to an increasingly aggressive US approach supported by the UK. US resolve was strengthened after the 11 September 2001 attacks on the US even though there was no clear evidence of a link between Saddam Hussein and Al Qaeda. Many countries voiced concerns about the US approach, notably Russia, China, Germany, France and Canada. Unlike the First Gulf War, or the war in Afghanistan in 2001, the war in Iraq, which started on 20 March 2003, had no explicit UN authorization and many questioned its legality under international law. According to US President George Bush and British Prime Minister Tony Blair the reasons for the war were 'to disarm Iraq of weapons of mass destruction, to end Saddam Hussein's support for terrorism, and to free the Iraqi people'. No weapons of mass destruction were subsequently found. United States military operations were conducted under Operation IRAQI LIBERATION, although 'Liberation' was soon replaced by 'Freedom' due to the unfortunate acronym 'OIL'. The main body of coalition forces met with little resistance due to massive air power and superior equipment and soldiers, and Baghdad was occupied on 9 April. The main fighting ended on 1 May but post-invasion conflicts still arose with insurgents and 'constructing the peace' was to be a formidable task over many years. Saddam Hussein was captured in December and was tried and hanged afterwards by the Iraqis.

At the start of the war, in early 2003, some 350 officers and soldiers – essentially all three rifle companies' combat power – deployed on the invasion of Iraq called Operation TELIC 1 by the British. The vast majority supported the 2nd Royal Tank Regiment Battle Group as part of 7 Armoured Brigade, but others were deployed with HQ 1 (UK) Armoured Division, HQ 102 Logistic Brigade and 32 Engineer Regiment. 'TELIC' means a purposeful or defined action, but as initial planning took place over the Christmas 2002 period, soldiers jokingly referred to TELIC as standing for 'Tell Everyone Leave Is Cancelled'. The Battalion's support also extended to the preparation for the operation with considerable manpower to the Port Task Group and the pre-deployment training package conducted for 7 Armoured Brigade. The commitment of A and D Company Groups to Operation TELIC 1 ended at the start of May with their return to Germany, fortunately without loss of life and only one serious injury, when Corporal Stesil lost an arm in an ammunition accident.

In July, the Battalion was formally warned to deploy on Operation TELIC 3 in November as part of the 20 Armoured Brigade operation. In August, the Brigade Commander confirmed that the 1LI Battle Group, which included B Squadron of The Queen's Royal Hussars and C Squadron of the 9/12 Lancers, would deploy to the Maysan Province within the Brigade area of operations and relieve the 1st Battalion The King's Own Scottish Borderers. D Company were detached to

Vehicles or Scimitars. The second was the training of the drivers for the 94 armoured vehicles on charge to the Battalion. The third and probably most important area was the integration of the armoured vehicles with the assault troops. Building on the success of their light-role experience in Edinburgh, the three rifle companies, Fire Support Company and Headquarters Company all exercised in their tactical role to complete their introduction to operations in the combined-arms warfighting environment. The culmination of the conversion programme was a two-week, armoured fighting vehicle gunnery camp at Bergen-Hohne, followed by two further weeks of field training based at Sennelager Training Area. This final exercise saw all of the components of the Battalion successfully attaining the required Collective Performance standard and was a key part in preparing for training in 2003 in Poland and Canada.

The First Gulf War had ended on 11 April 1991 with a policy of containment towards Iraq including numerous economic

GOC MND(SE) Commendation
B Company 1ˢᵗ Battalion The Light Infantry
Op TELIC 8 May – November 2006

The Old State Building (OSB) lies in the centre of Basrah City. From this small base the UK Multi-National Division gains significant intelligence, while the central location secures considerable oversight, insight and tactical influence for the ground-holding Brigade. The Militia recognise the symbolic and practical value of OSB and have consistently seen it as a threat to be destroyed.

B Company 1st Battalion The Light Infantry have held OSB for 7-months in the face of unrelenting enemy pressure. 132 mortar and rocket rounds and 121 Rocket Propelled Grenades have hit the compound, and B Company has also recorded more than 200 contacts involving sniper and small arms fire. Simultaneously the Improvised Explosive Device (IED) threat in the City increased, with 5 vehicles hit. The Militia sought to attack, harass, kill and break the spirit of B Company at every opportunity. It is testament to the resolute bravery, indomitable spirit and professional attitude of all members of the Company that the enemy failed miserably. This victory came at a cost; Corporal Cornish was killed, and 8 others wounded in action.

From the Officer Commanding to the newest private, every soldier has played their part; from the chef to mechanic, medic to storeman as well as those engaged in security operations. Their stoic acceptance of often appalling living and working conditions has been exemplary. The Company as a whole have epitomised offensive spirit and pride.

B Company has been consistently in the thick of the action. No other sub-unit have faced such an unrelenting, severe and demanding test of leadership, character and cohesion. Uncomplaining, ruthlessly professional and utterly brave, B Company deserve, uniquely as a group, the highest recognition.

Maj Gen
GOC MND (SE)

Above: Scenes from Op TELIC.

The Queen's Royal Hussars Battlegroup and deployed to the Northern Basra area of operations. After the required pre-deployment training, the 1LI Battle Group moved in from 19 October 2003 until April 2004.

The tour in Iraq was characterized by occasional attacks against members of the 1LI Battlegroup as the business of rebuilding the Iraqi security forces was carried out. In February, in Majar Al Kabir, a battle took place between locals of the town, reinforced by tribal elements coming in from surrounding areas, and various members of the Battlegroup as they arrived on the scene. The battle lasted three to four hours and was commanded by Major James Faux, Officer Commanding Fire Support Company; he was joined by members of several other cap-badges including The Argyll and Sutherland Highlanders, The Princess of Wales's Royal Regiment and The Parachute Regiment. Command and control were particularly difficult and enemy reinforcements appeared to be coming in from surrounding areas as the battle continued. However, after considerable expenditure of ammunition and political intervention from members of the Maysan Provincial Council, calm was restored. Minor casualties were sustained by members of 1LI but there were no fatalities.

A second upsurge in violence occurred towards the end of the tour after an influential rebel cleric, Muqtada Sadr, ordered his followers to attack members of the coalition after the mosque in the holy city of Najaf became surrounded by US troops. This manifested itself in an immediate series of ambushes and attacks on members of A Company who were patrolling in the town of Al Amarah. Warriors were brought into the town on many occasions to retain control but this was also balanced against the disruption they caused to many of the law-abiding inhabitants. The company base in the town was co-located with the Coalition Provisional Authority's offices and this, together with the Iraqi administrative building, became the focus for violence from Sadr's supporters. All sub-units in the Battlegroup were used to maintain control of the town over the few remaining days and weeks of the tour. This level of violence continued until 1LI Battlegroup handed over its area of responsibility to 1st Battalion of The Princess of Wales's Royal Regiment.

1LI had a year referred to officially as 'Other Tasks'! This is not an easy role, as it involves the provision of soldiers to other organizations for all sorts of tasks. Soldiers don't join the Army intending to conduct 'other tasks'! After July, things began to look up as a major training opportunity arose with a deployment to Altengrabow in the former East Germany and to Drawsko Pomorskie in Poland. War-fighting skills were re-learnt and the Battalion prepared to begin training specific to its deployment to Iraq in the spring. In addition to these major professional duties, members of 1LI were on operations in Iraq, Afghanistan, the Balkans and Sierra Leone while training teams and individuals deployed in support of units in the UK, Canada, Germany, Yemen, Belize and the Czech Republic. A significant part of D Company deployed to the British Army Training Unit at Suffield in Canada in support of 7 Armoured Brigade, and many smaller teams contributed to the pre-deployment training of 7 Brigade.

2006 was entirely devoted to the preparation for, and deployment to, the third tour of Iraq (on Op TELIC 8). Training for the operation began immediately on return from Christmas leave with all members of the 1LI Battlegroup – initially consisting of B and D Companies 1LI, A Squadron Queen's Royal Hussars (QRH), and 17 Bty 26 Regt RA – participating in a comprehensive Operational Training and Advisory Group (OPTAG) package that predominantly included tactical training

but also educated the Battlegroup on the cultural sensitivities of working in the country. In line with the Battlegrouping system, A Company 1LI was attached to the QRH Battlegroup and conducted their training with them. Early April saw the initial deployment of 1LI soldiers to Iraq, with A Company first off to Maysan Province with the QRH Battlegroup. This was followed by the 1LI Battlegroup taking control of the Basra City Area of Operations (AO). The Battlegroup was thrown very much into the deep end with an extremely successful detention-and-search operation against the Jaish Al Mahdi Militia headquarters elements, just two days after taking control. This was to be the first of many successful operations conducted by the Battlegroup and set the tone for the remainder of the tour.

The Battlegroup was split between the three multinational force bases within Basra City: the Shat-Al-Arab Hotel, the Old State Buildings and Basra Palace. This in itself presented numerous logistical challenges in addition to difficulties with command and control and communications. All of this was tested to the absolute limit when a Lynx helicopter was shot down over Basra on 6 May. 1LI soldiers were some of the first on the scene and spent many tough hours under attack in order to prevent local interference with the crash site, and allow the clearance of the wreckage.

Above: 1LI Desert Warriors, *painted by David Rowlands. The artist drew soldiers of The Light Infantry rapidly dismounting and attacking from Warrior armoured personnel carriers, and painted this scene from sketches he made on the spot in Az Zubayr, Iraq, 2003.*

The day-to-day work of the Battlegroup centred on the training and mentoring of the Iraqi Security Forces, and the implementation of consent-winning CIMIC (Civil Military Cooperation) projects all around the city. With such a large area of operations many thousands of miles were covered in both Warrior and Snatch vehicles – simply keeping them on the road was a task in itself and the soldiers spent many long hours hard at work ensuring that the Battlegroup could remain mobile. June saw a change in boundaries with the city being split into two – an acceptance of the sheer enormity of the original task; 1LI Battlegroup retaining the northern and western portions of the City and 2 R Anglian Battlegroup taking control of the south. All of the hard work produced by 1LI soldiers was set against a constant

Below: CSM 'Harry' Harrison, during the riots in Basra City.

background of violence and danger; improvised explosive devices and rocket propelled grenade/small arms fire attacks were an ever-present threat whilst indirect fire became almost a nightly theme, claiming the lives of two excellent soldiers – Corporal Matthew Cornish and Lance Corporal Dennis Brady. This never stopped the officers and soldiers from completing their tasks; it merely strengthened their resolve to succeed.

In October the Battalion returned to Paderborn. The announcement of the formation of a new Regiment, The Rifles, had already been made by the Ministry of Defence on 24 November 2005. It was implemented on 1 February 2007, four months after the return to Paderborn, and the era of The Light Infantry came to a close.

The Second Battalion
1968–2007

Montgomery Barracks, Berlin (1968–9)

Once it had been confirmed that a new Regiment was to be formed from the four Light Infantry regiments, Lieutenant Colonel Tony Elcomb, Commanding Officer, addressed the 1st Battalion King's Own Yorkshire Light Infantry at Montgomery Barracks, Berlin. He recalled how the officers of the 51st LI had presented a silver snuff box, in the form of a coffin mounted on a gun carriage, to mark their disapproval of the Cardwell Reforms of 1881. Now, 1 KOYLI would become the 2nd Battalion The Light Infantry. If 2LI were no better than 1 KOYLI, the fault would lie with those serving in the Regiment. There was no ceremony to mark the passing of the King's Own Yorkshire Light Infantry. Badges, signs and notices were replaced overnight with those of the new Light Infantry. This no-nonsense, down-to-earth 'WILCO' approach to soldiering was to be the hallmark of 2LI throughout its 39 years on the active Army List.

The 2LI story therefore starts in Berlin at the height of the Cold War. Part of the Berlin Infantry Brigade, the Battalion was to be found guarding the Allied Kommandantura, Spandau Prison, Sector Headquarters and British passenger and freight trains. Patrols of East Berlin, known as 'Flag Tours', designed to demonstrate British rights of access to the Soviet sector, and regular patrols of the border, formed the balance of the duties. Berlin was an exciting garrison in which to serve but they

were soon to be on the move. Shortly after Lieutenant Colonel Peter Sibbald assumed command in October 1968, news of an overseas exercise to Malaysia and a new posting to Colchester did much to raise morale, particularly among the single soldiers.

Brigadier RWL McAllister, Commander Berlin Infantry Brigade, conducting the Annual 'Fitness for Role' (FFR) inspection in March 1969, found:

'This is a hard, tough unit which should give a good account of itself anywhere on active service. Within Berlin's limitations the Battalion has, by a sustained effort over its two years here, maintained a high degree of physical fitness and tactical skill … The Battalion is relaxed, cheerful, happy, smart and proud of itself. It makes little attempt to 'show off', rather does it prefer to let its actions and successes speak for themselves. It is a thoroughly practical, professional unit with no frills.'

Meanee Barracks, Colchester (April 1969–March 1974)

In April 1969 the Battalion moved to Meanee Barracks, Colchester, and the 3rd Division's 19 Airportable Brigade. Around 120 men from the recently disbanded 4LI joined them.

By the end of May, 2LI was undergoing two months of jungle warfare training in Malaysia. Counter-revolutionary

Above: *The Freedom of Stockton accepted by Maj Gen David Tyacke, and (inset) commemorative stained-glass window from Dhekelia Garrison Church*

Left: *Maj 'Chalkie' White in Mess Dress (left) and Bugle Maj Graham Gilbert in No1 Dress Ceremonial (right).*

Opposite: *A slice of life in the Second Battalion.*

warfare skills were honed with helicopter deployments, long approach marches through the jungle and a series of ambushes, counter-ambushes and search-and-destroy operations. The final ten days in Malaysia offered superb opportunities to further explore the Far East, followed by return to Colchester.

Meanwhile, the deteriorating situation in Northern Ireland prompted some precautionary internal security training. After several false starts, the Battalion deployed to Belfast by ferry in September for its first Northern Ireland tour.

The Battalion quickly adapted to the mounting sectarian violence, rioting, petrol bombing, vehicle checkpoints, sniping and searches. Operating mainly in the Crumlin Road and New Lodge Road areas, 2LI was also responsible for the Unity Flats, or 'Lunacy Flats' as they were better known. Companies and platoons were regularly detached to other units, thus giving everyone a good feel for the situation across the city.

The so-called 'Battle of the Shankill', involving all three Light Infantry battalions, took place in mid-October and marked a turning point for the Army in Belfast. At the height of the battle, with rounds flying overhead and 3LI fighting their way up the road, the Commanding Officer and his group were at Unity Flats holding back the press. Lieutenant Tim Clarke and his platoon were deployed in the 'Disperse or We Fire' formation employed at the time. Tim Clarke radioed the Commanding Officer, asking if his platoon might take cover. The reply that they could kneel if necessary brought the quick answer: 'What I had in mind was lying down!' Perceptions changed that night. The next day 2LI was tasked to remove 'Radio Free Ulster' on the Shankill with five companies and two troops of Saladin armoured cars.

Having seen little of their families since April, 2LI returned to Colchester in January 1970 for a belated Christmas. The Battalion had undertaken three very different roles within a year and there was a considerable training backlog. They were also off to Malaysia again. With the war in Vietnam at its height, this exercise was designed to demonstrate the UK's ability to move forces rapidly to South East Asia and, after a short period of acclimatization and training, to support our allies on operations.

Based mostly at the Jungle Warfare School at Kota Tinggi from April to July, the exercise was the perfect antidote to

2LI TOURS

Montgomery Barracks, Berlin, February 1968 – April 1969

Meanee Barracks, Colchester, April 1969 – March 1974

Belfast, September 1969 – January 1970

Armagh, June – October 1971

Newry, February – March 1972

Londonderry, June – October 1972

Belfast, March – July 1973

Stornoway Barracks, Lemgo, March 1974 – December 1977

Londonderry, March – July 1975

West Belfast, July – December 1976

Abercorn Barracks, Ballykinler, January 1978 – August 1979

Gibraltar, September 1979 – July 1981

Weeton Barracks, Blackpool, July 1981 – November 1984

South Armagh, April – September 1982

Falkland Islands Coy Gp, August – December 1983

Peninsula Barracks, Deilinghofen, November 1984 – March 1989

West Belfast, July – December 1987

Lucknow Barracks, Tidworth, March 1989 – February 1993

Armagh, December 1989 – June 1990

Province Reserve Battalion, November 1990 – December 1990

South Armagh, August – September 1991

South Armagh, March – September 1992

MERGER OF 1ST, 2ND AND 3RD BATTALIONS 26 FEBRUARY 1993

Alanbrooke Barracks, Paderborn, February 1993 – December 1997

East Tyrone, June – December 1993

Bosnia, Op GRAPPLE, November 1995 – May 1996

Palace Barracks, Belfast, January 1997 – April 1999

Kiwi Barracks, Bulford Camp, April 1999 – February 2002

B Coy, South Armagh, January – March 2000

A Coy, South Armagh, March – April 2000

B Coy, South Armagh, April – May 2000

C Coy, Bosnia, October 1999 – April 2000

Kosovo, September – November 2000

Sierra Leone, June – September 2001

Alexander Barracks, Dhekelia, February 2002 – February 04

Falkland Islands B Coy, October 2002 – February 2003

Falkland Islands A Coy, February – July 2003

Iraq – Op TELIC 2, September – November 2003

Redford Barracks, Edinburgh, February 2004- January 2007

South Armagh, September 2004 – March 2005

Beirut – Op HIGHBROW, July 2006

Iraq – Op TELIC 8, October 2006

Afghanistan – Op HERRICK

FORMATION OF THE RIFLES, 1 FEBRUARY 2007

Belfast. The main exercise took place on the north-east coast near Kuala Terengganu. The climax was a brigade attack which highlighted the perennial problems of locating enemy positions, command and control and the heavy rate of attrition

Top left: Training in Tin City – the CO is captured!

when taking on well-defended ridge positions in jungle. Most of the Battalion returned by air but a small party came home on HMS *Bulwark* via Australia, Indonesia and South Africa.

After leave, courses and cadres continued. Marksmanship was accorded a high priority, although a month of public duties in London in the autumn intervened. Following a period of intensive drill under a saintly Grenadier Guards Drill Sergeant, the Battalion was deemed up to standard. A and B Companies provided the Guards for Buckingham Palace and St James's Palace, while Support and Command Companies carried out duties at HM Tower of London and the Bank of England. Although 2LI was never invited back, public duties were apparently much enjoyed but for one fact: the price of beer in London.

After several stints as 'Spearhead' battalion, 2LI 'hosted' the presentation of Colours to 2LI, 3LI and LI(V) by Her Majesty Queen Elizabeth The Queen Mother on 7 May 1971. The Commanding Officer, Lieutenant Colonel Peter Sibbald, commanded the parade. The Battalion's Colours were received from the Colonel-in-Chief by Lieutenants Richard Cousens (Queen's Colour) and Janusz Heath (Regimental Colour). Major Tony Wilson and Major Antony Makepeace-Warne commanded Number 1 and 2 Guards. It was an historic and memorable day, executed with pride, precision and panache.

The Battalion returned to Northern Ireland in June. Battalion HQ, Echelon, B and Support Companies were based at Gough Barracks in Armagh whilst A Company was based in

Enniskillen for a month before moving to Newry. D Company was based at Dungannon.

Operations for the first month were confined to patrols, roadblocks, ambushes and visits to vulnerable points. On 9 August, a Province-wide operation was mounted to intern all IRA suspects: 83 per cent of the targets in the Battalion area were arrested, the remainder being 'away from home'. Reaction was swift and violent. Street disorder and shootings were widespread, not least in Newry where A Company was reinforced with two batteries and an armoured car squadron.

On 15 September, Private Rudman was fatally wounded when a B Company convoy was ambushed at night on the road between Dungannon and Coalisland. Most casualties recovered quite quickly and returned to duty but Corporal Nicholas lost an eye in a bomb blast and Private Bryan was paralysed by a gunshot wound. The Battalion returned to Colchester at the end of October.

Lieutenant Colonel Robert MacGregor-Oakford assumed command in November 1971 in time for specialist cadres and preparation for a month on 'Spearhead'. There were rumours of Malta but, two weeks later, the Battalion was back in Northern Ireland following 'Bloody Sunday' to counter civil disturbance in the wake of the deaths of 13 civilians in Londonderry. A and B Companies were deployed into Newry to cover routes and to man barriers, D Company to the Mourne Mountains to establish roadblocks to capture escaped detainees, whilst the rest of the Battalion was held at ten minutes' notice in Ballykinler as airmobile Province reserve with six Wessex helicopters. 2LI was then moved to Londonderry to counter a threatened 'Day of Disruption' to mark the six-month anniversary of internment on 9 February. The day passed relatively quietly and 2LI returned to Colchester via the night ferry.

Right: A Northern Ireland aide-memoire – issued to all commanders – and the supporting 'cards'. The Yellow Card carried the rules of engagement.

Below: Snatch Squads training hard.

Below right: A multiple patrol in the Ardoyne, 1980s.

THE PEACEKEEPER

Our forefathers fused a thousand years of Light Infantry history in 1968. How was this child going to make its mark? The bushfire wars seemed over – Borneo, Malaya, Cyprus, Aden. But, still wet behind the ears, all three new battalions stood shoulder-to-shoulder on the Shankill as Ulster's Troubles erupted in 1969. And so a new generation of Light Infantrymen was born into an internal security background that re-ignited the regimental flame of self-belief. It was the perfect setting for giving the young JNCO and subaltern early operational confidence.

This was just as well, as the BAOR postings piled up, suggesting a 'heavy' future – Sir John Moore's descendants in decaying tin cans on the Hanoverian Plain? But the new breed forced through fast during successive emergency operational tours in Belfast, South Armagh and Derry, to become a byword for junior leadership excellence. By the 1980s, The Light Infantry had rediscovered itself. It has always been a lucky Regiment, and the advent of Airmobility gave the Regiment a second unequalled opportunity to excel.

As their pre-eminence in internal security and airmobility developed, The Light Infantry took on an enviable reputation that stayed intact throughout its short existence. Its subalterns were hand-picked from a handsomely over-subscribed application list, its serjeants' messes turned out dozens of superb Commissioned Officers and the soldiers really were Tina Turner's 'Simply the best' outfit. In 1987, 2LI won the BAOR Tickell Fitness Trophy, the Tickell Shooting Competition, the BAOR award for adventurous training and moved an armoured regiment into its vehicle accommodation while completing a six-month tour of Belfast. A Green Jacket GOC was to describe it as 'the best unit in BAOR'.

In 1988, the Ballygawley bomb wiped out a platoon of 1LI soldiers. Within a week, they were replaced by a full platoon of 2LI soldiers, who had only returned from post-Op BANNER leave a month before. They were picked from 100 volunteers answering the call and were operational before the Chain of Command woke up to splutter about an unauthorized deployment from 6 Airmob Bde to 39 Inf Bde.

The emergence of this 'just do it' self-confidence, never arrogant, occasionally risky, became a remarkable regimental characteristic.

And so, from three to two battalions and then the formation of The Rifles... Can that same, ancient Light Infantry thread survive? It seems so... But blow me down – they've kept that cap badge, symbol of the Cold War peacekeeper, second to none.

Brig Jim Parker

Opposite, clockwise from far left: Lt Col Jim Parker in West Belfast, 1987; Rural route clearance, Newry; Access Control, Belfast city centre.

Right: Soldiers of 2LI lining the decks of their sea transport to Northern Ireland.

Below: Cordon duty – long, tedious and very dangerous.

Below right: Page 3 girls were a regular morale raiser on operational tours.

THE LIGHT INFANTRY AT BISLEY 1976

At the regular Skill at Arms Meeting 1976, it is regretted to have to report that The Light Infantry put up its usual rather dismal performance. It is true that The Light Infantry Depot team came higher up in order, 10th out of 33, than any Light Infantry team for many years and that Cpl. Loveridge of 3LI did well to get into the Army Hundred, but as a Regiment it was a poor result.

It is sad to note that we appear to have the worst attendance record at Bisley of any similar Regiment over the last ten years. According to the ARA, the Depot has been six times, 3LI twice, 1LI once and 2LI never.

Formal pre-Northern Ireland training began again in April, but 240 men were sent to Yorkshire and County Durham to 'Keep the Army in the Public Eye' (KAPE). Large and enthusiastic crowds watched them march through Sunderland, Hartlepool, Durham, Wakefield and Pontefract. Back in Londonderry, 2LI assumed operational command of the western half of the city and country beyond out to the Irish border. Major Makepeace-Warne's company was established in a base within the Creggan 'no go' area, reached by a single road in and out. Major Dinwiddie's company occupied the adjacent Brook Park while the other companies responsible for the Shantallow estate and hinterland were based together with Battalion HQ in Fort George on the River Foyle. In the early weeks of the tour, all military operations were 'low profile' in order to facilitate a short-lived political initiative.

The provisional IRA (PIRA) declared a ceasefire in late June but the Battalion wisely did not lower its guard. On the very first night, two gunmen were shot as they moved forward at night to engage sentry posts. There were several similar incidents and Special Branch confirmed five IRA casualties. The ceasefire collapsed on 9 July and IRA activity increased. In a heated but effective firefight, A Company, led by Major Furness, disposed of a semi-permanent IRA roadblock on the Strabane Road. The Battalion took part in Operation

CARCAN on 31 July which opened up the Creggan and Bogside 'no-go' areas. On 25 August Serjeant Arthur Whitelock was shot dead by a sniper while on patrol in the Shantallow Estate. Corporal Nev Robson was to be awarded the Military Medal for his gallantry during the tour.

2LI were back in Colchester by mid-October, already aware that they would be returning for a fifth tour in Ulster in March 1973, this time in West Belfast. Here, the Battalion's outstanding surveillance teams delivered first-class intelligence which helped 2LI to virtually destroy PIRA's '2nd Battalion', capturing no fewer than 32 of its 'officers', including Gerry Adams. In the first two months the Battalion was involved in 80 shooting incidents, one rocket attack, 12 bomb hoaxes and 20 explosions, one of which, on 13 May 1973, mortally wounded Corporal Tommy Taylor and Private John Gaskell, and seriously injured Privates Henry and Barwell. However, 2LI had already arrested over 200 suspects, captured two gunmen red-handed and claimed five hits. As local government elections in Ulster loomed, the propaganda and shooting campaigns intensified. The Battalion came in for special attention thanks to its effective operational and public relations initiatives.

Private Roberts was killed by a sniper on 1 July and shortly afterwards Private Power was shot at close range by a sniper firing through the letterbox of a house in

If you go down to the woods today...

the Clonard. Immediate surgery in the excellent Royal Victoria Hospital saved his life. These incidents were to prove a turning point. Arrest operations followed and those responsible for the murder and attempted murder of two LI soldiers were all tracked down. Handing over to 3 RGJ on 26 July, Lieutenant Colonel Robert MacGregor-Oakford was subsequently awarded the OBE and Corporal Michael Thompson was to be awarded the Military Medal for his gallantry during the tour.

Stornoway Barracks, Lemgo (March 1974–January 1978)

After very nearly five years in Colchester, 2LI swapped barracks with 1LI in March 1974, moving to BAOR and Stornoway Barracks in Lemgo, Westphalia. Lieutenant Colonel Tony Hare assumed command in Lemgo. Under the watchful eye of HQ 20 Armoured Brigade, Battalion and company HQs were immediately launched on a series of Command Post Exercises (CPXs) while the remainder of the Battalion began training for their mechanized role in 432s. 2LI's first training season in BAOR culminated with Exercise 'Forefront (North)', the 20 Armoured Brigade phase of the annual divisional Field Training Exercise (FTX). The Brigade Commander reported, 'I was particularly pleased with the way in which 2LI, new to the role of mechanized infantry, took to their task'. Then came news of the Battalion's sixth Northern Ireland tour – Londonderry again – in March 1975.

2LI took over as Londonderry's Creggan battalion on 18 March 1975. Throughout the tour, a state of 'ceasefire' existed which required all ranks to exercise great ingenuity. Unusually, 2LI wore their own cap badges, patrolled at walking pace, stayed out of back gardens, did no house searches, or personality (P) checks, and suffered no serious casualties. No soldier fired his personal weapon at an identified target and no terrorist was served an interim custody order as a result of an arrest. For those who remembered the 1973 Londonderry tour, it was at best unnerving and at worst frustrating. It also conveyed a dangerously false impression to those soldiers experiencing Northern Ireland for the first time.

Having handed over the Creggan in June, the Battalion moved to Belfast to reinforce the garrison for the Loyalist marches of 12 July. Despite fine weather and a large crowd, the marches passed without incident and 2LI returned to Lemgo in mid-July, already warned for yet another Ireland tour in July 1976. It would be four years before 2LI was put through its mechanized paces and battlegroup field firing at BATUS. There was one consolation though: both Christmas 1975 and Christmas 1976 would be spent with the families.

In late August, 2LI began its second mechanized training season, undertaking various trials designed to test new 'battle' establishments. Training continued throughout the winter months and the Battalion was able to catch up with all the specialist cadres necessary to man the weapons, vehicles and equipment. A Battalion Revue, masterminded by the

THE CROSSING OF THE ESLA

The firm bonds of friendship between the 51st Light Infantry and the 15th Hussars were forged at the crossing of the River Esla on 31 May 1813 during the Peninsular War. The crossing was of no tactical importance but the river was in full spate. Holding onto stirrups and tails, the 51st Light Infantry were helped across the river by the 15th Hussars, saving many from a watery grave. The friendship endured and over time the crossing was commemorated by way of a sports competition whenever proximity and programmes allowed the two regiments (and their successors) to meet. The prize was possession of an oil painting, commissioned in 1932, which depicts the crossing. 2LI and the 15th/19th Hussars commemorated the crossing three times: June 1975 at Fallingbostel; April 1987 at Detmold; and April 1988 at Deilinghofen. The painting remained elusive and it is now with the Light Dragoons.

Bandmaster, was staged in the run-up to Christmas as well as an All Ranks Dance in the Schutzenhaus Halle. And, despite many administrative difficulties and unseasonably high temperatures on the slopes, 2LI and 3LI met at the end of March for The Light Infantry Ski Meeting, the first contest for ten years, at Grasgehren, Bavaria.

Although the Battalion had six tours behind it, such was the turnover of manpower that some 60 per cent of the rifle companies' private soldiers had no experience of the Province. The full Northern Ireland training package was therefore critical. Lieutenant Colonel Roger Preston took command of the Battalion before the West Belfast tour at the end of July 1976. Within an hour, a B Company patrol came under sniper attack, a warm welcome to what was to be a fortnight of serious disturbance – on a scale not seen by the Battalion since 1973 – to mark the anniversary of internment on 9 August. Most of the trouble – sniping attacks, rioting, vehicle hijacks and arson – was centred on the Falls Road, but all companies were involved. In all, 38 rounds were fired at 2LI, and 15 rounds returned. Five hundred and sixty five baton rounds

A LIFE ON THE OCEAN WAVE

The Light Infantry had an enviable reputation for offshore sailing during the late 1970s and 80s, and one man is indirectly responsible for setting these events in chain, surprisingly the late Major David Bower! He was responsible for sending one Sjt Jarratt and the then Lieutenant Ranald Blue on a cross-channel sailing trip on board *Kukri*, an Army Nicholson 55' Yacht. The idea being to get one of us qualified to act as Mate in order to take some Junior Soldiers on a sailing exercise in the Med. Well, both Ranald and I sat at the back of *Kukri* all the way to Cherbourg and back throwing up every bit of the way! 'Sod that for a game of soldiers' says I, 'unlucky, get back out there' says David Bower! To cut a very long story short, I got over sea sickness, Ranald as far as I know did not, and I ended up being bitten by the sailing bug very severely. Resulting achievements from a Regimental perspective were to have crews participating in countless offshore and ocean sailing expeditions, entering the Barmouth to Fort William Three Peaks Yacht and Running race twice, winning it the second time. Competing in the Alboran Race in the Med, the Fastnet Race, the Tall Ships Race, Services Offshore Races and many others. Hundreds if not thousands of Light Infanteers took part in offshore sailing during this time. They may have loved it, they may have hated it, but one fact is for sure, all would have been the better for the experience. These achievements would not have been possible without a hard core of Light Infantrymen who were willing to give up their leave and free time to learn to sail, become qualified and then take soldiers sailing. These include the late Tim (Admiral) Offley, Dave Lambert, Paul Butler, Sas Sore, Lee Potter, Bob Humphries to name a few.

Major Dave Jarratt

Above: *Dave Jarratt at the helm of Ensign Dyas.*

Right: *Anti-pirate drills on the Ensign Dyas in the Indian Ocean.*

were also used and eventually, in a seven-company Battalion operation, order was restored to the area and routes cleared. The Commanding Officer had a narrow escape in October when he came under fire in the Turf Lodge. A bullet hit the Land Rover door on the driver's side and lodged in the radio battery beneath the CO's seat. By the end of the tour, 47 people had been charged with serious offences as a result of arrests by 2LI. The Battalion returned to Lemgo in early December.

It was back to the vehicle parks in the New Year and preparation for PRE and ARU inspections. The exercise season was to be the Battalion's last chance to practise mechanized procedures, tactics and associated individual skills. In May D Company, the Bugle Platoon and the Reconnaissance Platoon deployed to Denmark for an exercise with 1st Prinsens Livregiment. National honour was momentarily upheld with the capture of a highly prized prisoner – a Dane in uniform carrying a marked map. Disappointingly, he turned out to be the local postman!

1977 was the year of Her Majesty The Queen's Silver Jubilee and on 7 July the mechanized might of the British Army of the Rhine paraded for a Review to mark the occasion. 2LI was on parade. The Review commenced with the march on of the Standard, Guidon and Colour Parties of 24 regiments to the Massed Bands, Corps of Drums, Pipes and Bugles (over 800 men). There followed an inspection by Her Majesty and a drive past of the vehicles on parade. During the afternoon the Battalion were honoured by a visit from Field Marshal and Lady Harding and Major General David Tyacke, the latter on his last official duty as Colonel of the Regiment.

The Battalion completed Northern Ireland training in the autumn. After Christmas, there was a final three weeks' refresher training before Stornoway Barracks was handed over to the 1st Battalion The Royal Welch Fusiliers, ending a ten-year association between The Light Infantry and Lemgo.

Abercorn Barracks, Ballykinler (January 1978–July 1979)

2LI took over Abercorn Barracks, Ballykinler, in the last week of January 1978. Situated just 500 yards from the beach and with views of the Mourne Mountains, all the married quarters were within the barracks perimeter, making security and administration that much easier.

There were four basic tasks required of the Battalion. One company was deployed in South Armagh under the command of the South Armagh battalion, a second company was on guard and the two remaining companies were known as Province Reserve 1 and Province Reserve 2. Throughout the two-year tour, Support Company operated as a rifle company. In theory, companies changed tasks every month so no married man would be away from his family for more than four weeks. In April, 2LI assumed responsibility for Newry, operating under command of the South Armagh battalion. A platoon was later deployed to Castlederg, on the border with the Republic, for two-week tours following the bombing of that village in November 1978. As the Battalion was never complete at any one time, short three-week NCOs' cadres were run, designed to teach potential patrol commanders the skills and procedures needed, and to assess their suitability for promotion to Lance Corporal.

Margaret Thatcher, at that time Leader of the Opposition, visited the Battalion early one Sunday morning. Corporal Moffat of the Bugle Platoon, a well-known advocate of trade union representation in the Army, received a long lecture by Mrs Thatcher on just how inappropriate that would be.

The end of the year brought the ARU, a pantomime and the usual Christmas parties. In his ARU report, Commander 3 Brigade, Brigadier David Thorne, concluded: 'I find it a very proper Battalion'. The pantomime received equally rave reviews.

Lieutenant Colonel Tim Bevan assumed command of 2LI at the end of January 1979. In May the whole Battalion deployed, in snow, to cover the polling stations during the General Election. Each polling station was visited by the Commanding Officer and the local Unionist candidate, Mr Enoch Powell. When the Castlederg commitment ended, the Battalion provided a platoon for 2 RGJ at Aughnacloy until the end of the tour. Other developments included the protection of convoys to Crossmaglen and Forkhill, patrolling the Dublin-to-Belfast railway line, and covering the Orange March in Newtownhamilton on 12 July. At the end of July, 2LI handed over Abercorn Barracks to 2nd Battalion The Parachute Regiment and departed on leave for a month before moving to Gibraltar in September.

Gibraltar (September 1979–July 1981)

After Northern Ireland, two years on the 'Rock' in the Mediterranean sun was a very attractive prospect. The Battalion soon slipped into the two-week duty cycle of military training, guards and ceremonial, administration and fatigues and adventure training. The Guard and Ceremonial Company was committed to the Convent Guard and the Frontier Platoon Guard which found a four-man ceremonial day guard by the frontier gates and manned three OPs along the border.

Adventure training was extremely popular, with inshore sailing, canoeing, sub-aqua, snorkelling, fishing, archery and clay-pigeon shooting on offer. During the summer two Safari Land Rovers were available for expeditions to Morocco. The Battalion also played an active part in the Colony's social calendar with cocktail parties and floodlit Sounding of Retreats on Lathbury Square and at Victoria Stadium, as well as the annual Queen's Birthday Parade on Naval Number 1 Ground in June. Salamanca Day in 1979 was marked with a Tattoo. After much effort, a programme lasting three and a quarter hours was produced, including acts by each of the three rifle companies as well as the Gibraltar Regiment, static displays and band performances. Raising nearly £250,000 for charity, some 3,000 people watched the Tattoo over three nights. A visit in October by the Regiment's affiliated ship, HMS

RUTHERFOORD BOWL/YORKSHIRE CANTER

During a visit of 1/4 KOYLI veterans in June 1986, Major Andrew Rutherfoord MC laid down a gauntlet to the Commanding Officer: he would present a magnificent silver rose bowl upon which would be engraved the names of anyone in the Battalion who could march 100 miles in 24 hours. The challenge was accepted and thus was born Exercise 'Yorkshire Canter', competed for in April 1987 for the first time. Success – 100 miles in 24 hours – eluded the Battalion at the first attempt but Corporal 'Coco' Cocoran completed an extraordinary 96 miles in the time, and 100 miles in under 25 hours.

Lieutenant Colonel Richard Cousens took command of the Battalion in October 1988 in time for Exercise 'Yorkshire Canter' at Sennelager. Lieutenant Richard Fullerton and Serjeant Cocoran both completed the 100 miles in 23 hours and 47 minutes, doubling the last mile to the Regimental double march, with the route lined by the entire Battalion. It was an incredible feat of physical endurance.

In October 1989 Exercise 'Yorkshire Canter' took place over two 50-mile circuits around the Somerset levels. Private Hiles secured his place on the plinth of the Rutherfoord Bowl by completing the 100 miles in 23 hours 55 minutes.

Above: Cpl Cocoran marches in on – and then deals with – a very sore pair of feet.

Invincible, added to the carnival spirit and justified three weeks of combined social and sporting activity.

A Battalion skill-at-arms meeting was held in the spring to identify the team to shoot at Bisley later in the year. A strong party was dispatched to the Infantry Demonstration Battalion (IDB) at Warminster for three months. Only the second time the Battalion had entered Bisley since 1968, the team came a creditable 36th in the Major Unit Championship and 23rd in the Infantry.

Because field training was so limited in Gibraltar, arrangements were made for the resident battalion to leave the Rock periodically. Each company returned to Salisbury Plain on Exercise 'Rocksand' for three and a half weeks to classify, field fire and conduct low-level tactical exercises.

In late 1979/early 1980, 2LI took part in two major exercises. The first of these, NATO Exercise 'Wintex', required the Battalion and other Army units in Gibraltar to undertake a number of tasks associated with transition to a war footing. These included exercises covering anti-hijack, major disaster relief, hostage release from caves and tunnels, KP manning, bomb-disposal procedures, and assistance to both the RN and the RAF. Two companies assisted the Royal Navy with their Exercise 'Spring Train', a dockyard internal security exercise to test the crews of HM ships on action to be taken when in a hostile port.

As a final fling, and with the Padre the only man in step, the Battalion marched through the town in the last week of the tour. A fitting end to the Battalion's two years on the Rock, salutes were taken by the Governor and the Mayor, both of whom were presented with silver bugles. In July 1981, duties were handed over to the 1st Battalion The Staffordshire Regiment, and 2LI moved to Weeton Camp near Blackpool where, on Minden Day, Lieutenant Colonel Mike Dru Drury assumed command.

Weeton Camp, Blackpool (July 1981–December 1984)

The sea and sandy beaches of Blackpool's Golden Mile were not a bad substitute for Gibraltar. Just eight miles from Blackpool, the former RAF camp at Weeton with its old Nissen huts was to be 2LI's home for three happy years. It was the Battalion's first 'home' posting since Colchester, with Yorkshire, the North East and Shropshire all within easy striking distance. Blackpool and the Lake District were also to make Weeton a popular posting. But there was training to be done and the immediate priority was to ensure that individual skills were of the highest order. Cadres were run and company exercises undertaken. This training should have culminated in a Battalion exercise at Stanford in mid-November but the Battalion was placed on standby to assist the civil authorities. In the event of a strike 2LI was to deliver fuel and oil to the industrial conurbations of the North West. The dispute was settled but it dragged on long enough to cause the cancellation of the Battalion exercise.

Training for the Battalion's next Ireland tour started in early February 1982. All platoon commanders and platoon serjeants attended the week-long rural techniques course run by NITAT, and the companies underwent a ten-day camp. A challenging Battalion exercise, which reproduced the contemporary operating environment of South Armagh, completed the training. The Battalion flew to Bessbrook in April by way of six Chinook helicopters, taking over the South Armagh TAOR from the 1st Battalion The Duke of Wellington's Regiment.

Battalion Tactical Headquarters, B Company, D Company and the Echelon were located at Bessbrook Mill. A Company was responsible for Crossmaglen whilst Support Company were based at Forkhill with responsibility for the central area of the border. A UDR platoon at Newtownhamilton was also under command. The eyes of the world were focused on the Falklands War but it was business as usual in 'Bandit

Country'. Missing no opportunity, PIRA erected a booby-trapped flagpole on which the Argentinean flag was flown in the hope that a passing patrol would pull it down with fatal consequences. 2LI's seasoned veterans spotted the ruse and the device was safely dismantled. Shooting incidents increased during the tour, including two attacks on Wessex helicopters. In September, 2LI handed over to the 1st Battalion Coldstream Guards and returned to Weeton by helicopter, having sustained no losses on the tour.

At the beginning of 1983, the Battalion role was changed from home defence to BAOR reinforcement. Although the Battalion was to remain under the command of 42 Infantry Brigade, its general war role as part of 24 Infantry Brigade meant that direction on training came from two brigade headquarters. During March the Battalion converted to the Milan anti-tank weapon and Clansman radios, both of which were to become firm 'friends' for the next two decades.

The threat of a fire strike led to a crash course for the Battalion on 'Green Goddesses' and fire hydrants, but they were not required in the end. The Battalion then formed a Guard of Honour for a parade at Imphal Barracks, York, on 16 May, before Her Majesty The Queen, to mark the 2nd Infantry Division's return to the United Kingdom.

With D Company deployed for four months to the Falkland Islands, the remainder of the Battalion headed for Otterburn for Exercise 'Red Grouse' where the Battalion had developed a company group live-firing exercise for Headquarters UKLF. A demanding 30-hour package was put together for a rifle company, supported by artillery, mortars, Milan and Fox, the final effects being added by US Air Force A10 aircraft.

The Battalion deployed to Kenya on Exercise 'Grand Prix' in the early autumn. Ten days' jungle training in the rain forest at Kathendini was followed by live firing at Mpala Farm, dry training at Dol Dol and an R and R period spent either at Lake Naivasha or Mombasa. The Band and Bugles played at two receptions marking the state visit to Kenya of Her Majesty The Queen and the Duke of Edinburgh. A Sounding Retreat was held at Nanyuki before the Battalion returned to Weeton and D Company came back from the Falkland Islands.

Lieutenant Colonel Colin Kaye assumed command just before Christmas, and the Battalion was immediately deployed at short notice to RAF Greenham Common, the scene of violent anti-nuclear demonstrations. Following six weeks on 'Spearhead' in the early spring, the Battalion turned to Exercise 'Lionheart', designed to demonstrate the UK's ability to reinforce BAOR in time of war. After months of preparation and a long journey beset with delays, 2LI occupied a defensive position west of the River Leine, south of Hanover. The battle, fought against German and United States forces, was somewhat confused due to the umpires' difficulties in controlling the enemy. The Battalion then completed an assault river crossing by night across the Leine. From a bridgehead, the Battalion started an extended advance-to-contact up the line of the

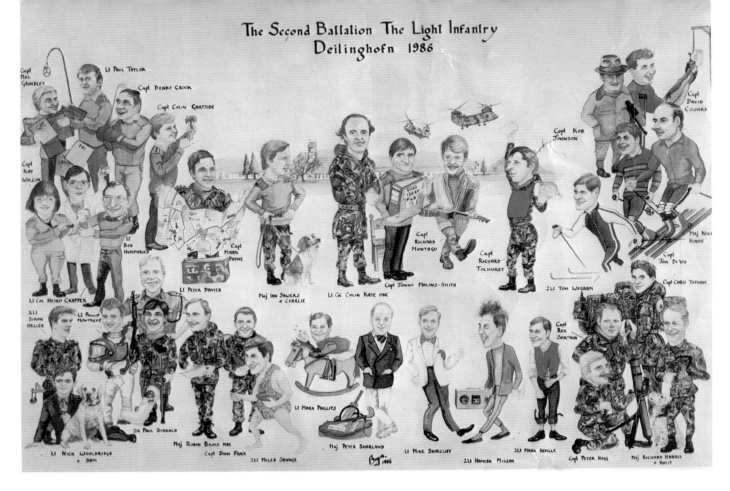

The Second Battalion The Light Infantry
Deilinghofn 1986

Left: Officers' Mess cartoons – always enjoyed by everyone.

autobahn, during which two companies were flown forward to destroy an enemy brigade headquarters.

On return, the Battalion started converting to the airmobile role, which saw the Anti-Tank Platoon increase from 24 to 42 Milan firing posts, whilst Weeton was readied for the handover to 1LI.

Peninsula/Barossa Barracks, Deilinghofen
(December 1984–March 1989)

2LI was complete in Peninsula Barracks, Deilinghofen, North Rhine-Westphalia, by Christmas 1984. Built by the Canadians in the 1950s and then handed over to the British in 1970, the barracks consisted of singularly unattractive pre-fabricated cream-coloured single-storey blocks. The Battalion came under the command of 6 Airmobile Brigade in 3rd Armoured Division. The Brigade's second infantry battalion, 1st Battalion The Gordon Highlanders, lived over the fence in Barossa Barracks and soon became firm friends.

Although the pressure was on to get the entire Battalion proficient in the airmobile role by July 1985, A and B Companies headed to Portugal for company-level training on the Santa Pargarida training area north-east of Lisbon. For the remainder, a full programme of adventure training was organized through the winter months. Every effort was made to establish good relations with the local population, the Battalion's affiliated Bundeswehr unit, 273 Fallschirmjaeger Battalion, and units of the Bundeswehr Airmobile Brigade, 27 Luftlande Brigade. Divisional and brigade study periods and CPXs ensured that everyone was fully conversant with the concept of operations.

The Regiment's tercentenary provided a welcome break in England in mid-June for the Colour Party and the Salamanca Band, but most made do with the Light Division hut at Steibis in Bavaria. Steibis proved a marvellous base for adventure

training in both summer and winter, and parties from the Battalion made frequent forays to canoe, windsurf, rock climb, hill walk and ski. In June the Battalion attained fifth place, and first mono-hull home, in the *Daily Telegraph* Three Peaks Race and also won the 1985 BAOR Army Cricket Cup.

Lieutenant Colonel Jim Parker assumed command in June 1986, as the Battalion embarked upon the final six months of the airmobile trial at Vogelsang in the Eifel and on Exercise 'Eternal Triangle', a 1st Armoured Division FTX. Company exercises at Ruhleben in Berlin and with the Alpini in Italy confirmed the low-level skills essential for airmobile operations.

The Battalion assumed responsibility for the West Belfast TAOR from 1st Battalion The Queen's Lancashire Regiment on 31 July 1987. After a five-year interval, this was to be 2LI's tenth Northern Ireland tour. The mission was to support the RUC in the defeat of terrorism, but the primacy of the RUC in all matters was now absolute. Battalion Tactical Headquarters and A Company were collocated at North Howard Street Mill. B Company was based at Girdwood Park with D Company split between Fort Whiterock and RUC Woodbourne. Echelon was at Musgrave Park Hospital.

The level of violence was similar to that of 1976 but the Battalion was very fortunate to suffer no fatalities. Quite early in the tour, a command-wire-initiated explosive device in the Ramoans Estate injured Second Lieutenant Andy Arkell and Private Rudd of D Company. Both were back on duty before the end of the tour. Private Alderson of A Company was shot in the chest and, receiving life-saving surgery for a very serious wound from Professor John Gibbons (formerly of 1/4 KOYLI), Alderson made a comfortable recovery and returned to duty in November. Lance Corporal Walters lost the sight of one eye in a Drogue grenade attack on his vehicle, just outside RUC New Barnsley, and Lance Corporal Fitzgerald was blown across

the Springfield Road when an explosive device was detonated whilst he was part of a cordon. Fortunately, he too escaped with shock but with some damage to his hearing.

The tour ended as busily as it had begun, with PIRA trying several 'days of disruption', consisting of coordinated attacks with small arms and live and hoax proxy bombs delivered to bases around the Battalion's area. These took up to 36 hours to clear. The West Belfast TAOR was handed over to 1st Battalion The Royal Scots in time for Christmas back in Germany and an all-ranks dance.

The Battalion was back into the airmobile role in the spring of 1988. A medals parade, at which Major General Edward Jones, the General Officer Commanding 3rd Armoured Division, took the salute, was held in March. Just as the Battalion was declared operational in role at the end of the month, 6 Airmobile Brigade became 6 Armoured Brigade. 2LI was to remain the only airmobile battalion in the Army until 24 Airmobile Brigade battalions took up the role.

2LI's primary task in 1988 was to provide administrative support for Exercise 'Summer Sales', the 1 (British) Corps biennial CPX, from May to July. A camp of 270 tents and 15 marquees was erected and administered in the hills overlooking Hameln and the river Weser with the Battalion's usual efficiency, style and the minimum of fuss.

Having borrowed the new SA80 and Light Support Weapons from the Grenadier Guards, 2LI qualified for RASAAM at Bisley where the team came ninth in the Major Unit Competition, their best-ever result. Elsewhere, the Salamanca Band and the Bugles spent August in Edinburgh where, in conjunction with the Normandy Band, they stole the show at the Tattoo. Meanwhile, the Battalion had upped sticks from Peninsula Barracks to the adjacent Barossa Barracks in order to make way for 3 RTR and their new Challenger tanks. Following the tragedy at Ballygawley, a platoon of 30 willing volunteers joined 1LI as Salamanca Platoon.

Lieutenant Colonel Richard Cousens took command of the Battalion in October 1988. In November the Battalion's airmobile role came to a close, playing enemy forces on 3rd Armoured Division's Exercise 'Iron Hammer'. There were long periods of inactivity for the companies but 2LI was able to execute two

battalion lifts, and the junior commanders were well tested in infantry skills. The Battalion's time in BAOR thus ended on something less than a high note, not helped by a six-inch fall of snow in 24 hours, which caused the exercise to be halted.

The Battalion then moved to Lucknow Barracks, Tidworth, in March 1989 and a change of role in the United Kingdom Mobile Force as a SAXON-mounted battalion.

Lucknow Barracks, Tidworth (March 1989–February 1993)

For a Battalion accustomed to the more basic end of military accommodation, Lucknow Barracks held no surprises. It had seen few improvements since it had been built in 1905 and what few funds there were went on refurbishing the stables. The Battalion's new mode of transport was the SAXON. Designed to be a cheap but efficient 'battle-taxi' for travelling from the UK to BAOR, it wasn't long before some budding Liddell Harts confused it with a high-spec AFV. One minor disadvantage soon became apparent: it was impossible to carry all the ammunition and equipment the Battalion would be expected to load on mobilization. Meanwhile, the Battalion got better acquainted with Salisbury Plain through SAXON driver training, company and Battalion exercises, as well as a District-wide clean-up of the Plain. True to form, D Company drew the short straw and ended up removing four 10-ton truck loads of rubbish from Beeches Barn.

The Battalion was chosen to represent the Light Division in a Central Television Military Skills Competition entitled *Combat 89*. The team was well trained but two unfortunate decisions during the early events caused them to be eliminated in the first round.

The Battalion – with Battlegroup assets – then headed for Canada on Exercise 'Pond Jump West' for a period of concentrated training over the summer at Wainwright in Alberta. The outstanding facilities and the unique flavour of adventure training at Jasper ensured that everyone enjoyed it. One day the Commanding Officer was driving from Wainwright to Edmonton when he passed a lonely, but familiar, figure hitch-hiking along the road. It was Private Paul Davies who had decided to go absent. After an animated exchange of views, he agreed to return to camp in the staff car and was not allowed to forget having been apprehended by the Commanding Officer.

On 10 January 1990 2LI started its eleventh tour since the Troubles began. As the Armagh Roulement Battalion (ARB), Support Company were based at Newtownhamilton, D Company at Crossmaglen, B Company at Forkhill and A Company at Newry. Battalion Tactical Headquarters was collocated with Headquarter Company and the Echelon at Bessbrook. The Battalion was reinforced by 4 (Sphinx) Battery Royal Artillery and D Company 2nd Battalion The Parachute Regiment.

Within ten days the base at Newtownhamilton was mortared but, fortunately, the four rounds failed to explode. Support Company made a number of very significant finds in well-concealed hides. In Crossmaglen D Company discovered that PIRA regularly stole mailbags, and A Company in Newry began

Below: The Light Infantry Salamanca Band and Bugles of 2LI, The Drums, Pipes and Regimental Band of the Gordon Highlanders with RAF Chinook and Puma and Army Air Corps Gazelle and Lynx helicopters. Deilinghofen, BAOR.

to understand why the trains never run on time in Northern Ireland: either the ticket office had been blown up or a bomb – hoax or real – had been placed on the track. B Company in Forkhill had a slightly quieter time but achieved considerable success with deterrent and disruptive operations.

The most exciting incident occurred in mid-February with the disruption of a major PIRA operation which involved hijacked cars, high-speed chases, machine gun and ammunition finds, and several arrests. A heliborne patrol landed after an observant pilot spotted armed and masked men in a car near Cullyhanna. The occupants of the car, realizing that they had been spotted, sped off pursued by the helicopter. The gang eventually split and two machine guns, radios, three automatic rifles and an assortment of ammunition were recovered.

The Battalion returned to Tidworth on 25 May and, after three weeks' leave, began re-learning their skills for the UKMF's primary exercise later in the summer. Amongst these preparations, the Battalion's Colour Party had the honour to represent the Regiment in June at a spectacular celebration of the Colonel-in-Chief's ninetieth birthday on Horse Guards. The UKMF exercise, 'Druids Drake', was chiefly remembered for the Assistant Adjutant, Lisa Tomlinson, successfully leading a Battalion night move across the Plain and a brigade attack executed to the sound of the Bugles.

An anticipated pre-Christmas upsurge in terrorist activity led to a Battalion three-week deployment to Northern Ireland on 30 November. Split throughout the Province, the companies were given worthwhile tasks and returned to Tidworth with a justified sense of achievement. The frequency of the Battalion's Northern Ireland tours was becoming so regular that the families began to refer to 'emergency tours in Tidworth'.

In January 1991, as the rest of the free world focused on Saddam Hussein's invasion of Kuwait, 2LI, ever independent in thought and deed, shipped out west to Fort Lewis, Washington State, for Exercise 'Trumpet Dance' and a month's training with the US Army. Field firing progressed from FIBUA drills in the Tire (sic) House to a demanding 36-hour live firing company group exercise at the Yakima Firing Centre – probably the biggest electric target range in the world – some 130 miles east of Fort Lewis. Arduous adventure training was conducted at the US Army Camp Bonneville. On return to the UK, the Battalion crammed two years of administration into two weeks.

The Battalion's focus then switched to preparations for the Presentation of New Colours on 31 May. With 1LI unable to leave Berlin and 3LI equally busy in Northern Ireland, the task of supporting the parade fell to the Battalion. The challenge of finding three Guards, providing the administrative support for the parade and organizing and running the Colours Ball absorbed every man in the Battalion and taxed the Quartermaster's Department to the limit. Lieutenant Colonel Richard Cousens who, on 7 May 1971 as an ensign in 2LI had received the new Queen's Colour from Her Majesty Queen Elizabeth The Queen Mother at Colchester, commanded the

GERMANY IN THE 90s

This event happened just prior to 2LI's deployment to Bosnia from Paderborn barracks. At the time the Battalion was working pretty hard and was taking any chance it could to have some fun before going on tour. On this particular Friday night I was orderly officer and was called down to the guardroom to meet the RMP town patrol who wanted to talk to me. I arrived at the guardroom and met a rather ruffled RMP corporal, and his RMP driver, who was there to let me know how badly the Battalion were behaving in town that night. I listened to him, and he left the guardroom in a better mood than he had come in. Unfortunately this was not to last. A few moments later he returned to the guardroom in a rage.

On returning to his Land Rover that was parked outside the guardroom he had discovered that someone had used the inside of his vehicle as a urinal. He was angry before but now he was furious. The livid RMP started demanding justice and to find out which one of 2LI's 'animals' was responsible. Rather unhelpfully and trying not to laugh I asked him was it locked? This was probably not such a good idea, and he only became angrier. He reminded me that there was a sentry on the gate, and insisted that we questioned him straight away, as the Land Rover was parked about 10 feet from where the sentry was standing.

The soldier acting as sentry was soon being interrogated by the RMP, and his answer was as close to genius as it gets. The sentry did agree that several soldiers returning from the town had come through the gate he was manning in the time the Land Rover was parked behind him, and yes he had seen the RMPs come in. The RMP asked the sentry had he seen who had pissed in his vehicle, and the soldier said straight away he had not. The RMP declared he could not believe him, as the soldier was only 10 feet from the Land Rover and it was just behind him. The sentry than calmly explained the arcs he had been given when posted, it was unfortunate but his arcs were to his front, and the now damp Land Rover was not in those arcs as it was behind him. The sentry declared it was therefore impossible for him to have seen what happened as he was observing his arcs, and only his arcs. End of chat, as people used to say in 2LI then.

Needless to say this did not please RMP chap, who then started ranting at me that I should jail the sentry and the rest of the guard and replace them. Not a very sensible solution around midnight on a Friday night just after the blokes had been paid. The guard were probably the only sober people in camp! This episode ended with the RMP corporal leaving after I reminded him that if he carried on the way he was, we did have room in our cells for one more. Happy days.

Sean Harris

Left: Battalion Headquarters in BATUS, 1995. Left to right: Capt Ben Tomkinson, Capt Mark Goldsack, Maj Ewen Turner, Capt Robin Davis, Capt Jonny Orchard.

'BONDI BEACH', BOSNIA 1995–6

B Company took over a derelict house next to the road. Toby Ellwood christened the crossing 'BONDI BEACH' after the Australian surfers' paradise – the name standing for warmth, warm water, constant sunlight and bikini-clad beach beauties; all notably absent anywhere in Bosnia at that time. The house had no windows or doors and only a few fragments of furniture. Soldiers painted the name 'BONDI BEACH' in letters four feet high on the bare walls, together with large red tropical palm trees. Lance Corporal Credland described how his platoon made the building habitable:

'The building we had to make our home was a detached house in the middle of the ethnically cleansed village of Sassina. Rooms didn't have any windows or doors. We began sealing the 'envelope' (surveyors' terminology) of the building. This consisted of wedging timber slats into the window void, cut to length using a rusty bow saw. Plastic sheeting was then nailed to the frame and then cut to size. The frame was finally sealed by using vast amounts of brown masking tape. Quality of finish varied considerably, from double glazing down to 'that will f---ing do'. Next priority was the door. Rugs were nailed to the existing frame. In view of the weather, possibly the most important pieces of kit were the wood fires that are in constant use throughout Bosnia. One appeared in every room.

Above: Cpl Dean Portman takes a bath.

The cookhouse was run by Corporal Shelley and Private Socks (a scraggy mutt of the four-legged type). Dinners were a big favourite with everyone.

Having filled up on all-in dinners day after day, inevitably the time would come when the excess would require disposing of. With health and hygiene a priority, the toilet was sited opposite the kitchen. It initially comprised a chair with the bottom smashed out and a black bin liner, but we progressed onto a 'Gucci' plastic thunderbox and soft bog roll.

We were fortunate to have a natural spring. A cast iron bath was propped up on bricks and six-foot pickets to allow a fire to be lit beneath it. We also constructed a shower. A metal trough was positioned midway between the basement wall and a showerhead attached at one end. A cement mixer was then filled with wood and used to heat the trough. Temperature control was a nightmare for both bath and shower.'

The BBC correspondent Martin Bell filmed a report from BONDI BEACH showing the bath in action.

[Extracted from *A Cold War*, by Brigadier Ben Barry.]

parade at which that Colour was finally marched off and new Colours received. The parade and associated festivities were a great success thanks to exceptional tolerance, good humour and impeccable planning and preparation.

Lieutenant Colonel Mark Elcomb assumed command in June 1991, the Battalion having just been warned of a 'Surge' operation in Northern Ireland in August and September, as well as a full Operation BANNER tour from March 1992. The aim of Operation BRONSKI in August and September 1991 was to refurbish the South Armagh surveillance towers and improve facilities at the base in Crossmaglen. A combination of static OPs, VCPs and mobile patrols was used to secure entry and exit routes and the towers themselves. Other than a 'come on' shoot onto an Anti-Tank Platoon OP, the operation went very smoothly.

On 24 March 1992, 2LI began its first six-month Northern Ireland tour in South Armagh. The Battalion's deployment was by now SOP: Support Company were based at Newtownhamilton, D Company at Crossmaglen, B Company at Forkhill and A Company at Newry. Battalion Tactical Headquarters was collocated with Headquarter Company and the Echelon at Bessbrook. At the peak of activity the Battalion had ten companies, 57 multiple patrols and over 1,000 men

Clockwise from above: Commanding a vehicle when it is -15; Sjt Jap Owen returns from the cookhouse despite the snow; A Company (left to right): Lt Will Hogg, Maj Jan de Vos, Simon Dring, Sjt 'H' Pattison.

under command. Their mission was to inhibit and deter terrorist operations by surveillance and offensive operations, restricting terrorist movement and causing attrition within the law, reassuring and protecting the population to support the long-term aims of the counter-terrorist campaign.

Throughout the tour a number of explosive devices were located and neutralized; some had already misfired and one had detonated early, wounding the terrorist assembling the charge. On 28 August, Private Turner was murdered by a sniper whilst on patrol in Crossmaglen. Private Turner had not even been born when 2LI had suffered its last operational fatality in Northern Ireland in 1973. 2LI handed over to 1st Battalion The Royal Scots on 25 September and returned to Tidworth.

The period immediately following the return to Lucknow Barracks saw a significant reduction in the strength of the

Above: A Coy Warriors on route to Mirkonic Grad.

BOSNIA, 1995–6

Mass graves, ethnic cleansing, systematic rape, medieval brutality in a country closer to London than Finland or Greece.

We trained hard in Sennelager and BATUS for every eventuality including a fighting withdrawal which was not inconceivable given the UN's impotence, no more clearly demonstrated than in July 1995 when Serbs slaughtered thousands of Muslims in a UN 'safe haven' with 400 Dutch soldiers powerless to stop it.

The beautiful countryside was marred by burnt-out houses, some still burning as we watched. We were little more than military sightseers, sometimes used as hostages (as had happened to Captain Paul Sulyok on a previous tour). The situation changed when we became part of NATO and were able to use force to enforce the Dayton Agreement. We changed base regularly and soldiers never ceased to amaze me with their ingenuity in creating a comfortable temporary home even in what became known as the Mud Factory which had to be cleared of dead pigs and mines before we occupied it.

On Christmas Eve while I was writing 'blueys' to home by candlelight, Captain Ed Creswell, on attachment from the RDG, miraculously and generously produced a giant Fortnum & Mason hamper and despite the cold and the squalor around us life suddenly seemed good. Then we were being shot at. The guard were tasked to deal with whoever it was who had been rude enough to interrupt supper. It turned out to be a local farmer waving an old AK47 in the air, drunk as could be.

As the Chief Liaison Officer I had up to 60 interpreters working for me in addition to the 220 strong Support Company. On one occasion I instructed, via an interpreter, the Chief of Police of Banja Luka to tear down his police checkpoints by Wednesday or we would destroy them. The roadblocks in Bosnia had been a significant source of power and control for many years. I subsequently discovered that my interpreter was so frightened that he had diluted my message

to ask if the Chief of Police wouldn't mind considering my 'request'. I sacked the interpreter – which was a bitter blow for him given the income it represented and little alternative employment, but any misunderstanding could easily escalate into violence. I returned the next day and reinforced the message – for once we were not offered coffee or slivovitz. We had succeeded in establishing a fragile peace, separating the warring factions and now were determined to implement the Dayton Agreement by force if necessary.

We had gone to Bosnia not knowing what to expect, many believing that we would have a routine tour as the harsh winter slowed down any military operation and turned the Chobham-armoured Warriors into 30-tonne sledges. In fact there were no routines, no groundhog days. As we stepped into the Hercules to take us home to Paderborn and beyond we all had a great sense of a job well done, that people in England would not be able to understand what had happened on their doorsteps but that we had made a difference.

Ian Baker

Above: Lt Peter Chapman negotiates a crossing point.

TRANS-ATLANTIC ROWING RACE 1997

In early 1995 2LI was based in Paderborn. In May I was back in the UK on leave when I saw in the papers that Chay Blyth was planning the first-ever ocean rowing race, across the Atlantic from the Canaries to Barbados, to start in October 1997. I sought out a fellow LI officer, Martin Bellamy (aka Bumper), to tell him I'd found something I thought would interest him. We then planned our modus operandi to get the Army and the regiment on-side. All the planning would have to be fitted around six months in Bosnia (November 1995–May 1996) and a move to Palace Barracks, Belfast, in January 1997. We began by getting Peter de la Billière on board (as a prominent Light Infantryman) and then the Queen Mother, as Colonel of the Regiment. She was superb and not only sent a personal cheque as a donation but, unprompted, sent us a good luck telegram the day before we set off (which now hangs proudly in my loo). Ranulph Fiennes agreed to become our patron and we bored every senior officer we could find with our plans. Our new CO, Tim Martin, was a great support and kindly gave us the time off with the words 'no-one is indispensable'.

The boat itself was 7mm marine plywood, 7 metres long and 2 metres wide. She came in kit form and we built her (an adventure in itself) in a boatyard on Mallorca where we based ourselves to prepare throughout 1997 (while the rest of the battalion stagged on in Belfast)!. We called her 'Salamanca', quickly shortened to Sally. There were thirty boats in the race, from all over the world, although we were the only soldiers.

The voyage itself was 2,500 miles from Tenerife to Barbados; it lasted 74 days and was not without mishap. The supposedly state-of-the-art water maker on board broke down on day two and never worked again, thereby drastically reducing our daily water intake (from a recommended 8 litres each to 2) and meaning we never had fresh water to wash in. Unlike boats today we had no sat phone and weather forecasting came from a French radio station.

Likewise, having only 45 days' worth of food on board led to some severe rationing and the catching of fish to boost the calories. On day 54, still 900 miles from land and in daytime temperatures touching 100 degrees Fahrenheit, we stopped a passing oil tanker and took on welcome supplies. Nevertheless, each of us lost in the region of 3 stone in weight by the time we rowed into Barbados at first light on Christmas Day 1997.

Mark Mortimer

Battalion. With the PVR ban lifted for the first time in 18 months and in spite of the deep recession, 14 soldiers took advantage of the opportunity to leave the Army. The manning implications of the impending merger began to take on a more immediate significance as men started to move across to 3LI in Paderborn, and the opportunity was taken for the first time in 18 months to send a number of junior and senior NCOs on career-enhancing postings. Within two months of leaving South Armagh, the Battalion was 225 men below establishment.

Inkerman Day provided the only opportunity to celebrate a Regimental Day in true style. It was marked with a Battalion bonfire party, funfair and disco, based on the NAAFI Junior Ranks Club. The guy was marched to the bonfire to music from the Salamanca Band and suffered total immolation to the strains of Handel's *Music for the Royal Fireworks*. With a guest night in the Officers' Mess the following night, Inkerman Day was felt to have been suitably celebrated, the 'old' 2LI's social activities ending on a high note. The Commanding Officer, Adjutant and Regimental Serjeant Major all relinquished their posts on the same day.

Alanbrooke Barracks, Paderborn
(February 1993–January 1997)

Over in Germany at Alanbrooke Barracks in Paderborn, the 3rd Battalion, under the command of Lieutenant Colonel Martin Grubb, renumbered as the 2nd Battalion on Merger Day, 26 February 1993. Brigadier Jim Parker took the salute as the 3LI Colours were marched off the snow-covered square and the 2LI Colours were marched on. The Battalion then doubled off behind the 'new' Colours and straight back to armoured infantry training. No fuss.

2LI deployed to Northern Ireland in July 1993, the seventeenth time that 2LI (old and new) had done so. This time it was to East Tyrone and the bases at Dungannon, Coalisland, Pomeroy and Auchnacloy. It was to be a tour of unsuccessful mortar attacks, improvised explosive devices and weapon finds.

In January 1994 the Battalion reformed in Paderborn and began to reorganize and re-train as an Armoured Infantry battalion with gunnery and Driving and Maintenance (D&M) to the fore. Lieutenant Colonel Ben Barry assumed command in June. Training on the Canadian Prairie at BATUS from May to September enabled more advanced battlegroup training, resulting in a formal report which stated that 'the final impression was of a well-organized and fully effective battlegroup which was more than capable of undertaking the operation with which it was tasked'. It was also the first time a Light Infantry Battlegroup had deployed to BATUS in 21 years. The three rifle companies deployed again to BATUS the following summer with the Queen's Dragoon Guards Battlegroup, made all the more entertaining by Tactical Engagement Simulation (TES). By the end of the year, the Battalion was claiming to be 'more experienced in armoured warfare than any other battalion in the Army'.

The international community's deployment of military forces to 'keep the peace' and 'nation-build' in the former Yugoslavia since 1992 bought time for the diplomats and politicians to determine and agree courses of action which were to eventually bring peace to the Balkans. The 'new world order' brought optimism and uncertainty in equal measure. During the Cold War, the UN had seemingly presided over almost 45 years of peace where Western casualties had been few and genocide in Europe unthinkable. When war broke out in southern Europe, few could believe what was happening and fewer knew how to deal with it. It was the 'peacekeepers' who broke new ground. The UN Protection Force (UNPROFOR) was not just a peacekeeping force: it was an instrument of international diplomacy – although events on the ground shaped it for much of the time.

Against this backdrop, 2LI deployed to Bosnia on Operation GRAPPLE in November 1995 for a six-month tour as part of UNPROFOR. Training in Canada earlier in the summer was topped up in the autumn with more specific training geared to the particular requirements of Yugoslavia. The Dayton Agreement, signed in Paris in December 1995, brought to an end three and a half years of war in Bosnia-Herzegovina, a switch from UNPROFOR to IFOR and the redeployment of the Battalion from the Mount Igman and Vitez area to the north around Bihac. Blue berets were swapped for green and the Warriors re-painted. Working with French, Greek, Slovak, Indonesian, Czech, Austrian, German, Hungarian, Romanian, Malaysian and New Zealand contingents, everyone gave of their utmost and gained reciprocally, whether in maturity, confidence or experience. They gained wide respect amongst both their international colleagues in IFOR and amongst the local populations where firm and friendly action was welcomed. It was a unique and extremely arduous experience in an arena where creature comforts were virtually non-existent. The Regiment commissioned an oil painting by Hugo Grenville to commemorate the tour. The Colonel of the Regiment, Major General Mike Regan, presented the Battalion its medals on 23 May 1996 in Paderborn.

Lieutenant Colonel Tim Martin took command in October 1996 as the Battalion prepared, after seven years in Alanbrooke Barracks, to hand over to 2 RGJ and relocate for a two-year residential tour in Northern Ireland at Palace Barracks, Belfast. Sixty-eight NCOs and soldiers – mostly for domestic reasons – volunteered to remain in Germany to reinforce 2 RGJ.

Palace Barracks, Belfast (January 1997–January 1999)

On the outskirts of Belfast, Palace Barracks was considered to be the best resident battalion location in Northern Ireland. It is close to the airports and the ferry terminal as well as being in a pleasant cultural and social area of the Province. The accommodation was mostly excellent and, with all the families living on camp, there was a great sense of community spirit.

Above: The Recce Platoon – route proving or lost? It was always difficult to tell.

The Battalion operated a four-month cycle, rotating companies around four tasks and changing approximately every four weeks. One company was permanently deployed out of barracks to North Belfast; one was the first-line reserve, normally deploying 50 per cent of the time; a third maintained the barracks' local security; and the fourth was generally deployed out of Province on exercise, adventure training, recruiting drives or leave. Despite the ceasefire, activity levels remained very high, but relative peace enabled many soldiers to get away to ski in Norway, France, Austria or Scotland. A lucky few undertook expeditions to the Himalayas and to Cyprus.

Dramatic changes to the political situation in Northern Ireland set numerous challenges to both commanders and soldiers alike. The Battalion's first year focused on the summer marching season and the general and local elections in May. Intense public order training ensured that the Battalion was well prepared for a summer of disorder in the Ardoyne, the Ormeau Bridge and elsewhere in support of the RUC's Belfast Region. Community relations events, including an Open Day, were also to the fore to 'help drive a wedge between the terrorist and ordinary decent people'. The Battalion were witness to the historic Good Friday Agreement, signed on 10 April 1998 and endorsed by a referendum the following month. The Agreement would bring about the disarming

Left: 2LI Northern Ireland Multiple, Bessbrook Mill, 2005. LCpl Thomas (back row, 2nd from right) was later killed in Iraq.

of all paramilitary groups, the end of Operation BANNER and the reform of the Police. But it would take another nine years for the Army to be fully withdrawn from the Province's security architecture. So the pace of life and training tempo remained high, as the Battalion found itself on the one hand trying to maintain its Northern Ireland skills and on the other beginning the transition to the new mechanized role.

As 'Notice to Move' restrictions relaxed, so The Light Infantryman's lot improved. There were recruiting drives in Yorkshire and the North East, one company exercised in the USA with the 101st Airborne Division, and there were further adventure training exercises in Cyprus, Gibraltar and Cumbria. The final months at Palace Barracks were characterized by a distinct change in operational tempo with the withdrawal of routine military support to the RUC in Belfast. The training focus switched to the Battalion's new role in 1 Mechanized Brigade.

2LI handed over to 1 RGJ in March 1999. A number volunteered to remain in Northern Ireland, having married local girls and/or keen to retain the better pay and allowances (the average private soldier was £200 a month better off in Ulster). Lieutenant Colonel David Wood assumed command in January 1999 of a highly resilient, widely respected Battalion, justifiably proud of its achievements and reputation in the Province.

Kiwi Barracks, Bulford (March 1999–May 2002)

By March 1999, the Battalion had moved to Kiwi Barracks, Bulford, in Wiltshire and continued converting to their new mechanized role. It was a welcome return to England and some more traditional soldiering. To ring the changes and better meet the challenges of this new role, the Battalion was reorganized into six companies. A, B and C Companies remained as rifle companies but with just two platoons each. D Company was resurrected as Command Company with armoured recce, patrols, sniper, signals and training platoons. E was for Echelon Company under the Quartermaster's command, whilst F was for Fire Support Company with mortars and three Direct Fire Groups (Milan and GPMG (SF)). Just as that training was complete, training began again for the commitment as standby battalion for deployment back to Northern Ireland!

In many ways the training concentrated not so much on skills as a change in the 'mindset' from the Northern Ireland requirement to a more dynamic mission command approach to both operations and the preparation for them. There was a drive to retrain the Battalion in basic infantry soldiering skills as well as the more specialized tasks. Leadership and command, fitness and shooting were the three core strands. The sight of the whole Battalion spread out along the Bulford Road, with all its weapons, carrying out its Friday morning eight-mile forced march was a regular and quietly admired spectacle. The incentive was a long weekend!

Right: The Adjutant in Dhekelia – Captain Will Follett.

C Company deployed to Banja Luka, Bosnia, in October 1999 for a six-month tour as the Banja Luka Operations Company. Their task was to patrol Banja Luka and the surrounding countryside, monitoring all military and civilian activities as well as to provide security for the 'Metal Factory', home to HQ Multinational Division (South West).

There were three distinct phases for 2LI in 2000: commitments to Northern Ireland and Bosnia; training for and completing a high-intensity test exercise (TESEX 2000 – Exercise 'Wessex Warrior') in their primary mechanized role; and a short-notice deployment, including the move of all equipment and vehicles, to Kosovo for the build-up and aftermath of the October 2000 elections. In Northern Ireland, A and B Companies deployed consecutively to South Armagh, although at one stage both were in the Province together. In the latter half of the year the Battalion formed the Kosovo Force (KFOR) operational reserve, alongside a Greek mechanized infantry company! (History does not relate how communications were resolved.) Part of the Battalion was separately deployed under command of the Multi-National Brigade (Centre) with which they conducted joint operations.

On returning to Bulford from Kosovo, 2LI faced an uncertain time as deployments wavered between Canada, Sierra Leone, Gibraltar and the move to Cyprus. Not so much a case of 'on the bus, off the bus' but 'just which bus do you want me on'! In the event, one company spent a month in Gibraltar, relieving the Gibraltar Regiment to permit it to complete mandatory training in the UK. The move to Cyprus was delayed until February 2002 and the main effort was therefore pitched at the forthcoming operational tour to Sierra Leone, West Africa. Lieutenant Colonel Peter Davies took command in January 2001.

Following nine years of brutal civil war, a UK Joint Task Force had restored peace to the former British colony in June

2000. Rich in diamonds, this tropical country struggled to manage the exploitation and export of these precious minerals. 2LI deployed to Sierra Leone in late May 2001 and took over from the 1st Battalion. This auspicious and unique occasion was marked with a joint Bugle Breakfast and an exchange of silver palm trees. The Battalion's primary purpose was to train Sierra Leone Army recruits at Benguema, some 20 miles from the capital, Freetown. Those who had joined The Light Infantry for travel and adventure were not disappointed as they patrolled the African savannah and rain forest in stripped-down Land Rovers, mounted with Browning .50 machine guns, in temperatures averaging 26°C. By the time the Battalion left in October 2001, they had trained almost 2,400 men, contributing enormously to Sierra Leone's stability.

Returning to Bulford, the Battalion prepared as quickly as it could for the arms plot move to Cyprus. On St Valentine's Day 2002 Kiwi Barracks was handed over and, in far sunnier climes, the Regimental flag was run up at Alexander Barracks, Dhekelia, in the UK's Eastern Sovereign Base Area in Cyprus.

Alexander Barracks, Cyprus (February 2002–April 2004)

The expression 'sunshine' posting conjures up images of Empire, gently swaying palm trees, brandy sours, exotic bars – but operational commitments on island and constant changes in 'notices to move' combined to make this residential posting busier than any since the Battalion had been in Paderborn. Imaginative and careful leadership was required to ensure that the Battalion was able to make the most of what the island had to offer whilst maintaining professional infantry standards.

Joint training between the Resident Infantry Battalions and the SBA Police was a regular part of the programme. Language difficulties, command and control issues, operational sustainability and stringent safety training precautions

placed on the SBA Police made such training complex and challenging. August 2002 was marked by a return to war-fighting training as C Company prepared to deploy to Jordan in September and B and A Companies prepared to go to the Falkland Islands in November and March respectively. Although the purpose of the infantry company in the Falkland Islands was to demonstrate British sovereignty through overt patrols, it also allowed for some demanding and invaluable warfighting training from section to company level. Cyprus also proved to be ideal for regimental soldiering. The Battalion was able to mark The Queen's Golden Jubilee, and celebrate Salamanca, Minden and Inkerman Days.

In July 2003, 2LI was warned to deploy a rifle company group to Iraq to support coalition forces in an internal security role. C Company deployed in the first week of August to Basra under command of the 1st Battalion Queen's Lancashire

Top left: The Old State Building (OSB) RPG Sangar, Central Basra, Op TELIC 8.

Above: A Company disembark in Beirut from HMS Gloucester, 2006.

Regiment. A Company then relieved C Company who became 19 Mechanized Brigade's Operations Company. Battalion Tactical Headquarters and Fire Support Company deployed a week later with the final elements, including B Company, bringing up the rear in mid-September.

With Battalion Tactical Headquarters deployed to the Al Fawr peninsula to assist the US Marine Corps (USMC) with anti-smuggling operations, A Company patrolled round the clock in the town of Az Zubayr, B Company deployed initially to the Iran–Iraq border and then to Al Amarah, whilst Fire Support Company provided escort teams to the Coalition Provisional Authority and Government Support Teams which took them across Multi-National Division (South East)'s entire Area of Operations.

Lieutenant Colonel Ted Shields assumed command at the tail end of Iraq. The Battalion was complete in Dhekelia by the end of November. The operational statistics give some

idea of the intensity of activity for the Battalion in Iraq: 11 shooting incidents; three bomb incidents, one mortar attack, over 280 weapons seized; eight oil tankers and barges seized on suspicion of smuggling and 96 arrests made.

2LI was well manned, confident in itself and thus able to meet all operational commitments as well as undertake career training and a wide variety of sporting and adventurous training. Following a farewell cocktail party or two, the Battalion moved to Edinburgh.

Redford Barracks, Edinburgh (April 2004–February 2007)

Redford Infantry Barracks, Colinton, was built between 1909 and 1915. Its imposing Edwardian façade has given rise to 'an apocryphal urban myth . . . that the Barracks' design was originally intended for use in India due to its distinctive Indo-Saracenic architectural features, as well as the high ceilings, doorways and airy rooms throughout the main blocks.' Close to the North East and Yorkshire, 2LI's Edinburgh experience was happily no different to that of the 1st Battalion's three years before. With the move complete by the end of March 2004, the taxpayer was saved a few pounds by the cancellation of an exercise to Belize and replacing it with six weeks of 'back to basics' conventional warfare training in Scotland and Otterburn. Training concluded in Galloway with 52 Infantry Brigade's induction test – the 24-mile Advanced Combat Fitness Test. In September, it was back to Northern Ireland again; South Armagh to be precise – the Battalion's ninth tour in that area and The Light Infantry's last of the Troubles.

Despite the Good Friday Agreement, South Armagh remained 'different' and the police still required routine military support. Smuggling and other illegal activities, especially cross-border fuel smuggling, were endemic. Based once more in Bessbrook Mill, companies had functional as opposed to geographic responsibilities: A Company deployed

Right: Dockside in Beirut, 2006.

Below right: Battalion Headquarters, 2007.

Below: The Recce Platoon – 'found' in the jungle – Ex 'Grand Prix', Belize, September 2005. Sjt Scott (5th from left) and LCpl Kirkness (3rd from right) were both subsequently killed in action in Op HERRICK 11.

as Bessbrook Security Company; B Company as Patrols Company; C Company as Surveillance Company (manning the hill-top observation towers); and Fire Support Company deployed as Out Stations Company with responsibility for the bases at Crossmaglen, Forkhill and Newtownhamilton. Multiples rotated every four to five weeks around these tasks. Returning to Edinburgh in March 2005, the Battalion was back in the Province in June, training in public order for the summer marching season.

A few expeditions conceived in the depths of the South Armagh winter came to fruition. A Company went trekking in South Africa on the Sani Pass and took the opportunity to visit Hlobane and Khambula where the 13th Light Infantry had so distinguished themselves in March 1879. Another tour to the Peninsula took in Talavera, Badajoz (where Ensign Dyas of the 51st Light Infantry stormed the breach) and, of course, Salamanca.

Being over strength, the Battalion was tasked to reinforce Iraq-bound 1st Battalion The Cheshire Regiment with a rifle platoon. A composite platoon (Salamanca) of volunteers was quickly formed and deployed in April 2004. In the five months since 2LI had left, the security situation in Iraq had deteriorated significantly. Lance Corporal Taff Thomas was killed during an assault on a militia position on 17 August. He was buried with full military honours at Castle Caereinion near his family home. The platoon subsequently re-joined the Battalion in South Armagh in November.

Edinburgh provided a number of high-profile opportunities for 2LI at which the 30-strong Bugle Platoon were often well to the fore. The Edinburgh Tattoo in August 2005 was one such highlight which saw a concentration of Light Division buglers unparalleled since Sounding Retreat on Horse Guards

Parade in 1993. The Battalion then deployed to Belize in September 2005 to prepare for Spearhead. Basic procedures in the jungle progressed through mobility, patrols and live-firing. After a strenuous final exercise and perhaps one too many river crossings, the Battalion left the jungle for the delights of Cancun in Mexico and the Belizean Cayes.

2LI's last Commanding Officer, Lieutenant Colonel Ralph Arundell, assumed command in April 2006, two weeks into the Spearhead roster. It would not quite rival the Duchess of Richmond's Ball before the Battle of Waterloo but the Warning Order for 2LI to evacuate UK nationals from the Lebanon arrived in similar fashion at the Officers' Mess Summer Ball on Saturday 15 July. Days later, C Company and Battalion HQ deployed to Cyprus on Operation HIGHBROW. C Company then deployed forward to Beirut. Having identified the various locations required for the Evacuation, C Company defended and ran the Evacuee Handling Centre in the Forum de Beyrouth, a conference centre in the centre of the city. Here a total of 6,000 people were processed in five days, including every single UK evacuee and a number of other nationals, including Germans and Swedes.

Meanwhile, A and B Companies deployed to Iraq as part of the Rear Operations Battlegroup, based on The Queen's Dragoon Guards. The Battlegroup provided base security at Shaibah Logistics Base; patrols into Basra city; escorts for a variety of convoys between Kuwait, Shaibah and all British locations in Iraq; security for the headquarters of the Senior British Military Representative in Iraq in Baghdad; and security for the Divisional Temporary Detention Facility.

On return to Edinburgh, Battalion HQ and C Company completed their training for Iraq or Afghanistan. C Company was finally sent to Afghanistan in early November 2006, for

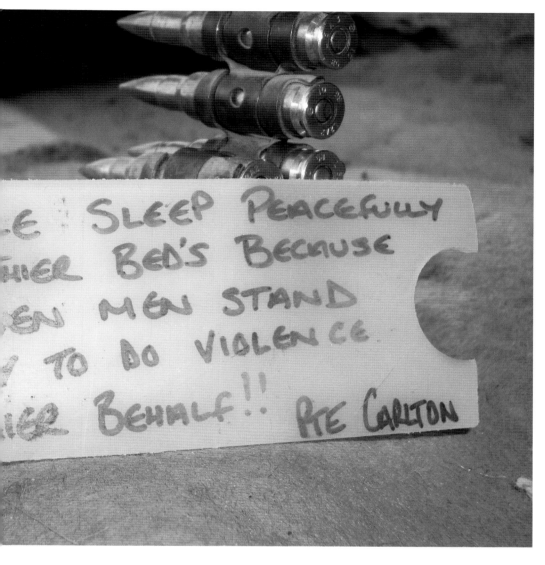

Above: A message from Sangin.

Opposite far left: Major Ben Lampard and Capt Colin Oliver at a Shura.

Opposite left: The Light Infantry flag is lowered for the last time in Sangin, 23 February 2007.

Right: US Commander's coin – handed out by US forces.

THE END OF AN ERA

On the night of the merger to become The Rifles, 2LI was deployed on operations in the Middle East. The majority of the Battalion was based in Iraq, however C Company was relishing its independence having been sent to bolster 42 Commando during its volatile tour of Afghanistan.

The Company had already experienced a busy year having been deployed as the Spearhead Lead Element to conduct a non-combatant evacuation operation in Beirut. They now found themselves defending the strategically important District Centre of Sangin in the Helmand Province. The town sat on a vital main supply route and was under constant threat from Taliban forces who sought to control the area. Cut off from road movement and rarely re-supplied by air due to the threat, it soon earned itself the name of the Alamo!

In an attempt to honour the final moments of the Regiment in the confined and austere conditions of the base, Private Duncan cleverly rigged up a crowd control speaker to play the Last Post from his music system. As the Company stood to at last light, the bugle notes sounded across the town and the Company legend, Private 'Fathead' Hague, ably assisted by his side-kick Private Neeves, lowered the regimental flag. It was the end of an era but what better place to finish it than whilst serving on operations?

To mark the occasion, it was decided that a Bugle Breakfast should be held the following morning. Despite the limited resources, Colour Serjeant Ayton and Serjeant Teale turned their skills to the kitchen and miraculously produced a monumental fry-up for all the officers and SNCOs from an eight-man ration pack.

When the now Riflemen were asked how they felt about the merger and the end of the Regiment, in true Northern dourness they replied 'bugger all, I've still got to stag on in the front sangar!'

Ben Lampard (OC C Company 2006–8)

what was initially understood to be a 60-day deployment in support of the 3 Commando Brigade, Royal Marines. C Company first moved to Camp Bastion in Helmand Province and into a force protection task in order to better familiarize themselves for more demanding work. Battalion HQ deployed in late November 2006, taking over from the previous Theatre Reserve Battalion HQ in a mentoring role in the Iraqi Security Forces' Provincial Joint Coordination Centre (PJOC) in the Ar Rabbat district of central Basra. They were the focal point for coordination between the full range of Iraqi Army and emergency services in Basra Province. On 21 January 2007, Private Michael 'Tenchy' Tench, 18, died as a result of injuries sustained from an improvised explosive device on a roadside in Basra. He was the last 2LI soldier to be killed on operations.

So on 31 January 2007, 2LI's last day before merger and a new name, the Battalion was to be found on operations in Iraq and Afghanistan. Typically, in the words of the Commanding Officer, it was a day of 'no fuss and no nonsense'. No one who had ever served in 2LI would have had it any other way. 2LI reformed in Edinburgh in March 2007 as the 3rd Battalion The Rifles. The Colours were laid up in the Town Hall in Durham City on Sunday 17 February 2008. Eight former Commanding Officers were present amongst many others who had had the privilege of serving in the 2nd Battalion. In the words of a song, popular around the time of the Cardwell Reforms: 'But whatever the change, one thing is the same, It's the Regiment we love no matter the name.'

The Third Battalion

1968–1993

Terendak Camp, Malacca (August 1968–April 1969)
When The Light Infantry was formed on 10 July 1968, the 3rd
Battalion (3LI) was based at Terendak Camp near Malacca in
Malaysia as part of 28 Commonwealth Brigade, with companies
detached on internal security duties in Mauritius; an operation
for which the Battalion was subsequently awarded the
Wilkinson Sword of Peace. This operation is covered in some
detail later on in the section on Operations. The last elements of
3LI left Mauritius in November 1968 and the Battalion moved
to Seaton Barracks, Plymouth. In Terendak Camp A Company
were heavily involved in making the film 'Ambush Patrol' which
nearly brought Battalion routine to a standstill and revealed
some hitherto unsuspected dramatic talent. On return from
Mauritius, C Company had been placed under the command
of 1st Battalion Royal New Zealand Infantry Regiment to act as
enemy force on a 99 Brigade exercise. This composite Battalion
performed very well and escaped detection by the Gurkha force
attempting to locate them. The last three months in Terendak
Camp were extremely busy. In January and early February,
platoons undertook a number of adventure training projects, a
last chance to take advantage of being in the Far East. This was
followed by the inter-platoon competition for the Reade Shield,

THE JUNGLE

As I spent a mere six months in the Far East with the Battalion, and two of those
were on a course in Singapore, I only went on a couple of exercises in the jungle.
I was in awe of the skill of my fellow infantrymen and tried hard to learn from
them. The final jungle exercise held by the Battalion in Malaysia was one I took
part in, when Support Company played the part of 'the enemy'. In the final stages
of the exercise we, the enemy, closed up the base camp and tidied up the area
at the foot of the hill. A large pit was dug and we threw all our rubbish in and
set fire to the hole before shovelling soil over the top. The word came through
the Battalion was arriving and we bolted up the hillside and into our trenches.
As we sat waiting holy hell broke loose below, blank shots by rifles and machine
guns. Thunderflashes (training grenades) exploded and we heard the shouts of
command. The attack started on the hill and the rifle companies made their way
up the very steep slippery jungle covered slope. It is always difficult to make
training exercises realistic, and the umpires, wearing their white armbands, control
events. Those with the attacking troops would tap a soldier on the shoulder and
inform that individual that they were dead or wounded. Below our position a
frustrated Company Commander, Major Nicholas, shouted 'Radio Operator!' 'I'm
dead, Sir!' 'Corporal Smith!' 'I'm dead, Sir!' The major swore and called 'Serjeant
Major, come over here!' 'I've had my leg blown off, Sir!' 'Well,' the furious officer
replied, 'F---ing crawl over here!'

An umpire, whilst this was going on gathered
three of us 'enemy' together and gave the following
fire order, 'Five rounds rapid at the officer with the big
voice! Fire!' He stood up and pointed at the major and
ordered 'You're dead, Sir!' The officer violently and
verbally disagreed. We roared with laughter! After the
exercise the Colonel ordered the Regimental Police
Sergeant, Sgt G Griffiths known as 'Griff the Stick' to
clear enough ground for a helicopter to land to take
away the 'wounded'. Four Companies of fit healthy
light infantrymen were making their way down the
hillside towards Griff the Stick. Here was his work force!
He lifted his voice and shouted: 'Right you Herberts!'
he bellowed to draw our attention; 'I want a heli-pad
cleared here!' He indicated the area, 'All those with
gollocks start cutting back the undergrowth. Those
without gollocks borrow one from those who have!' Six
hundred soldiers burst out laughing!

Cpl Jim Parker

Above: 1968 Mauritius – C Company on Point Pieter Both.

Far left: A typical river patrol in Borneo.

Left: Carrying a casualty across the helicopter landing site.

won by a composite platoon from C Company commanded by Second Lieutenant Nick Kench. In early March the Battalion took part in what was to be the final exercise conducted by 28 Commonwealth Brigade, lasting for almost two weeks and involving most of the land forces in Malaysia and Singapore and massive RNAS, RAF and RAAF air support.

Seaton Barracks, Plymouth (April 1969–November 1971)
The main body of the Battalion left Terendak Camp in April, coinciding with the arrival of a strong draft from 4LI, and was fully stretched until the Battalion reformed in Plymouth on 23 June as part of 24 Airportable Brigade and the strategic reserve. It then found that an exercise in Libya planned for mid-October had been cancelled and that they would be Spearhead battalion from 13 August. The late summer and autumn of 1968 had seen a series of increasingly violent marches and demonstrations in Northern Ireland under the auspices of the Northern Ireland Civil Rights Association (NICRA). By August 1969 the situation required the deployment of 3LI to guard key facilities in the Province and by the autumn all three regular battalions were on operations in Northern Ireland, with elements of each being involved in the so-called 'Battle of the Shankill' in Belfast in October 1969.

Inevitably, once the decision had been made to send more troops to Northern Ireland, the Spearhead battalion would be one of the very first units to move. It therefore came as no great surprise when, having been told that no movement to Northern Ireland was imminent and all transport (namely civilian buses) had been dismissed, the order to move to Northern Ireland was received. Staging through the Movement Control Check Point (MCCP) at Devizes, the leading company group arrived in Belfast on 15 August, after a short pause between the airport and Belfast to purchase street maps of Belfast from a filling station!

After concentrating in Palace Barracks, Holywood, the main body deployed next day and was immediately pitched into a severe disturbance between Catholics and Protestants on the Crumlin Road. Over 100 Catholic houses, shops and pubs were burned to the ground. Firearms were used by both communities

3LI TOURS

Terendak Camp, Malacca, July 1968 – April 1969
Mauritius, July – November 1968
Seaton Barracks, Plymouth, April 1969 – November 1971
UNFICYP, April – November 1970
Belfast, August – November 1969
Belfast, February – April 1971
Clifton Barracks, Minden, December 1971 – August 1976
Belfast, November 1972 – March 1973
Belfast, April – August 1974
Belfast, November 1975 – March 1976
Alma Barracks, Catterick, August 1976 – April 1980
Belfast, June – October 1977
UNFICYP, November 1978 – May 1979
Dhekelia, Cyprus, April 1980 – April 1982
Aliwal Barracks, Tidworth, April 1982 – January 1985
Belfast, October 1982 – February 1983
Lisanelly Barracks, Omagh, January 1985 – November 1986
Weeton Barracks, Blackpool, November 1986 – February 1990
Alanbrooke Barracks, Paderborn, February 1990 – May 1991
West Belfast, May – November 1991

MERGER OF 1ST, 2ND AND 3RD BATTALIONS 26 FEBRUARY 1993

and the B Specials. The arrival of the Battalion restored some sort of peace, much to the relief of the Catholics, some of whom had hoped for military intervention from the Republic. Indeed, the Dublin government had called up reservists and stationed troops along the border. By late September the Battalion was permanently established in the north-west sector of the city which included the Shankill and Ballygomartin districts and the Crumlin Road. Violence by militant Protestants broke out in the Shankill area in mid-October and the Battalion was fully engaged for four consecutive days and nights, with elements of nine different units under command at one stage. The most violent and premeditated incident took place on the night of 11 October when a large crowd used firearms, petrol bombs and missiles against the Army.

THE BATTLE OF THE SHANKILL

For those who have read *Holy War in Belfast*, the evening of Saturday 11 October 1969 could very well have been an evening 200 years ago. The same street names, the same crowd intent on a similar purpose; the only substitutions were the RUC for the Irish Constabulary and the Life Guards for the Dragoons.

A crowd of Protestants was moving towards the Catholic Unity Flats at the city end of the Shankill. The RUC had a strong cordon across the road but it was obvious they would not be able to hold the vast mob. The RUC were backed up by a company of ours and 2LI around the flats, but the Brigade Commander told us to thump the crowd from the flank. Thus began a memorable night.

We moved into the Shankill down two parallel streets, Upper Townsend and Israel, and cordoned the road fifty yards in front of the RUC. Bricks and bottles were rained at us and, after warning that CS gas would be used, we donned respirators. The noise from the mob was thunderous and was only increased when we fired our first four rounds of CS canister at 2330 hrs. At this time some shots were fired from the crowd resulting in one policeman shot dead, two injured, and one Bugler shot through the leg. After more CS and shots from the mob it was obvious they were more determined than on previous occasions and different tactics must be employed.

We took cover in side streets and doorways while the 'heavy squad' was used for the first time. The first charge, covered by a blanket of CS, accounted for two arrests, and was quickly followed by more charges. By this time petrol bombs were being thrown and more varied weapons were joining those already in use by the mob. It is difficult to describe this utterly incredible scene in a British city: a howling, drunken mob, half bricks and broken flagstones bouncing down the street, petrol bombs and now automatic weapons joined in the fray. The stench of CS gas, the old-type respirator constantly misting, and the realisation that this was to be no ordinary excerpt from *Keeping the Peace Part II*.

This was the pattern for the remainder of the night: CS, an advance behind the armoured cars smashing through the new barricades of cars erected by the crowd, parties detailed off to cover side streets, and the 'heavy squad' constantly raising their score of arrests. Our casualties were heavy. In all, almost half the force suffered gunshot wounds from various calibre weapons, the most unfortunate being Lieutenant Colonel Bruce Robertson, the CO designate who was present as an interested spectator, and the luckiest being CSM MacCreedy with two 0.45 bullets from a Thompson sub-machine gun which struck his 9mm pistol and a pocket book.

We reached the junction of Northumberland Street and the Shankill at about 0400 hrs, where Brigade told us to 'go firm', which we did under constant sniper fire which eventually faded away at 0500 hrs. We now realised that it was cold and possibly had been for some hours: our damp clothes were uncomfortable and we had the grisly thought that dawn was still two hours away.

With the aftermath of a fairly intense battle all around us, dawn brought a look of the blitz to Belfast. Unshaven but alert soldiers, the majority of whom had never even cocked their weapons, were huddled in doorways and behind vehicles. The Shankill people acted as if that Saturday night had never been (except for the entry of the troops) and their bigoted and unnatural Sabbath day began.

This was not the end of the Shankill for us. We endured two more days of rudery and delivered yet more CS gas to a crowd on the Sunday night. The sheer volume of the CS had a remarkable effect and the mob disappeared behind the barricades. More shots were fired at us but none returned. During the 52 hours spent in the Shankill an unknown number of snipers and petrol bombers were shot and over 70 arrested by the 'heavies'. Our own unbelievably lucky casualties totalled 20 shot, of whom 14 were admitted to hospital with no lasting after-effects. A total of 68 rounds of 7.62 mm, 394 CS gas cartridges and 52 grenades were expended, and we estimate that over 1,000 rounds of assorted calibres were fired at us, plus a couple of hundred petrol bombs and half the pavement on the Shankill! We were not sorry to hand over this area to 1 PARA during the early hours of Tuesday and return to our well-ordered areas and our beds.

On 16 August 1969 the Battalion had carried out its first operation by entering Belfast down the Shankill to scenes of tumultuous welcome akin to that reserved for liberating armies. On 17 November 1969 the last men of the Battalion drove out of Belfast via the Shankill Road to utter indifference by the local people.

Indeed, this was probably one of the last occasions on which the old fashioned 'Keeping the Peace' procedures were adopted when the Police, after one of their constables was shot dead, formally informed the military that they could no longer contain the situation and requested the military to assume command, whereupon the time-honoured order 'Disperse or I fire' was given.

Major General Antony Makepeace-Warne
From Exceedingly Lucky: The History of The Light Infantry 1968–1993
(Bristol, 1993)

Above: *3LI on the streets of Belfast, August 1968.*

A very brief stay in Plymouth between tours in Northern Ireland gave 3LI the opportunity to lay up the Colours of 1KSLI in Bridgnorth on 16 April 1970, after which the Battalion moved to Cyprus for a six-month UNFICYP (United Nations Peacekeeping Force) tour, returning in October 1970.

On becoming part of UNFICYP the Battalion joined military contingents from six nations: Canada, Denmark, Finland, Ireland, Sweden and the United Kingdom. Support for the force came from an Australian Civil Police detachment, an Austrian Field ambulance, UK helicopter squadron and a UK armoured car squadron commanded by His Royal Highness the Duke of Kent. The UNFICYP roles were to prevent a recurrence of inter-communal fighting, to seek the restoration and maintenance of law and order, and to encourage a return to normal conditions through constant surveillance and maintenance of the status quo. Keeping the peace was still the precarious business it had been when the United Nations Force was so hastily assembled on the island six years previously. Quite minor inter-communal troubles, arising from real or imagined grievances, could escalate rapidly to incidents involving loss of life and damage to property. Without the presence of UNFICYP to defuse these local disputes, the situation could have deteriorated very quickly.

The Battalion was spread across two civil administrative districts, Limassol and Paphos, with Battalion Headquarters and two companies at Polemedhia Camp, Limassol, and the remaining company at Ktima Camp, Paphos. The Battalion was responsible for keeping the peace over an area of some 111 square miles – quite a change from the six square miles they had looked after in Belfast the previous summer! 3LI occupied seven permanent platoon/section OPs at likely flashpoints and the urban areas were regularly patrolled in conjunction with the Australian Civil Police. Platoons were rotated through the posts every three weeks to provide variety and renew interest.

The tour was relatively quiet and on 25 September, the Battalion paraded at Polemedhia Camp before the Force Commander, Major General Prem Chand from India, for the presentation of their UN medals. The parade was followed by a floodlit Sounding of Retreat: the last time that Bugle Major Alan Armstrong – for ten years the DLI Bugle Major – would lead the Bugles on parade. In mid-October 3LI handed over their UNFICYP responsibilities to 3 RGJ and returned to Plymouth. In his half-yearly report to the Colonel of the Regiment the Commanding Officer, Lieutenant Colonel Bruce Robertson, remarked, 'We are hoping to spend a more settled year in Plymouth with our families before moving to Minden, BAOR, in November 1971.'

Above: Capt Antony Pile (left) and Cpl Falp at Fort George, Derry, 1972.

Above left: The RFA Sir Bedivere delivers 3LI to Belfast.

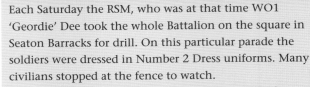

THE RSM

Each Saturday the RSM, who was at that time WO1 'Geordie' Dee took the whole Battalion on the square in Seaton Barracks for drill. On this particular parade the soldiers were dressed in Number 2 Dress uniforms. Many civilians stopped at the fence to watch.

Geordie had the whole Battalion in three ranks facing him, when he ordered the Battalion to 'Ground Arms'. He then ordered the front rank to remove their left boots. This revealed a multitude of coloured socks. One soldier was wearing a pair of fashionable red 'dayglo' socks, which the RSM could hardly miss! He closed in on the unfortunate man. Geordie pointed out that the Army was kind enough to issue each soldier with several pairs of grey or green knitted woollen socks. 'We don't mind if you wear brown or black socks!' he shouted, and then in a frenzy 'But, not f---ing dayglo red socks!' As the soldier was marched away to the Guardroom Geordie ordered the centre rank to remove their jackets. Most soldiers wore army-issued grey braces. A pair of red braces held up one man's trousers. Geordie homed in on him. 'The government is kind enough to issue you with grey braces!' the RSM informed the trembling soldier, 'But you know better. You wear red braces!' At that point legend says that the RSM ordered the Battalion to moon at the gawping civilians.

THE FIRST NI TOUR

On Friday 15 August 1969 at two o'clock in the morning we were woken by the sound of a bugle blowing one short tune over and over again. Big Fred Kunadomo, a Fijian Lance Corporal in the Assault Pioneers, came stumbling out of his bunk wanting to know what the noise was all about. No one recognised the bugle call. Fred opened the window and with us crowded around him shouted to the bugler below, 'Bugle, what's the call?' The bugler stopped blowing and shaking his head shouted back, 'General Alarm, for Christ's sake!'

The Battalion was being turned out to go to Northern Ireland. Half of us thought it was a joke and the other half simply an exercise to practice Active Edge. One of our tasks on call out was to pack some equipment for the Battalion HQ. We were told to pack our kit, but still we thought it was just an exercise. Sitting around doing nothing waiting for the next order, George Gutteridge started to pack his kit, and for something to do the rest of us in that room did the same. That was lucky really!

I would like to stop here and explain. Who in 1969 thought we would be called out for active service in the United Kingdom? Belfast, Manchester, Dundee, Liverpool and Newcastle are all British cities, who could believe armed troops would be sent to any of those?

Twenty-four hours after the bugle call, 3LI was in Northern Ireland. The main body of troop were in a barracks in Belfast, we of Support Company were sent to HQ Northern Ireland, in Lisburn. We were billeted in the gymnasium, and if I remember we had to erect our own double bunk beds. I know we spent a short time practising 'anti-riot' drills as the Battalion had done in Malaysia. Then we were in open four-tonne lorries into Belfast. We drove through streets littered with debris. Cheering people behind improvised barriers greeted us. Some threw cigarettes at us. Support Company moved into the Church Hall on Crumlin Road. My first 'duty' was to stand on the street across the road from the Church Hall. Pte Meston who had served in the Royal Marines, and was somewhat older than the rest of us, partnered me. The general public were very glad to see us, and came up to speak and shake hands.

Cpl Jim Parker

In fact, following their return from Cyprus, 3LI were to have only five weeks' leave and nine weeks' duty before finding themselves again in Belfast as emergency reinforcements. Fortunately the Battalion had been fully prepared for an airportability exercise when the word was received to move immediately to Belfast on 5 and 6 February 1971 to become the province reserve. After drawing IS stores and training with newly introduced equipment, several days were spent at short notice reinforcing the city battalions. C Company's rapid reinforcement of a company of 3rd Battalion The Queen's Regiment in the Ardoyne, after two RUC men were killed on 26 February, drew very favourable comment. For the last month, Headquarters 39 Infantry Brigade allocated an area of the city – almost identical to that which 3LI had in 1969 – with Support Company at Ligoniel, C Company at Leopold Street and the balance of the Battalion in Flax Street Mill. Parties from 1LI began to arrive on 16 March and the handover, marred only by the tragic death of Private Eastaugh, was completed on 25 March when operational responsibility for the area was handed over to 1LI.

On 7 May 1971 Her Majesty Queen Elizabeth The Queen Mother, the Colonel-in-Chief, presented new Colours to 2LI, 3LI and LI(V) at Colchester. In June 1971 3LI had the task of organizing the parade and other ceremonies associated with the departure of the Army from Plymouth and move of Headquarters 24 Airportable Brigade to Barnard Castle.

Clockwise from left: On watch at the Divis Observation Post; Catch and search; Breakfast on a bonnet – always a relief on cordon.

Clifton Barracks, Minden
(December 1971–August 1976)

In November 1971 3LI moved to Clifton Barracks in Minden, West Germany, to become a mechanized infantry battalion. In preparation for this over 100 of all ranks were sent on courses for the tracked APC (Armoured Personnel Carrier), the Stalwart high-mobility load carrier and the Ferret scout car. The Mortar and Anti-Tank Platoons joined the Demonstration Battalion at the School of Infantry, Warminster, for two weeks to familiarize themselves with mechanized techniques. Unit-level familiarization training was carried out in December. It was a full-time job adjusting to the new barracks, making the worn-out equipment and vehicles serviceable, and changing internal administration. During January 1972 each company spent a week at Sennelager, providing a valuable opportunity to get the APCs on the road and do some field training and platoon field firing. In barracks, training consisted largely of Armoured Fighting Vehicle (AFV) recognition and nuclear, biological and chemical (NBC) drills, with Battalion Headquarters venturing into the field for its first Command Post Exercise (CPX) in February. Very generously, 2 RGJ offered to share their ski hut at Steibis on the Austro–German border in Bavaria. It was much enjoyed by all who went there and some 140 men had learned to ski by the end of the skiing season. An unusual sporting achievement was the winning of the Divisional table-tennis competition!

The Deputy Colonel-in-Chief, Her Royal Highness Princess Alexandra, visited the Battalion at Sennelager on 24 May and, after lunch, flew to Minden to meet the families. The Officers' Mess lived extremely well throughout this period, partly due to the fact that the Second-in-Command and all three rifle company commanders were bachelors, but more importantly because the Mess Corporal, Corporal Edwards, was a Master of Wine and insisted that the food should be of the requisite standard to complement his cellar. As a consequence 3LI were regularly called upon by Divisional and Brigade Headquarters to host VIP visitors!

At the beginning of October the APCs were locked away and intensive training started for the forthcoming third Northern Ireland tour. Northern Ireland training commenced with two exercises: 'Red Hand', an internal Battalion exercise, and 'Gaelic Holiday', the brigade exercise. The Battalion took over smoothly from 1LI. Their arrival in Belfast coincided with the decision to reduce force levels to those which had existed before Operation MOTORMAN. As a consequence, the Battalion area increased substantially: A Company took over the Ardoyne bus depot, New Ardoyne, Glenbryns and Ligionel; while B Company occupied Leopold Street RUC station with responsibility for the Shankill. Prospect Mill, Flax Street, was shared by the Echelon and C Company who were responsible for the Old Ardoyne and the Alliances, while Support Company settled into the relative luxury of Finniston School to look after the Catholic and Protestant Bone. Battalion

(1976) EXERCISE SISYPHUS – A COY 3LI

Nude body weighing at sunrise and sunset, measuring all the water and food consumed and further weighing of all body waste added up to the more unpleasant aspects of Exercise Sisyphus. Forty soldiers of A Coy 3LI were involved in this APRE designed exercise to test the water requirement of soldiers in an NBC environment. The wearing of NBC suits and respirators in temperatures of 80 degrees Fahrenheit and more whilst digging slit trenches, reduced weight more effectively than any sauna, although they lacked the accompanying massage. Amazingly the only soldier to fall out on the exercise had measles but the scientists supervising the experiments, who dressed in shorts only, did worse – one had to retire with malaria. The results of the two weeks' work were never known (and I don't think A Company were interested anyway), but soldiers on leave, who had participated, were able to boast to their nearest and dearest in the pubs from Camborne to Consett that they had 'performed' (or words more explicit) for Britain!

Tactical Headquarters was located at Tennent Street RUC station. By way of introduction some 800 rounds were fired at Battalion posts during their first Sunday in the Province, but the Battalion settled down very rapidly and, by the end of the tour, had arrested or detained 20 of the wanted men on the 'shopping list' of IRA terrorists left by 1LI. Lieutenant Christopher Downward received gunshot wounds to the left leg during his hot pursuit of terrorists following an incident in the Old Ardoyne. Lance Corporal Kennington was killed on 28 February while on 'lollipop' patrol guarding children. Private Mason, Bugler Blackburn and Lance Corporal Hodge were all wounded while on similar duties. All recovered, but sadly Bugler Blackburn lost the sight of one eye. It was not one-way traffic: following a shooting incident in the Crumlin Road, A Company shot dead James Fox, a

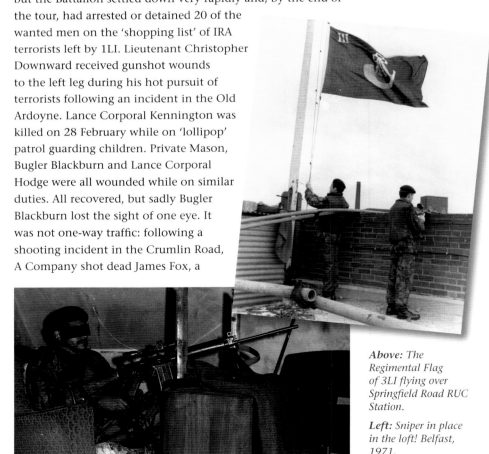

Above: The Regimental Flag of 3LI flying over Springfield Road RUC Station.

Left: Sniper in place in the loft! Belfast, 1971.

Above: Cpl Bradley meets HRH Princess Alexandra in 1972.

JELLALABAD DAY (7 APRIL)

During the 1st Afghan War (1839–42), one of the worst setbacks inflicted on British power in the region, it was the 13th Light Infantry (later the Somerset Light Infantry) who alone upheld British honour. Besieged by a greatly superior force of Afghans in the town of Jellalabad (80 miles east of Kabul) from 12 November 1841 to 13 April 1842, the 'conduct of the Regiment during the siege and the courage of all ranks was legendary.' After the relieving force failed to reach the fortress, General 'Fighting Bob' Sale took the decision to break out. This was successfully accomplished on 7 April 1842 when the Regiment (together with the 35th Bengal Infantry) defeated an Afghan rebel force estimated to be six times greater in number. News of the courageous breakout soon reached England. Queen Victoria was so impressed that she ordered that the Regiment – 'that Illustrious Garrison' – should henceforth be known as 'Prince Albert's Regiment of Light Infantry' after her Consort.

wanted gunman and leading IRA Fiannah youth member, and wounded his companion. At the end of the Battalion's tour, a number of NCOs from the Reconnaissance Platoon, some of whom subsequently were to receive gallantry awards, were left behind and, in conjunction with volunteers from other units, were to form the core of counter-terrorist operations in the Province. A total of 53 weapons, 12,000 rounds of ammunition and 1,100lbs of explosive were recovered during the tour.

At the end of July 3LI Battlegroup, comprising C Squadron 3rd Royal Tank Regiment, 97 Battery (Lawson's Company) 4 Field Regiment Royal Artillery, and other supporting units,

went to Soltau to train in preparation for battlegroup training in Canada. It was a busy ten days and excellent training, in the course of which Corporal 'Jessie' James, George Medal (GM), was required to demonstrate his bravery for a second time. As the driver of the Commanding Officer's APC, he took advantage of a brief halt on the march to lash a tin of composition rations to the exhaust pipe to warm it up. On being ordered to drive on he failed to remove the can and some five minutes later it exploded, covering the Commanding Officer with boiling steak and kidney pie. James halted the vehicle, leaped out and ran into an adjacent thicket from which he refused to emerge until persuaded that the Commanding Officer had calmed down! For 3LI the month at the British Army Training Unit Suffield (BATUS) in Canada offered not only unparalleled battlegroup training but also the opportunity to do some challenging adventure training.

In mid-January 1974 3LI returned from leave, put the APCs in preservation and reorganized once more for Northern Ireland training. The training package covered the skills and procedures needed to meet every conceivable type of incident that might possibly occur in Northern Ireland. They were to be practised again in Exercise 'Red Hand' at Sennelager and Exercise 'Gaelic Holiday' in Minden.

During the first week of the tour there were two serious outbreaks of rioting on the Falls Road, which included the by-now traditional hijacking and burning of vehicles, often accompanied by some shooting. Protest marches had become a recognized weekend occupation with organizations from both communities taking to the streets, often accompanied by a ragbag of fringe organizations such as the Political Hostages Release Committee, People's Democracy, Belfast Gay Liberation Society and the Divine Light Mission. On 21 April an illegal march to the city centre resulted in serious rioting outside Battalion Tactical Headquarters which had to be dispersed by 'Wurzel Force', an ad hoc force. Although the incidence of shooting was much reduced since the Battalion's last tour, there were a number of serious shooting incidents, particularly in the Lower Falls area. The Battalion achieved two particularly notable successes which showed the fundamental importance of a properly zeroed weapon. In early May a patrol from B Company was fired at and immediately took follow-up action. Simultaneously, a patrol from A Company was in the Divis Flats and a soldier with a starlight scope saw two gunmen at a junction trying to clear a Thompson machine gun. He fired two shots, hitting both gunmen. The B Company patrol, still moving rapidly forward, arrested the two men and seized the weapon and ammunition. Another incident took place toward the end of the tour and involved a soldier from B Company in a night-time OP (Observation Post) killing with one round a terrorist, Martin Skillen, armed with an Armalite rifle; a patrol on the ground then captured a further two men with their ammunition. It was upon the junior NCO and young soldiers that the main burden of operations fell and the quality of their response to the challenge was of the highest order. Private Paul Broome of B Company was Second-in-Command of his section when, on 21 May, an OP was hit by a grenade which wounded Private Morris. During the relief of the OP, the Section Commander, Lance Corporal Overton, was also wounded in a firefight. Broome, a young and relatively inexperienced rifleman, took command of the section, directed the follow-up and organized the evacuation of the two wounded soldiers. He was awarded the Queen's Gallantry Medal for his actions. Private Wayne Smith, also of B Company, was part of a patrol in Distillery Street on 14 May when they came under fire. He noticed a small child move onto the street and, despite the incoming fire, dashed out and bundled the child into a doorway, saving its life. Smith was subsequently awarded the Queen's Gallantry Medal. Sadly, since leaving the army Wayne Smith has died. His medals are on display in The Light Infantry Museum at Bodmin.

In Belfast the 12 July marches to mark the victory at the Battle of the Boyne, and the numerous Orange Lodge marches which precede this event, passed peacefully although requiring a major deployment of RUC and Army. The spectacle of thousands of Orangemen on the march was sobering and depressing evidence that the divide between the two communities was as deep and uncompromising as ever. The 13 weapons and 2,500 rounds of ammunition found by the Battalion in the Sandy Row Orange Hall seemed to be rather beyond the realistic needs of the Lodge.

Having had a full fourteen months away from Northern Ireland 3LI moved to Londonderry in November 1975. Prior to deployment the Battalion reorganized and began the now familiar Northern Ireland training package. As always, despite the wealth of experience in the Battalion, there were many soldiers who had not served in Ulster and many new techniques, tactics and legal procedures had to be learned. There was added interest this time as 3LI had not hitherto served in Londonderry, an area which covered both urban and rural operations. Just before the Battalion's departure for Northern Ireland it was announced that 3LI would move to Catterick in August 1976. This news was greeted with delight as many of the single men would at last find themselves close to home. On 11 November 3LI relieved 1st Battalion The Prince of Wales's Own Regiment of Yorkshire as Creggan Battalion in Londonderry. The handover did not go smoothly. A 250lb bomb at the Buncrana VCP (vehicle check point) delayed the takeover by Support Company until an ATO (Army Technical Officer) had neutralized the device. The bomb at the Buncrana VCP was a foretaste of what was to come two weeks later at the same VCP. A lorry was driven into the centre of the VCP and the driver leaped out shouting that there was a bomb on board which would shortly detonate. Captain Chris Downward, who was in command at the time, took swift action to evacuate the site and, half an hour later, 200lbs of explosive detonated, destroying the whole VCP but

Above: A 3LI patrol leaves for the Ardoyne in January 1973. The handwriting notes that one hour after the photo was taken, the officer arrowed was shot in the leg.

CATTERICK 77

In early January 1977 The Royal Scots Dragoon Guards moved from Germany to Catterick. During the move the Regiment suffered the sad loss of their regimental goat which had to be put down. The goat had been the companion of Trojan, the Regimental drum horse, which had been presented to the Regiment by Her Majesty The Queen and was now in serious danger of pining to death. As a welcoming gesture it was decided to present a replacement goat – a gift from the Battalion to The Royal Scots Dragoon Guards – and the Assistant Adjutant was duly directed to effect the necessary purchase. To maintain The Light Infantry county affiliation a large, and somewhat aggressive, long-haired Durham billy goat was acquired, the Second-in-Command complaining that it was over a month before he got rid of the smell in his Land Rover. Under the watchful eye of the Regimental Serjeant Major, the goat was groomed into some semblance of military respectability, and on the day of the presentation the two Commanding Officers (one on crutches) formed up in front of their respective commands. Dense fog failed to mar the occasion and 'Henry' the goat was duly introduced to Trojan. The latter took instant exception to his new Geordie companion and galloped across the square, scattering the orderly ranks of dismounted dragoons like chaff before the wind. He was last seen heading toward the Officers' Mess with his astonished groom in tow, 'skiing' across the icy parade square on the end of the leading rein.

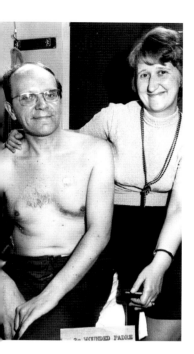

Above: The wounded Padre.

Above: The Band and Bugles sound retreat below Mt Kenya.

Right: The Band plays before dinner.

Far right: The Officers' Mess laid out for a Dinner Night.

causing no casualties. The period of apparent calm that had prevailed in Londonderry since Christmas continued, with a slight increase in activity following the death of Frank Stagg, the PIRA hunger striker, in Wakefield gaol. Some minor 'aggro' took place periodically in the Creggan and was dispersed by C Company using baton rounds. A vehicle patrol from A Company in the Shantallow was ambushed by terrorists who detonated a 100lb bomb as one of a pair of Land Rovers passed. A small piece of shrapnel hit Private Ivor Tunks in the eye, which sadly he subsequently lost. Prompt action by the medical team saved the other eye and Tunks made a good recovery. In the enclave west of Londonderry, PIRA concentrated their efforts on the disruption of traffic to and from the Republic. They blew up the customs posts at Moss-side and Killea, and the Gardai found two milk churns packed with explosive by the side of a road just across the border. A vigorous programme of patrolling, vehicle checks and searches did much to control the level of violence. The searches did not yield much compared with Belfast, but sufficient weapons and ammunition were found to deter PIRA. The Battalion handed over to 1st Battalion The Cheshire Regiment on 16 March and returned to Germany.

In July 3LI finally became non-operational and all efforts were directed to preparing the barracks, vehicles and equipment for handover to 1st Battalion The Duke of Wellington's Regiment. On 6 August, after nearly five years in BAOR, the last flight left Gutersloh.

Alma Barracks, Catterick (August 1976–April 1980)

In March 1976 3LI returned to Minden and, after a flurry of exercises, moved to Alma Barracks, Catterick, in August 1976 as a home defence battalion. In September 3LI was tasked to find the guard at Edinburgh Castle, a duty which was much enjoyed and which lasted until early January 1977.

In May the Battalion had to blend the preparations for receiving the Freedom of Stockton-on-Tees with training for Northern Ireland. 3LI assumed responsibility for the West Belfast area from 2nd Battalion The Royal Anglian Regiment on 28 June, deploying Battalion Tactical Headquarters at Springfield Road RUC station.

On 29 June, the day after the Battalion became responsible for the area, a shooting incident took place in North Howard Street in which Private Richard Turnbull and Private Michael Harrison were killed and the Commanding Officer, Padre and Lance Corporal Georgeson were wounded. The Padre's wounds were very severe and he never returned to duty with 3LI. The wounds of the Commanding Officer and Lance Corporal Georgeson were slight and they were soon able to resume duties.

Largely because of its layout, the Ballymurphy estate was traditionally one of the most difficult and dangerous areas to control and proved to be a very active area. Close coordination of operations was necessary with 45 Commando Royal Marines, responsible for the neighbouring – and in some areas dominating – Turf Lodge estate, to prevent patrols being engaged from across the inter-battalion boundary. There were a number of shootings by PIRA, both at static posts such as OPs and at foot patrols. On 9 August 1977 Private Lewis Harrison of A Company was killed while part of the cordon protecting the ATO working on a hoax explosive device on a lorry. Private Dixon, also of A Company, was shot through the chest but somehow managed to recover after skilled medical attention.

There were other narrow escapes and the level of PIRA activity remained high throughout the early part of the tour, reaching peaks on the anniversary of internment on 9 August (when 113 arrests for rioting were made, of whom 63 were later charged), and the week of Her Majesty The Queen's visit to the Province. There was a well-coordinated PIRA sniping attack when a sangar at McCrory Park was engaged and, whilst the sentry was distracted, another sniper fired at a Royal Engineer Land Rover. A cordon covering a planned search in the Whiterock came under fire from five gunmen in three separate firing positions: 27 rounds were returned and, from the bloodstains on the floor, the follow-up substantiated the claim that three terrorists were hit.

The searches were rather more productive than those on the previous tour in Londonderry had been: C Company on a planned search in the Clonard found an Armalite AR180 and a Remington Woodsmaster, both linked by forensic evidence to previous shootings. An A Company patrol, in the follow-up to a shooting incident in the feud between the Official and Provisional IRA (OIRA/PIRA), arrested three men in possession of an M1 Carbine and an ACP sub-machine gun fitted with a silencer. The most eye-catching find was by C Company, when a patrol stopped a man carrying a plastic guitar case. In the case they found two AR15 Armalite weapons, a Garand rifle, a Colt revolver and ammunition for all the weapons. Perhaps even more grotesque was the finding of nine American grenades in a bathroom in the Ballymurphy.

The second half of the tour was rather quieter, but there was still quite enough PIRA activity across the Battalion area to keep everybody active, and the Battalion was fortunate to have further lucky escapes. Less fortunate were Private France, who was shot in the forearm whilst photographing a rally in the Westrock area; Private Woodman, who sustained slight shrapnel wounds to his buttocks when a round fired at him hit the floor of the APC, causing splintering of both bullet and floor, and Private McGowan, who lost an eye when a bottle was thrown at his vehicle. In the last two months of the tour, 28 people were shot in the kneecap by PIRA in a programme of punishment shootings. On the bright side, the success rate and morale of the RUC continued to rise and there were signs of albeit grudging acceptance of the RUC in some of the republican areas.

In June 1977 3LI returned to the now very familiar streets of West Belfast for another four-month tour at the end of which, in late October, almost without drawing breath, the Battalion found itself deployed in a fire-fighting role in Tyne and Wear. An industrial dispute, which had been brewing for some time in the Fire Service, seemed likely to develop into a total strike with the Government obliged to call on the armed forces to maintain a basic fire-fighting capability. Indeed, the Battalion reconnaissance group flew straight from Belfast into Newcastle airport to open up a tactical headquarters and design a command-and-control system incorporating the police, fire authorities and local government. Under Operation DIGEST, the Battalion collected 19 'Green Goddess' fire engines and, under the guidance of Mr Philip Shepherd, the Army Fire Service Chief Officer in Catterick, began to develop their fire-fighting techniques. In parallel with the fire-fighting preparations, the Battalion planned to parade in Durham on Remembrance Sunday. The purpose of the parade was to give thanks for the Battalion's safe return from Ulster, and to

ANZIO DAY (THE SECOND FRIDAY IN MAY)

This Regimental Day commemorates the 1st Battalion The King's Shropshire Light Infantry's distinguished and protracted action at Anzio from 23 January to 25 May 1944. By the end of 1943 the allied 15th Army Group (British 8th Army and 5th US Army) advancing north from the toe of Italy had ground to a halt in front of the formidable Gustav Line. General Alexander, supported by Churchill, devised a plan to carry out an amphibious landing in the area of Anzio with the aim of outflanking the Gustav Line and hopefully shortening the war in Italy. This task was given to the 6th US Corps of General Mark Clark's 5th US Army and the British 1st Division, in which 1KSLI were serving, was placed under command of the US army for the operation. The landings achieved complete surprise but were not subsequently developed with the necessary speed and determination. The Germans brilliantly rushed reserves to the area from all over Europe and rapidly developed plans to push the Allies back into the sea. 1KSLI with great dash reached the important road/railway junction at Campoleone, 12 miles inland, before heavy German counter-attacks drove the allies back by 5 February to a tight perimeter around the original landing area, which was completely dominated by the Alban Hills. For nearly four months, bitter fighting continued in the 'wadis' in conditions and attrition rates closely resembling the trenches the First World War. Eventually, on 22 May the Allies, sufficiently reinforced, began the breakout battle and 1KSLI took part in General Mark Clark's triumphal, but highly controversial, advance on Rome, which was liberated on 4 June. The KOYLI were also awarded the Battle Honour 'Anzio'.

remember those who did not return from Ireland and from earlier campaigns. The occasion also offered an opportunity for 3LI to exercise the Regiment's Freedom of the City of Durham. The service in the cathedral, attended by the whole Battalion and the families, was immensely moving. It was conducted by The Very Reverend H W Heaton, Dean of Durham, who in his address made special mention of Privates Richard Turnbull, Lewis Harrison and Michael Harrison. Two Buglers sounded

Above: The Otter was the centrepiece of the exceptional collection of silver animals started by the KSLI and continued by the Third and Second Battalions, before being passed on to The Rifles.

'Last Post' from the gallery below the great west window and the entire Bugle Platoon took up 'Reveille' from the triforium above the nave.

At five o'clock in the morning on 14 November, the Battalion deployed to their fire-fighting locations in Tyne and Wear. The area of deployment was supposed to be a strict secret but, given the number of Geordies in the Battalion, the announcement appeared to come as no surprise whatsoever to the soldiers!

As the strike dragged on, the problem of continued separation for the married men increased. Extra hands were called in from all over Catterick garrison to produce the requisite number of crews and permit everyone to have five days' leave at either Christmas or the New Year. It was with

considerable relief that, after nine weeks fire-fighting, the emergency ended and the 'Green Goddesses' headed toward Catterick. The Battalion had dealt with a total of 1,531 calls during its tour of duty and had done much to enhance the name of the Regiment in the North East.

A very memorable Sounding of Retreat took place at Richmond Castle on 24 June, culminating in the Massed Bands and Bugles playing Tchaikovsky's *1812 Overture*, supported by four field guns from the local TA artillery regiment and the church bells of all three churches in Richmond. Fifty-two Buglers lined the Castle walls and a full rifle company provided the musket fire. The Retreat concluded with the Flying Bugles, the regimental free-fall parachute team, appearing to land in the River Swale!

RHODESIA – GUERRILLAS AT RUKOMECHI

In December 1979 Captain Richard Hodson and sixteen selected NCOs from 3LI flew to Rhodesia as part of the ceasefire monitoring force. The 3LI party was deployed to the Rukomechi assembly point in the north west, where some 300 armed guerrillas of the Zimbabwe Peoples' Revolutionary Army (ZIPRA) were assembled in the early stages of the ceasefire. Captain Hodson was subsequently awarded the MBE. This is his account:

Below: On parade at Rukomechi.

Bottom: Sjt Rann and a new friend!

An abandoned Tsetse Fly research station stands desolate in the middle of the Mana Pools game reserve on the Rukomechi River. This area of the Zambezi Valley is still largely uncontrolled, and remains the natural habitat for large numbers of game normally found in this part of Africa. During the war years it was also used as one of the main infiltration routes by the guerrillas based in Zambia. Code-named Papa, this was the assembly place that became the crude and primitive home for 1,946 Zipra guerrillas and 30 members of the monitoring force.

At 0730 hrs, 28 December 1979, Papa was established by 13 members of the 3rd Bn The Light Infantry, one vehicle mechanic (38 Engineers) and three Royal Signallers from 8 Field Force. Two Zipra liaison officers, recently based at Lusaka, followed shortly afterwards. During the first week

the guerillas poured in by bus loads, laden with vast quantities of assorted ammunition and a whole host of mainly obsolete Soviet weapons, including mortars, anti-tank and anti-aircraft guns. Hercules aircraft, clearly marked with white crosses, droned constantly overhead dropping supplies and equipment to house, feed and heal these reluctant, suspicious and temperamental men who constituted Joshua Nkomo's ragged Army of 'Liberation'. 'Papa' became the largest Zipra camp and the third largest in Southern Rhodesia.

Our initial priorities were to establish some form of working relationship with them and a semblance of order. Muster and sick parades got off the ground. Medicine became a great healer for them – and for their attitude towards us. The sick numbered some 250 a day. The walking wounded were badly infected through lack of proper medical attention and had to be casevaced six days after their arrival. Some weren't so bad: 'Comrade, there is something terribly wrong with me – I faint in my sleep!' Establishing cordial relations with them wasn't an easy proposition. The entire operation ran on a shoestring for the first month. Shortages of food, an insufficient water supply and promised camp stores that arrived long after they were due, prompted accusations of 'Dirty British' or 'Rhodesian collaborators systematically starving the forces of liberation'. At dawn, 3 March 1980, 26 men from the monitoring force 'recovered' to Salisbury. They left well satisfied. Relations between ourselves and the Patriotic Front had become excellent – patience, time and cinema shows, etc., had seen to that. The Rhodesian security forces had arrived, at long last, to commence the initial integration process between the Armed Forces. Once bitter enemies, the two opposing sides were now drinking beer and recounting their war experiences together and toasting the new Zimbabwe. The six-man liaison team left behind for a few more days witnessed the calm acceptance of the totally unexpected election result by all assembled at 'Papa'. Everybody then relaxed with the grim satisfaction that the war was, at least, at an end.

After an exciting and interesting exercise in Kenya, during which links were renewed with the Kenya Rifles, 3LI moved to Cyprus in November 1978 for a six-month tour with UNFICYP. Initially A and B Companies took over the UN commitments, while C and Number 4 Companies started off in WSBA at Dhekelia. Life in UNFICYP Sector 2 was rather more restricted than in WSBA with little time for training or recreation, and the two companies were fully stretched, manning some 16 OPs and checkpoints between the Turkish and Greek Cypriot ceasefire lines. Accommodation in the OPs varied from requisitioned bungalows, with 16 soldiers sharing one bathroom, to huts built by the Royal Engineers. Sector Headquarters and Eastern Company Headquarters were in St David's Camp, an old hutted camp and one-time detention centre for EOKA terrorists, to the west of Nicosia. Western Company was based in a former box factory partitioned off into rooms. In the early part of the tour the weather was quite unpleasant with parkas and windproof smocks required at night in the OPs and four-wheel drive and great care needed when driving on the muddy patrol track linking the OPs.

The halfway point of the tour was marked by the rotation of rifle companies on 11 February, followed on 20 February by the medal parade, at which the UNFICYP Force Commander, Major General Quinn, presented every member of the Battalion with their UN medal. Before leaving the island, the Battalion Band and the Band of The Queen's Lancashire Regiment combined to give a spectacular floodlit performance in the magical setting of the amphitheatre at Curium. The Battalion was relieved by 41 Commando Royal Marines in May 1979 and returned to Catterick for two weeks' disembarkation leave. On 21 June Lieutenant Colonel Stephen Caney assumed command, just in time to command the Battalion on Exercise 'Tristar', a NATO SAS exercise in Northumberland, in which 3LI provided the hunter force in the tactical movement and escape and evasion phases. The exercise provided excellent training in low-level tactics and was the first time for several years that the Battalion had operated as a Battalion in the field. The results were very encouraging and 85 of the multinational escapers, nearly 60 per cent, were captured. On return to Catterick, 3LI was detailed for Spearhead battalion duty from 13 August to 7 September. On 29 September the Battalion represented the Regiment at the granting of the Freedom of the City of Leeds to The Light Infantry, previously granted to the KOYLI on 7 June 1945. In November and early December reciprocal exercises took place with the Jamaica Defence Force (JDF). In December Captain Richard Hodson and 16 selected NCOs from 3LI flew to Rhodesia as part of the ceasefire monitoring force. On 30 January 1980 Her Royal Highness Princess Alexandra visited 3LI in Catterick.

Salamanca Barracks, Dhekelia Garrison, Cyprus (April 1980–April 1982)

On 23 March the advance party arrived in Cyprus and started to take over Salamanca Barracks in the WSBA from 1st Battalion The Queen's Lancashire Regiment. By the beginning of May, 3LI was complete in Cyprus and had assumed the responsibilities of resident battalion. These required the maintenance of the security of WSBA at all times, with a squadron of 13th/18th Hussars under command, together with the holding of an IS company at short notice to move, and the deployment – for three-week periods – of one company to Ayios Nikolaos in support of the ESBA battalion. The remainder of the Battalion was at six hours' notice to transfer from a training to an operational role.

The heightened threat of terrorist activity was causing increasing concern in Cyprus. By May 1981, 3LI had completed the construction of a series of permanent OPs on the hills covering the Northern approaches to Episkopi garrison. Routine operational tasks, including patrolling, surveillance and static guards, continued to involve two companies at any given time in WSBA, ESBA and the Troodos Mountains. Rifle companies continued to devote much time to arduous and imaginative training, frequently making use of the RAF helicopters and the launches and Mexeflotes (powered rafts) of 10 Port Squadron, Royal Corps of Transport.

The Battalion was deployed on a major Land Forces Cyprus IS exercise in May, and deployed Battalion tactical headquarters and lower controls for the British Forces Cyprus CPX in June. A battalion group amphibious counter-insurgency exercise was held in August, using the visiting Landing Ship (LSL) *Sir Lancelot*, for a dawn beach assault landing at Lara Point. Maximum use was made of all available air support, and the opportunity was taken to exercise battalion battle procedures and deployment of supporting armour.

Below: Two members of the Machine Gun Platoon of 3LI on United Nations duties in Cyprus.

In the latter part of 1981 there was a change of emphasis in Battalion training, to take account not only of the IS (Internal Security) threat in Cyprus, but also of the Battalion's forthcoming tour in Northern Ireland.

On 8 January 1982 Lieutenant Colonel Michael Regan assumed command of the Battalion. In March a complete rifle company was deployed to act as civilian population and insurgents for a major RMAS FTX. The Band were heavily engaged in training for their war role as medical assistants, but also had an increasing number of musical engagements. The final Sounding of Retreat included a 'Son et Lumière' interpretation of The Light Infantry Battle Symphony *Salamanca*. The Band and Bugles, silent drill squads and fireworks display combined to produce a widely acclaimed performance, a fitting end to the tour. The duties of the WSBA resident battalion were handed over to 1st Battalion The Argyll and Sutherland Highlanders on 5 April.

Aliwal Barracks, Tidworth
(April 1982–January 1985)

The Battalion reassembled in Aliwal Barracks, Tidworth, in May, under the command of 1 Infantry Brigade, which was the major component of the UKMF. 3LI did not, however, participate in any of the associated training during 1982 because of the impending Operation BANNER tour of duty in Fermanagh.

The Commanding Officer had been informed, strictly on a 'need to know' basis, that once the Falkland Islands had been recaptured, the Battalion's tour in Fermanagh would in all probability be cancelled and 3LI would form the Garrison on the Islands. He was also required to earmark a company (C Company) as battle casualty replacements. Several months were therefore spent training for a role quite different from that anticipated by the Commanding Officer! In the event, the decision was taken that the Fermanagh tour should proceed as planned, and that 1st Battalion The Queen's Own Highlanders should go to the Falkland Islands.

At the beginning of October, 3LI assumed responsibility for the Fermanagh TAOR from 1st Battalion The Parachute Regiment. A good working relationship was quickly established with both the RUC and UDR, the latter principally responsible for North Fermanagh. Battalion Tactical Headquarters was based at Fort St Angelo on the edge of the airstrip to the north of Enniskillen.

The Battalion was to support the RUC in the maintenance of law and order by a combination of reassurance, deterrence and attrition. The number of incidents in the Fermanagh TAOR had traditionally been lower than in the rest of the Province, the chief activity being smuggling rather than terrorism. However, the blowing up of an RUC constable as he drove out of Enniskillen at the beginning of the tour, and the lucky escape of a reservist when his booby-trapped car failed to explode, served as vivid reminders that there could be no relaxation in the campaign. This was underlined by the death of Corporal David Salthouse, employed at Headquarters 8 Infantry Brigade, in the 'Drop Inn Well' bomb outrage on 6 December.

During the latter part of the tour two improvised explosive devices were discovered, and there were several fairly elaborate hoaxes and an unsuccessful attempt to booby-trap a reserve constable's car. A 550lb device near the village of Donagh was discovered, and an ambush laid on the site. Subsequently, a terrorist was detected at the firing point, wounded and arrested, the device being rendered safe in a very successful operation thereafter. The policy of reassurance, deterrence and attrition worked well with all ranks clearly understanding the policy, and their good humour, patience and professionalism earned respect throughout the TAOR.

Order appeared to have been restored and, when the Battalion left on 13 February 1983, it was not replaced by another roulement battalion.

On return from Fermanagh in early 1983 3LI concentrated on their primary role in the UKMF (United Kingdom Mobile Force), taking part in major exercises in Denmark during the late summer and autumn and, in the latter part of the year, being deployed to RAF Greenham Common where the 'Greenham Women' had established a camp.

A period of Public Duties in London, the second in the history of the Regiment, was undertaken by 3LI in January and February 1984.

Below: 'Slim' *Appleyard (right) and* 'Jesse' *James chillin'.*

Lisanelly Barracks, Omagh
(January 1985–November 1986)

In January 1985 3LI moved to Omagh for a two-year tour as a resident battalion; a busy and very successful tour.

In January 1985 the UKMF role was handed over to 1st Battalion The Duke of Wellington's Regiment, and 3LI took over from 1st Battalion The Queen's Regiment as part of 8 Infantry Brigade in Omagh. The Battalion operated a monthly rotation of the four rifle companies: Operations Company, Brigade Reserve Company, Guards and Duties Company, and Leave and Training Company.

The Battalion maintained a very high work rate, providing reinforcements both for its own operations and other battalions. The greatest commitment was over the period of the Orange marches. On 12 July, the Battalion formed five company groups – with one company still on leave in England!

In early summer, 6UDR assumed responsibility for providing the patrol section for the Castlederg Salient, which was in any case in their TAOR, previously found by the Brigade Reserve Company. This allowed the Brigade Reserve Company to take on the guarding of Rosslea RUC station from Guards and Duties Company. On 31 March, there was a grenade and small arms attack against an RUC mobile patrol in the Lisnaskea area. In

their routine inspection of likely mortar baseplate sites around the Lisnaskea base, the RUC had unwittingly established a pattern. A clearance operation was mounted and coordinated by B Company and fortunately, although the vehicle was damaged, there were no casualties. On 1 May, PIRA set fire to a house in Newtonbutler, intending thereby to provoke an RUC investigation. However, the RUC did not respond and, in a clearance operation mounted by A Company (Major Andrew Mortimer), a 450lb home-made, command-wire-detonated explosive device was found and neutralized.

On 13 September the QRF (Quick Reaction Force) provided to 6UDR were involved in the follow-up to a car bomb explosion which had taken place two days earlier in Omagh. During the autumn, there was a marked increase in the use by PIRA of mortars to attack RUC stations and security force bases in the Province. The increased terrorist threat and bombing campaign against border RUC stations of December 1985–January 1986 provoked Operation COUNTERPOINT. This caused the Brigade Reserve Company to be permanently deployed in the Battalion TAOR, based with C Company 6UDR in the Deanery, Clogher. Two reinforcement infantry battalions were sent to the Province under Operation CARA CARA and, from 18 March, Battalion Tactical Headquarters and the Echelon of 1st Battalion The King's Own Scottish Borderers were located at Lisanelly Barracks, Omagh, with one rifle company, under the operational control of 3LI, meeting the Clogher commitment. The deployment of additional battalions to Omagh was to continue throughout the rest of the Battalion's tour, the King's Own Scottish Borderers being followed by three more battalions at roughly three-monthly intervals.

Left: Public Duties, 1983.

Below left: The Ceremony of the Keys at the Tower of London.

Below: Marching into Buckingham Palace, led by Maj Nigel Jones.

Above: 3LI soldiers dismounting from a Lynx helicopter in Northern Ireland.

On 11 February four masked men carrying a blast incendiary entered the 'Talk of the Town' public house at Maguiresbridge, shot dead an RUC Constable and a civilian, and departed leaving the incendiary device which subsequently exploded, gutting the building. C Company were involved in both the immediate follow-up and the clearance of the escape vehicle, found two days later. The Protestant backlash, provoked by the Anglo-Irish Agreement, required an increased commitment by the Battalion to support the RUC during local government elections and the loyalist 'Day of Action' on 3 March.

In the early hours of 31 March, a patrol from Support Company of the King's Own Scottish Borderers, under operational control of 3LI, disturbed terrorists in the act of planting a command-wire-initiated explosive device in the Favour Royal Forest near Clogher. Although the terrorists were not apprehended, the device, approximately 60lbs of home-made explosive, was neutralized successfully the following day. Easter saw the start of the traditional marching season, and, on Easter Sunday, the Brigade Reserve Company was deployed to cover a large Republican rally at Carrickmore while, at Lisnaskea, A Company (Major Nigel Davenport) covered another at Donagh. Both passed without incident.

On 24 April, a routine patrol from D Company (Major David Thomas) was conducting a route check of the main road into Rosslea prior to an RUC shift changeover. A member of the patrol discovered a hidden culvert under the road containing a fully assembled 800lb command-wire-initiated explosive device. An operation was mounted and, on 26 April, fire was directed at two men in the area of the device, killing one,

Seamus McElwaine, and wounding the other, J J Lynch. The entire explosive device was recovered intact, together with an FNC rifle, a Mini-Ruger rifle and two radios. On 20 May, a patrol from C Company was conducting route checks through Donagh prior to local by-elections, when an explosive device behind the wall of a derelict building in the village was remotely detonated, causing blast injuries in the face and upper body to Corporal Jones, the second-in-command of the patrol. On 21 August, a radio used in the attack was found in Donagh graveyard by a patrol from D Company. Constable McVitty was murdered by two gunmen while he was off duty working his fields near Rosslea. Elements of B Company and the ARF were deployed in the follow-up operation but without success.

The traditional marches took place in July and August, with the whole Battalion being deployed to Dungannon on 12 July. A substantial find of arms and ammunition was made in Newtownbutler on 7 August, and a further find of ammunition and bomb-making material in Aghalurcher graveyard on 30 September.

Taking advantage of a visit by the Corunna Band, a Sounding of Retreat and cocktail party were held at Lisanelly Barracks on 26 September as the Battalion's formal farewell to the Province. On Sunday 16 November, the Chaplain General to the Armed Forces, the Venerable Archdeacon W E Johnstone, dedicated The Light Infantry window in the garrison church. The window was based on a design by the Education Officer, Captain Gill Wing, depicting scenes from the Regiment's recruiting areas.

The last two months of the tour were quiet operationally and, having handed over the Omagh commitments to 1LI, 3LI moved to Weeton Camp in late November.

Weeton Barracks, Blackpool (November 1986–February 1990)

For 3LI, an intensive period of training with the Saxon wheeled troop-carrying vehicle was necessary before the Battalion could take its place on brigade exercises. This training was interrupted in February by a deployment to Salisbury Plain to cover an exercise by the Ground Launched Cruise Missiles (GLCMS) of the US Air Force. A strong detachment from 3LI was required to support the Cardiff Tattoo in July and August, but by October the Battalion was ready to move to Germany with its Saxons for Exercise 'Keystone'. In March 1988 one company from 3LI was deployed to the Falkland Islands to join the garrison; the balance of the Battalion followed shortly thereafter on a reinforcement exercise, Exercise 'Fire Focus'. In July 3LI was tasked to provide security for the newly opened temporary prison at Rollestone Camp on Salisbury Plain and subsequently, with some relief, moved to Kenya for the long awaited Exercise 'Grand Prix'. For 3LI the early part of 1989 was filled with a host of commitments arising from the Regular Army Assistance Table, but the Battalion did escape to take part in Exercise 'Key Flight' in Germany in September.

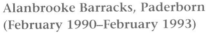

Alanbrooke Barracks, Paderborn
(February 1990–February 1993)

In February 1990 3LI moved from Weeton Camp to Paderborn to become a mechanized battalion with the new Warrior infantry combat vehicle. However, any prospect of mechanized training was removed when the Battalion was tasked with the training of reinforcements for the Gulf War. All available Warrior vehicles having been transferred to the Gulf, it was decided to bring forward the 3LI tour in Northern Ireland and the Battalion deployed to West Belfast in May 1991. It was 13 years since 3LI had last deployed in West Belfast and much had changed in the conduct of operations.

The level of terrorist activity was the highest it had been for some years, and the Battalion was kept fully occupied dealing with a huge diversity of incidents across the area. On 25 May an explosive grenade was thrown into the dog kennels area of North Howard Street Mill, killing Corporal O'Neill, Royal Regiment of Fusiliers, and severely wounding Lance Corporal Swift, Royal Green Jackets, who were dog handlers attached to 3LI. Two new weapons had entered the terrorist armoury: the projected recoilless improvised grenade (PRIG), a 'throwaway' launcher which would project a Semtex-filled warhead some 50 to 100 metres, and the 'coffee jar', or mark 15 grenade, a simple but effective device formed by filling a glass jar with Semtex explosive with a fuse which detonates as the jar breaks on impact.

On 16 June, in the area of the Ballymurphy estate, Private Williams, a member of an A Company foot patrol, found what he thought was a command wire. As a result of this discovery

by an alert soldier, a formal clearance operation was mounted and a 2kg charge of Semtex discovered. On 1 July a 3LI foot patrol, reinforced by members of the Royal Military Police, was in the New Lodge when a mark 15 grenade was thrown at the team commanded by Corporal Pattison. Despite the fact that he had been close to the seat of the explosion and that two members of his team had been injured by the blast, Corporal Pattison mounted a determined and aggressive pursuit. Unable to catch the thrower, he returned and supervised the treatment and evacuation of the wounded.

A vehicle patrol from C Company was passing through Turf Lodge on 11 July when one round from an RPG7 rocket launcher was fired at the vehicle. The round missed the vehicle and Private Thompson, the 'top cover' sentry, fired one round immediately from the vehicle, dismounted and fired a further round, narrowly missing the firer of the RPG who made a hasty escape. Although the terrorist escaped, Private Thompson's rapid response and accurate fire did much to deter similar attacks.

15 August, the 22nd anniversary of the deployment of troops to Northern Ireland, was marked by an unusually high incident rate. During the course of the day, 11 vehicles were

Clockwise from top left: Crossing the Weser – a constant theme of any large Cold War exercise in Germany; Op ROGER, 1987 securing Greenham Common; Op ROGER, 1987 (2); Op ROGER, 1987 (3); FIBUA Building entry – Imber Village.

Left: Infantry section dismounted from their Saxon Armoured Personnel Carrier with MB Tank in the background.

SOUTH GEORGIA, FALKLANDS – 1987

Despite a series of briefings and a wide range of specialist skills training, the first sight of the Island was like a Gothic dream. Jagged peaks, glaciers, a vision betwixt Purgatory and Hell. 3 RGJ whom we were relieving were ecstatic on our arrival and after a three-day handover, the Bugle gained ascendancy on this tiny corner of the Empire. To the Northwest, 800 miles away, lay the Falkland Islands and in all other directions, water, for miles. Sharing home with Major Graham Whitmore and the Recce Platoon were a doctor, a Royal Marine Mountain Leader and a handful of Sappers and Signallers. Home was actually King Edward Point which lies in the same cove as the disused whaling station of Grytviken. Early good weather allowed the updating of local maps before the snow came, and reports to the Battalion told of frequent wildlife sightings, with seals in particular.

All manner of training could be carried out, including the full range of mountain and arctic warfare skills, but insufficient snow was available for ski qualifications. Patrols had not only to contend with the local weather conditions but also to master movement across differing mountainous terrains, as well as deployment by Rigid Raider. The patrols visited various sites, checked routes, safety huts and hidden caches. Usually they came back with an interesting wildlife encounter too. The normal programme of APWT, Field Firing and a variety of Cadres continued unabated when not on patrol. OC Troops also had the exacting civilian tasks of Postmaster, Magistrate, Harbour Master and Customs and Immigration Officer thrust upon his plate. Supplying First Day Covers to the world proved to be an exacting task, as did the unloading of supplies from a variety of ships that resupplied or simply paid a call. These visits of course provided some amusement and diversion from the normal routine as a good dinner on board was usually included into the bargain as well, including being

the recipient of some 'Glasnost' when a Soviet research ship with 2 x HIND helicopters on deck paid a visit. Air resupply by Hercules was also carried out to ensure that all supplies got through, particularly the mail, though the men in blue were not impressed to hear the strains of the 'Dambusters' being hummed as they started their final run in for a drop. Other entertainment was provided by the sheer challenge of the place, to explore it, photograph it and record events. Much of the time, through a mixture of videos, quizzes, potted sports, barbecues and certain 'off beat activities' such as 'hairdressing', proved to be sufficient diversion for most. Perhaps South Georgia is one of the few truly unique postings in the world and the challenge to learn and master a new range of skills, live in a very different way and be virtually isolated for four months will undoubtedly have left its mark on all those who were fortunate enough to serve there.

Graham Whitmore

Below: Training on South Georgia and (below right) digging snowholes.

Right: Maj Graham Whitmore.

THE LIGHT INFANTRY ETHOS VS THE CHAIN OF COMMAND

While stationed at Weeton Barracks, 3LI completed Exercise 'Grand Prix' in Kenya in December 1988. This was a golden opportunity to extend the Battalion and create a realistic training experience. The standard package was a typical rotation through a number of training areas including live firing. We decided to do something completely different and Martin Grubb, the Second-in-Command, was sent to Kenya to negotiate a movement area where we could run a full Battalion-level operation over a substantial piece of real estate. He succeeded brilliantly and also enlisted the support of the British Army Training Team and the High Commission, who in turn gained the approval of the Kenyan Government and Army.

We were set to cover some 240km over four weeks, chasing up a live enemy and conducting tactical operations such as 24-hour ambushes that nobody had done since Malaysia days. The companies rotated out of the line for R and R and the whole expedition concluded with a Battalion assault high up in the Matthews Mountains in northern Kenya. Because of the possibility of encountering armed Somali bandits, all commanders carried live ammunition, which was of course a break in the normal rules of 'blanks only'.

Some months before we were due to deploy I was visiting the Recce Platoon in South Georgia when a very excited signaller came up to me and told me that he had received an 'eyes only' coded signal for me and would let me have it once it had been decoded. This naturally caused some excitement: was it war? Was an Argentinian submarine on the prowl? To my utter astonishment it was a signal from UKLF telling me that the Field Army Commander had reviewed our plans for Kenya and forbidden us to carry out the exercise. The reason for this was that 'The men will not enjoy any exercise that lasts for longer than 14 days'.

Needless to say we complied with the great man's absurd command in a typical Light Infantry manner. We just split the Battalion exercise into three phases and continued as before, conveniently obscuring the fact that the phases were continuous. The High Commissioner visited us in the field and liked what he saw, which was significant because he had hitherto been much against these exercises and there was considerable tension between the Ministry of Defence and the Foreign Office. The Battalion performed magnificently in very harsh conditions, completing what the Kenyan Army liaison officers initially thought was an impossible task, but one that to LI or Rifles battalions in Afghanistan would be routine.

Above: Sjt 'Gripper' Growden (left) in the assault.

Unfortunately (as I was told at the time) the High Commissioner took it upon himself to write to London to say that all would be well in Kenya if future exercises could be run like ours. Protocol passed the letter to UKLF. The cat was out of the bag and the powers that be were unamused. We had lost a company's worth of mosquito nets, buried a couple of new 4-ton trucks in the sand of the Seyia River, and on our return a small number of men went down with malaria (later established to be from drug-resistant mosquitoes). GOC NW District was ordered to investigate 'the apparent failure of leadership in 3rd Battalion The Light Infantry' and I went to Cyprus, never to return.

Richard Sale *(CO 3LI at that time)*

(Editorial Note: It is worth noting that the experience gained from this exercise directly influenced a number of young officers. It is perhaps no surprise therefore that the development of the overseas battle camp at the Infantry Battle School and the current format of battalion overseas exercises in Kenya closely resemble the style and ethos of this 'Trailblazer'.)

CO's Tac Group have tea with a Samburu scout.

The Ops Officer, Capt Tim Evans, enjoying a ride.

The Mortar Platoon advances into the Ndoto Mountains with the aid of a camel train.

Right: 3LI faces, 1990.

Below: A house search in the Ballymurphy, and (inset) Pte 'Slug' Pickering – ready for anything.

delivered to various parts of Belfast, each of which required the mounting of a formal clearance operation. There were eight separate shooting incidents against the security forces and two large explosions, one of which resulted in the death of a bystander. The whole series of incidents lasted about nine hours and no casualties were sustained by the Battalion.

On 23 September, PIRA initiated an elaborate 'come on' in the area of Corry's Woodyard, to which the Battalion responded by mounting a formal clearance operation which yielded a 3.3kg Semtex charge, a timer unit and electric detonator.

On 11 October a large proxy bomb, comprising some 170kg of home-made explosive in a Skoda car, was intercepted by the RUC in the Donegal Road and cleared. The Battalion had a major find of arms and ammunition in a flat in Forthriver Crescent on 24 October. On 2 November a terrorist bomb exploded at the Musgrave Park Hospital, causing a number of casualties and considerable damage. Although the Echelon and elements

of Headquarter Company were based at the hospital, the explosion occurred in an area not used by 3LI.

On 8 November responsibility for West Belfast was handed over to 1st Battalion The Prince of Wales's Own Regiment of Yorkshire and 3LI was complete in Paderborn by the end of that day.

On 31 May 1991 Her Majesty Queen Elizabeth The Queen Mother presented new Colours to the three regular battalions at Tidworth. With the outcome of the 'Options' studies very much in mind, but yet to be announced, it was to be a particularly memorable regimental occasion, even though the 1LI presence was much reduced and 3LI could only spare a small party from operations in Northern Ireland. 1992 was spent finally reroling as an Armoured Infantry Battalion some two and a half years after arriving in Germany. It was a over this period that 'Options for Change' came to a head requiring a reduction in the number of infantry battalions in the British Army. The decision by the Army Board to back single battalion parochialism led to the large regiments carrying the brunt of the cuts. On 25 February 1993 the three regular battalions merged to become two, a major reorganization achieved with a smoothness and efficiency that does nothing but credit to the 'large regiment' concept. 1LI occupied the barracks occupied by 2LI, and 3LI renumbered as 2LI and remained in Germany. Merger Day was marked by a simple yet poignant parade, during which the 3rd Battalion Colours were marched off for the last time and the Colours of the 2nd Battalion marched on. Brigadier Jim Parker, Deputy Colonel of The Light Infantry (Yorkshire), was the Inspecting Officer.

The Fourth Battalion

The summer of 1968 found 1 DLI serving in Cyprus as part of the United Nations Force in Cyprus (UNFICYP). The Battalion was responsible for a large area of southern Cyprus.

A helicopter became an almost essential means of visiting the outlying companies; each manning a series of observation posts (OPs). Only a small part of the Battalion was therefore able to be present at the Vesting Day parade.

On the evening of 10 July, the moon was shining on a calm Mediterranean Sea as the guests assembled by the parade ground in Polemedhia Camp. Not only were the leaders of the Greek and Turkish Cypriot communities present – an unusual event even in the neutral ground of a UN camp – but also Major General A–E Martola, the Finnish officer commanding UNFICYP, the commanders and a representative party of officers from all the UNFICYP contingents: Canada, Sweden, Denmark, Finland, the Republic of Ireland, Austria and Australia.

The parade was introduced by the Second-in-Command (Major Micahel Benson) who explained the significance of the occasion. After a rousing fanfare sounded by the Bugles, the Band and Bugles marched on, their white tropical dress tunics standing out on the floodlit parade ground. The first part of the parade consisted of the Band and Bugles playing the regimental quick marches of the four Light Infantry regiments and finishing with the DLI regimental slow march, 'The Old 68th'. The parade ground lights were then extinguished and a spotlight picked out the Commanding Officer's Bugler,

Corporal Brown, who sounded the 'Last Post' as the DLI flag was lowered. The Band then played the regimental hymn 'Abide With Me' and, after a pause, the Buglers sounded 'Reveille' and the new Light Infantry flag was raised. 1 DLI had become 4LI.

After a bugle display, the playing of the 'Keel Row' and 'Light Infantry', Bugle Major Walker requested permission from Major General David Lloyd Owen, the General Officer Commanding (GOC) British troops on the island, for the Band and Bugles to march off. After this moving ceremony the Battalion's guests were entertained in the various messes.

4LI, commanded by Lieutenant Colonel John Jacob, continued to carry out its UNFICYP role in Cyprus, observing the relationship between the Greek and Turkish Cypriot communities and seeking to prevent violence. The task was very manpower intensive and gave little opportunity for more than the shortest breaks. Superficially an easy task, there were

Below left: 4LI Final Parade, Durham, 12 December 1968. Princess Alexandra speaks to Sjt Lynn (A/CSM A Coy) with Lt Col Jacob, CO.

Below: Laying up the Colours in Durham Cathedral.

A TOUR WITH UNITED NATIONS, 1968

Extract from *The Silver Bugle*

As we (The 4th Battalion) go to press our tour with the United Nations Force in Cyprus is coming to an end. For six months we have formed a part of UNFICYP where we are one of six contingents; the others being from Ireland, Finland, Sweden, Canada and Denmark. The Australian Civilian Police also have a representation in the Force. Each contingent is responsible for a portion of the Island, ours being a large part of the South West stretching from Larnaca round as far as Polis in the North West. Our role as members of the United Nations Force in Cyprus covers many aspects. Our main tasks are to maintain posts in sensitive areas between Greek and Turkish communities and so prevent both by our presence and by negotiations, any further outbreak of hostilities. Secondly, to contribute to the restoration and maintenance of law and order, and thirdly to contribute to a return to normal conditions. It has become necessary to disregard normal Battalion organization and for companies to lose

their identification. Company Headquarters have become District Headquarters with many outposts scattered around the hills and villages of their areas. To avoid boredom and subsequent loss of efficiency, platoons rotate throughout the various Districts once every two weeks. (This also enables platoons to have an opportunity of seeing the countryside and of enjoying the varied amenities.) Living conditions vary, from the house occupied by Lord Kitchener when he was a subaltern officer mapping Cyprus in the 1870s and now part of the MT Platoons accommodation, to tents of all shapes and sizes situated on hilltops. Those who were in Borneo with the Battalion quickly settled into their new accommodation having already learned how to look after themselves in restricted surroundings. Apart from providing quarter guards for visiting dignitaries, our first big parade was Vesting Day held on 10 July. The parade was attended by the Force Commander, the C. in C., the G.O.C. and a number of civilian personalities. This was followed by the UN medal presentation parade on 6th August, taken by our Chief of Staff Brigadier Michael Harbottle (Late Oxfordshire and Buckinghamshire L.L). The qualifying time for this medal is 90 days, and the ribbon is United Nations blue with a dark blue stripe enclosing a white bar. Our commitments have kept us very busy, and there has been little or no opportunity to get away on leave. However there has been a variety of sports and pastimes, all of which we have taken part in. During the six months each contingent has sponsored some activity. Our event was a falling plates competition, combined with a Tug-of-War. We are pleased to record that we won the falling plates, but were not so fortunate with the Tug-of-war. Because of our close proximity to the sea full advantage has been taken of all forms of water sports and, indeed, over 120 men have learnt to water ski. The Battalion moves back to UK at the end of October and will immediately go on three weeks' leave; upon return much of the time at Colchester will be spent in preparation for the Battalion's final parade in County Durham on 12 December. From 2 January onwards the Battalion will gradually run down to final disbandment by the 31 March 1969.

Anonymous Geordie

Above: A young Pte 'Blondie' Lawton gets paid.

long periods in which nothing happened and sentries, who were required to salute any car flying a UN flag, had to be constantly alert. There was no major incident between the two communities during the Battalion's tour on the island. That was in no small measure due to the vigilance displayed by the junior officers, NCOs and men in the OPs. No minor incident was allowed to develop into a significant incident. Relations between the contingents within UNFICYP were extremely good and exchanges of officers and NCOs were arranged with the Canadian and Irish battalions, those on exchange being

expected to carry out the duties they would have performed in their own battalion. The only hitch occurred when an Irish soldier had his rifle stolen by a Turkish Cypriot and the Irish contingent commander felt it would not go down well with the Dublin newspapers if a British officer had to give evidence at the subsequent court martial.

In 1968 the Finnish Army celebrated the 50th anniversary of its re-formation in 1918 and the Band and Bugles were asked to play for the parade to mark the occasion. The Finns march rather slowly and, as the Band played, a Danish colonel

Left: The final parade in Cathedral Close.

was heard to remark, 'Ah! British ceremonial, very slow and dignified'. He was somewhat taken aback when the time came for the Band and Bugles to march off parade – at a brisk Light Infantry pace. After the parade, the Band played during a lunch given by the Finnish contingent. Before leaving the lunch the Band's choir sang 'Finlandia', a gesture immensely appreciated by the Finns and which established a very special relationship which endured throughout the rest of the tour.

In July, the Vice Chief of the General Staff (VCGS), Lieutenant General Sir Victor Fitzgeorge-Balfour, visited Cyprus and on his return to Britain wrote to Major General Abdy Ricketts, the Deputy Colonel for Durham, saying that he had heard nothing but praise for the way the Battalion was carrying out its role in UNFICYP.

During the latter part of the tour, preparations were beginning to be made for the disbandment of the Battalion. The Regiment had good reason to be grateful to Colonel David Colbeck, the officer in change of infantry records at Exeter (and formerly a member of The Royal Northumberland Fusiliers with whom the DLI had long shared a Depot at Fenham Barracks, Newcastle upon Tyne) who interviewed every single man in the Battalion to establish his posting preferences. This helped immeasurably to ensure a smooth disbandment.

The Battalion returned to Meanee Barracks, Colchester, in October. After three weeks' leave, preparations began in earnest for the laying up of the 1 DLI Colours in Durham Cathedral on 12 December. The opportunity was taken to parade the Colours through Batley and Hartlepool to show that, in spite of the passing of the old Light Infantry regiments in Yorkshire and Durham, the spirit of The Light Infantry and the historic Light Division lived on. By 10 December the Battalion was complete in Barnard Castle, which was to be the Battalion base for its short stay in the North.

On 12 December the Battalion formed up outside the Gilesgate Drill Hall, Lieutenant Tim Harris carrying the Queen's Colour and Second Lieutenant Rex Stephenson the Regimental Colour. The Band and Bugles, under the Bandmaster, Warrant Officer Class I Ron Berry, played the Battalion out for the last time. As the Battalion marched under their Commanding Officer, Lieutenant Colonel John Jacob, to Palace Green, the Mayor of Durham took the salute in the Market Square. The Battalion formed up on Palace Green and was inspected by Her Royal Highness Princess Alexandra, Colonel-in-Chief The Durham Light Infantry, and now Deputy Colonel-in-Chief The Light Infantry, before the Colours were trooped for the last time.

After the parade, at a very moving service in the cathedral, the Commanding Officer handed the Colours to two former padres of the Battalion, The Reverend G Parr MC (1st Battalion) and The Reverend D E Rice MC (2nd Battalion), who then passed them into the custody of the Dean. A memorable address was given by the Rt Rev John Leonard Wilson, Bishop of Birmingham, who had served in the Durham Light Infantry in the First World War and, as Dean of Singapore, had been taken prisoner by the Japanese in the Second. He was soon identified by his captors as one of the leaders of the prisoners in Changi gaol and tortured by them in a vain endeavour to break his spirit. His chief torturer was imprisoned as a war criminal and, on his release, saved up enough money to come to England to be baptized by the man he had so brutally tortured.

After the service, the Battalion was most generously entertained by the County of Durham. Many past and present DLI officers lunched with the Princess in the Grand Hall of Durham Castle and the Battalion was given a magnificent lunch in Bede College Hall, where the men were visited by the Princess before she left the city. On her departure, the Geordies, to quote a contemporary report, 'slipped down to

TRANSITIONAL ECHOES

It was with a degree of apprehension and pride that I drove into Colchester to join my Regiment 1st Battalion The Durham Light Infantry as the last commissioned officer. I recalled, what seemed a lifetime ago, the Regimental Board at Sandhurst when that group of young officer cadets went to be interviewed and selected for the last time for the old County Light Infantry Regiments. It was with great pride that I heard the news that I had been selected for 1 DLI but also with a sense of apprehension over the future. Change was in the air with Duncan Sandys' Defence Review and the political battles just starting with 'Mad Mitch' and Save the Argyles.

The scene changes – sitting on Mandria Hill, a UN post on the outskirts of Paphos, in Cyprus, watching the sun sinking over the Mediterranean and marvelling at the change of events. Independent of the clutches of barracks life and surrounded by some 30-plus Geordies commanded by Serjeant Corkie Kirkbride (I was just an appendage then), the realization hit me with some pride of how privileged and lucky I was but also with apprehension that I still really did not understand 'Geordie'. As far as I was concerned Geordie was an official language and when in full spate was far more secure than the current radio secure speech format (SLIDEX). Anyway I had six months to understand them and hopefully secure their trust.

Isolated in my UN posts in Paphos, Kophinou, Skarinou Bridge, Polis, Ayios Theodoros and Limassol, I was blissfully unaware of the seismic change that was being invoked upon the structure of The Light Infantry, but this was to impact on all of us. When the emotional parade took place on Vesting Day in Limassol it was doubly poignant as 1DLI became 4LI and the new large Light Infantry Regiment was formed. I returned to my platoon to find that my Geordie world had not changed apart from a new cap badge and a very grumpy and disheartened Serjeant Corkie Kirkbride.

Back with my company again (now C Company 4LI), I had to discuss with my large platoon their individual futures after disbandment. I have no idea why I was posted to 1LI but it was my first choice at the time. It was all somewhat surreal at the time for those who expected a lifetime of Geordie soldiering. However this again all changed when news reached me that being the full stop of the DLI I would be carrying the Regimental Colour on disbandment. This is when reality really kicked in.

Later, we stood hesitantly at the door of 1LI officers' mess anteroom in Ballykinler. It was coffee break and the room was filled with papers and smoke. Uncertain, we moved in. A voice behind a paper said 'The Durhams have arrived' and life moved on. What fascinated me most was the interaction between the Geordies, the Somerset lads and the Cornishmen. All so different, but unique in their special ways. We did not have much time to test this, for on return from Kenya we were fully engaged in a baptism of fire that was the initial riots in Belfast at the start of the Troubles. There was no time to look back. 'Events, dear boy, events' had taken charge and we all gelled together in this new Light Infantry Regiment.

Rex Stephenson

Below: Firing an Energa Grenade – Cyprus, 1968.

their favourite pubs to benefit from the extended licence; there to drink and remember, in their most natural surrounding, the passing of their own distinctive Regiment'.

The Battalion returned to Colchester after Christmas leave and set about the task of disbandment as directed: 'I am commanded by the Army Board of the Defence Council to inform you that 4th Battalion, The Light Infantry is to disband at Colchester with effect from 31st March 1969. Further detailed instructions on the disbandment are to be issued separately to those concerned.'

The Colonel of The Light Infantry, General Sir Geoffrey Musson, received the following message from the CGS: 'On the occasion of the disbandment of your Fourth Battalion I send you and your Regiment my warm regards and deep sympathy. This is a sad occasion for all of us who honour and respect the brave and distinguished service that regiments from The Light Infantry have given to the Crown for so many years. The whole Army mourns your loss. I know that the fine traditions of the four regiments from which you are formed will be firmly carried on by the remaining three battalions.'

The Volunteer Battalions

On 1 April 1967, one year before Vesting Day and with very little fanfare, the first new Light Infantry battalion came into existence. The Light Infantry Volunteers was formed from 5 DCLI (the Territorials having kept their single county affiliations even after the regular SCLI formed in 1959), 4 KSLI, 4 KOYLI, 1 Herefordshire LI, and 8 DLI. With companies in Truro, Bodmin, Shrewsbury, Wakefield, Hereford and Durham, the LI Volunteers covered almost every historical recruiting area and fully embodied the emerging vision of a new, national, Light Infantry regiment, based on the historical county footprint.

This is a gross oversimplification, of course. Many other Territorial units with Light Infantry heritage existed alongside the new LI (V) and some would subsequently contribute manpower, history or real estate to the Battalion and later units. To pick an example: as D Company LI Volunteers formed in Durham, 6/8 DLI in Horden merged to form a company of the Northumbrian Volunteers alongside the County of Durham Regiment Royal Artillery, themselves formerly 5/7 DLI. However, these historical Light Infantrymen would not join the new regiment until 7LI swept them up in 1975. To follow another example, in Somerset, the only Light Infantry recruiting area not represented by LI (V), 4 Som LI merged with the North Somerset Yeomanry and the West Somerset Yeomanry to form the Somerset Yeomanry and Light Infantry. This scenario was not uncommon, and not only created a web of confused links in its own right but in this case also drew in connections with the Royal Tank Regiment, the North Somerset and Bristol Yeomanries, the Royal Artillery, the Royal Horse Artillery and the Royal Signals! The West Somerset Yeomanry had spent the Great War on the Western Front as 12 Somerset LI, so had as much claim to a Light Infantry heritage as a Yeomanry one; nevertheless, the Territorial Army has become used to simplifying competing threads of regimental history into a straightforward narrative, otherwise things become unworkable. Most TA Company Commanders will have experienced having to gently explain to an association chairman that their links with the modern regiment really are too tenuous now, even if we did take over the old TA Centre and some of the paintings; or in other words, while we must acknowledge the rich background from which the TA Light Infantry has emerged, there is simply not space to tell every detail of the story here.

Left: Pure grit – WO2 Clive Jackson on an Assault Course at Sennybridge, 1992. This photograph won the TA Photograph of the Year.

From confusing beginnings the LI Volunteers emerged into a confused and uncertain period in the TA's history. The future of the reserves had been hotly debated since 1965, with senior figures in the Regular Army, notably Generals Sir John Hackett and Michael Carver, arguing that there was little role for Volunteers and Territorials in the nuclear age and advocating scarce defence resources be directed towards the Regular Army and Regular Reserve. As Vesting Day came and went, the Territorial organization was under consideration for complete disbandment and the future of the LI Volunteers was by no means certain. The term 'Territorial' at that time denoted Territorial Army Volunteer Reserve band 3, or TAVR III, which were home defence units, equipped with bolt-action rifles and

Winning Skill at Arms competitions was a constant feature of life in all the Volunteer Battalions!

under 50,000 five years later. The year 1970 saw a change in government and a change in fortunes, however, as the new administration announced a 10,000 increase in Group A manpower to support NATO deterrence, secure the home base and provide a basis for military expansion in wartime. On 1 April 1971, 20 so-called 'Heath Battalions' were formed from the residual cadres of TAVR III units disbanded three years before. One of these was the Somerset Yeomanry and Light Infantry and the new unit was designated 6th Battalion The Light Infantry (Volunteers), with its headquarters in Bath and companies in Yeovil, Falmouth and Penzance. The following year the LI Volunteers was renamed 5th Battalion The Light Infantry (Volunteers) and from that point on all Light Infantry TA battalions embraced the convention of forming numbered battalions within the new large regimental family, unlike some TA units, which retained their own names, cap badges and exclusive traditions.

For the next three years 5 and 6LI formed the Volunteer element of The Light Infantry, 6LI providing a General Reserve (essentially home defence) battalion, and 5LI retaining their more demanding NATO support role. Greater NATO support was required by the Army, but the portmanteau nature of many TAVR III cadres resurrected in 1971 did not offer a credible basis for a cohesive battlegroup that could take its place alongside the regulars. One such cadre was the Northumbrian Volunteers, a mishmash of an artillery battery and four infantry companies wearing three different cap badges, DLI among them. Two companies and the battalion headquarters were selected to form the basis of a third Light Infantry TA battalion, combined with one of 5LI's two Durham companies. Another cadreized battalion, the Yorkshire Volunteers, provided the final rifle company in the form of E (KOYLI) Company in Wakefield, and 7th Battalion The Light Infantry (Volunteers) took its place on the order of battle and among the regimental family.

5 and 6LI also reorganized. Having given up a sub-unit, 5LI absorbed a company from The Light Infantry and Mercian Volunteers based in Wellington in Shropshire, which brought the battalion back up to strength and took the first steps towards consolidating a centre of gravity in the old KSLI heartlands of the Welsh Marches. 6LI merged its two Cornish companies, giving up Penzance, and stretched its West Country credentials to take on another Light Infantry and Mercian Volunteers company from across the Bristol Channel in Ross-on-Wye. This apparently illogical grouping had the advantage of drawing one more historical Light Infantry company into the regimental fold, where it was subsequently placed more rationally with 5LI during the next round of reorganizations. These took place in 1981, with 5LI transferring their Truro company to 6LI in return for Ross-on-Wye and their remaining Durham company to 7LI, gaining Wakefield in return. By the end of 1981, therefore, the 6th Battalion was firmly established as The Light Infantry in the South West, the successors to the SCLI; 7LI were unambiguous

1940s battledress, and undertook only limited training, much of which was unpaid. 'Volunteer' units like the LI Volunteers were TAVR I (the 'Ever Readies') and TAVR II, much better equipped with modern uniforms and weapons and with a considerable paid training commitment. This enabled them to mobilize to fight outside the UK alongside the Regular Army, where they typically carried out lines-of-communication security tasks and formed a reserve for BAOR, the British Army on the Rhine. As the first regular Light Infantry battalions formed in 1968 the TAVR reorganized again, first disbanding TAVR III – although many units clung on in more or less unofficial cadre form – and then creating the two TA groupings that endure today: Group A, which had a liability to serve overseas if mobilized, and whose members formally retained the title 'Volunteer'; and Group B, comprising everyone else. From this point on, the distinction between 'Volunteers' and 'Territorials' began to fade and the two terms became increasingly interchangeable until the title 'Territorial Army' was officially resurrected by the Reserve Forces Act of 1982.

As a Volunteer, 'Ever Ready' TAVR I and finally Group A unit, the LI Volunteers endured, and even prospered, in part from an influx of former TAVR III Light Infantrymen as the Territorials drew down. Annual Camp in 1969 even saw C (Herefordshire) Company deploy to Germany to train alongside 3 RGJ in Celle. However, motivating troops cannot have been easy during this depressing period, as the TAVR reduced from a strength of more than 116,000 in 1965 to

Left: Annual Camp.

Far left: Her Majesty The Queen inspects the troops.

This event was a great success, although courted disaster when the pike bearing the Queen's Colour struck a low arch at Light Infantry speed, badly buckling both the finial and the Ensign to the Colour, Lieutenant Graham Pickering, as the pikestaff was driven into his groin at 140 paces to the minute.

The fact that all three Volunteer battalions had their own Colours by this point, and that they had been presented by no less personages than Her Majesty Queen Elizabeth The Queen Mother (to 5LI (as LI (V)) in 1971 and 6LI in 1979) and Her Royal Highness Princess Alexandra (to 7LI in 1978), was an indication in itself of how far the TA Light Infantry had come, both in prestige and permanence. Not only capable of performing their wartime roles, the Volunteers increasingly found themselves the natural link between The Light Infantry and the counties: representing the Regiment at freedom parades, receptions and events like county shows

heirs to the Durhams in the North East, which made some small reparation for the shabby treatment of the regular DLI; and 5LI represented The Light Infantry in Shropshire, Herefordshire and the West Riding of Yorkshire.

By the early 1980s the TA Light Infantry had grown from an unpromising start to the point where NATO-roled elements were fully equipped to regular scales and would routinely deploy to Germany to take part in major exercises. Less glamorous than the NATO units, even General Reserve battalions filled a vital operational niche and were well furnished with modern equipment. The LI (V)'s first Annual Camp had been a relatively subdued affair at Sennybridge, but since then TA Light Infantrymen had attended camps as far flung as Belgium, Cyprus, Germany and Gibraltar, no small thing in an age of limited overseas travel. Exercise 'Crusader 80' showed how far things had come, with all three Volunteer battalions engaging fully in one of the major NATO acts of deterrence of the Cold War. 5LI deployed to BAOR as part of 5 Field Force, training for two weeks near Bielefeld, while 6LI supported the home defence element of the exercise, guarding key points and reacting to 'enemy' incursions in the South of England as part of 8 Field Force. They concluded the exercise with a brigade-sized assault on Imber Village, a scale of activities hard to imagine for the modern TA. 7LI supported both the Germany- and UK-based elements of the exercise, and also found time to send a company to Gibraltar, and with 5LI form a Guard of Honour for Her Majesty Queen Elizabeth The Queen Mother's 80th birthday celebration visit to Durham.

Left: Helping out after floods.

THE LIGHT INFANTRY REGIMENTAL ASSOCIATION

The Regimental Association was established to promote the efficiency of the Regiment and maintain comradeship amongst past and present members through a branch network, by means of reunions, and by the publication of regimental literature such as *The Silver Bugle* and newsletters. All soldiers on leaving the Service were given details of The Light Infantry Regimental Association; a copy of this is set out below:

'Now that your service in The Light Infantry has come to an end and you are returning to civilian life, we hope you will keep in touch with the Regiment and with the friends you

have made. The Light Infantry Regimental Association exists for this purpose. Its primary aim is to foster and maintain a spirit of comradeship among all who are serving or have served in The Light Infantry. It does this by providing an organization through which members of the Regiment, past and present, can keep in touch with each other, and through which, in the event of need, they can obtain help and advice. This help may range from advice on finding employment to the provision of financial or other aid through the Regimental Secretaries at Light Infantry Offices.

There is a Light Infantry Office in each of our five counties (Durham, Yorkshire, Shropshire (including Herefordshire), Somerset and Cornwall). In addition, there are numerous branches of the Associations of former Light Infantry Regiments in each county as well as Light Infantry branches, plus one or two elsewhere, each organising and promoting social functions as well as providing focal points for contact between all Light Infantrymen. The addresses of the various Light Infantry offices are below. Addresses of branches can be obtained from Light Infantry offices and from The Silver Bugle.'

The Light Infantry Regimental Association is now more than simply a collection of branches. It is part of a wider regimental family and, depending on the membership of any particular branch, can span the entire spectrum of Light Infantry service from a former county regiment all the way through to The Rifles. In addition there is a vibrant online community working though both the Association pages of The Light Infantry website and on social networking sites like Facebook. The centrepiece of the Association's year has been firmly established as the Reunion Weekend celebrated annually in the summer at Copthorne Barracks, Shrewsbury.

Above: A celebration during the first Gulf War.

Right: A group of Chelsea Pensioners enjoys the reunion.

and Remembrance parades. As the threat from Northern Ireland began to push the Regular Army out of everyday public view, both for security reasons and because the regulars were so often away on operations, the Volunteers filled the gap, necessitating the two categories of Light Infantryman should be indistinguishable ceremonially as well as operationally. Buglers proved to be among the biggest assets for keeping The Light Infantry on show in the recruiting areas, but they were not established posts, thus there was constant friction between them attending military training in their official capacity and ceremonial events in their unofficial role. The same friction was magnified across all ranks when big ceremonial events were planned, and permanent staff raised their blood pressures to dangerous levels trying to ensure maximum attendance at mandatory military training as well as the parade, or vice versa.

Despite the angst, and often over the still-twitching body of the Training Major, the TA Light Infantry battalions embraced their representation role, furnishing both their own troops and hosting the regular battalions and bands. In 1983, for example, 6LI hosted a Sounding of Retreat by the Massed Bands of The Light Infantry over two nights at Bath's Royal Crescent and also participated in the freedom parade granted by the city to The Light Infantry. Some 11,000 people turned out to watch, and in the same year 7LI hosted a similar event in Durham, where the North East supported the event in even greater numbers. 7LI also went a step further and formed The Light Infantry Burma Band, an unofficially established addition to the bands of The Light Infantry with more time to devote to the Battalion's counties, which first performed publicly in 1985. This innovative approach to representation was typical of the TA battalions, 5LI leading the way in 1975, when they were instrumental in forming and manning The Flying Bugles parachute display team, together with the LI Depot at Shrewsbury. The Flying Bugles proved to be a key recruiting and representation asset for the whole regiment, manned by both regulars and Territorials. It embodied the notion of a unified regiment until tightening defence budgets meant funds could no longer be found to support them.

The TA Light Infantry battalions also provided bases and life-support for various regular regimental recruiting initiatives. Names of these changed over the years but tended to be variations on the theme of Regimental Recruiting Team or Regimental Support Team and comprised a small group of regular personnel with a vehicle and a transportable recruiting stand. These teams operated out of Light Infantry TA Centres, under direction from Regimental Headquarters but administered by their TA host. Over time, TA battalions learned to attach their own recruiters to the team, and sometimes to include cadet representation as well, so that they would be able to offer something to every person that approached them, whatever their circumstances. The more canny ones would even group LI Association members with the team so that they could do their own recruiting; and coincidentally deflect chatty candidates of the wrong age group away from The Light Infantry recruiters!

The most important links between the regular and Territorial Light Infantry, however, were the permanent staff attached to the Volunteers from the three regular battalions; and the non-regular permanent staff, or NRPS. These were long-serving ex-regulars who had transferred to TA Group B, where they provided essential administrative support to enable the TA and their regular advisors to concentrate on training. Theirs was an often unglamorous and thankless task, working long hours ensuring that TA Centres, stores, weapons

Left: 5LI, Barry Buddon Camp, Scotland. Visit by HRH Princess Alexandra. Gen Bush, Lt Col Simon Furness, CO (with the 'CO's Boot'). This was the boot of former 5LI CO Col Beath, highly polished and mounted on an ammunition box, it was subsequently competed for annually in a variety of competitions, heavily fought for from individual to Section, Platoon and Company level.

Below left: On exercise in support of NATO, 1970s.

Right: Members of 7LI Mortar Platoon who took part in the Newcastle to Paris (The Whitbread Beerjolais Race), helping to raise £8,500 for the Spastics Society.

Below: Volunteers manning the WOMBAT.

and vehicles were available when needed, and that as much of the day-to-day administrative burden as possible was lifted from their Volunteer counterparts. NRPS could be appointed from any regimental background, but in practice The Light Infantry ensured that enough high-quality candidates filled the majority of posts, although a relocation of a TA Centre or one of the many re-groupings could throw a spanner in the works. Having Light Infantry NRPS was much to be preferred, as they came steeped in regimental traditions that the Territorials were hungry to absorb, and they provided another strong link between the full- and part-time battalions. NRPS had to maintain a difficult balancing act: as the permanent presence in the TA Centre during the working week they frequently had to act on behalf of their Territorial counterparts; the trick was to avoid doing their job for them. With their long experience and more time to spend on a problem, most NRPS were more than capable of doing any job better themselves; but the best ones learned where to step back and let the Volunteers take up the strain, even if this meant things not running as smoothly as they might. Those NRPS that managed to achieve this difficult balance might be surprised by the affection with which they are remembered by the Territorials they mentored.

The same is also true of the regular Light Infantrymen attached to the Volunteer battalions as training instructors. Each Territorial company would have one or two Senior Non-Commissioned Officers grouped with them on two-year

postings, while battalion headquarters had a regular Adjutant and Regimental Serjeant Major. The key regular appointment other than the Commanding Officer (who might be a regular or a Territorial) was the unique TA post of Training Major, which effectively fulfilled the role of Battalion Second-in-Command, although this post was officially held by a Territorial officer. The Training Major was the focal point for all training, including recruit training, and other events and was also the budget manager for 'Man Training Days', the mechanism through which the Territorials' part-time pay was managed. If the Commanding Officer was a Territorial the Training Major could also find himself mentoring and standing in for him, which made the appointment even more critical and fraught with pitfalls. Unlike a regular Battalion Second-in-Command, a Training Major did not have a full-time battalion's worth of people around to support him, and could not even call in his company training staff for a meeting without hundreds of miles' worth of motor-mileage claims. Added to this was the constant uncertainty as to exactly how many Territorials would choose to attend any given training event, and what ranks, range or training qualifications or even driving licences they might hold. Training Majors were thus usually characterized by being rather younger than the Territorial majors they served alongside, but looking rather older.

The same was not true of another category of Light Infantryman that emerged within the TA during the 1980s, the Home Service Force or HSF. HSF companies or platoons were raised in all infantry battalions, starting in 1982, specifically to support home defence operations and counter an increased threat from Soviet sabotage operations during a build-up to hostilities. They were exclusively recruited from ex-services personnel and, as Group B Territorials, had generous age limits and reduced commitments that made it an attractive proposition to settled but bored former soldiers looking for adventure. HSF companies therefore tended to be piratical bands of ancient Pistols, Bardolphs and Nyms, some of whom looked as old as God but were brimming with youthful mischief and enthusiasm. They often outperformed their younger counterparts and brought a level of guile and

cunning to home defence exercises that suggested that they would have given the Spetznaz a run for their money if it had ever come to it. HSF companies attached to the LI battalions wore The Light Infantry cap badge and trained both independently as a separate force and alongside their host battalions as additional rifle companies or platoons. While they tended to be most closely integrated within General Reserve battalions, such as 6LI, who shared an essentially similar home defence role (5LI only ever had a platoon of HSF in any case), the HSF brought another dimension to the regimental family until they stood down in 1992. Their experience was formidable, and frequently leavened the Territorials battalions with valuable operational knowledge, particularly important in a period when very few Volunteers were permitted to serve in operational theatres.

The 1980s were a high-water mark for the Territorial Army's power and significance, culminating for The Light Infantry in the creation of a fourth TA Light Infantry battalion, 8LI(V), at the beginning of 1987 and their presentation of Colours by the Colonel-in-Chief the following year. The new Battalion was raised around the Yorkshire companies from 5LI, which had the very welcome effect of creating a Light Infantry Volunteer battalion for each of the historical recruiting areas and firmly establishing regimental representation in Yorkshire. This resurgence of The Light Infantry in the historical home of the KOYLI was marked by a Sounding of Retreat at Pontefract Racecourse three months before the battalion officially formed, with the 7LI Burma Band on parade. Considerable investment was made in rebuilding the TA Centre in Wakefield to house the new battalion headquarters.

Wakefield also accommodated the Anti-Tank platoon equipped with state-of-the-art Milan guided missiles, another symbol of how well equipped and capable the NATO-roled TA Light Infantry had become. Their structure and equipment mirrored that of regular battalions, with a full complement of vehicles and support weapons, including 81mm mortars, general purpose machine guns (GPMGs) and Milan, and Assault Pioneer and Reconnaissance platoons. General Reserve home defence battalions were not so generously equipped and this could cause a certain amount of friction, particularly if companies were re-assigned from a NATO-roled unit to General Reserve, as with A Company 5LI when they became D Company 6LI in 1981. Veterans of such moves recall even now the frustration of having to hand in equipment like GPMGs and modern Clansman radios, in return for Brens and cumbersome Larkspur communications, even though they were still parading at the same TA Centres under the same cap badge; but by the end of the 1980s even General Reserve battalions had been brought up to date. Nevertheless, they still lacked the full complement of support weapon platoons enjoyed by their NATO counterparts, which meant that NATO-roled battalions still offered greater variety and opportunities for career progression for their Volunteers, whose

Above: Exercise 'Marble Tor IV', June 1992. The 7LI Burma Band and Bugles pose for a photo on top of the Rock.

entire service would typically be seen out within a relatively local geographical area. Because of this, support weapon and specialist platoons were spread across a battalion's footprint, collocated with rifle companies rather than in a single Support Company location, so that soldiers could have access to a variety of jobs and opportunities within the same TA Centre.

On the face of it, NATO-roled battalions also offered a guarantee of overseas travel, to Germany at least, as their camps were frequently held near to their general deployment positions. The scale of some of those deployments is mind boggling now; when 5LI took part in Exercise 'Lionheart' in 1984, for example, the Battalion put over 600 men into the field as part of a Corps-level exercise in Germany. The Battalion initially deployed to secure the Teutoburger Ridge near Osnabruck in Northern Germany, then cleared the village of Borgholzhausen in a battlegroup attack followed by a 100km night move to relieve a regular battalion on the River Leine. From there they conducted an assault river crossing, a battlegroup wood-clearance operation, and took part in a battlegroup-plus sized operation to clear another village, supported by armour, then recovered to the North of England, all as a single annual camp! Some idea of how successfully Light Infantry Territorials performed alongside their regular counterparts can be gained from a remark overheard from a very senior officer during Exercise 'Keystone' in 1987: 'If 7LI can cross the start line on time, why can't 24 Brigade?'

It was not just the NATO battalions that deployed beyond

the UK, however. During this period of strong investment in the TA even General Reserve battalions like 6LI achieved an impressive amount of overseas training, sending Light Infantrymen to Belize and Gibraltar in 1981, Germany in 1982, Gibraltar again in 1983 and 1986, Canada in 1986 and Cyprus in 1989, where 426 members of the Battalion deployed on Exercise 'Lion Cub', the first occasion in which a complete TA battalion had trained on the island. In addition, and admittedly stretching the term 'overseas' to its limit, the battalion trained on the Isle of Wight in 1983, 1984 and 1986 in a series of exercises that were largely the brainchild of Major Chris Bull, the Battalion Second-in-Command, who demonstrated that Territorials could often match their regular counterparts in results, as long as they had the time to devote to the job, and the support of their permanent staff to fall back on when they did not.

The Regular Army permanent staff had a critical role in developing and maintaining the quality and ethos of the TA Light Infantry battalions. A recruiting poster of the time showed two soldiers, one Volunteer and one regular, advancing side by side in combat dress and asked the question, 'If you were the enemy, could you tell the difference?'. There was none visible, and the TA themselves were keen to live up to the standards of the regulars, insofar as training time allowed. To them it was the regular permanent staff that embodied Regular Army standards and their quality and professionalism were therefore crucial factors in the TA perspective of what was 'right'. They possessed enormous referent authority and their advice would be sought by private soldiers and field officers alike, who would often defer to their greater experience. Unlike a regular battalion, where good role models would always dilute the bad, one wrong man in the job could do a

Below: 'Show Knees' – high jinks at Annual Camp.

great deal of damage. Happily the close relationship across the regular and Territorial branches of The Light Infantry ensured a steady supply of high-quality regular permanent staff, although the less conventional candidates in Regular Army terms often found the relatively unstructured nature of a TA battalion afforded them an opportunity to excel. Conversely, the best candidates for a post in a regular battalion were not always suited to the TA, so close liaison across all parties was essential at manning conferences. As with NRPS, many regular permanent staff would be surprised to learn how long their influence endured after they had moved on, and how the best are still remembered fondly, decades later.

If the formation of 8LI at the end of the 1980s was the high-water mark in the fortunes of the TA Light Infantry, that wave broke against the reunification of Germany in 1990, effectively ending the Cold War and heralding a decade of defence cuts and an ever-ebbing tide. The defence review of 1991, 'Options for Change', reduced the regular Light Infantry from three battalions to two, and there was little doubt that the four Territorial battalions would be in the firing line when the details of the planned cuts to the TA were finalized. Regimentally the biggest fear was that 7 and 8LI might be merged or cut, with echoes of the unfair treatment of the Durhams in 1968, and leaving The Light Infantry unrepresented in Yorkshire yet again, despite being the only infantry regiment to have actually been raised in that county. The threat to 5 and 6LI seemed negligible, and accordingly huge efforts were directed towards lobbying on behalf of the two northern battalions. In County Durham, the Colonel of the Regiment received a strong message that if the DLI were to be disbanded again, not just The Light Infantry but the army as a whole would find it difficult to recruit in the North East ever again!

The restructuring of the TA battalions generated far more public attention and political sensitivity than the merger of the regular battalions; but this was only to be expected, because The Light Infantry had formed as a large regiment without any specific county affiliations for its regular battalions precisely so that it could contract or enlarge without fuss. The TA battalions on the other hand were rooted in the counties from which they sprang, and had vigorously pursued a policy of ensuring the counties felt close ties with 'their' regiment. This had been reinforced in 1988 when each TA battalion had been granted permission to include their county names within their full title; thus, 8LI had become 8th (Yorkshire) Battalion The Light Infantry (Volunteers), and 7LI the 7th (Durham) Battalion The Light Infantry (Volunteers). If nothing else, the strength of feeling displayed by the counties during the period showed the success of the TA representation effort and vindicated the risk taken in 1968 to drop any obvious link between the name of the new regiment 'The Light Infantry' and the counties from which it recruited.

The lobbying effort placed a huge strain on both battalions, which not only had to live under the expectation of swingeing cuts, but also had to continue training to the same high standards as before while ramping up their representation efforts to unprecedented levels. The effort paid off in full, however, when the Ministry of Defence accepted the case for retaining both 7 and 8LI; but only on the basis that 5LI reduce to a single company and be incorporated within a non-Light Infantry unit, a totally unexpected threat for which no contingency had been made. As the regimental history *Exceedingly Lucky* put it:

> *There was an almost audible gasp of astonishment across the Regiment: delight at saving the two northern battalions was coupled with disbelief at the proposal for 5LI(V) which was unwelcome and, of all possible outcomes, the least expected. Indeed, the Regimental Council was caught flat-footed, having never even considered such a possibility at any of their meetings. An immediate, and very vociferous, campaign to preserve 5LI(V) was mounted with the Honorary Colonel, Sir Peter Gadsden, playing a crucially influential part.*

As the focus now shifted toward saving 5th (Shropshire and Herefordshire) Battalion The Light Infantry (Volunteers) from the axe, there was a sense that whatever happened The Light Infantry would not be allowed to retain all four of its TA battalions, whatever the logic for doing so. The agony

continued throughout the year, with various proposals being put forward and rejected by both the Regimental Council and the Ministry of Defence, none of which boded well for the future of the 5th or 6th Battalions, whose futures now seemed linked as the only two Light Infantry TA units 'up for grabs'. It is extraordinary that throughout this desperate and depressing year all four battalions continued to train as hard as ever; 5LI, for example, deploying both to a command TEWT in Germany and annual camp in Belgium as well as winning the Western District GPMG(SF) competition, re-equipping with the SA80 weapon system and re-roling from a NATO to a national defence battalion! Finally, on 10 December 1991, the regiment was put out of its misery by an announcement in the House

Below left: *Maj Gen Barry Lane, GOC South West District, with Cpl Scott, inspects the 6LI Colour Guard, Bath.*

Below: *Soldiers from 5LI display the full range of modern equipment deployed by a NATO-roled TA Battalion.*

'BRIGADIER HEMSLEY I PRESUME …' 5LI VISITS KENYA

It was early in December 1982 when the Battalion 'Rumour Control' first started to mumble about some sort of trip to Kenya in the offing. However, unlike others, this rumour gained size and detail rapidly, until the easily fooled of HQ Company actually believed that Brigadier Hemsley and his wife were going to drive from Capetown to London and that 5LI had been asked to provide a re-supply of fuel on the Kenya–Sudan border. Just to prove the old adage 'every dog has his day', the rumour indeed proved true, so the easily fooled strutted round with 'I told you so!' smirks, and the unbelievers went into shock.

By a process of natural and democratic selection (ie the Training Major took who he wanted), the six to pile into a minibus for Heathrow Airport were Major Tim Harris, Captain Doug Dee, WO2 Andy Carney, C/Sjt Taff Turner, C/Sjt Dave Jones and Cpl 'SAS' Holloway. As we gratefully clambered aboard our jumbo jet bound for the sun, we discovered that the MOD had amazingly given us 'Club' seats. Everybody on the plane enjoyed the sight of pretty stewardesses, but those in 'Club' seats had something far more important – free drinks. Suffice to say we had a pleasant flight out.

On landing at Nairobi we were met by a friendly face in the shape of Major Ian Park-Weir. He escorted us to his empire which rejoiced in the title of British Army Training Liaison Staff Kenya (BATLSK), consisting of a force of some 20 All Ranks residing in part of Kahawa Camp, about 10 miles north of Nairobi. Kahawa Camp was certainly not the prettiest place in the world, but it proved to be one of the most efficient. By tea-time we had obtained the vehicles, petrol, rations and sun-tan cream that we needed and were ready to leave at first light the following day.

Within 15 miles of Nairobi we discovered that what the Kenyans call a main road was the sort of track any self-respecting farmer would be embarrassed to have up the side of his field. What stretches of tarmac there were contained World Championship standard potholes. Cpl Holloway was convinced they were some sort of elephant trap, and my behind was inclined to agree with him.

Lokichokio village sits in the middle of a tongue of Kenya, surrounded on three sides by Uganda, Sudan and Ethiopia. As these borders are mere lines on a map, the locals quite happily wander from country to country as the mood takes them. Cattle rustling from a neighbouring country has been quite common, with the raiding gangs using machine-guns and mortars in aid of their larceny.

Despite not having heard from the Brigadier since we left UK we were sure he would get to us on time. Considering the red tape the Brigadier had conquered in organising his expedition so far, we thought that travelling half-way up Africa and being bang on schedule would be child's play to him. Our opinion proved well founded as, almost to the hour, a white Range Rover containing a very fresh-looking crew, swept into our little camp. The vehicle was quickly fuelled and watered, while our two guests were treated to that world famous delicacy – Compo all-in stew. Just to add a little 5LI style to the meal I had managed to 'obtain' a bottle of champagne on the way out to Kenya. Not only did it survive the trip but, thanks to the local Kenya Police Inspector, it was even quite cool.

Within 45 minutes of arriving the Brigadier and his wife were on their way again into Sudan, well pleased, we trusted, with the little bit of help we had given them. Our job done, we gladly broke camp and retraced our steps south to the cooler climate of Nairobi and our old friends, BATLSK.

In conclusion, we had helped Brigadier Hemsley set a few driving records and had seen more of Kenya than any millionaire safari could hope to see. Finally, we had once again proved that The Light Infantryman (Regular or Territorial) is capable of doing an unfamiliar job at short notice, anywhere in the world!

Doug Dee

---

of Commons that all four Light Infantry TA battalions would remain, although each would reduce to three rifle companies only, and in the case of 5LI one of these was to be a company from the Worcester and Sherwood Foresters. While not ideal, it could unquestionably have been much worse.

Sadly the reprieve, such as it was, proved only temporary and the next round of cuts that were to characterize the decade fell in 1994, when the TA Review of that year announced that 8LI would re-role to form a Light Reconnaissance Regiment within the Royal Armoured Corps. The name of the new unit, The King's Own Yorkshire Yeomanry (Light Infantry), or KOYY(LI), was small consolation and although every effort was made to retain Light Infantry links with the new regiment when it formed

in 1995 there is no doubt that this was a huge blow regimentally. The sum total of the two reorganizations of the first half of the 1990s was to have lost, in effect, more than two battalions' worth of manpower and the key Light Infantry presence in Yorkshire.

For the TA Light Infantrymen themselves restructurings could offer mixed blessings. On the one hand they would certainly agree with the assessment of the Regimental Colonel in his report that year that *'Flexibility and the ability to react to the unexpected lie at the very heart of The Light Infantry ethos; however, unrelenting structural change creates uncertainty, erodes morale and ultimately manifests itself in high wastage and poor retention of both quality officers and highly trained soldiers and NCOs'.*

On the other hand, change could sometimes mean new equipment and tactics to master and new opportunities. The inherently territorial nature of the Territorials also meant that an apparent regimental success, such as not losing a whole battalion, might still mean a personal disaster if their nearest company or TA Centre was lost. TA soldiers are nothing if not enthusiasts, however, and there is no doubt that across the Volunteer battalions Light Infantrymen everywhere made the best of things, even if this meant changing cap badge to continue serving, or finding a different way to contribute to society, perhaps by supporting the cadets or the regimental associations.

One group of TA Light Infantry for whom the uncertainties of change were magnified was the peculiar anomaly of Light Infantry*women*: Light Infantry cap-badged female soldiers within the TA battalions. The Women's Royal Army Corps had disbanded in 1992 with little consideration to the impact on the TA, where female recruits presenting themselves to a TA Centre had simply been recruited into the WRAC administratively but had then continued to parade and train with whatever unit was based there. With the WRAC gone, some female soldiers in TA Light Infantry battalions found themselves in posts from which they could simply transfer to a new cap badge and continue as before, or near TA Centres that housed non-infantry units, which could accept female soldiers. Many did not have these options, however, but could not legally be discharged without an amendment to TA Regulations, which would not catch up with the demise of the WRAC for some years to come. The only solution in the meantime was to bring these troops onto The Light Infantry's strength, creating the unexpected sight of female soldiers wearing The Light Infantry cap badge and decades of headaches for Adjutants, who had to try and manage an infantry career path for soldiers that the infantry insisted could not be in the infantry. The issue was never fully resolved and for the remainder of The Light Infantry's history it was technically possible to recruit female Volunteers into the

Above left: 5LI Recce Platoon crossing the river Leine during Exercise 'Lionheart', 1984.

Left: 7LI Exercise 'Marble Tor IV', 1992. Members of 7LI on the return flight from Gibraltar to the UK. A Hercules flight – not exactly British Airways!

Below: 7LI live firing MILAN at Otterburn.

regiment, a situation that often generated mixed feelings. In the end the women themselves tended to solve any difficulties by proving capable, valuable and often glamorous members of the team; and many of them challenged preconceptions by performing better than the men during training.

Perversely, although the 1990s were primarily characterized by cuts and reorganizations to the TA, they were also characterized by increasing numbers of Territorials deploying on operations. Small numbers of TA Light Infantrymen had always supported the regular battalions on operational tours, through the medium of an 'S Type' engagement; but typically these were one or two individuals at a time, who had to be discharged from their TA engagement, enlisted into the Regular Army and then be discharged once again to re-enlist back into their previous TA post. The main operational theatre was Northern Ireland and there was genuine concern that if TA troops were perceived as directly supporting the Regular Army with manpower then mainland TA Centres would become targets for the IRA. This made having a clear

Below: 7LI Annual Camp, Scotland. Soldiers crossing an Infantry Assault Bridge.

separation between regular and Volunteer service necessary; and the potential threat was underlined by an IRA bomb attack in 1992, which devastated the KSLI Regimental Museum in Shrewsbury. However, S Type was a cumbersome and tedious process that did not encourage participation. The TA Review of 1994 that oversaw the demise of 8LI had also called for greater active use of the TA, and the following year 5LI deployed 30 soldiers to support the Falkland Islands guard force and a further 40 Light Infantrymen from all the TA battalions deployed to Bosnia in support of 2LI. For more and more Volunteers the option of serving operationally became realistic and was embraced enthusiastically; particularly once the 1996 Reserve Forces Act simplified mobilizing individual TA soldiers rather than whole units.

In between the reorganizations and deployments the TA battalions continued to train and provide representation as before, although restrictions on equipment and man-training finance began to make themselves felt and exercises were nothing like on the scale of the 1980s. Nevertheless, exciting training did take place, with 5, 6 and 7LI holding camps in Belgium and 7LI in Minnesota with the US National Guard, as well as many adventure training expeditions, to destinations as diverse as France, Spain, Norway and the Himalayas. The training staff also took every opportunity to make training interesting, for example 6LI's 1996 camp in Thetford involved a beach assault using landing craft, although in choppy seas and an onshore breeze the RLC coxswains' seamanship drew some unfavourable comment from a spectating member of the public. When asked if he thought he could do better, the elderly gentleman announced that he had, on Gold Beach in 1944, which rather ended the conversation. In 1997 they went for the less contentious option of an Entebbe-style air assault on West Freugh airfield before linking up with the nuclear submarine HMS *Vanguard*, safely out of public view.

With only two regular Light Infantry battalions remaining, representation assumed even greater importance for the remaining Volunteers, with the Colonel of the Regiment observing in 1993 that 'Our TA battalions occupy an increasingly important part in our regimental life. As the Regular Army reduces in size and commensurately fewer people join, so the contact of the local community with their County Regiment, and their identification with it, becomes more and more dependent on the TA'. Further refinements to the names of the TA battalions were made that year to cement their connections with the counties and their antecedent regiments. 5LI were styled the 5th Battalion The (Shropshire and Herefordshire) Light Infantry (Volunteers) (rather than 5th (Shropshire and Herefordshire) Battalion); 6LI the 6th Battalion The (Somerset and Cornwall) Light Infantry (Volunteers); 7LI the 7th Battalion The (Durham) Light Infantry (Volunteers); and 8LI the 8th Battalion The (Yorkshire) Light Infantry (Volunteers). While these changes built on the success of the earlier incorporation of the county names into the battalion

C (DLI) COMPANY OP TELIC 2 (2003)

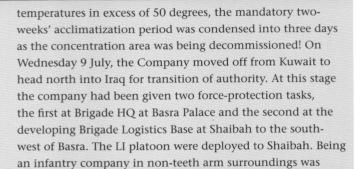

Various signals received on 23 May finally confirmed that the much talked about mobilization of a Tyne Tees rifle company in support of Op TELIC 2 had been given the green light. This was immediately followed by the arrival of numerous call-out papers received from the next day with a reporting date of 14 June. A few days before mobilization we were grateful to receive an excellent presentation from the members of 1LI who took part in Op TELIC 1 with the RTR battlegroup. This proved to be a fantastic evening with some pertinent messages for us all as we prepared to leave for sunnier climes. Over fifty members of C (DLI) Coy paraded at Bishop Auckland before departing to Chilwell after the obligatory send-off from the families and some encouraging words from Col Peter Catesby, whose own daughter was still in Iraq from Op TELIC 1.

Having passed through the well-oiled machine known as RTMC Chilwell, a total of 47 Light Infantry soldiers were mobilized as part of the TELIC company and joined 68 other Tyne Tees soldiers from the GH and RRF. The 115-strong Company then moved off to Grantham for a week of ITD training covering first aid, weapon training, NBC and a briefing day. Final confirmation of the ORBAT was made with the LI contingent forming 2 Pl, the strongest platoon of the Tyne Tees Company, before moving off to Warcop for some hastily arranged pre-deployment training. The week-long training package proved an excellent opportunity to learn and practise various incident drills, search procedures, mine awareness, the disciplines of operational administration and to fine-tune weapon skills on the Warcop ranges. As the main body prepared to move to Catterick to practise their skills on exercise, the advance party departed for 3 Div HQ at Bulford before flying out to Iraq. On arrival at Basra airport, the advance party were promptly shipped out to concentration area RIPPER in Kuwait and were joined by a fourth platoon from the East of England Regiment (EER). The main body arrived in Iraq on 5 July 2003 and joined the advance party in CA RIPPER just in time for the logistic experts to locate our vehicles and CAMS stores! With daytime

temperatures in excess of 50 degrees, the mandatory two-weeks' acclimatization period was condensed into three days as the concentration area was being decommissioned! On Wednesday 9 July, the Company moved off from Kuwait to head north into Iraq for transition of authority. At this stage the company had been given two force-protection tasks, the first at Brigade HQ at Basra Palace and the second at the developing Brigade Logistics Base at Shaibah to the south-west of Basra. The LI platoon were deployed to Shaibah. Being an infantry company in non-teeth arm surroundings was certainly interesting and we have had to become accustomed to the way the corps do their business, especially as we were accommodated in a sandy, tented city with a REME Battalion.

Shaibah airfield is an RAF base from the 1930s and certainly was in better condition then! The 17km boundary was marked by a series of fence posts with no fence remaining as the local Iraqi populace had stolen it along with several thousand rounds of ammo from the ammo compound. 2 Pl worked around the clock on observation post, mobile patrols and quick reaction force tasks and in eight weeks apprehended over 400 local thieves and recovered some ammunition and other stolen equipment. The LI platoon also established strong links with the local villagers who provided a valuable source of intelligence and sweet tea, mainly for Cpl Whitfield's section, although Cpl Simpson did excel himself with donkey impressions while attempting to communicate with one party of trespassers. Just as the air-conditioning arrived to tackle the 50+ degree heat, and the new boundary fence was completed, 2 Pl completed their eight-week stint at Shaibah and moved off to Basra Palace to work with 3 (RRF) Pl in providing security for the Brigade HQ. Immediately impressed by the lack of sand and dust, the platoon quickly settled into a new routine which included gate guard, sangar guard and OFF tasks. There were no dramas, the only incident of note involved Pte Hodgson who was turned away from the pay office after being mistaken for a local due to the copious amount of sunbathing!

titles they were a constant headache for Adjutants, who had to enforce everyone using the up-to-date names and stationery. To make matters worse the Army also formally dropped the (V) suffix for TA unit abbreviations (although (Volunteers) remained in the full title), thus making 8LI the correct form, rather than 8LI(V). For some reason it took even longer for this to sink in.

Name trouble notwithstanding, the Territorial battalions continued to represent the regiment and support recruiting admirably. 7LI assisted 1LI in accepting the freedom of Darlington in 1995, the last major town of County Durham to grant the honour to The Light Infantry; and 6LI began forming

the Gibraltar Band in 1996, intending it to raise the regimental profile in the South West as the 5LI Bligny Band and the 7LI Burma Band had done in the Midlands and the North East. In truth, though, this profile raising was as much in their own interests rather than for the wider regiment, as by that stage it was becoming clear that a reduction in TA manpower must be inevitable and full manning and strong community support might help deflect cuts away from The Light Infantry. This proved a forlorn hope, as the 1997 Strategic Defence Review saw little need for the TA infantry, reducing it from 33 battalions to 15, all to be composite units with regional cap badges retained only at company level. Effective from 1 July

1999 but a reality from the middle of 1998, The Light Infantry no longer had any TA battalions.

Of the new TA battalions formed, only two were affiliated to the Light Division, and only one of these, the Rifle Volunteers, contained Light Infantry Companies. The Rifle Volunteers, whose abbreviation 'Rifle Vol' was to cause even more problems than dropping the (V) from LI(V), contained two Light Infantry companies, formed from the contraction of HQ and B Company 6LI in Somerset and C and D Company in Cornwall. Elsewhere, HQ and C Company 5LI in Shrewsbury and Hereford contracted to form E (Light Infantry) Company The West Midlands Regiment, while B and C Company 7LI in Bishop Auckland and Washington contracted to form C (Durham Light Infantry) Company The Tyne Tees Regiment (whose battalion headquarters remained in the Gilesgate Armoury). A consolation was the reinstatement of HQ and C Squadron KOYY(LI) as Light Infantry, who merged to form Minden Company The East and West Riding Regiment in Wakefield and Batley. Despite the swingeing cuts, or perhaps because of them, the five Light Infantry Volunteer companies still provided some 42 soldiers to support the regular battalions on operations during the reorganizations in 1998. Emphasizing the paradox that characterized the 1990s, as the new, less-capable battalions officially formed the following year, the whole of the TA stood on the brink of their first general mobilization since the Suez crisis, as NATO poised to enter Kosovo.

Above, top and right:
The Rifle Volunteers
at war. Salamanca
Company on Op
TELIC 4.

The First Battalion, The Royal Gloucestershire, Berkshire and Wiltshire Light Infantry

On 27 April 1994 the 1st Battalion, The Royal Gloucestershire, Berkshire and Wiltshire Regiment was formed in Catterick from an amalgamation of The Gloucestershire Regiment and The Duke of Edinburgh's Royal Regiment (Berkshire & Wiltshire). A few weeks later they deployed to Gorazde in Bosnia. General Charles Guthrie, the Chief of the General Staff, commented following a visit to the Battalion: *'They are outstanding, the best unit I have visited in the last two years'*. 1RGBW went on to serve in Cyprus, Colchester (as part of 24 Airmobile Brigade and then 16 Air Assault Brigade), Ballykinler and Hounslow. During that time they completed operational tours of Bosnia (1994), South Armagh (1998), Kosovo (1999), Northern Ireland (2000–2), Northern Ireland (2003) and Kosovo (2004) as the Spearhead Land Element.

On 16 December 2004 it was announced that 1RGBW would be disbanded as part of Future Army Structures – the Gloucestershire element, along with The Devonshire and Dorset Regiment would be merged with The Light Infantry; the Berkshire and Wiltshire elements would be merged with The Princess of Wales's Royal Regiment. However, in March 2005, it was announced that this disbandment of 1RGBW would not take place; instead, the Regiment would merge completely with The Devonshire and Dorset Regiment and

become 1st Battalion, Light Infantry. In preparation for this, the regiment was moved from The Prince of Wales' Division to The Light Division and renamed The Royal Gloucestershire, Berkshire and Wiltshire Light Infantry. This change followed a visit to 1RGBW by the Chief of the General Staff, General Mike Jackson. Having been on the receiving end of some barbed comments from the Warrant Officers and Senior NCOs, Jackson also pledged that 1RGBWLI would deploy to Afghanistan on a final operational tour. The Royal Gloucestershire, Berkshire and Wiltshire Regiment became The Royal Gloucestershire, Berkshire and Wiltshire Light Infantry (RGBWLI) on Friday 22nd July 2005, the anniversary of the Battle of Salamanca.

On 24 November 2005, the Ministry of Defence announced further changes to the amalgamations. The regiment would still merge with The Devonshire and Dorset Light Infantry; however, they were now to join a new large regiment created by the amalgamation of The Light Infantry and The Royal Green Jackets. This new regiment was to be called The Rifles and would be formed in 2007. The battalion resulting from the merger of The Royal Gloucestershire, Berkshire and Wiltshire Light Infantry and The Devonshire and Dorset Light Infantry would become 1st Battalion, The Rifles.

A MESSAGE FROM THE COLONEL-IN-CHIEF

HRH The Prince Philip, Duke of Edinburgh Colonel-in-Chief, The Royal Gloucestershire, Berkshire and Wiltshire Light Infantry

The British Army has had to endure a number of major changes in recent years. The creation of a large Light Infantry Regiment brings together The Devonshire and Dorset Regiment with The Royal Gloucestershire, Berkshire and Wiltshire Regiment. I hope it is a good omen that this change takes place on the anniversary of the Battle of Salamanca on 22 July, when the Regiments fought side by side in that famous battle, along with The King's Shropshire Light Infantry and The Duke of Cornwall's Light Infantry.

I send my best wishes for the future to all the members of The Royal Gloucestershire, Berkshire and Wiltshire Regiment as you become Light Infantrymen.

Below: The 28th (North Gloucestershire) Regiment of Foot at Quatre Bras (Lady Butler).

Right: The Last Stand of the 66th Foot at Maiwand (Peter Archer). The dog, Bobbie, received a medal from Queen Victoria in 1881, but was run over by a Hansom Cab a year later.

Below right: Cpl Ben Stiley, second-in-command of MOT Romeo immediately following the ambush which killed LCpl Sherwood and seriously wounded his patrol commander, Capt Cay. Despite having been shot in the shoulder, Cpl Stiley commanded the indident follow up and the evacuation of casualties.

Afghanistan – Op HERRICK 3 (2005–6) and Prelim Ops in Helmand Province

1RGBWLI deployed to Afghanistan in September 2005, with the Battalion task organized as follows:

- The Operations Company (QRF) for Regional Command North, based at Mazar-e-Shariff.
- The Provincial Reconstruction Team (PRT) and Mobile Observation Teams (MOTs), also based at Mazar-e-Shariff.
- The Kabul Patrols Company based at Camp Souter in Kabul.
- The Afghan National Army Training Team (ANATT), based at the Kabul Military Training Centre in Kabul.

There was also the requirement to provide force elements to preliminary operations in Kandahar and Lashkar Gah for the British takeover of Helmand Province in early 2006.

Although Op HERRICK 3 did not compare in intensity to subsequent Op HERRICK tours in Helmand Province, it was apparent from the start of the tour that Afghanistan was firmly in the grips of an insurgency. The principal threats were ambush, IED and suicide attacks. Significant events from the tour include:

28 Sep 05: A suicide bomber rode a Motor-Cycle-Borne IED (MCBIED) into a group of ANA soldiers outside the Kabul Military Training Centre, killing nine ANA soldiers:

29 Oct 05: Mobile Observation Team (Romeo) was ambushed while transiting through Mazar-e-Shariff. LCpl Steven Sherwood received a fatal gun shot wound and was killed instantly. The Patrol Commander, Captain Andy Cay, and the Patrol Medic were both Very Seriously Injured (VSI) while the Patrol Second-in-Command, Corpora113l Stiley, and driver of the lead vehicle also suffered gun shot wounds.

14 Nov 05: A suicide bomber drove into a German ISAF vehicle killing a German Lieutenant Colonel and German Warrant Officer. During the confusion immediately following the incident, a secondary Remote-Controlled IED was placed at the seat of the initial explosion: 90 minutes later a second suicide bomber drove towards the western cordon position. When this suicide bomber detonated, it caused the sympathetic explosion of yet another, previously concealed, secondary IED. This double explosion resulted in the death of 17 Afghan civilians and the injuring of approximately 40 more.

25 Nov 05: A team of Swedish Special Forces soldiers based at the UK Forward Support Base were transiting back from Mazar-e-Shariff when the lead vehicle was contacted by an RCIED: This attack resulted in the death of two Swedish Special Forces soldiers.

14 Dec 05: A suicide bomber detonated outside the Blue Mosque in the centre of Mazar-e-Shariff: Fortunately, there were no civilian or ISAF casualties.

1 Feb 06: 1RGBWLI became the first British Infantry unit to deploy soldiers to Helmand province in support of Preliminary Operations. This included a platoon to Lashkar Gah PRT (Provincial Reconstruction Team) to provide security and protected mobility for the PRT Commander, Lieutenant Colonel Henry Worsley RGJ.

7 Feb 06: Following mass protests in response to Danish cartoons of the Prophet Mohammed, an attack was mounted on the Norwegian Provincial Reconstruction Team at Meymanah in north-west Afghanistan: The 1RGBWLI Operations Company deployed by air to Meymanah, conducting a link-up and relief in place with the besieged Norwegians.

Above: The Cap Badge and Back Badge of the Royal Gloucestershire Berkshire and Wiltshire Light Infantry.

27 Mar 06: Lance Corporal Craddock, a team commander in Lashkar Gah was killed when the WMIK he was commanding collided with a tractor whilst providing depth protection and mutual support to a combined UK and US Special Forces convoy transiting to the Tactical Landing Zone to the south of Lashkar Gah.

During the tour, six ISAF soldiers were killed in the 1RGBWLI Area of Responsibility, including Lance Corporals Sherwood and Craddock from 1RGBWLI with a further eleven ISAF soldiers injured, of which six were UK personnel. After returning to UK in April 2006, 1RGBWLI prepared for amalgamation with the DDLI (who were deployed on Op TELIC in Iraq) and subsequent merger to become 1st Battalion, The Rifles.

Above: Multiple Patrol, Lashkar Gah.

Below left: Capt Matt Baker, Lashkar Gah.

The First Battalion, The Devonshire and Dorset Light Infantry

The Devonshire and Dorset Regiment, usually just known as The Devon and Dorsets, was formed in 1958 by the amalgamation of two county regiments – The Devonshire Regiment and The Dorset Regiment. In the 2004 re-organization of the infantry, it was announced that The Devonshire and Dorset Regiment would cease to exist; it would be amalgamated with The Royal Gloucestershire, Berkshire and Wiltshire Regiment to form a new battalion of The Light Infantry. As part of the preparation for this, the Regiment moved from The Prince of Wales' Division to The Light Division, and on 22 July 2005 was renamed The Devonshire and Dorset Light Infantry. On 24 November 2005, the Ministry of Defence announced further changes to the amalgamations. The regiment would still merge with The Royal Gloucestershire, Berkshire and Wiltshire Regiment resulting in a single battalion; however they were now to join a new large regiment created by the amalgamation of The Light Infantry and The Royal Green Jackets. This new regiment was to be called The Rifles and was to be formed in February 2007. The battalion that resulted from the merger of The Devonshire and Dorset Regiment and The Royal Gloucestershire, Berkshire and Wiltshire Regiment was designated 1st Battalion, The Rifles. As part of becoming a rifle regiment, the Regiment laid up its Colours in Exeter Cathedral on 27 January 2007. For most of its short existence the Regiment was committed to preparing for and then deploying on operations in Iraq.

Op TELIC 8 – 1 DDLI (Basra Rural South Battlegroup)

During Op TELIC 8, 1 DDLI Battlegroup was responsible for the vast tracts of land to the west and south of Basra, the Iraqi second city.

A Company was responsible for the largest town, Al Zubayr, a thriving satellite city located 10km south-west of Basra. In a Shia-dominated south this town formed a Sunni enclave with about 30 per cent of its half million

Above, above right and right: 1 DDLI, Op TELIC 8.

FIRST PATROL IN IRAQ – A PRIVATE OF 1DDLI

It was my first patrol in Iraq. There were eight of us going out to conduct a night standing observation post. Our mission was to kill or capture insurgent rocket teams trying to attack Camp Abu Naji. I wouldn't say I was complacent, because it was my first patrol but I don't think any of us were expecting what was waiting for us and what we were going to face.

We were dropped off by Warrior AFVs a few kilometres away from our first RV. The Warriors were very loud and I don't know whether the enemy heard us getting dropped off but they obviously knew we were coming. We dismounted from the Warriors and used the cover of darkness and tabbed off into the night. We had to take our time as it was hard not to make a noise as we patrolled through woods and also had to cross electric fences and small roads.

After we had been patrolling for about an hour, stopping occasionally to conduct nav checks, we came to a small housing estate on the edge of the city. We went firm because we heard dogs barking. Tom came over the radio and said 'he was nervous and thought we should take a different route'. Everybody knew Tom was scared of dogs but there wasn't any other way to go so we cracked on. We were paying particular attention to the backs of the houses, and as we patrolled out of the cul-de-sac we came to a long wide road. Until we started to cross the road I didn't realize how illuminated we were, even wearing desert combats.

I then heard loud automatic gunfire just behind me. I froze for a split second; I think I was in disbelief. I saw bullets hitting the ground right by my feet. I returned a rapid rate of fire. I looked over my shoulder and saw my team commander peeling back straight away. We went into our eight-man contact drills. The enemy were on the rooftop of a house firing at us with heavy machine guns. They had the upper hand as we were in new strange territory and their ambush was set and we were in their killing zone. Luckily we managed to take cover in some dead ground and used that to extract to a rally point. We peeled left for three, maybe four hundred metres giving each other cover and fire as we were still being contacted even as the Quick Reaction Force arrived at the scene.

We were lucky to get out alive. It proved that the training we are taught works and something as simple as a peel left can get you out of the mire. I wouldn't say I would want to be in that situation again but that night I put my training to good use and did my job. The contact was in the papers a couple of days later. A member of the MOD staff said that it was a platoon of men, but there were only eight of us, and we had killed three and injured up to another ten.

population being Sunni. In the early days and during times of heightened sectarian tension much of the Company's efforts were directed at reassuring the Sunni populace. A Company also patrolled the Rumaylah oilfields and protected the Corps' main supply route Tampa. B Company was based in one of Saddam Hussein's former palaces in the suburbs of Basra city and was responsible for the Al Faw Peninsula. This was the scene of intense fighting during the Iran–Iraq war, with prolific debris from this conflict still apparent. The town of Abu Al Khaseeb, on the banks of the Shatt Al Arab waterway, housed a significant Sunni minority. At the tip of the peninsula is the Manifold Metering Station, a big valve at the terminus of the numerous oil pipelines. From here the flow of export oil is controlled, with an estimated 90 per cent of Iraq's wealth passing through this one location, making it a key infrastructure site for Iraqi economic regeneration. Umm Qasr is Iraq's only deep-sea port and was the home of C Company. In addition to the port, C Company was responsible for Safwan town and the nearby border crossing site with Kuwait. Safwan is a typical border town with the associated lowlifes and smuggling gangs, all of which kept the Company busy.

With about two months to go the Battlegroup was reinforced by two companies from the Theatre Reserve Battalion (2 RRF). This freed B and C Companies from their static commitments allowing the whole Battlegroup to carry out more focused and ambitious operations in the city in support of the Basra Security Plan. Support Company was re-roled early in the pre-deployment training to form the Brigade Surveillance Company (BSC). The fact that this was the first time the TELIC BSC was formed entirely from one unit says a

Left: Hearts and minds.

Below: *Drums and Bugle Platoon, SF live firing, Sennybridge.*

Above: A private enjoys a takeaway in his Snatch Land Rover.

Above right: Cooling off in Basra Palace.

great deal for the depth of quality in the Battalion, particularly considering that three rifle companies were fielded at the same time. The BSC worked directly to Brigade Headquarters and was involved in a myriad of covert operations gaining information on likely targets. Sustaining and directing all this activity was the Headquarters and Echelon grouping in Britannia Lines, Shaibah Logistics Base. Here the vehicle fleet was maintained, stores delivered and pushed forward, mouths fed and operations planned!

Above right: River patrol on the Shatt al Arab.

Right: Brigadier Tim Gregson inspects the Pass Off Parade.

Far right: Laying up DDLI colours, Exeter Cathedral.

A MESSAGE FROM THE CO

Operation TELIC 8 was a Regimental milestone. It was the last operational tour for The Devon and Dorsets, the last time that a Battalion wore our cap badge on active service. It was fitting then, but will come as no surprise, that the tour was conducted with the professionalism, flair and thoroughness that our fine Regiment has become famous for over the years.

But to remember it only because of its unique timing fails to acknowledge the enormous challenge that such a dangerous and dynamic operational environment presented to our soldiers. We came into theatre as Iraq struggled to emplace a government of national unity. Any optimism however soon gave way to reality as Shia parties continued to vie for power in Basra Province. Brutality between competing sections of society, intimidation and victimization of Sunni minorities and militia violence against coalition forces were everyday occurrences and omnipresent threats. But despite this our soldiers persevered and in every area of the operation made very real progress. Robust security operations resulted in the arrests of many active terrorists and the recovery of countless arms, ammunition and bomb-making components. Such strike operations, delivered alongside training and development of the Police, Army and other Iraqi security force organizations, backed up by carefully managed relationships with key local civic leaders and the delivery of myriad community projects, made a really positive difference to our little corner of a very troubled country. For this all the men and women who served with the Battlegroup can be well satisfied. I am hugely proud of them.

For the families and loved ones left behind I also have the utmost admiration. They had to deal with many anxious moments, often waiting for news after another tragedy had been announced in the media. More prosaically but just as significantly they had to cope with managing home, household and often children single-handedly, having to do so without a helping hand or a shoulder to cry on. Also left behind, without the glamour and excitement of the operational theatre, was the Rear Party. We could not have coped without either, who together with the wider Regimental family formed that all-important home base.

As well as all the achievements, the tour brought tragedy when it robbed us of a much-respected friend and colleague, Corporal John Johnston Cosby, or George as many of us knew him.

Having had the privilege of commanding such a fine Battlegroup I know that the last-ever operational tour of The Devon and Dorsets will be chronicled as an exemplar of service, professionalism and sacrifice in the finest tradition of our Regiment and as a worthy prologue to the formation of The Rifles.

PART 3
The Wider Regiment

Training

Introduction

In describing the evolution of soldier and officer training over the period of the Regiment's life, this chapter will show that even in the relatively short lifespan of our Regiment, The Light Infantryman of 2007 was prepared for service with his Battalion in a markedly different way than his forebears in 1968, largely due to that ever-present feature of British Army life, 'change'. Whatever the drivers for that change have been, the training base has invariably been in the vanguard of doing things differently. In 1968, we trained our soldiers at the Regimental Depot in Shrewsbury and drew in Juniors from one of three separate training battalions in Oswestry, Rhyl or Shorncliffe. The story of both adult and junior training through to 2007 is notable for the number of locations used before the Regiment finally settled, with the rest of the Infantry, at Catterick, with a small stream of Juniors continuing to flow through Harrogate and Bassingbourn. We have seen skill-at-arms and tactical command training for our NCOs eventually collocate and establish firm roots in Brecon together with the Platoon Commanders' Division. As for young officers, we still drew subalterns from both Sandhurst and Mons in 1968, but by 2007 not only were all young officers drawn from Sandhurst, but they were now also the product of a common commissioning course which included training alongside female cadets.

Adult Recruit Training – The Early Years
Light Infantry Depot, Sir John Moore Barracks, Shrewsbury 1968–83

Originally built as the Depot for the King's Shropshire Light Infantry in 1877–9, Copthorne Barracks was to become the Regimental home of The Light Infantry in 1968. In addition to the adult recruits delivered by Training Company, the Depot also trained Junior Soldiers, including Junior Buglers and Junior Bandsmen. In 1972, the Recruit Syllabus was changed to reflect the demands of operations in Northern Ireland; a new 16-week course now included counter-insurgency training with the final exercise introducing recruits to scenarios that would prepare them for service in Northern Ireland. This package would be extended to 18 weeks in length in 1974, with the highlight being two weeks of intensive field firing at Sennybridge at the end of the course. Copthorne Barracks is now the home of Headquarters 5th Division.

Light Division Depot, Peninsula Barracks, Winchester 1983–5

Following closure of The Light Infantry Depot, recruit training moved to Peninsula Barracks in Winchester. This former home of The King's Royal Rifle Corps and The Rifle Brigade now changed its title from The Rifle Depot to The Light Division Depot. Initially there were four platoons training all adult recruits for The Light Infantry and Royal Green Jackets,

Above: The CFT – a brutal eight-miler. 2LI push it out on the Pentlands, Edinburgh, 2005.

Left: Kit Check on final Battle Camp, Sennybridge.

Previous pages: Maj Mark Winston-Davis, the Combined Services and Army waterski champion.

Above: Military Assistance to the Civil Community.

unusual for a section commander to have 18–20 recruits in his charge, which compares markedly with today's strictly enforced ratio of 1:12. Not only were the section commanders feeling the strain, but so was the infrastructure in a tired old barracks not designed to cope with in excess of 400 recruits at a time. By 1985, recruits were completing a 20-week course with over 25 days spent in the field, many of them in Wales, including the live firing and final exercise at Sennybridge culminating in an unforgettable 27-mile march/run.

Today Peninsula Barracks is a spectacular residential site. Apartments and townhouses are set in wonderful grounds and at least one property has been sold for £1 million! Additionally, the barracks also house a number of military museums and Regimental Headquarters, including those of The Rifles.

and at its peak there were some 290 recruits under training in the first year. The Platoons – Cassino, Tobruk, Kohima and Pegasus – were named after LI and RGJ battle honours and the training teams were a mix of instructors from both regiments. An additional training team was also formed to train TA recruits on a two-week basic course and prepare JNCOs from the regular battalions for their Tactics Course at the School of Infantry. In 1984, additional JNCOs were posted in to increase the number of sections in the platoons from four to six in order to cope with the very high numbers of recruits joining for training – platoons were forming up with well over 80 recruits at a time. During the final year of training at Peninsula Barracks, recruit numbers continued to rise markedly with some platoon intakes reaching treble figures and one peaking at 113. It was not

Adult Recruit Training – The Later Years

In 1990, a review of the Army's training base was initiated with the aim of making a 30 per cent budgetary and manpower saving across the Army Training Organization. The result saw a significantly different approach being taken to soldier training. For the Infantry this meant the end of the old Divisional Depot and a move to separate Phase 1 and Phase 2 training establishments. Phase 1 training would now be conducted at one of five new Army Training Regiments at Bassingbourn, Glencorse, Lichfield, Pirbright and Winchester, with Phase 2 special-to-arm training being conducted at respective Arms centres. For The Light Infantry recruit, initial training would still take place in Winchester, but from April 1993 this would be under the banner of Army Training Regiment (Winchester). Infantry Phase 2 training was to be centred on the Infantry Training Centre (Catterick) using Helles and Vimy Barracks, which had for many years delivered Phase 1 and 2 training for the Royal Corps of Signals. However, significant work would be required to develop the site in order to give it both the necessary capacity and training infrastructure to meet the demands of supporting Phase 2 training for the entire Infantry. As an interregnum, all Infantry Phase 2 training in the period 1993–5 would be conducted at three separate Infantry Training Battalions (ITBs) in Catterick, Ouston and Strensall. In this period, Light Infantry adult recruits would complete their training at ITB Ouston in Northumberland and TA Light Infantrymen would train at ITB Strensall on the outskirts of York.

Light Division Depot, Sir John Moore Barracks, Winchester 1985–93

Sir John Moore Barracks was built at Flowerdown on the outskirts of Winchester on a site that had variously been used by the Royal Flying Corps, the Royal Air Force, the Royal Navy and the Army between 1914 and 1976. The new barracks were unique at the time as the only modern, purpose-built training establishment in the UK. The barracks were officially opened by Her Majesty The Queen and Her Royal Highness Princess Alexandra on 27 November 1986. The new Depot would train all

Right: Digging in on Salisbury Plain takes its toll.

Light Division recruits, including Juniors. Initially, the ORBAT comprised two adult recruit training companies, each of four platoons, though these would be bolstered by the addition of a Junior Soldiers Company and then a Junior Leaders Company, each of three platoons, in the second half of 1986. In addition to a TA training platoon, the Depot also trained recruits for the Army Air Corps and Royal Army Pay Corps. 1990 saw the adult recruit course extend from 19 to 21 weeks. Not to be forgotten was the steady trickle of potential officers who completed eight weeks of training in an adult platoon as O-Type entrants before attending the Regular Commissions Board at Westbury.

Army Training Regiment (Winchester), Sir John Moore Barracks, Winchester 1993–2002

ATR Winchester was formed on 2 April 1993. Like the other newly created ATRs, Winchester was to deliver recruit training through a common 10-week course known as the Common Military Syllabus (Recruits). The course would be completed alongside recruits destined for the Royal Armoured Corps, the Army Air Corps, the Intelligence Corps and the Adjutant General's Corps. For the first time, this would also see Light

Infantry recruits training alongside a sizeable female recruit population. Initially, the ATR had three training companies, but a fourth was established in January 1995 to provide a permanent home for the Army Air Corps and the Intelligence Corps. The Light Division was fortunate enough to have its own Company from the off which did much to engender the right ethos with our recruits and, as the only infanteers in the ATR, the training teams quickly established a formidable reputation for professional excellence amongst their peers. In an effort to further bear down on wastage the course was extended from 10 to 11 weeks in October 1996, in order to de-heat the programme for recruits. In December 1996, in yet another attempt to further reduce wastage in training, the Army Foundation Scheme was launched. This initiative aimed to ensure that recruits were physically and psychologically ready for successful completion of Common Military Syllabus (Recruits) by gently inducting them into Army life over a period of two to three weeks before they joined a training platoon.

Infantry Training Battalion, Albermarle Barracks, Ouston 1993–5

Infantry Training Battalion (ITB), Ouston, opened for business in January 1993. Since Albermarle Barracks was previously the home of the Junior Infantry Battalion for the Scottish and King's Divisions, the site was ideally suited for its new interregnum role as an ITB conducting Phase 2 training for recruits from the Light, Scottish and Queen's Divisions as well as Pioneers from the Royal Logistic Corps. Whilst Divisional integrity was maintained at platoon level, the ten training platoons were spread across three companies, all delivering the Combat Infantryman's Course, which was to move from an 11- to a 12-week package by the time the ITB passed out its last recruits in May 1995. Albermarle Barracks is now the home of 39 Regiment RA equipped with the MLRS.

Far left: LI Depot Anti-Tank Field Firing Range 'Continuation Training'. Platoon Commander Lt B M Elliott takes lunch with his Platoon.

Below left: Assault Course. The 12-foot wall.

Left: Building character in the pool complex at Sir John Moore Barracks, Winchester.

Above: 'On guard!'
Bayonet training at
the ITC.

Infantry Training Centre, Catterick, 1995–2007

In April 1995, ITC Catterick took responsibility for delivery of all Phase 2 Infantry training. The ITC comprised ten recruit companies spread across three separate training battalions. At this stage only the Foot Guards and the Parachute Regiment trained in their own Divisional Companies – this a result of their own longer courses to cover the requirement to deliver respectively an enhanced drill package and preparation for and completion of parachute selection and training. However, where possible, cap badge integrity was retained at platoon level with Light Division recruits invariably being trained by a Light Division training team. The Combat Infantryman's Course (CIC) was now 14 weeks long and focused heavily on skill-at-arms, fieldcraft and fitness with almost 50 per cent of the course spent in the field using the local training areas around Catterick Garrison and key exercises being conducted in Otterburn and Garelochead, while field firing took place at Warcop.

In May 2000, ITC Catterick began to trial a combined Phase 1 and 2 Course of 24 weeks. The driver was again reducing wastage in training; in 1999, the wastage rate for a split Phase 1 and Phase 2 training regime was 38 per cent, which was neither acceptable nor sustainable. This trial would ultimately lead to the roll-out of the 24-week Combat Infantryman's Course (CIC) from the end of 2002. With ITC Catterick now delivering a common course for all Line Infantry, the focus in 2003 switched to seeking further improvements to the delivery of training; the key output of this work was the introduction of training within Divisional companies. The Light Division Company was established in the 1st Battalion ITC in 2004 and would eventually comprise eight training platoons with each platoon forming up with 44 recruits. The Company would also take responsibility for training recruits destined for the Royal Irish Regiment.

As well as having responsibility for all Regular and Territorial Army initial training for the Infantry, ITC Catterick is also home to the School of Ceremonial, which delivers Phase 3 training for Infantry Drummers and Buglers. In early 2007 the All Arms Drill Wing also moved up from Pirbright. The training conducted at the ITC is on a scale not seen since the days of National Service. Not surprisingly, Headquarters School of Infantry moved to Catterick in 2001 and this one-star headquarters has command responsibility for the ITC, the Infantry Battle School in Brecon, the Support Weapons School in Warminster, the School of Ceremonial and the School of Bagpipe Music and Highland Drumming in Edinburgh.

Junior Soldier and Junior Leader Training

In 1968, the Regiment drew Juniors from one of four locations: Junior Leaders from Oswestry and Junior Soldiers from Rhyl, Shorncliffe and the Regimental Depot in Shrewsbury. In 1974 the Infantry Junior Leaders' Battalion in Oswestry and the Junior Tradesman's Regiment in Rhyl closed. Shorncliffe now became the home of Junior Leader training and all Junior Soldiers would now be trained at The Light Infantry Depot in Shrewsbury. Regardless of where a Junior completed his initial training, he would always complete a period in Training Company at the Depot before joining his Battalion. In due course, all Juniors would be trained at Winchester, before further Army changes led to a single adult intake. However, between 1993 and 1998 the only Juniors recruited into the Army were those destined for a technical trade in the Royal Electrical and Mechanical Engineers, with their training conducted at the Army Technical Foundation College in Arborfield. This is significant because when the decision was taken in 1996 to reintroduce the Infantry Junior Entry through the Armed Forces College, Harrogate, there would be insufficient capacity at the new site to meet demand. The result was that for a two-year window in 1998–9, a small number of Infantry Juniors were trained at Arborfield until both AFC Harrogate and ATR Bassingbourn had fully come on line.

Infantry Junior Leaders' Battalion, Oswestry, 1968–74

Located at Park Hall Camp in Oswestry, the Infantry Junior Leaders' Battalion opened in 1960, and was responsible for training all of the Infantry's Junior Leaders. Initially, boys would join from 15.5 years of age and follow a seven-term course. With the raising of the school leaving age to 16 in 1972, the course was shortened to a four- then subsequently a three-term package lasting a year. On joining the Battalion, Juniors would first complete basic training in Z Company before moving to their parent training company. The Oswestry era has often been referred to as the 'golden years' on account of the very high number of Junior Leaders who went on to become warrant officers and Late Entry officers in all parts of the Army.

Junior Infantry Battalion, Sir John Moore Barracks, Shorncliffe, 1968–85

Sir John Moore Barracks began training Junior Infantrymen from the Scottish, Queen's, King's, Prince of Wales's and Light Divisions in September 1967. The course lasted six terms and was conducted at a comparatively leisurely pace. Juniors spent at least two years at Shorncliffe between the ages of fifteen and seventeen. In August 1974, Shorncliffe assumed responsibility from Oswestry for the training of Junior Leaders. The new course was initially four terms long but was later reduced to three terms and completed in a year. The original five Divisions of Infantry were now expanded to incorporate the Junior Leaders from the Guards, the Parachute Regiment, the Royal Pioneer Corps and, for a short time, the Royal Military Police. Over the next decade innovations such as the Junior Army Education Certificate, the Education for Promotion Certificate for Young Entrants and a new system of progressive leadership training were introduced. Junior Leaders were expected to achieve rapid promotion to NCO rank on joining their battalions. Indeed, a Shorncliffe Junior Leader was three times more likely to achieve warrant rank after only 12 years service compared to 17 years for an adult recruit joining in the same year.

Above: Internal Security Training.

Junior Tradesman's Regiment, Kinmel Park Camp, Rhyl, 1968–74

In 1962, two Junior Tradesman's Regiments were formed: one at Rhyl in north Wales and the other at Troon on the west coast of Scotland. Juniors heading for The Light Infantry trained in Rhyl alongside other Infantry cap badges and those destined for careers in many of the Corps. The purpose of the Regiment was to train drivers, driver/radio operators and clerks. On joining, boys spent their first term in Basic Training Company before moving to one of three Regimental companies where they began their trade training as well as undertaking significant amounts of education. Sport and adventure training also featured heavily on the programme. After a year in training, some boys would qualify in more than one trade, with driving being extremely popular – static trainer to Austin 1-Tonner and then on to Bedford 3-Tonners on the camp circuit before progression onto the open road. A small number would also learn to ride motorbikes.

specialist platoons also existed for training Junior Buglers and Junior Bandsmen. After initial training in one of the two junior training platoons, boys would eventually move into the senior training platoon where they were prepared for transition to an adult recruit platoon in Training Company at the point they reached 17.5 years of age. Those individuals completing their Junior Service in Oswestry, Rhyl and Shorncliffe would also come to the Depot and, alongside the Shrewsbury element of the senior platoon, be tested and assessed in order to determine which week of adult recruit training they would be best suited to join.

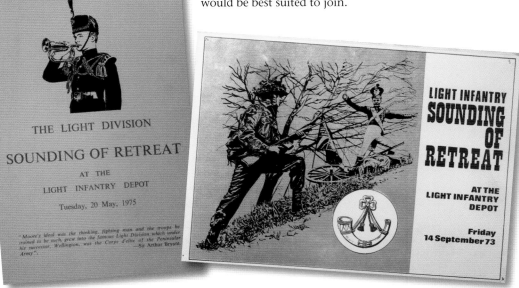

Light Infantry Depot, Sir John Moore Barracks, Shrewsbury, 1968–83

Although the Regiment had Juniors training at four separate locations during the early years of this period, by far the majority of Junior Light Infantrymen began their service in Junior Soldier Company at the Depot in Shrewsbury, where

It was the 9th September 1975, and having completed the hugs and kisses with my mum, brother and sister on the station platform and received the final firm handshake from my dad, I got into the train carriage with my small suitcase containing the required items as listed on the joining instructions – mostly coathangers and bootbrushes. As the train pulled away, I leant out of the window to wave goodbye. I was leaving home at 16 with Shrewsbury as my destination. I felt a bit of a dipstick because my dad insisted that I wore a jacket and tie – this would become significant when I got to Shrewsbury. Filled with both apprehension and excitement I found a seat opposite a young boy of similar age and dress to me. This was 'Bondy' and he was also off to Shrewsbury to join The Light Infantry. As we walked out of Shrewsbury station there were lots of other lads being put into groups and then loaded onto 4-Tonners. On arrival at Sir John Moore Barracks, we were lined up on the square and then a big bloke, Sjt Mac McLaughlin, came down the line and started selecting individuals. Both Bondy and I were selected and put into a group where it quickly became apparent that most lads were wearing jacket and tie – we had just been selected for the Bugle Platoon! Having been taken to our accommodation, we then met the Bugle Major, Bill Jones, who was both impressive and scary. He quickly instilled immense pride in the group and gave us a massive sense of belonging. During the first couple of weeks we were taught to shave by Cpl Alan Howarth, spent hours in the Drill Shed with Cpls Brian Holman, Stan Wilkinson and Chuck Smiley, were allocated nicknames and locked in the Keep until we could pass the '5 Note Test'. We learnt to iron our itchy KF shirts and shave the insides, bull our boots and gaiters (puttees had not yet been issued!) and spend endless hours (wax on, wax off) getting the floor in our accommodation to mirror standard using the universal bumper. We did all of this for £5 per week, which did not go very far. Cash paid at one desk, barrack damages taken

Clockwise from below: Changing collar badges on Vesting Day; A wet and cold Pass Out Parade; Peter de la Billière talks to Best Recruit.

off at the next followed by a trip to the NAAFI for more kiwi black polish, a can of starch, a packet of Maltesers and a pint of milk – roll on the next payday! However, this system did impose a non-negotiable savings scheme by way of credits which meant that when Leave came round, we received our credit savings cash lump sum and we were rich!

Reflections on Joining The Light Infantry Depot in 1975 by Major Graham Gilbert.

Light Division Depot, Sir John Moore Barracks, Shrewsbury, 1983–5

For a brief two year period, 1983–5, Shrewsbury became the home for all Light Division Junior Soldier training. Training Company comprised five Junior Soldier platoons, and separate platoons for Junior Buglers and Junior Bandsmen. At this stage, the course was still 42 weeks long but soon extended to a 52-week programme with the Junior Soldiers posted straight to their battalions on completion. The last Junior Soldiers passed out in the summer of 1985.

Light Division Depot, Sir John Moore Barracks, Winchester, 1985–93

In 1985, the decision was taken to combine the training of Junior Leaders and Junior Soldiers on a regional/divisional basis, and in 1986 Light Division Junior Leaders moved to the new Light Division Depot in Winchester where they were joined by the Junior Soldiers who had previously trained in Shrewsbury. On arrival from Shrewsbury and Shorncliffe respectively, Junior Soldiers and Junior Leaders continued to be trained in separate companies, each of three platoons. The Junior Soldier Course was significantly reduced from a 42-week to a 32-week programme in 1987 and, in the following year, the Junior Leaders Course was completely re-written with the aim of reducing the perennial problem of wastage through Discharge as of Right. The course moved to three 14-week terms with the third term notable for the increased emphasis on leadership skills and confidence-building periods. However, further change was just around the corner and, as we entered the 1990s, the training of all Juniors morphed into a single 42-week course and all trainees were now known as Junior Leaders.

Army Training Regiment (Bassingbourn), 1999–2007

In 1999, a Junior Entry system was established at ATR Bassingbourn. This Phase 1 course lasted 20 weeks with Junior Entrants being trained in all-arms platoons with instructors drawn from across the Army. On completion of this course, all Infantry Junior Entrants moved to ITC Catterick to complete their Phase 2 special to arm training.

Did You Know? The barracks was previously The Queen's Division Depot and before that a RAF flying station. However, Bassingbourn is probably best known for its connection to the

big screen. During World War Two, it was a flying base for US B-17 bombers, including the 'Memphis Belle' immortalized in the movie of the same name. The barracks was also used to film part of Stanley Kubrick's Vietnam blockbuster 'Full Metal Jacket'.

Army Foundation College, Harrogate, 1998–2007

The Army Foundation College was established in 1998 on the site of the old Junior Apprentice College for the Royal Corps of Signals. Initially, the College only trained Junior Soldiers for the Infantry, the Royal Artillery and the Royal Armoured Corps, although this was subsequently changed in 2004 to include all cap badges except the Royal Military Police and the Intelligence Corps. The College has two intakes per year, forming up with 18 platoons in September and nine platoons in January. The aim is to develop qualities of leadership, character and team spirit through a progressive 42-week course that combines the Common Military Syllabus (Recruits) with Vocational Education and Leadership and Initiative Training. On passing out from the College, all Infantrymen move to ITC Catterick to complete their Phase 2 special-to-arm training.

In the last two weeks of the Course a Junior RSM is appointed. Between 1998 and 2007, The Light Infantry had the unique privilege of producing more Junior RSMs at the Army Foundation College than any other cap badge – a remarkable achievement in so short a time. They were: JRSM Wheatley in August 1998, JRSM Thompson in December 2001 and JRSM Taylor in August 2003.

Infantry Training Centre, Catterick, 1999–2007

All Juniors leaving Bassingbourn and Harrogate completed their Phase 2 special-to-arm training Infantry training at the ITC. For those graduating from Harrogate there followed a 10-week course and for those from Bassingbourn a slightly longer 14-week course – this reflecting a much shorter time spent in training at Phase 1. Throughout their time at Catterick, Junior soldiers were accommodated and trained separately from adult recruits and, although this meant that the training platoons were multi-cap badge, the Light Division Company within the ITC played an active role in Regimental nurturing and preparing the young Light Infantryman for his arrival into Battalion life.

Officer Training

1968–72: Royal Military Academy Sandhurst and Mons

In this period there were still two distinct routes to commissioning: the first through a two-year course, with significant academic content, at the RMAS, and the second by completing officer training at the Mons Officer Cadet School in Aldershot. Mons was a throwback to the days of National Service where the limited return of service for a young officer precluded lengthy training. It also catered for the Regular Short Service Commission officer. Following the abolition of National Service in 1960, Mons assumed responsibility for all Short Service officer cadets and university graduates. A shrinking Army together with the increasing popularity of a faster commission achieved through Mons was the catalyst for major change. In 1972, Mons moved from Aldershot to New College in the RMAS. The original intent was for the two organizations to be collocated but this quickly proved to be unfeasible and the entire system of officer training was re-structured.

1972–2007: Royal Military Academy Sandhurst

The new system saw all cadets complete the six-month Standard Military Course. Short Service officers then left the Academy whilst their Regular counterparts were required to stay on for a further five months to complete the Regular Career Course (RCC) which majored on International Affairs and War Studies. In due course officers were able to return to Old College to complete this course after a period at Regimental Duty. Also, those Short Service officers wishing to convert to a Regular Commission would need to return to the Academy to complete the RCC. For university graduates there were two subtly different routes to a commission at this stage: the Army Undergraduate Cadets Course was for probationary second lieutenants who had been granted a sponsored place at a university by the Army and consisted of three weeks at RMAS prior to university, followed by a 17-week course on graduation;

Above left: The Light Infantry Depot, Copthorne Barracks, Shrewsbury. Seen from the top of the Keep. Officers Mess (left); Serjeants Mess (centre); Junior Soldiers Block (right).

Below: The Light Infantry Depot, Shrewsbury. The Junior Soldiers Bugle Section.

Above: Final Battle Camp, Brecon, 2005. NBC suits have given way to body armour.

Above right: Mock Gas Attack during Battle Camp in the 1980s.

and the 20-week-long Direct Entry Course for graduates with no military experience. In 1976 the RCC was extended from 18 to 23 weeks and a year later saw the introduction of the 'infamous' Pre-RMAS (Rowallan Company) Course designed to develop leadership qualities in those candidates identified by the Regular Commissions Board before joining their respective commissioning course. In 1982 the Standard Military and Standard Graduate Courses were established, with both running for 28 weeks. At the same time the RCC was reduced to 14 weeks and would be undertaken after between 24–50 months' service. Further change came in 1987 with the Standard Military Course being extended to 42 weeks and the RCC being replaced by Phase 1 of the Junior Command and Staff Course. Finally, a 42-week common course for all, simply known as the Commissioning Course, was launched in 1992.

It will come as no surprise that Light Infantrymen consistently shone at the Academy. A steady succession of Light Infantry Colour Serjeant instructors left their mark on generations of young cadets and in turn returned to their battalions on a fast-track route to the Regimental Serjeant Major's appointment. We were also hugely fortunate in attracting officer cadets whose hallmark was a welcome blend of professionalism and style. Not surprisingly, the Regiment featured strongly on the list of those achieving honours at the Academy with no fewer than nine winners of the Sword of Honour and two winners of the Queen's Medal. Sword of Honour: MJC Payne, August 1980; DGS Livingston, August 1992; JAD de Labillière, August 1994; RAJ Chisolm, December 1996; DN Graham, April 1999; CB Martin, April 2001; DJ Flanagan, April 2003; MJ Devenish, December 2005; JAB Edwards, August 2006. Queen's Medal: AAJ Fyfe, August 1990; DJ Flanagan, April 2003.

Every year some 60 or more SNCOs hand picked from across the Army attend the RMAS Cadre Course in the hope of becoming one of 20 successful candidates who will be formally posted to the RMAS in order to train the future generals of the Army. These SNCOs have already proved themselves to be at the leading edge of their own peer group; they now face the toughest challenge of their lives.
The Cadre consists of six weeks of intense testing whilst being placed under immense pressure; the aim is to ensure that only the very best survive. The Cadre replicates a compressed version of the officer cadet syllabus to ensure that the future instructor is fully aware of the key mental and physical challenges faced by those they are about to train. Others have described the Cadre as a mini Brecon tactics course, skill-at-arms and drill course rolled into one. By the end of Week 2, the Cadre was down to 40 SNCOs and only 30 would make it through to the end. On the

penultimate day, Cadre Detail was published, detailing 10 SNCOs to report to the Academy Adjutant at 1000 hours the following morning. Also at 1000 hours was the Cadre final photograph in full No2 Dress. This was the Academy's peculiar way of telling those 10 men that they hadn't made it! Phew, my name wasn't on the list.

New instructors would be split between 'Drillers', those who were to be Platoon Colour Serjeants and 'Skillers', those who would work in the Academy Skill-at-Arms Wing and teach weapon and range skills. I was one of the lucky ones to be selected as a platoon Colour Serjeant on completion of the Cadre of 1985. Having received my first 35 young officer cadets, I was soon out to place my stamp on what could be the future top brass of the Armed Forces. I remember early on in training that young university graduates would simply not be motivated by me screaming obscene words of displeasure into their delicate ears. After some serious thinking, I soon learnt that foul-mouthing educated young men wasn't the way to succeed at this unique establishment. Instead, I learnt the Christian names of all of my cadets and, when discipline was required, I would publicly embarrass an individual in

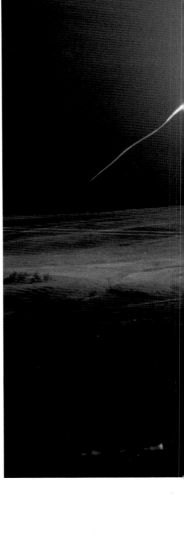

front of his fellow cadets. For instance, if a cadet turned up late for a range day and had forgotten his rifle magazines, he would be brought out in front of the Platoon to hear 'Giles, it's really kind of you to join us today but how disgraceful it is of you to forget such an essential piece of equipment for such an important day's training'. Giles would never be late or forget his kit again.

Reflections on life as a Colour Serjeant Instructor 1985–7 by Lt Col Bob Pickford

Infantry Battle School, Dering Lines, Brecon

Rather like Sandhurst, Brecon has a reputation founded on professional excellence and not a little mystique. The Dering Lines site was originally a tented camp in World War One and a wooden-hutted infantry training centre in World War Two. Little used after the War, it was not until 1961 that Dering Lines started to function in a recognizable Battle School form as the Parachute Regiment Battle School. It would not be until 1968 that formal centralized tactical training for NCOs from the rest of the Infantry would begin in earnest. Over the years, formal skill-at-arms courses have also slowly gravitated to Brecon via homes in Hythe, Warminster, Strensall and Aldershot. In 1973, Brecon's broader pan-Infantry focus saw the Parachute Regiment Battle School re-named the Senior NCOs' Tactical Division of the School of Infantry. A number of iterative name changes followed before the sign at the gate welcomed visitors to the Infantry Battle School in 2004.

Evolution to the Platoon Sergeants' Battle Course (PSBC)

In 1968, the delivery of centralized tactical training for infantry sergeants was a relatively new concept. The eight-week course began life as a bolt-on to the existing Parachute Regiment Battle School package and would be the catalyst for the creation of the Infantry NCOs' Tactics Division. At this stage, completion of the course was not a pre-requisite for promotion to sergeant or employment as a rifle platoon serjeant. The course has continued to evolve over the years and significant milestones include: the eventual joining of separate skill-at-arms and tactics courses in 1986 into what we now recognise as the PSBC – and the deployment of the course to Kenya in 2004 to battlecamp its final exercise, though resource constraints would see this exciting initiative being relatively short-lived.

Lemgo, October 1978: the Commanding Officer has just told me that I am off to Brecon to complete the Platoon Sergeants' Battle Course. Wow! I quickly started doing extra fitness training and sought out extra information about the Course. The only advice I got from my own platoon serjeant who had recently returned injured from Brecon, was to see the MO quickly, get a sick note and don't go – not very helpful, but there were many times in the next four months when I wished I had taken his advice!

Left: Platoon Serjeants Battle Course.

Above: *Tracer lights up the Brecon Beacons during a night attack.*

Above right: *'Fan Dance' – climbing Jacob's Ladder up to Pen y Fan (top right).*

After completing an excellent pre-course training package at the Depot in Shrewsbury, I arrived at Brecon in January 1979, where one of my first memories is of running around Dering Lines at least three times with my fellow students before reporting to the Senior Division Office where the Sergeant Major then placed us all into our platoons. It was at this stage that we were also told which weapon system we would carry for the course – I was informed that I had the ideal build to carry the 84mm Carl Gustav and the SMG!

At that time, Dering Lines was comprised of World War Two-style wooden huts which looked terrible from the outside but they were generally warm and fit for purpose. I entered the 2 Platoon 3 Section hut, found an empty bed and met my fellow students for the next eight weeks. They were all a great bunch, including the sergeant from 2 PARA who was clever enough to turn up with four sets of 58 pattern webbing. I was grateful that he loaned me a set. Anyone who has ever used 58 pattern webbing will testify to its great water-absorbing qualities and its ability to shrink and generally compress your chest like steel bands.

The Clansman Radio had just been introduced into the Army and this was Senior Division's first course using the new kit which had replaced the Larkspur A40/ A41 range. We found that this new equipment broke very easily and the bills for broken or lost items were horrendous. The other item that proved to be totally unsuitable was the infamous DMS boot. After the first hour on the Sennybridge Training Area, everyone's feet would be soaked and the boot reduced to a lump of wet leather and cardboard. Why it took the Falklands War to finally address the issue is anyone's guess?

On reflection, I fully enjoyed myself at Brecon. I learnt a great deal about myself and others in a high-pressure scenario that has stood me in good stead during many years of service. Most importantly, as I learnt my trade as a rifle platoon serjeant, others were ultimately being prepared for the hardships of the Falklands War, which was just around the corner.

Reflections on the Platoon Sergeants' Battle Course in 1979 by Major (Retired) Paul Evanson

Evolution to the Section Commanders' Battle Course (SCBC)
It was not until 1975 that centralized tactical training for all Infantry JNCOs was launched. Rather like the SNCO model, the new course, which was initially seven weeks, was developed from an existing Parachute Regiment Battle School package. Within a year the course would become a week longer and become known as the Infantry Section Commanders' Course. Like its senior brother, the SCBC that we recognize today was created in 1986 through the linking of separate skill-at-arms and tactics courses to be delivered in sequence at Brecon.

Platoon Commanders' Battle Course (PCBC)
For many years, platoon commanders conducted their special-to-arm training in Warminster. Until 2003, young officers had only the briefest of flirtations with Brecon and its surrounding hills when deploying for exercises such as the aptly named Ex 'Grim Reaper'! However, all changed in December 2003 when the Platoon Commanders' Division moved from ITC Warminster to ITC Wales and the first Brecon-based PCBC got underway in January 2004. By this stage, the culmination of the course was a battlecamp conducted in Africa. Kenya and Malawi have been well used and there is little doubt that the product of the PCBC in 2007 was a young officer much better prepared for the challenges and uncertainties of 21st-century operations.

Regimental Headquarters

As elsewhere in the British Army LI Regimental Headquarters existed predominantly to provide the staff support to the Colonel of the Regiment to allow him to direct domestic regimental affairs, financial and benevolence policy, recruiting, to disseminate news and information, seek assistance and advice for the security of the Regiment, and collect and maintain historical records, artefacts and property for succeeding generations.

In the case of The Light Infantry, the Colonel of the Regiment remained as the key individual responsible for personal contact with the Colonel-in-Chief – formerly Her Majesty Queen Elizabeth, The Queen Mother, subsequently HRH The Princess Alexandra – and it has been to her that he addressed annually a 'state of the nation' Report. These responsibilities can perhaps more readily be expressed as the five 'Rs' – representation, recruiting, resettlement, retirement and research.

Few would doubt that the single most important task for any regiment, outside operations and training for them, is to recruit. The Light Infantry was, perhaps by virtue of its unique ancestry, consistently extraordinarily successful in this (where permitted by government) and not only managed largely to keep itself within reach of full strength but also to support others. But recruiting successfully could not have been achieved without representation in the communities from which we traditionally drew our soldiers and some of our officers, and back to which at the end of their service we returned them. It is here that the advantages of having a representative regimental office in each of the key counties in which our founding Regiments were based really came to the fore. The importance of this presence dramatically increased when the TA was reorganized in 1968. From the original Light Infantry Volunteers in which Major General Peter Bush established the individual companies in each of the counties, the expansion of our Territorial Battalions to four, based in Shrewsbury, Taunton, Durham and Wakefield, gave real visibility to the cap badge. Furthermore, the Battalion Headquarters of each took on many of the more public tasks in the communities and added a powerful arm to regimental advertising and recruiting. It was a major blow to the Regiment when these very well-recruited Reserve units were axed, to be replaced by Light Infantry Companies within multi-cap badge Regiments. With the best will in the world, and with only one or two regular staff, they simply did not have the capacity to support the same level of activity. Indeed the County Offices had to pick up much of the liaison and planning formerly done by a regular Commanding Officer and his battalion headquarters team. The importance of the County Offices therefore rose in direct comparison with their workload. They were staffed to the absolute minimum, were considered to be a seriously endangered species and their continued existence was a surprise to many.

Resettlement is a task for which there is a professional organization but there were always those who needed help outside the normal sphere and RHQ always encouraged

Left: Princess Alexandra compliments Martin Grubb.

Below: Presentation of Colours to the First Battalion at The Light Infantry Depot, Shrewsbury, 25 May 1972.

Opposite, top: Band training at Shrewsbury with the Kenya Rifles.

ALLIANCES

Canadian Armed Forces – The Royal Hamilton Light Infantry (Wentworth Regiment)

The Regiment originated on 11 Dec 1862 when 'The 13th Battalion Volunteer Militia (Infantry), Canada' was authorized to be formed from seven rifle companies. During the Fenian raids the 13th Battalion Volunteer Militia (Infantry) took part in the engagement at Ridgeway, 2 June 1866. Subsequently it provided volunteers for the Canadian contingents during the South African War, 1899–1902. It seved with distinction in both the First and Second World Wars.

Canadian Armed Forces – The North Saskatchewan Regiment

The Moose Mountain Scouts and the Battleford Infantry Company were raised for, and served during, the campaign in North West Canada, 1885. The modern Regiment originated on 3 July 1905 and incorporated the following regiments: The Battleford Light Infantry (L6th/22nd Saskatchewan Horse), The Prince Albert Volunteers, and The Saskatoon Light Infantry.

Canadian Armed Forces – Le Regiment de Maisonneuve

The Regiment originated on 4 June 1880 when the '85th Battalion of Infantry' was authorized to be formed from five independent infantry companies. It was redesignated '85th Regiment' on 8 May 1900 and then 'Le Regiment de Maisonneuve' on 1 April 1920. It seved with distinction in both the First and Second World Wars.

New Zealand Army – 2nd Battalion (Canterbury and Nelson Marlborough and West Coast) Royal New Zealand Infantry Regiment

The alliance between The Durham Light Infantry and 2nd Battalion RNZIR has always been fairly elastic owing to the distance involved. The association between the two Regiments was officially established in 1913 and since that date every opportunity has been taken to maintain contact.

Pakistan Army – 11th Battalion The Baluch Regiment

The alliance between the 11th Baluch and The Durham Light Infantry was achieved after the 1939–45 war, 11th Baluch and 1st Battalion The Durham Light Infantry having fought side by side in the same brigade throughout the Italian campaign.

Pakistan Army – 1st Battalion The Sind Regiment

In July 1962 the Adjutant-General wrote to all Colonels of Regiments asking them to accept alliances with the Pakistan Army. From a list supplied, General Goldsmith on behalf of The Somerset and Cornwall Light Infantry submitted three choices to the Adjutant-General, who allocated the 13th Baluch. Final approval by Her Majesty The Queen and the President of Pakistan was given in April 1966. Army Order 27 of 1966 published the authority. 13 Baluch were re-named as 1 SIND in 1980 as part of the ethnic reorganization of the Pakistan Army.

Kenya Army – 1st Battalion The Kenya Rifles

The Kenya Army was formed in 1963. The First Battalion, The Kenya Rifles was formed in 1964 and they invited Brigadier A J Hardy CBE, late KSLI (at that time Army Commander) to use his good offices to secure agreement from the Colonel of the Regiment (General Sir Geoffrey Musson) to an alliance between themselves and The King's Shropshire Light Infantry.

Mauritius – The Mauritius Special Mobile Force

In November 1970 an alliance between the Mauritius Special Mobile Force and The Light Infantry was approved. The alliance was requested by the Government of Mauritius in recognition of the services of the 1st Battalion The King's Shropshire Light Infantry whilst stationed there in 1968 for which they were awarded the Wilkinson Sword of Peace.

Australian Military Forces – Monash University Regiment

In September 1981 an alliance with the Monash University Regiment of the Australian Citizen Military Forces (Army Reserve) was approved. The alliance was requested by Brigadier I H Lowen OBE ED, Honorary Colonel, Monash University Regiment.

South African Defence Force – The Rand Light Infantry

The Rand Light Infantry originated shortly after the South African War when, on 1 October 1905, The Transvaal Cycle Corps was formed as a volunteer regiment after the British troops had sailed home. The RLI were allied to The Duke of Cornwall's Light Infantry in 1932. This alliance fell into abeyance during the period of secession and was resurrected in April 1995 with The Light Infantry.

BONDS OF FRIENDSHIP
HMS *Invincible*

An affiliation between The Light Infantry and HMS *Invincible* was approved by the Commander-in-Chief Fleet (Admiral Sir James Eberle KCB) on 18 December 1979. As formal affiliations between HM Ships and other branches of the British Forces are not now recognized, this is now termed a Bond of Friendship.

HMS *Cornwall*

An affiliation between The Light Infantry and HMS *Cornwall* was formalized in April 1988. Again this is now referred to as a Bond of Friendship.

TWINNING
Army of The Republic of France – 7th Bataillon Chasseurs d'Alpin

A 'Twinning' arrangement, to enhance co-operation with the French Army, was established in 1999 by MOD. Under this arrangement, The Light Infantry was 'twinned' with the 7th Bataillon Chasseurs d'Alpin based at Bourg St Maurice, Isère. Twinning activities are at the discretion of commanding officers. Twinning formally commenced on 1 June 1999.

soldiers on retirement to get in touch with their local County Office if in need of support. Retirement is not an easy business, particularly in a tight employment market, and 'family' contacts can sometimes make all the difference to an individual looking for work. Some of this support came, and still does come, from the Regimental Association. Whilst all the branches are autonomous, the coordination of their activities and the management of the overall finances is another responsibility of the County Secretaries as is the management of reunions, battlefield tours, and assistance with the maintenance of memorials, property and other inherited goods and chattels.

The distribution and management of benevolence, both to the serving and to the retired elements of the Regiment, added considerably to the workload throughout the life of The Light Infantry. The aim has always been to provide assistance at the point of need and within a short timeframe, ideally of five days. The County Offices were always instrumental in achieving this, through their contacts with the Association Branches and through the various support Charities such as SSAFA, ABF and RBL. The management of the finances and investments

Left: Lt Gen Sir Peter de la Billière.

Below left: The Queen's and Regimental Colours of The Light Infantry, 1971.

to support this aspect of regimental life and indeed all other demands on the funds rested with a Finance Committee whose decisions were implemented by the staff at RHQ. Much of the strong foundation of those investments was laid down in the early life of RHQ and the Regiment by Lieutenant Colonel Richard Osborne, and The Light Infantry owed much to his skill and perception in determining the policy.

A very considerable task was also achieved at this time, to wit the accumulation and cataloguing of all the property of the former regiments under one (written) archive and the centralization of its maintenance and insurance within RHQ. That archive has proved absolutely invaluable in tracking the whereabouts of individual items of silver, the phased repair and maintenance, as well as the history, of all of the silver bugles as well as the gallery of pictures. The Regiment owed what is probably the best record in the infantry of all its goods and chattels to one key individual, Major Ron Berry.

Finally, it was of course the task of the regional offices to oversee the management of the Regiment's history within the Museums, and to provide facilities for access to the archives. This was a never-ending and excessively time-consuming task for which the offices really were not equipped in terms of manpower. Much of the research is still carried out by volunteers or, in some cases, the archives have been handed over to the relevant County Council and its resources.

DEER STALKING IN THE REGIMENT

From 1981, members of the Regiment of all ranks converged annually on a number of deer forests in Scotland. For the first 21 years, Glens Lochay and Lyon were the focus of operations with John Sinclair, the head stalker in control. He once famously said 'I've never had a Brigadier and a Colonel as my ghillies before!'

Deer stalking in the highlands is essentially a cull of the surplus Red Deer, in wild, mountainous country, amidst superb scenery, sometimes in snow or heavy rain, using skills that are fundamental to an Infantryman – fieldcraft, use of ground and wind direction, concealment and accurate shooting, combined with a reasonable level of fitness; all with people you know and whose company you enjoy. It can be very exciting.

Over the years the party has been housed in a variety of large lodges and farm houses, we feed well and enjoy fine whisky and shot over 300 stags, a few hinds with over 45 first stags, not to forget a couple of salmon and a few trout and the occasional grouse and one year some grey partridge.

So many have stalked with us over the years – Tim Bevan, Gage Williams, Rupert Nicholas, Nick Gaskell, Peter Jackson, John Marsham, Mark Watts, Martin Smith and Jeremy Hooper, and of the younger generation Mark Adams, Ted Shields, Johnny Bowron, James de Labillière, Edward Hooper, Ben Dyer, Tome Hext to name but a few regulars and not forgetting the intrepid girls Penny Bevan, Nikki Gaskell and Susie de Labillière who have all shot stags.

In recent years and continuing to this day the exercise has continued to flourish. Mark Adams, having entertained members of the Edinburgh Battalion at Corrour, now has his own deer forest at Glasnock on Applecross, Tim Bevan and Nick Gaskell still mastermind a large party at Auchs and now Atholl, while Rupert Nicholas and Peter Jackson continue to stalk with John Sinclair in the Glens to the west of Killin.

Rupert Nicholas

Modern data management practices and in particular the digitization of records do allow far faster searching, but often there is no substitute to sitting down with the files and reading the original letters and texts. RHQ has digitized the whole of *The Silver Bugle* and this provides an excellent prime resource about people and places. Also recently completed has been the digitizing of the complete regimental photo archive. RHQ's file records have been transferred to Bodmin, with The Light Infantry Museum Collection, and the aim is to proceed with digitization and to employ an archivist/researcher there as funds permit. Access to these will eventually be available on the Web.

Over the past 20 years in particular, the Army has gone through a massive period of change in the way it does its business and the Regiment was not been immune to this. The reduction from the 1992 position of seven battalions, two regular, one TA Band, a Depot and a Headquarters Light Division, down to the 2007 strength of two regular battalions and two independently badged TA Companies was dramatic and vastly changed the role of RHQ. In many ways the loss of the Depot and all the coordinating functions that it carried out on behalf of the whole spectrum of regimental life was the most noticeable change. The Depot moved from what many still feel to be the spiritual home of The Light Infantry in Shrewsbury to the new Light Division Depot at Sir John Moore Barracks in Winchester, which was formally opened in 1986. Much effort was put into making this showpiece training establishment a real home for both The Light Infantry and The Royal Green Jackets. It also housed the RHQs for both Regiments. RHQ LI moved under the control of Lt Col Richard Osborne firstly to Peninsula Barracks and then to Sir John Moore Barracks in 1985. Co-location with the Depot, HQ Light Division and the main home base was obviously a sensible decision but it was with a considerable emotional wrench that we said goodbye as the home of RHQ to Copthorne Barracks. However, from the point of view of physical space, the new Sir John Moore Barracks was not an ideal location, and as accommodation suddenly became available in the recently refurbished Short Block at Peninsula Barracks both The Light Infantry and Green Jacket RHQs moved back into the centre of the city. The space made available by the move of the old RGJ Depot and Light Division Headquarters was also utilized for an expansion of the RGJ Museum and for the establishment of a new Light Infantry Museum, opened by HRH Princess Alexandra in 1991. The closure of all infantry divisional Headquarters to be replaced by a Lieutenant Colonel and a vestigial staff at Warminster, and the translation of regimental recruit training to Army Training Regiments, removed yet another important level of support to the battalions, to the Regimental Headquarters and indeed to the whole regimental system. Further coordination responsibilities devolved on to RHQ; the team, then consisting of three Retired Officers and two full-time clerical staff, found themselves moved very much further into the forefront of regimental life.

Support to all the pillars of the Regiment has been a sine qua non for everyone within the overall RHQ structure throughout the nearly 40-year life of The Light Infantry. The spectrum of work that has been covered is far too varied to

THE COLONEL-IN-CHIEF'S FUNERAL

Her Majesty Queen Elizabeth, The Queen Mother was a national treasure and our Colonel-in-Chief. When she died at a great age, sadness was accompanied by a genuine celebration of her long life. Her funeral ceremonial incorporated the Procession from St James's Palace to Westminster Hall for the Lying-in-State from Friday 5 April 2002 to Tuesday 9 April 2002, and the Procession to Westminster Abbey for the Funeral Service. The arrangements had been planned under the operational code name Taybridge. The details were kept on a strict need-to-know basis, with only the Colonel of the Regiment and Regimental Secretary in the knowledge. Colonels of Regiment to which Her Majesty was Colonel-in-Chief, and Royal Navy and Royal Air Force equivalents, were pall bearers. Also involved were Captain Adam Anderson, the bearer of HRH's Insignia and WO2 McBurney, LCpl Thompson and Pte Mawston as Escort Buglers. The two Buglers who sounded The Last Post and Reveille were Sjt Sullivan and Cpl Arnold. Huge crowds lined the streets for the Processions on Friday 5 April and Tuesday 9 April. In keeping with the occasion spring sunshine with just the lightest breeze made the silence of such large crowds very special and moving. The events were carried out with the precision that Her Majesty would have wanted. She too would have enjoyed some 'moments' in rehearsal which might be expected to accompany so many senior people gathered together. HRH the Duke of Edinburgh's eye for detail had many a senior officer tested on the correctness of his uniform. And the Garrison Sergeant Major putting the pall bearers through their paces with a spot of extra drill inside an empty Westminster Abbey at 6am on the Sunday morning was a sight to behold. The overriding impression was one of dignity, splendour and huge admiration for a much loved member of the Royal Family.

cover in an article such as this. The mantra was always one of providing the best possible service, with a personal and human face, from the somewhat limited resources, and indeed this responsibility continues with a massive volunteer effort across all our Counties, which is coordinated and directed from The Light Infantry Committee, currently under the leadership of Lieutenant General Robin Brims.

Royal Colonels-in-Chief

In 1927 King George V appointed the Duchess of York, the wife of his second son, to be the Colonel-in-Chief of The King's Own Yorkshire Light Infantry (KOYLI). So commenced a link with The Light Infantry which was to endure for 75 years until her death in 2002. In 1927 there was no hint that through the hand of fate she would become the future Queen of England during one of the most dangerous periods of British history, or that her steely determination and innate ability to mix with

everyone would make such an important and inspirational contribution to the maintenance of the morale of the British people during World War II. After the untimely death of her husband King George VI in 1952, when she was only 51, she maintained, as the 'Queen Mother', a remarkable position in the Royal Family and the country for a further 50 years and was perceived by many as the rock around which a turbulent sea of social and cultural change flowed in the second half of 20th-century Britain.

Deeply admired and much loved, Queen Elizabeth, The Queen Mother, was the unanimous choice of all the Regimental Colonels of the forming regiments to be Colonel-in-Chief of The Light Infantry. The new regiment was twice blessed when HRH Princess Alexandra accepted the invitation to become Deputy Colonel-in Chief of the new regiment. Thus, from the outset, The Light Infantry had at the head of the 'family', two people who had a long association with

Below: The Lucknow Tureen and its mutineers' musket ball. The Tureen (in its packing case!) formed part of the barricade put up to defend the Lucknow Residency during the Indian Mutiny. The ball is perhaps evidence that Regimental silver plays more than just a ceremonial part in a regiment's life. In memory of the action the Tureen and its musket ball have been preserved unrepaired.

Above: HRH Princess Alexandra discusses the exhibits with Col Richard Cousens, Chairman of the LI Museum Trustees and Lt Col Mike Rescorle.

THE LIGHT INFANTRY COMMITTEE

When The Rifles formed, The Light Infantry Council handed over their responsibilities to The Rifles Council. At the same time a new committee was created: The Light Infantry Committee. It is charged with looking after the reputation and heritage of The Light Infantry. Most important among this is the need to look after the interests of Light Infantrymen.

The Committee has organized itself to attend to The Light Infantry Association and related Reunion events; The Light Infantry Club; and specific projects, one project being the production of this book led by Colonel Mark Goldsack and his sub-committee of helping hands. Indeed the formation of sub-committees is the way that projects are developed and implemented. The creation of a Light Infantry memorial at the National Arboretum is another example.

The Committee will represent issues as necessary to The Rifles. Whilst having no formal responsibilities to the former Light Infantry regiments it will represent their views if their Trustees so wish.

The funds of The Light Infantry were handed over to The Rifles who inherit the benevolence responsibility. Some £200,000 has been ring-fenced to enable the Committee to organize the Annual Reunion weekend. Currently this weekend is run by a sub-committee led by Lieutenant Colonel Ron Bevan and is proving to be very popular and well attended. Significant additional funding is provided by a draw initially launched and run by Doc Halliday from Telford.

It is hoped that many Light Infantrymen will wish to be involved with these activities for many years to come. It is good to gather, reflect on shared experiences, remember the fallen and celebrate good fortune. Equally through such gatherings we should be able to identify those less fortunate who might need help. Helping each other was, and is, at the core of The Light Infantry values.

Robin Brims

former light infantry regiments, who took a deep interest in our affairs and who possessed a great sense of duty, natural dignity, enormous charm and a wonderful sense of fun. In consequence, every visit undertaken by our Royal Colonels became relaxed family occasions, which were always memorable for those involved.

The Royal Colonels shared their responsibilities and a pattern of events involving them became a regular feature in the regimental calendar. They were assiduous in keeping themselves well informed about the affairs of the regiment; receiving and commenting constructively on annual reports, giving audiences to successive Colonels of the Regiment and all Commanding Officers on assuming and relinquishing command. The Light Infantry spanned the history of the most recent troubles in Northern Ireland and visits to the families during periods of separation gave tremendous moral support and they consistently showed compassion and concern when casualties were incurred.

The range of events and visits undertaken by the Royal Colonels was both varied and extensive, ranging from Presentation of Colours in 1971 and 1991, taking Royal Salutes at Retreats on Horse Guards Parade, attending receptions and luncheons in London, visiting the Training Depots at Shrewsbury and Winchester and annual visits to Regular or Territorial battalions in the UK or abroad. Queen Elizabeth always portrayed a happy and mischievous spirit and thrived on the unexpected. On a visit to the 3rd Battalion in 1983 at Tidworth she was delighted, in the days before the now ubiquitous mobile telephone, to hold a surprise radio conversation with her housekeeper at the Castle of Mey arranged 'by kind permission' of the Signals Platoon. In 2007 The Light Infantry became one of the forming regiments of The Rifles and it was both reassuring and appropriate, in the interests of continuity, that Princess Alexandra accepted the invitation to become The Royal Colonel of 3rd Battalion The Rifles, an erstwhile battalion of Light Infantry. In our Royal Colonels-in-Chief The Light Infantry was indeed 'Exceedingly Lucky'.

THE FAMILIES

The support of one's family (given and taken) is a fundamental part of Regimental life. In acknowledging the essential contribution made by the families a vignette from the 2LI tour in Bosnia illustrates the symbiotic relationship perfectly.

The Families Officer, Captain Mick Garner, and his team were co-ordinators, trouble-shooters and my representatives in Paderborn. Whenever our tenuous communications allowed, Mick had a daily dialogue with the adjutant and many prospective welfare problems were nipped in the bud.

Many families went back to England for a period, particularly at Christmas, but most had school-age children and spent the majority of their time in Germany. At times mail was very slow and telephone calls home were difficult or impossible to arrange. Mick described the work of Rear Party in the *Silver Bugle*:

'Rear Party is actually a six-month tour in itself. Day to day administration continued. All those people arriving back from posting or going on posting from Bosnia staged through Paderborn. People were discharged and new recruits were inducted and prepared to go straight out.

Sunday lunches were held twice a month, quiz nights were run, trips were organised and at times the Rear Party staff felt like a travel agent organising travel to and from the UK for families and their relatives. Throughout the tour the wives ran a coffee shop each morning which became a focal point for all those left behind in Paderborn. Families were kept in touch with the situation through a Bosnia

Information Board. The wives also collected clothes for Bosnian children and at Christmas raised over DM700 carol singing for an orphanage in Banja Luka. Needless to say there were rumours and most of them were corrected through this forum. Sheets of paper were put up on notice boards for wives to write messages to their husbands. Some of these were very subtle and cryptic; others were not and were definitely risqué. They were a real boost to morale at both ends of the system.

It is not a glamorous job to stay behind whilst the majority of the battalion is making modern European history, implementing the peace in a war-torn country. But somebody has to do it.'

Brigadier Ben Barry

From *A Cold War: Front Line Operations in Bosnia 1995–1996*
(Stroud, 2008)

Opposite: A sporting scrapbook from The Light Infantry's back pages.

Above: The Colonel-in-Chief, HRH Princess Alexandra, with Diane Turner during a visit to Paderborn.

Left: The Wives Club enjoys some Heavy Metal.

The Bands and Bugles

During the life of The Light Infantry some fundamental changes to the relationship between battalions and their respective musical heritages occurred. In 1968 the importance of military music as part of the regimental glue that holds a unit together and deliverers combined military effect on a wider basis was undisputed. The result was that each battalion had its own Band which lived and played alongside it. Over time however resource constraints reduced this scaling progressively to the point at which on becoming The Rifles the entire regiment shared The Band of The Light Division with The Royal Green Jackets.

1st Battalion, The Light Infantry

The Vesting Parade to celebrate the birth of the new Regiment was held by the 1st Battalion at Gravesend on 6 July 1968. The Band continued mostly unaffected by the change. In its ranks was David Marshall, who had enlisted in 1960 and who left in the early 1970s to attend the bandmasters' course at Kneller Hall; in his final year there he won a total of eight prizes including the medal for best all-round student, a haul that indicated the great future that awaited him, first at the Worcester & Sherwood Foresters and then in the Coldstream Guards.

The last Bandmaster in the history of what had been The Somerset and Cornwall Light Infantry was Mr K W Napier, appointed in 1974. Under his baton the Band played at such major events as the massed bands display for the Armex '75 show in Harrogate, the Hong Kong Silver Jubilee celebrations in 1977 with the Brigade of Gurkhas and the Hong Kong Police Band, and a one-day Services Spectacular at Wilton House, Salisbury in 1978. In 1984 the Regiment decided that rather than have three small battalion bands each of 21, it would prefer two larger bands each of 35. The Corunna and Salamanca Bands thus came into being.

2nd Battalion, The Light Infantry

In July 1968 what had now become the Band of the 2nd Light Infantry staged a floodlit pageant in Berlin, in which the histories of the four constituent parts of the new Regiment were depicted and the four regimental marches performed. The following year, Mr M Cadwallader was appointed Bandmaster, a post he held until the arrival of John Simmonds in 1974. The strength of the Band in this period can be judged from

the fact that by 1982 there were three student bandmasters at Kneller Hall from the Battalion, together with five pupils; of the former, Tex Carlton went on to become Bandmaster of the Black Watch, and Bob Hatton that of the 15th/19th Hussars.

In 1981 Mr Simmonds took a regimental commission and was succeeded by A S 'Jack' Leeming, a former bandsman of the Yorkshire Light Infantry who had gone on to become Bandmaster of the 3rd Green Jackets. He in turn was followed by Bandmaster D Burton. When The Light Infantry decided to form two bands instead of three, Mr Burton became Bandmaster of the new Salamanca Band.

3rd Battalion, The Light Infantry

Stuart James had been appointed Bandmaster of the Shropshire Light Infantry in 1967, and it was under his baton that the Band beat retreat in Terendak in July 1968 to herald the new incarnation of the Regiment. As a student at Kneller Hall, Mr James had been School Band Serjeant Major and it was thus entirely appropriate that his first role when he left the 3rd Light Infantry in 1974 should be to return as School Bandmaster.

Left: The bugles of 1LI.

Opposite: *Bugle Major Ingram.*

LIGHT INFANTRY BANDMASTERS 1968–94

1LI	1968–74	WO1 (BM) Slater E
	1974–84	WO1 (BM) Napier K
2LI	1968–9	WO1 (BM) Offard J
	1969–74	WO1 (BM) Cadwallader M
	1974–80	WO1 (BM) Simmonds J
	1980–3	WO1 (BM) Leeming AS
	1983–5	WO1 (BM) Burton D
3LI	1968	WO1 (BM) Ridings RA
	1968–74	WO1 (BM) James S
	1974–81	WO1 (BM) Evans M
	1981–4	WO1 (BM) Lever M
4LI	1968–9	WO1 (BM) Berry R

The Light Infantry Salamanca Band

1985–91	WO1 (BM) Burton D
1991–4	WO1 (BM) Taylor M

The Light Infantry Corunna Band

1985–90	WO1 (BM) Lever M
1990–4	WO1 (BM) Keeley E

The Band and Bugles of The Light Division

	Directors of Music	Bandmasters
1994–7	Capt R Owen	WO1 (BM) Keeley E
1997–2000	Capt G O Jones	WO1 (BM) Knox A
2000–3	Capt C G Gray	WO1 (BM) Norley P
2003–5	Capt C G Gray	WO1 (BM) Barringer D
2005–7	Maj C G Gray	WO1 (BM) Mathews J

The Band and Bugles of The Rifles

2007	Maj C G Gray	WO1 (BM) Mathews J
2007–10	Capt M D Purvey	WO1 (BM) Kingston A

The Light Division SOUNDING RETREAT HORSE GUARDS PARADE at 6.30 pm 12th, 13th and 14th JUNE 1979

Below: The Massed Bands on Horse Guards.

His replacement was Michael Evans, who was to take the Band through the next seven years, until he was succeeded by Bandmaster Michael Lever. Amongst the latter's tasks was the welcoming of ships back from the Falklands in 1982, including the frigate *Brilliant*. In 1984 Mr Lever took over the newly formed Corunna Band.

4th Battalion, The Light Infantry

In July 1968 what had become the Band of the 4th Battalion of The Light Infantry was stationed in Cyprus. It was here that a parade was staged to herald the DLI's absorption into The Light Infantry; under the direction of the Bandmaster Ron Berry the Band played the regimental marches of the four constituent regiments.

The incarnation as the 4th Battalion, Light Infantry was to be very short lived. Within the year the battalion had been disbanded and the traditions of the 68th and 106th Foot were passed to The Light Infantry.

The Corunna Band

Bandmaster Lever, formerly of the 3rd Battalion, was succeeded in 1990 by Ed Keeley. That same year the Band participated in perhaps the biggest-ever engagement of any Light Infantry band: a performance of Roger Waters' work *The Wall*, staged in Berlin and attracting a television audience estimated at millions of people. As the transformation of Germany continued, the Corunna Band also made an exchange visit with a Red Army Band in the East, where it was presented with a brass T62 Soviet tank and played in Karl Marx Platz for the unification ceremony.

The Corunna Band left Berlin in 1990 and joined 3LI in Paderborn where further overseas bookings saw the Band spend six days in Poland in 1991, a visit centred on the Krakow Music Festival, and an excursion to Canada for the 125th Nova Scotia International Tattoo the following year. In 1993 the Division staged its last Sounding Retreat parade on Horse Guards, and the next year the Band relocated to Winchester and took part in the Royal Tournament which witnessed the last-ever performance by the four Bands of the Light Division, before they were merged to form the new Band demanded under 'Options for Change'.

The Salamanca Band

Bandmaster Burton moved from the 2nd Battalion to lead the new Band, and spent the next four and a half years based in Germany. It played every year at the Corps Commander's concert in Sonthofen, appeared at the Halle Munsterland massed bands show, and made visits to Belgium and Holland.

Returning to England in 1989, the Salamanca Band found itself deploying on Operation GRANBY. The Band was attached to 24 (Airmobile) Field ambulance from Sept 1990 until March 1991. Three musicians were awarded Mentioned In Dispatches: Bandsmen Bennett, Lawson and Mair. After Operation GRANBY the Band was busily engaged on regimental duties but also played for such events as the Liberation Parade in Guernsey in 1992. The same year it played in the Massed Bands and Bugles of the Light Division, sounding Retreat at the historic depot in Winchester, before the depot was transformed into the Army Training Regiment, Winchester.

The Band took part in the historic Sounding of Retreat on Horse Guards Parade in 1993 and with the Corunna Band and 2RGJ Bands paraded for the last time at the Royal Tournament, marching off from the final performance at 220 paces per minute.

Senior Bugle Majors

Traditionally the position of Senior Bugle Major was a Divisional post and was located with the Depot Buglers in Shrewsbury and Winchester. He would take the lead on all Massed Bands and Bugles events and was the subject matter expert on all things ceremonial. When the Light Division Depot closed and transformed into the Army Training Regiment Winchester, the training of Buglers moved to ITC Houston as part of the Army School of Ceremonial. It was not until the formation of the Light Division Band in 1994 that the position was formally established. The Massed

SENIOR BUGLE MAJORS	
1972–74	B/Maj Jock Kent
1974–81	B/Maj Jones, 1LI
1981–83	B/Maj Wilkinson S, 1LI
1983–85	B/Maj Ingram T, 3LI
1985–87	WO2 (B/Maj) Bygraves, 3LI
1987–88	Sjt (B/Maj) Thornton S, 2LI
1988–90	WO2 (B/Maj) Wilkinson T, 1LI
1990–92	WO2 (B/Maj) Ingram T, 3LI
1992–93	WO2 (B/Maj) Plumridge J, 1LI
1993–94	WO2 (B/Maj) Holman B, 3LI
1994–94	WO2 (B/Maj) Green C, BEM, 7LI (Royal Tournament)
1994–96	CSjt (B/Maj) Wells A, 1LI
1996–99	CSjt (B/Maj) Goodwin G, 2RGJ
1999–2002	WO2 (B/Maj) Wells A, 1LI
2002–4	CSjt (B/Maj) McLeod V, 1RGJ
2004–6	CSjt (B/Maj) Morris J, 2LI
2006–7	CSjt (B/Maj) Flavin SP, 2LI

Below left: The Light Infantry Salamanca Band and the RGJ Normandy Band prepare to play carols in Winchester Cathedral. The Bandmasters are Mark Taylor (LI) and Ian MaGilligot (RGJ).

Bands and Bugles paraded for the last time at the Royal Tournament in July 1994 and were led by Bugle Major CM (Nosher) Green. This was to be his last parade after 37 years service and was very nearly his last moment! On 30 July 1994, in front of the Queen, he led the Massed Bands and Bugles out of the arena to 'Black Bear'. Speeding up to 220 paces to the minute, he brought the audience to its feet and himself almost to his knees! It is said that he was still out

t453 of 196

of breath when he was presented to HM The Queen some time after the performance.

The Band of The Light Division was based at the Army Training Regiment Winchester and, as all Buglers were located with the Battalions, The Light Division Bugle Platoon was formed. The Senior Bugle Major was appointed by selecting the highest ranking Bugle Major in the Division, usually CSjt-WO2. Four Buglers from each of the four regular Battalions were attached to the Band under the command of the Senior Bugle Major. The platoon not only provided musical support but offered the Band the capability to conduct military training by providing instructors. The Bugle Platoon would also provide force protection when the Band and Bugles visited any Operational Theatres such as Northern Ireland, Bosnia, Kosovo and Op Telic. The strength of Light Infantry Bugling is demonstrated by the number of Light Infantry Senior Bugle Majors selected over the Years.

Above: The Salamanca Band on Op GRANBY, 1991.

THE 1994 ROYAL TOURNAMENT

The 1994 Royal Tournament was a highly anticipated event because sadly we all knew it was to be the last appearance of the Massed Bands and Bugles of The Light Division. It was also the last parade for WO2 (B/Maj) Nosher Green as he was retiring after 37 years' service. So it was with a buzz of excitement that the Massed Bands and Bugles descended on Sir John Moore Barracks in Winchester for rehearsals. By the end of a week of hard graft on the square a worthy display had been constructed which included all the tunes synonymous with The Light Division and of course, the debut of 'Zorba The Greek'. As we departed for London we passed the landlords of the India Arms and the Baker's Arms rubbing their hands in glee as they counted the week's takings!

We arrived at Earls Court to find that the Bands had bagged accommodation in Hounslow, leaving the Bugles to slum it in the mini garrison that had been created inside the Earls Court exhibition hall. Determined to make the most of it, the Buglers of The Light Division cracked on and set up home in the warren of 20-man rooms that had been carefully constructed by that age-old method of banging up a flimsy wooden frame and sticking a bit of cardboard over the hole.

Earls Court itself had no showers, so a field shower unit was constructed and a rota produced. Using their typical initiative, though, the Light Division Buglers found some sinks that were well hidden by a rear exit of the complex. After each performance the race was on to get out of uniform and sprint to the sinks for a 'birdbath' with the intention of getting down to the bar before the rest of the performers. Unfortunately on the night of the Royal performance the ritual sprint coincided with HM The Queen leaving Earls Court via the same exit. Consummate professionals, the Light Division Buglers instantly lined up smartly to attention, with their towels held to cover their dignity. A very bemused Queen was left wondering if the looming defence cuts had already had an impact on the dress of her usual Guard of Honour! Needless to say from that point birdbaths were forbidden until all VIPs had left the venue!

To pass the time the RGJ Buglers soon acquired a small TV and as there was no TV signal, videos of Sharpe's Rifles were constantly showing. One night, returning from the basement bar, LCpl Shitty Brown and Bgr Greg Meadham needed to relieve themselves and to save the long walk to the toilets they found a lone portacabin to go behind. As they both looked up mid-flow they found themselves looking right into the eyes of the Duty Policeman sat behind his desk in what they then recognized as the Joint Service Police Station! Their collars were felt and the RMP soon realised they were dealing with someone special when the Buglers gave their names as Richard Sharpe and Obadiah Hakeswell. They were duly returned to their accommodation in Cardboard City and put to bed, but the next day the message came over the Earls Court intercom: 'Richard Sharpe and Obadiah Hakeswell are to report to the show RSM immediately'. This left most people confused but LCpl Brown and Bgr Meadham immediately doubled off to the RSM's cardboard office and could be seen shovelling horseshit from the Arena for the rest of the morning!

The 1994 Royal Tournament was a great success and it was the performance by the Massed Bands and Bugles of The Light Division which stole the show. The introduction of 'Zorba The Greek' caught the audience's imagination to such an extent that for the first time in the Tournament's history an encore was demanded every night.

Bugle Major Steve Flavin

The Regiment's Cadets

The third pillar of the Regiment could be said to be its cadets, the affiliated ACF detachments and CCF contingents, many having been formed over a century ago. In numerical terms they were probably the largest pillar, there being in recent times nearly five thousand cadets, all proudly wearing the Regiment's badge, in some one hundred and fifteen ACF detachments and twenty CCF school contingents, spread throughout its Counties from Penzance in the South West to South Shields in the North East.

During their time as cadets they would have trained under their officers and NCOs at least once a week, have attended weekend and annual camps on a military training area, visited the regular Battalions and taken part in a whole range of activities such as fieldcraft, first aid, shooting, adventure training, various sports and military music. They may have attended leadership courses at the Cadet Training Centre at Frimley Park, have participated in competitive shooting at Bisley, have been on an Exchange Visit to Canada or India or on a challenging overseas expedition to such places as the Himalayas, climbing to heights of 22,000 ft, or camped amongst lions and leopards on safari in Botswana, or have been rafting in South America, and on their return given a presentation to The Royal Geographical Society in London covering their experiences.

A fair number of these cadets enlisted to serve in the Regiment. They proved of immense value, having been nurtured in the Regimental ethos, and as a consequence of their commitment, physical fitness, and the many skills they had acquired as cadets. Some were decorated for gallantry, others achieved significant advancement in rank, to RSM and even to Colonel of the Regiment, like General Sir John Deverell, in retirement the current President of the ACFA.

With the constant reductions in the Regiment's Territorial battalions so the cadets, in particular the Army cadets, came to play an increasingly important role in representing the Regiment within their local community. Participating at local civic and Regimental occasions, parading and marching through their cities, towns and villages on Armistice Sunday, featuring in the local press on account of some achievement, raising funds for SSAFA and other causes, in attendance as a Lord Lieutenant's Cadet on Royal and other occasions, all helped

Above: Nothing like a lorry-load of smiling faces and the end of a day's activities!

Left: Confidence building on the assault course.

ACF AND CCF UNITS

Army Cadet Forces
City and County of Bristol
Army Cadet Force
Cleveland Army Cadet Force
Durham Cadet Battalion
Humberside & South Yorkshire
Army Cadet Force (Doncaster Det)
Shropshire Army Cadet Force
The Cornwall Cadet Battalion
The Hereford Cadet Battalion
The Royal Alderney Militia
The Somerset Cadet Battalion
Yorkshire Cadet Battalion

Combined Cadet Forces
Adams Grammar School, Newport
Barnard Castle School, Barnard Castle
Batley Grammar School, Batley

Clifton College, Bristol
Downside School, Somerset
Durham School, Durham
Ellesmere College, Ellesmere
Herefordshire Cathedral School,
  Hereford
King Edward's School, Bath
King's College, Taunton
Malvern College
Monkton Combe School, Nr Bath
Prior Park College, Bath
Rivington School
Shrewsbury School, Shrewsbury
Taunton School, Taunton
Wellington School
Wells Cathedral School, Wells
Wrekin College, Telford
Writhlington School, Radstock

Right and far right: Canoeing and climbing lie at the heart of the cadet adventure training syllabus and provide invaluable development skills.

to connect localities and their people with the Regiment. And there were two other important, additional ways in which this was achieved. First, through the ACFA Outreach programme through which the County Cadet Forces engaged with other young people within their communities who were experiencing difficulties in their lives, making their facilities and resources available, providing leadership, and using senior cadets as mentors and role models. Not only did this provide precisely the training, discipline, fun and confidence building such youngsters benifited from but it strengthened the Regiment's and Army's contacts and image with those schools and local institutions being supported. Secondly, with the Regiment reduced to a single Band the cadet Bands and Bugles, noticeably in Somerset and Durham, came to the fore, providing music not just for local military orientated occasions but in entertaining school audiences and the general public with various performances, concerts, and Sounding Retreat.

The standards attained by these Bands and Bugles, particularly the Borneo Band and Bugles of Durham ACF, which was acclaimed the best in the land, was such that they virtually matched their counterparts in the Regular Army and were hugely appreciated and applauded wherever they went.

The Regiment had every reason to be exceptionally proud of the youngsters privileged to wear its badge, and grateful to them too for the contribution they made to its reputation and well-being.

141

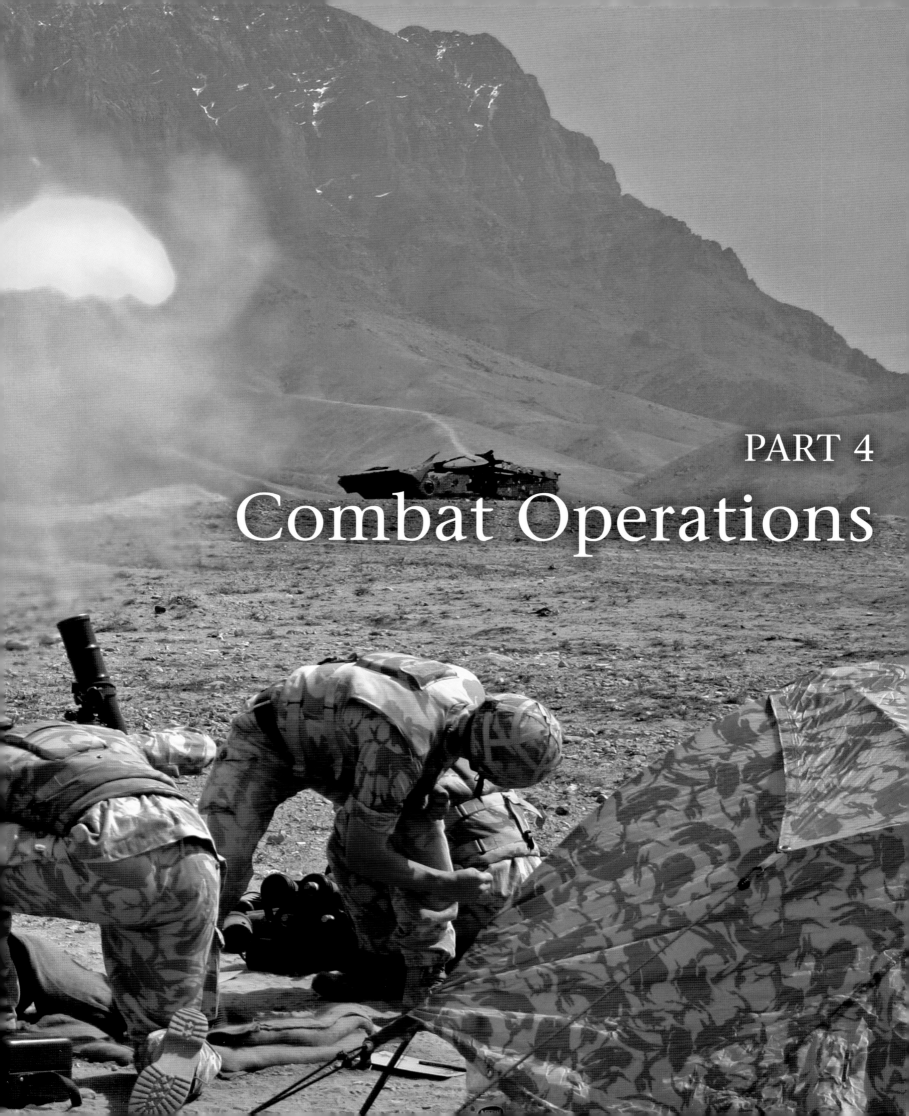

PART 4
Combat Operations

Mauritius

The emergency deployment of elements of 1 KSLI to Mauritius on 22 January 1968 took place five months before Vesting Day and it was a further four months until all the companies of 3LI were to return to Malaysia. Thus the final operational commitment of 1 KSLI became the first such experience for 3LI.

There is no doubt that this operation taught those involved, in the initial stages, some valuable lessons concerning the importance of low-level command and control, initiative by junior NCOs, the importance of close liaison with police and the handling of large crowds with minimal force, all of which were to prove of relevance in Northern Ireland the following year. It is perhaps more than a coincidence that the three NCOs from 3LI who subsequently gained gallantry awards in Ulster all served with the leading company sent to Mauritius (Cpl Bradley DCM, Pte Czepukojc QGM, Pte James GM).

The *Times* described the deployment from Malaysia to Mauritius as 'the swiftest service mobilization in British experience'. 1 KSLI was not the Far East Spearhead battalion, or on any form of operational warning, indeed it was awaiting the arrival of Lt General Sir Geoffrey Musson, Colonel of the Regiment, on an official visit. The officers and their wives were preparing for a formal dinner when a phone call from Major Peter Sibbald, then GOS 2 Ops at HQ FARELF, was picked up on the Officers' Mess telephone at 1750 by Major Brian Lowe who as PMC was checking the arrangements for dinner. The message was a friendly warning that 1 KSLI might be getting orders to deploy a company very shortly. The CO, who was watching a hockey match was alerted and he instructed Brian Lowe to get his company together. At 1810 the official order from HQ FARELF came through, ordering a company to move to Singapore in four hours' time for emplacement for Mauritius.

By 0430 the next day B Company had collected their married men from Tampin 17 miles away and the bachelors who were spread all over the brigade camp and had packed up and moved 150 miles to RAF Changi in Singapore. Ammunition, IS equipment and baggage were loaded onto two C 130 Hercules aircraft. The first aircraft took off at 0700 and landed at Mauritius some 12 hours later; a second Hercules with the balance of the company landed 30 minutes later and a third with two Sioux of the Battalion's Air Platoon on board arrived 48 hours later.

On arrival in Mauritius some 24 hours after being stood to, the company were met by the Commissioner of Police (Bernard

Above: On patrol in Port Louis.

McCaffrey), Sandy Ward, the CO of the Special Mobile Force – the locally recruited paramilitary riot police, together with an assorted collection of Land Rovers and lorries drawn from the Water Board and Police which were to be the sole means of mobility for the company.

A quick briefing by Kevin Rooney, the charming Military Intelligence Officer who had accepted a posting to Mauritius on the assumption that nothing untoward was ever likely to happen there, gave an update on violence in the capital and the Police Commissioner made it clear that B Company backed by the SMF was to restore order as quickly as possible to enable the police to resume their proper duties.

With a force of only 142 all ranks to bring an end to violence in Port Louis, a city of over 150,000, it was imperative that the troops acted swiftly and firmly to stamp out racial attacks and intimidation. Major Lowe decided that by mounting the maximum possible number of mobile patrols in the Muslim and Creole areas he would create the illusion that his force was much bigger than it was in reality. This tactic had the added advantage that all ranks got to know the layout of the city quickly. After driving in convoy to Port Louis the company left two platoons to unload stores and to make a barrack block in the

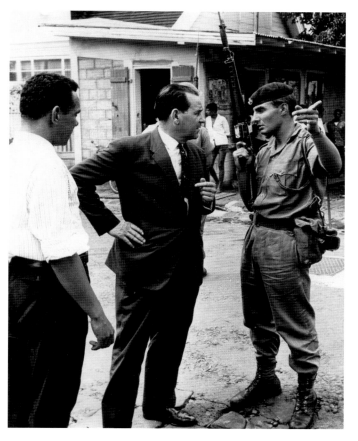

Right: Briefing the Governor.

PARLEZ VOUS FRANCAIS?

Mauritius is a largely French-speaking island and so we faced a few problems teaching the soldiers some basic phrases. 'I am an English soldier' – *Je suis soldat Anglais* – was rapidly mastered until a night patrol led by young Robinson was challenged by a Mauritian policeman. Robinson replied in perfect French, albeit with a Geordie accent, and was promptly shot in the leg, the policeman arguing that he could not be English; he spoke in French! 'Stop or I fire' was a touch more difficult, but 'Harriet Harriet who shit here' seemed to work quite well!

Police Headquarters at Line Barracks, constructed by Napoleon Bonaparte for his garrison in the 1790s and not noticeably updated since, into the company base. The remaining three platoons were dispatched to patrol an area of the city.

The fact that French was the common language in Mauritius presented the company with a problem from the outset. As

OPERATIONAL OVERVIEW

Mauritius is a substantial island of nearly 800 square miles, some 500 miles east of Madagascar in the Indian Ocean. Formerly a Dutch, then a French colony on the sea route to the East, it became a British colony during the Napoleonic wars. By the 1960s the population of mixed races was just under one million. The island was due to achieve independence within the Commonwealth in March 1968.

In January 1968, however, hatred between Muslim and Creole gangs flared into serious sectarian violence. More than 20 people were murdered and about 1,000 people, fearing for their lives, fled from their homes. On Monday 22 January, the British Governor, Sir John Rennie, requested military assistance. With the assistance of 3LI, all was calm by Independence Day on 12 March.

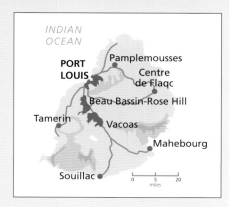

most soldiers had only a sketchy idea of English grammar there was little prospect of them all mastering basic French. A simple phonetic system was adopted for the less gifted linguistically. Thus the caution 'Arretez! Arretez! ou je tire un coup de fusil' became 'Harriet! Harriet! who shit here!' Captain Jeremy York, who spoke fluent French, and Major Lowe, who had been attached to the French Army in Madagascar, dealt with more complicated instructions to the locals.

Once B Company had made its presence felt in the city by removing roadblocks and driving crowds off the streets, the gangs adopted a lower profile and contented themselves with opportunist looting and arson. In order to deprive both sides of their weaponry a number of cordon-and-search operations were conducted. The first cordon was to isolate Plein Verte, a Muslim residential area. The plan was to surround the rectangular area quickly to prevent any gang leaders getting away, thus the cordon was inserted from all cardinal points simultaneously. One platoon was assigned to each side of the area to be sealed. Platoon commanders carefully studied the routes they were required to take to their positions, noting the French names of all the streets they would traverse. On the order to deploy the platoons sped off but to their horror discovered that ten days earlier all street signs in the Muslim area had been replaced with ones written in Arabic. Notwithstanding, the cordon was in place exactly as planned and a large quantity of crudely fashioned weapons, acid bombs and Molotov cocktails recovered.

To combat arson and looting at night time, a curfew was introduced, in which the two Sioux helicopters played a major role, spotting fires and directing patrols to arrest those seen running away from the scene.

Despite patrols being seriously outnumbered, a number of unruly mobs were speeded on their way with wooden baton rounds or tear gas. No serious casualties were suffered save for 2/Lt Bill Barneby shot by a SMF sentry who could not believe that an Englishman could have responded to his challenge in such excellent French. Happily his injuries were not severe.

The pressure of operations had its effect. Terrorists never knew where they were going to be hit next and many concluded that a helicopter overhead could spot every move below. The last and most successful operation followed the abduction of a 17-year-old Muslim girl by Creoles. An informant told the Police that the girl could be found by the Latanière Bridge over the dried-up bed of the Latanière river which marked the boundary between the Muslim and Creole areas of the city. Sjt Mick Kemp was dispatched with a Land Rover patrol to investigate and discovered the naked girl bound with barbed wire beneath the bridge. By this time a crowd of Muslims had formed at one end of the bridge with an antagonistic group of Creoles at the other. Sjt Kemp appreciated that the Muslims would become incensed if they discovered the condition of the girl. Parking his vehicle to block the centre of the bridge, he posted two soldiers at either end of the bridge to keep the rapidly growing crowd of spectators apart and radioed Company HQ for orders. By this time it was growing dark, which afforded an opportunity to evacuate the girl without the Muslims becoming aware that the girl was under the bridge, as her presence would certainly have given rise to a major riot which would have overwhelmed Sjt Kemp's patrol. The crowds at each end of the bridge had grown to several hundred and were taunting each other, making reinforcement of the patrol virtually impossible. It was decided to send two patrols to another bridge 200 yards upstream, from which they could move along the boulder-strewn river bed with a stretcher to recover the girl out of view of both Muslims and Creoles. No lights were to be used, and as soon as the girl was evacuated to the upstream bridge a helicopter would fly in to whisk her off to hospital. The operation went without a hitch and much credit is due to Sjt Kemp for his coolness in a very dodgy situation.

By the end of February the police were able to resume normal duties in Port Louis although B Company remained very much in evidence to reassure the population and deter any attempt to undermine the Independence ceremony on 12 March for which two platoons formed a Guard of Honour with the Special Mobile Force. Two days later B Company was relieved by C Company and the Bugle Platoon and returned to Malaysia.

Apart from continuing to ensure that Port Louis remained quiet, subsequent operations placed emphasis on cooperation with the police and SMF in countering the drug trade.

A RAID – WRONG DOOR, SIR!

A drugs raid in support of the police on an illegal hilltop night club/brothel was planned. Starting off before dawn the force climbed the hill and, on arrival, the Commander confidently strode forward to the obvious entry point only to find it locked. A young bugler tapped him on the shoulder: 'Wrong door sir!' and led him to a much less obvious, but open door! Quite evident where the buglers spent their R&R! As the raid went in, rumour has it that the size of the dance band doubled as some very English-looking musicians took up instruments and played on with great gusto. The night club was out of bounds to the British military!

Gandhia, the local cannabis, was widely grown in clearings created in the middle of sugar fields. The Sioux helicopters could readily spot the Gandhia plots from the air and direct troops to the right spot to destroy the plants. Similar raids took place to detect illicit rum stills as the steam rising from the stills could be easily spotted from the air.

The final stages of military activity in Mauritius was in the field of hearts and minds where the platoons of B Company had started to assist in refurbishing part of a Cheshire Home; sponsoring an old people's home and running an Outward Bound camp for teenagers. Meanwhile the Air Platoon, while evacuating the Muslim girl, had discovered a blind boy in a cage at a missionary outpost adjacent to the helicopter landing site. They were so appalled by the boy's situation that they raised the funds to send him to South Africa for a successful operation to restore his sight. These activities resulted in 3LI being awarded The Wilkinson Sword of Peace in July 1969 eight months after the withdrawal to Malaysia.

A GANDHIA TRIP

An operation to find and destroy 'Gandhia' (a narcotic drug, marijuana) grown illegally in the hills, started by locating the growing plot from the air using the Sioux helicopter, which then 'talked in' a patrol on the ground. Once the patrol arrived on site, the plants were cut down, piled up and set on fire. On one occasion, one Pte Davies (on whom the 3LI silver statue of a soldier in jungle gear with an Armalite is modelled) unwisely stood downwind of this bonfire and rapidly went into a Gandhia-induced trip with a fearful headache to follow! Never again!

Below: Searching suspects.

Cyprus

The Light Infantry and Cyprus

The Light Infantry was involved with Cyprus from the very start as on Vesting Day 4LI was deployed as part of UNFICYP. This involvement was focused around three separate military tasks. On the one hand there was the requirement to provide a garrison for the two Sovereign Base Areas. This required at its core a Resident Infantry Battalion (RIB) in each SBA and The Light Infantry fulfilled this role for both areas on three occasions. Secondly there was the United Kingdom's commitment to support the UN Force in Cyprus (UNFICYP),

a role that the Regiment carried out four times. Finally there was the overseas training function enabled by the SBAs and manifested through the 'Lion Sun' Exercises. All the battalions – Regular and Territorial – benefited from these. Often regarded as 'sunshine tours' because of the proximity of the beaches, the quality of the brandy sours and the triviality of much of the military activity, these commitments actually represented a very serious contribution to the United Kingdom's military efforts. Securing the SBA was a strategically significant task. The outstations on Mount Olympus and at Ayios Nikalaos were

Below: Field Firing on the Akamas Ranges.

147

always at the core of what British Forces Cyprus delivered, but the significance of RAF Akrotiri as a staging post has grown out of all proportion in recent years due to the operations in Iraq and Afghanistan. Given the location of Cyprus in the Middle East there was always a credible threat to the bases and on top of that there is the small but vociferous Cypriot 'Brits Out' movement. The RIBs have not only secured the areas during periods of extreme intercommunal unrest but have latterly provided both a garrison for the Falkland Islands and an acclimatized reserve to operations in both Iraq and Afghanistan. 1LI and 2LI supplied Reinforced Infantry Companies to the Falklands Islands. Based at RAF Mount Pleasant the tours were generally welcomed as a break from the tedium of garrison duties in Cyprus (independence from the Battalion and the excellent training and field-firing opportunities were the headlines) although it should be noted that a number of families were less than impressed with the separation. 2LI deployed to Iraq on Op TELIC 2 – a task that subsequently developed for both RIBs into acting as the Reserve Battalion for both Iraq and Afghanistan. The UN tours served by the various battalions took place during the most serious periods of intercommunal confrontation, the task being handed off to non-infantry units once the level of threat had subsided. The overseas training opportunity was a prescient investment in hot and dry training given the commitments in Iraq and Afghanistan over the following years.

The Sovereign Base Areas

The Sovereign Base Areas of Akrotiri and Dhekelia are two British-administered areas comprising a British Overseas Territory on the island of Cyprus administered as Sovereign Base Areas of the United Kingdom. The bases were retained by the United Kingdom because of the strategic location of Cyprus following the granting of independence and the eventual transition of Cyprus from a crown colony to an independent sovereign state in 1960. The SBAs were retained in 1960 as military bases under British sovereignty, not as ordinary colonial territories. The two SBAs are assigned as West (WSBA) and East (ESBA). Under the 1960 Agreement the United Kingdom agreed not to develop the Sovereign Base Areas for other than military purposes. To that end the bases are administered by the Administrator of the Sovereign Base Areas, who is the Commander of British Forces Cyprus. The Administrator has all the executive and legislative authority of a Governor of an overseas territory.

UNFICYP

The UN Peacekeeping Force in Cyprus (UNFICYP) was established as a result of the segregation resulting from the intercommunal violence that broke out in December 1963. The basic mandate called upon UNFICYP to operate 'in the interest of preserving international peace and security, to use to its best efforts to prevent a recurrence of fighting and, as

OPERATIONAL OVERVIEW

Cyprus, before being placed under British administration in 1878, was under Ottoman Turkish rule for three centuries. The island's population includes a majority (more than 70 per cent) of people of Greek origin who have never been reconciled to the Turkish minority and vice versa.

UNFICYP ON PARADE

There was a well established precedent for the British contingent to produce the most polished of the contingent medal parades and, after a week of rehearsals, a floodlit parade by the Battalion took place in United Nations folklore as a result of the wish of the Commanding Officer, as Parade Commander, to include a drive past which featured every type of vehicle run by UNFICYP. At the Commanding Officer's insistence the Battalion's 'S–t Gobbler' was included in the column of vehicles. This was an elderly but essential vehicle whose humble, albeit vital duty was to evacuate the cesspits at all the outposts located along the 'Green Line'. Despite the fact that it had been scrubbed and polished until it gleamed, an unpleasant aroma wafted along in its wake. During every rehearsal it managed to break down before reaching the saluting base, causing major dislocation to the Cavalry in their armoured scout cars who were echeloned, somewhat unhappily, behind it. The Adjutant, tactfully but with increasing firmness, advised its removal, but the Commanding Officer, adamant that 'it was sure to be all right on the night', was only reluctantly prepared to concede that the 'Gobbler' be relegated to the rear of the column.

When the great evening arrived the parade passed like clockwork, until the closing moments when the unfortunate 'Gobbler' broke down right in front of the main VIP stand in the full glare of the floodlights. The odour had a lingering quality and the glittering array of dignitaries did not appear to do justice to the food at the post-parade reception.

1st Battalion The Light Infantry
UNFICYP November 1979 – April 1980
Episkopi Garrison April 1997 – April 1999
2nd Battalion The Light Infantry
Dhekalia Garrison February 2002 – April 2004
3rd Battalion The Light Infantry
UNFICYP, April – November 1970
UNFICYP, November 1978 – May 1979
Dhekalia Garrison, April 1980 – April 1982
4th Battalion The Light Infantry
UNFICYP, July – October 1968
Residential Tours
Emergency Tours

THE BATTLE OF EPISKOPI

In March 1997 1LI deployed to Episkopi Garrison as the Resident Infantry Battalion replacing the 1st Battalion The Royal Gloucestershire, Berkshire and Wiltshire Regiment. The military task of defending the Sovereign Base Area with which the Battalion was charged was taken seriously but by 1997 the security situation in Cyprus was as quiet as it had ever been.

As the OC and CSM strode out of Coy HQ at midday the 2 IC stuck his head out of Battalion Headquarters and asked how fast the company could be got ready to move as Episkopi Police Station had just been overrun and Support Company were to recapture it and restore order. This had come from nowhere and was initially put down to the 2 IC's famous sense of humour. Having been assured however that 'I'm not ****ing about', Support Company was on the way to Episkopi Police Station within 15 minutes – 'just turn left out of camp and go about a mile and a half and you can't miss it'.

The Mortar, Anti-Tank and Recce platoons doubled down the road out of camp and along the clifftop road to find the police station. The fast-thinking CSM and CQMS joined the column with a 1-tonner loaded with the Internal Security pack (riot shield, truncheons, weapons) and as much 'plastic' as the CSM could find. The Recce Platoon were thrown out front as screen and by the time the Mortar platoon reached the Police Station it was clear that it had indeed been captured by Greek protesters – "undreds of 'em Sir". A quick clearance was ordered – the Mortar platoon under Captain Piers Gorman and Colour Serjeant Atkinson formed a baseline with the 1-tonner on the main road and the Anti-Tank platoon climbed over the back fence and cleared the police compound of all the Cypriots, during which Support Company finally realized that the Sovereign Base Area Police were not British but Greek which was why a group of the protesters had seemed to be quite determined to climb back in to the Police compound every time they were evicted! Fortunately the plain-clothes officers were not too seriously hurt. The cause of the riot had also been established by this point: the Sovereign Base Area Police had arrested an individual on charges surrounding gambling and prostitution. His 'supporters' had mobilized and attacked the Police Station to break him out. This sort of behaviour was completely out of character and unpredicted – hence the surprise!

Support Company then set about securing the area and with the SBA Police Inspector (known to all as Charlie and a superb operator) started to disperse the crowd. At this point a little Suzuki jeep arrived at the back of the rioting Greeks. Early that morning a group of wives had set off for a shopping trip into Limassol. On their return they found the coast road blocked by the protest. Fortunately the Greeks are gentlemen. The leaders of the protest approached the Baseline waving their arms and calling for a truce. The OC stepped forward of the Shield Wall and the Greeks explained that the wives wanted to get home so if we stopped for a couple of minutes the baseline could open to let them through and the protesters would wait until the wives were clear before restarting. The passage of lines then passed peacefully followed by the enthusiastic re-engagement on both sides five minutes later. After a further two days of excitement the incident faded into history marked only by a three-line piece in the *Times* noting a 'small riot' had occurred. Meanwhile the balance of the Battalion arrived, the camp followers deployed to the beach, the various headquarters returned to their normal battle rhythm, the local Cypriots reopened all the restaurants and bars to welcome the new battalion, Inspector Charlie was promoted and Colour Serjeant Atkinson was awarded a Joint Force Commendation (as were three others) for his control of the Baseline.

MG

necessary, to contribute to the maintenance and restoration of law and order and a return to normal conditions'. Up until 1974 UNFICYP troops were deployed throughout the island between the Greek Cypriot and Turkish Cypriot communities acting primarily as mediators between the two. In July 1974 the Greek military junta in Athens staged a coup to bring about their nationalist dream of 'Enosis' – the union of Cyprus and Greece. Although the coup ultimately failed it led directly to the Turkish invasion and occupation of northern Cyprus with some 40,000 soldiers and 200 tanks. UNFICYP was unable to prevent either the 'Greek' coup or the Turkish invasion, operations that in any case exceeded both the UNFICYP mandate and its military ability. Immediately following the 1974 hostilities, UNFICYP played both a humanitarian role including exchange of prisoners and a peacekeeping role along the UN Buffer Zone.

Since then the two rival communities have been living in mainly peaceful separation. The international community recognizes only the Government of the Republic of Cyprus (ROC) as the legitimate authority on the island. UNFICYP personnel maintain peace and stability through a system of static observation posts and mobile and standing patrols, ensuring the UNBZ is kept under constant surveillance. The civilian police contingent of UNFICYP functions as a liaison between the two communities' police forces and maintains law and order in the buffer zone.

Above: Cyprus 1981–2: Punk supergroup Phil Sick and the Vomits pose for the cameras. Behind the greasepaint (front L to R) 2Lt Mark O'Hanlon, Lt Philip Hadfield, Maj Rex Stevenson. Bringing up the rear, RSM Jones.

Northern Ireland

1968 was a dangerous year in Western democracies. Actions by the Civil Rights movement in the USA, student riots on the streets of Paris and in German cities, were followed by the Czech uprising, crushed by Soviet tanks. Civil violence in Northern Ireland broke out.

The long complex history of divisions in Ireland, and particularly the province of Ulster, which comprises Northern Ireland and remains part of the United Kingdom, is a story in itself. The social and political inequalities, which characterized the rigidly separate lives of the Catholic 'nationalist' and

Protestant 'loyalist, unionist' communities, led to four decades of 'troubles' from 1968. These re-echoed earlier 'troubles' – those of 1798, 1916 and 1918–22, before the establishment of the Irish Free State, later the Irish Republic. The Republic's constitution was written with an aim for eventual 'reunification' with the Northern

Above: *Internal Security Training.*

Left: *In the aftermath of a bomb.*

OPERATIONAL OVERVIEW, 1968–90

The Light Infantry were there at the very start of 'the troubles'. In August 1968 1LI was deployed for a tour which lasted for nearly two years. They were swiftly joined by 2LI and 3LI on emergency 'internal security' tours (as the mission was then termed) in Belfast.

Whilst the province of Ulster was and remains about two-thirds Unionist / Loyalist / Protestant, there exist both urban and country areas with exclusive concentrations of Republican / Nationalist / Catholics. In Londonderry, there are two nationalist enclaves, the inner city Bogside and the Creggan estate to the west. In Belfast the Shankill road runs east–west through the Greater Shankill area comprising some 20,000 loyalists, between the republican areas of the Falls Road and Ardoyne. In the countryside, the area which became known as the 'bandit country' of South Armagh was dominated by PIRA. Also areas in County Fermanagh near the border with the Republic of Ireland – often a means of safe escape – were often problematic to the Security Forces.

The first period of 'the troubles' was marked by rioting, petrol bombing, and shooting in the cities – often with intense exchanges of fire between opposing paramilitaries and the Army. Army units were deployed in urban positions to control the violence. Operating with foot patrols, armoured and light mobile patrols and reserves, as well as using permanent checkpoints and setting up instant road-blocks, the Security Forces attempted to use minimum force and make arrests, so that due process of law could be followed. It was certainly a war dominated by 'minor tactics', and it came to be known as the 'corporals' war' because the lowest levels of command so often were the most effective, NCOs being able to take the immediate initiative. Significant politico-military events and factors in the early years included internment without trial of terrorists in Long Kesh, later the Maze prison (1971); the 'Bloody Sunday' civil rights march and shooting of 13 civilian / paramilitaries in Londonderry (30 January 1972); Operation MOTORMAN (31 July 1972), in which four battalions of infantry and bulldozer tanks of the Royal Engineers were used to open up 'no-go areas' established by the PIRA in Londonderry, with a further 11 battalions acting in Belfast; and internal struggles within the paramilitaries.

By the mid 1970s, the Army, UDR and RUC had reduced the power of the paramilitaries to act freely. They continued, however, to operate on an opportunity basis for many years, with assassinations, shootings and revenge killings. Particularly effective were the planting of remote-controlled bombs in cities and on country roads, where they could use surprise to great effect – such as the Warren Point bomb (August 79) killing 18 members of the Parachute Regiment, and the Ballygawley Crossroads bomb of 1988, which resulted in the deaths of eight and wounding of a further 28 members of 1LI. The PIRA also took their bombing campaign to mainland Britain, with explosions and casualties inflicted in London, Aldershot, Guildford, Birmingham and later at Warrington.

While there had been open talks and secret contacts by the British government with the parties involved since at least 1973, the political 'tipping point' has been identified by historians as the prison hunger strikes, culminating in the death of elected Sinn Fein MP Bobby Sands, in 1981. The middle period of 'the troubles' was thus characterized by containment by the Army, but also by significant terrorist organization actions, seeking to increase their politico-military power.

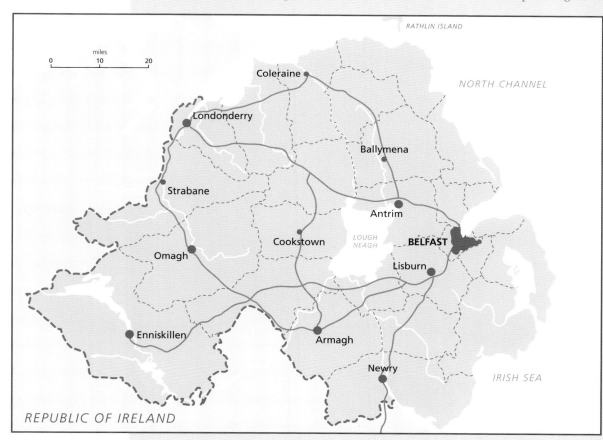

CLOSE OBSERVATION PLATOON, EARLY 1980s

In the early 1980s Battalions (Bn) deployed to Northern Ireland (NI) with a Close Observation Platoon (COP). It was manned by mature Recce-type soldiers carefully selected as they had to be extremely fit, able to work in very small teams and the type of soldier who was not scared to take calculated risks or to carry a Bergen of well over 100lbs! Observation Posts (OPs) also required a high degree of fitness as the individual could be in the prone position for anything up to ten days and then be required to react like a coiled spring as the situation changed. All members of the Platoon grew their hair and sideboards in order to blend in when deployed in civilian clothes and two of the administrative staff grew beards. Well before the tour started the rest of the Bn regarded the COP as cowboys.

All had to learn the skill of entering a rural or urban OP leaving no signs behind – all rubbish and human waste was bagged and carried out. The main COP missions were to provide Special Branch (SB) with intelligence in the form of photographs and video films, to provide protection for individuals under terrorist threat and to provide back-up for other specialist agencies. The reputation of the Unit's COP meant everything. Successful jobs helped the COP to get more high-level operations, many involving Special Forces.

Ken Kennedy

province of Ulster, naturally supported by the Catholic minority in the North.

The first Catholic protest took place on 5 August, following a number of well-publicized protest events in Derry (or Londonderry to unionists) earlier in the year. The dispute was initially about housing. On 5 October there was another march, in Derry itself, followed by three days of rioting. In Belfast there were marches against 'police brutality' and a reaction from the Protestant community with counter-demonstrations. The violence got out of hand. The Royal Ulster Constabulary (RUC, mainly Protestants) were unable to contain the situation. Military Aid to the Civil Power was invoked. British Army units were deployed. At first welcomed by the Catholics, being seen as protection from the violence of the Protestants, soon the Army found itself the targets of abuse, physical violence, fire-bombs and bullets from both sides. Members of both communities armed themselves in due course, forming paramilitary units. They were the Provisional Irish Republican Army (PIRA, a newly invigorated offshoot

Above: Sgt Hardy, 2LI, attends to the victim of a shooting.

OPERATIONAL OVERVIEW, 1991–2007

Although the intensity of attacks against the Security Forces and sectarian killings continued into the early 1990s there was a growing sense of fatigue with terrorism in both communities. There were early signs of political engagement across the sectarian divide and between London and Dublin and Washington. It was therefore not a total surprise when a ceasefire was announced by the Provisional IRA in the early 1990s. Whilst much of the world's security effort and public reporting was focused on events in the Balkans, the 'talking about talking' was taking place in troubled Northern Ireland.

These early talks broke down due to a lack of confidence on all sides and the Provisional IRA (PIRA) returned to the bullet, its armed struggle against the British Government. Even though this violence was deadly, there was a feeling that it was a tactic which might be reversed given the right circumstances. PIRA was bankrupt and its leaders were approaching their sixties, looking to build their retirement homes in County Donegal. The role of the Security Forces became increasingly delicate and had to be calibrated very carefully at the political and operational level. If the Northern Ireland campaign had been dubbed the Corporals' War during the 1970s, it became the Company Commanders' War in the mid-1990s. The presence of soldiers 'on the ground' had become part of the problem, rather than the solution, but the RUC could not operate without military support.

When the Provisional IRA ceasefire was restored in summer 1997, encouraged perhaps by the change of British Government, a period of intense negotiation eventually led to the Belfast Agreement, better known as the Good Friday Agreement. Within this framework the Army became part

Below: 1LI, early 1970s at Flax St Mill in the Ardoyne, Belfast. An 'own goal' by the IRA, who in attempting to float a bomb under the mill, succeeded in blowing up the Celtic Club. The device was either badly timed, or got stuck somehow before reaching its target.

of the negotiating equation. Somehow it had to support the RUC in confronting splinter terrorist groups, such as the 'Real IRA', who were responsible for the Omagh bomb that September, and help to maintain public order, when there was considerable unrest on both sides of the sectarian divide. At the same time it had to make itself less and less visible. Whereas the mere existence of Army patrols was a confidence-building measure for the RUC and many within both communities, it was a stumbling block as far as PIRA was concerned. The desirability of 'demilitarization' was acknowledged by all but its timing was fraught. This was a high-wire balancing act for all parties involved.

It also led to several bitter pills to be swallowed under the terms of the Good Friday Agreement, the release of convicted murderers being one of the more obvious. Reform of the RUC into the Police Service of Northern Ireland and disbandment of the Home Service battalions of the Royal Irish Regiment followed thereafter. But the rewards of peace made these pills essential. Throughout this period the Army provided a bedrock of support despite the new demands of Iraq and Afghanistan, until Operation BANNER came to an end in August 2007. As a regiment The Light Infantry more or less coincided with the Troubles. We should take pride in our part in this long campaign, conducted with fortitude and ingenuity but at great cost. We will not forget our fallen and wounded Light Infantrymen, from Belfast to Londonderry and from Ballygawley to South Armagh.

By 2007, 763 members of the British Army had been killed and about 6,100 injured during Op BANNER, of which Light Infantry battalions had lost 32 – their names are listed in the Roll of Honour on page 9.

of a long-standing organization and military wing of the republican 'nationalist' Sinn Fein political party), the 'loyalist' Ulster Volunteer Force (UVF, dating from 1966) and Ulster Defence Association (UDA, from 1971, some of whom were known as the Ulster Freedom Fighters, UFF). All these groups became 'terrorist' organizations in the eyes of their opponents. To assist the Regular Army, the Ulster Defence Regiment was established in 1969 as a neutral, part-time force. The UDR was an integral part of the Army and fully under command of the General Officer Commanding in Chief, whose Headquarters were at Lisburn, outside Belfast.

Operation BANNER was the name given to Army deployments in Northern Ireland from 1969 to 2007. Infantry battalions and other arms' units deployed on 'emergency tours' of up to six months, or served for up to two years, usually accompanied by families, as part of the 'permanent garrison'. The collective term 'Security Forces' (SF) was given to the Army, RUC and other statutory bodies.

Airmobility

A simplistic introduction to NATO's defensive strategy...
It is hard to think, some 30 years after the height of the Cold War, that once upon a time there was a real concern that the Warsaw Pact (WP) would choose to launch an attack on the West. From the perspective of a British infantry battalion in BAOR the threat presented by the exercise planners for the annual exercise programme was the Group of Soviet Forces in Germany (GSFG) and more especially 3 Shock Army. The exact composition and capability of these forces was the specialist theme of the intelligence community and BRIXMIS of whom we knew little and saw less, but their output was manifest in the latest (classified) photographs of WP equipment used for Armoured Fighting Vehicle (AFV) recognition lectures and lessons and in the regular upgrades of our own vehicles, weapons and equipment to counter the latest threat increase.

For four decades this reciprocated practice of matching the threat had resulted in heavier, faster and larger numbers of armoured vehicles and in larger numbers of more capable anti-tank systems. NATO's defensive posture advocated a strong line of forward defence backed up by modest mobile reserves, with national corps taking their share of the front: 1(BR) Corps for example would deploy on the Inner German Border (IGB) with a German corps to their north and the Belgian corps to the south. This strong defensive 'crust' left little combat substance in the rear areas and placed significant reliance on the capability of NATO air power to write down WP forces attacking on a broad front, whilst land forces fought a delaying battle to deny ground. If either air or land operations failed, a significant Warsaw Pact advance would be halted by the use of tactical nuclear weapons at which stage on exercise, ENDEX would be called and all troops returned to barracks. In retrospect, the concept of nuclear Mutually Assured Destruction (MAD) was truly incredible.

The 1980s witnessed a new threat in WP capability with the introduction of the concept of the Operational Manoeuvre Group (OMG) – not new weaponry or technology, but a change of offensive tactic, massing armour and artillery to punch a narrow hole through NATO's forward defensive line and to exploit as fast and as deep as momentum would allow to unhinge NORTHAG operational command. Such a force would operate inside the decision/action cycle of any NORTHAG tactical reinforcement and would not constitute a large enough target to justify a nuclear response with its drastic strategic implications. Such mobility and combat power could not be countered by the use of an armoured reserve, nor could ground attack air power be guaranteed to be available or effective. Enter airmobility!

The Third Dimension

The delivery of land forces into operational areas by air had been under development since the invention of powered flight, conventionally and tactically by parachute or helicopter, and strategically by air transport. The British Army has included in its inventory at various times airborne, airportable and airlanded brigades, but the decision to convert 6 Armoured Brigade to conduct an airmobile trial in 1983 was the first time that light infantry had been committed to close working with Army and RAF helicopters in a setting as formal as NORTHAG's concept of operations. Airmobile and air assault operations were familiar from the US experience in Vietnam, but no similar capability had been attempted in BAOR and certainly not in the British Army.

The justification for major expenditure and the structural shift in the British component was that the OMG threat would be countered by a force whose reaction and deployment times were sufficiently short to allow the commitment of a credible and potent anti-armour force. Air delivery would allow the battlefield frictions to be overflown thus ensuring rapid deployment; drills would allow procedures to be reduced to a minimum; and the deployment of an infantry force heavily armed with anti-tank weapons would provide a strong counter to an armoured

Below: A Gazelle drops off the Ops Officer.

154

Right: *6 Airmobile Brigade on the move with Chinooks.*

threat. For the trial 6 Brigade was reorganized with two infantry battalions, one artillery (light gun) regiment and an engineer squadron, calling upon army Aviation and the RAF Support Helicopter Force to provide the mobility for quick deployment.

The Regimental Reality

1LI arrived in BAOR in 1981 as part of 5 Field Force. No sooner had this formation become 24 Infantry Brigade, than the Battalion was transferred to 6 Armoured Brigade. It was then almost immediately sent to West Belfast and returned in October 1983 to find the Brigade re-roling as an experimental airmobile formation. Phase 1 of the airmobile trial was intended to confirm the organization of the Brigade and Battalions and included Exercise 'Lionheart'. During this phase the primary role of the Brigade was seen as that of destroying enemy armoured thrusts by deploying rapidly to occupy counter-penetration positions on the expected enemy line of advance. 1LI spent summer 1983 until May 1984 in a high grade training progression culminating in a Battalion FTX. This was the only time in the whole training year when fog completely prevented air movement! In June 1984, half the battalion deployed to Normandy for the D Day Anniversary. Colour parties, company guards and the Band and Bugles were all moved from parade to parade by Chinook. July saw the whole airmobile Brigade really operating for the first time. The Brigade FTX was designed to practice 1LI in the defence of a counter-penetration position. At the start of the fly-out the whole Battalion was airborne within nine minutes of the arrival of the first helicopter and each of the three assaulting companies landed simultaneously at their drop off points. The summer heat, hilly country of the Sauerland and sheer speed of the exercise made it one of the most challenging ever experienced. Even those who had been most sceptical

about the airmobile concept were forced to admit that once the helicopters and troops actually came together, the Battalion could be moved much more smoothly than they had imagined. A further work-up exercise in September gave 1LI a chance to shake-out before Exercise 'Spearpoint'. This was the climax of the first phase of the trial and completely vindicated the long hours spent on joint training earlier in the year. Few could remember such a period of concentrated yet correctly ordered training, starting with the individual and then progressing through sub unit to battalion and formation exercises. The CO's own last experience of such a well-structured training year had been in Malaysia in 1967!

1LI's tour came to a close when 2LI took over their G1098 accounts on their arrival in Hemer/Deilinghofen in December 1984. 2LI was to further test and develop airmobile procedures and exceptional numbers of soldiers were trained to meet the new establishment requirements, without which there could be no field training. The conversion of two battalions of infantry to operate Milan as a section weapon when it had hitherto been a specialist anti-tank missile system presented a major challenge to both traditional thinking and the professional jealousy of Milan platoons in 'conventional' battalions, but with (fading) memories from Lemgo of a Swingfire platoon, 2LI had sufficient confidence to accept the challenge. Practical training built up from platoon drills to the major brigade exercise north of Osnabruck in 1985, using any helicopters that could be found from UK, US and Germany as well as the familiar 'heli-Bedford'. Loading trials found that soldiers could carry unrealistic weights over short distances only – so drills and procedures were developed to land companies as close as possible to their deployment positions. Even so, a landing site in the middle of a company position could still leave Milan detachments up to 1000 metres away from where they would dig in: and digging was the major part of the infantryman's lot, given the enemy's artillery capability. Loads of over 90 lbs were not uncommon and the Milan and GPMG detachments carried significantly more, placing significant strain on backs, knees and other joints. The BAOR trial formally concluded in 1987 by which stage the concept had been proved as feasible. 2LI remained in Hemer for a further year during which 6 Brigade returned to its armoured ORBAT. 1988 culminated in participation in two major FTX – the 1(NL) Corps Exercise 'Free Lion' and 3 Div Exercise 'Iron Hammer', the last ever divisional FTX on the 1 (BR) Corps scale. In both, the battalion played a unique part as an airmobile OPFOR.

Trial outcomes and 24 Brigade

It was decided that a continued airmobile capability should not be based in BAOR but be provided by 24 Airportable Brigade who would re-role and move from Catterick to Colchester. The helicopter community had built up real confidence in 6 Brigade's aviation and SH planning and handling ability as a result of the investment of thousands of flying hours and joint planning time in BAOR, and was required to repeat the process with a new formation and new units in the UK. Redeployment of a significant part of the support helicopter force from RAF(G) ensured that much air component experience was transferred, but it was not the same for the Army elements who converted from scratch. Human nature meant that it was not a simple matter of passing the 6 Brigade SOPs to the new user, because the wheel needed to be reinvented by the new custodians and the training cycle was repeated. The 6 Brigade trial proved the need for integral artillery, engineer and logistic capability and the 24 Brigade ORBAT thus built up to two infantry battalions, two AAC regiments, one light gun regiment and an engineer field squadron with logistic support provided by a combat service support battalion, a provost company and a field ambulance. 1LI (formerly 2LI) returned to the redeveloped airmobile role, moving to Meanee Barracks in Colchester from Tidworth in 1994, returning to a barracks familiar to 1DLI, 4LI and 2LI in the airportable role 25 years earlier.

By 1994 the brigade training cycle was well established with new units and personnel properly supported by the in-place capability. Airmobile experience was valued and protected, the brigade staff was formally established and trained, jointery was practised *regularly* and a comprehensive exercise programme ensured that the capability was properly tested and evaluated. A rigorous brigade and battlegroup trainer programme kept staffs at all levels up to date with developing procedures, and sufficient field training with adequate support ensured that the practicalities of working with helicopters were catered for.

This was not to mean that the future was seen through a rosy glow of optimism: 24 Brigade was a big organization to run, although with its aviation and FAC component its operational capability was significant. The brigade road tail was immense, with time past a point for a single route road move of some 20 hours; the real-estate demands of the brigade were significant

Left: Light Strike Vehicles of Screen Company 1LI.

and the space needed to exercise fully the capability required concurrent allocation of a significant proportion of the UK's principal training areas: it was not unknown for exercises to run from Thetford to Cornwall, or from Salisbury Plain to Otterburn.

The brigade earned its operational spurs in 1995 when, under the command of Robin Brims, it deployed to Ploce at extremely short notice to provide 'on the horizon' support to the UK component of UNPROFOR in the uneasy and early days of the Bosnia peacekeeping mission: but whilst its strategic mobility was proved without doubt by deploying a capable force over 1,500 miles in a short period of time, the tactical capability was not called upon. Robin Brims handed over to Mark Elcomb in 1996, whose time in command saw the early shift towards accommodating the awesome capability of the attack helicopter. Indeed it was in order to take forward the essential work for this strategic shift that the brigade was replaced on the Bosnia roster in 1997, although brigade units continued to provide sub-unit and individual reinforcements for operations throughout. Vigorous debate tested the ways in which the attack helicopter should be grouped, tasked and supported. Airmobility formally left the British Army's list of capabilities in September 1998, when 24 Brigade converted to the current structure of 16 Air Assault Brigade which owes much to this debate and the experience developed in the previous ten years.

Below: The fly forward – the Chinook will carry up to 30 troops.

The Balkans

BOSNIA

The break-up of Yugoslavia and especially the Bosnian civil war, between April 1992 and December 1995, brought about the start of a new world disorder that made demands upon international institutions originally born after the Second World War and refined in the context of the Cold War. The Army found itself deployed into Bosnia's multi-sided and vicious civil war as the international community deliberated the wisdom of intervention, the notion of peacekeeping or peace enforcement, and stumbled through so-called safe havens.

Under a United Nations banner, first logistics and medical support, but quickly infantry battalions, became involved in operations in Bosnia under these circumstances in 1992 and 1993. For most British soldiers of the day this was a new type of expeditionary warfare. And it was set in a multinational context where allies had very different experiences and practices. The ingenuity of the troops was much admired but in truth there was little peace to keep and the so-called international community was disparate. Meanwhile the media reported warring factional atrocities, and a sense that something must be done was growing strongly in 1994 into 1995. By this time the British had a brigade-sized force deployed in South West Bosnia.

KOSOVO

The province of Kosovo, with its large Muslim Albanian majority, had always been a problem for Belgrade, the Serb capital where the power of the Yugoslav state had resided during the communist years. The Kosovo Liberation Army (KVA) was formed in 1997, seeking secession from Yugoslavia, and it was countered vigorously by Serb forces, being Christians with links to Russia. There followed many acts of atrocity, which for centuries have been endemic in the Balkan states. NATO's plan, initially agreed at the Rambouillet Conference of early 1999, was for NATO to administer Kosovo 'as an autonomous province within Yugoslavia'. It was rejected by Belgrade. From March to June 1999 NATO waged a bombing campaign against Yugoslavia. British troops formed part of an invasion force in June, which occupied Kosovo virtually unopposed, and seized the provincial capital, Pristina. The added danger was that the Russians were ambivalent about which side they supported. In the end they too joined in the capture of Pristina from Serb control.

Bosnia

In the summer of 1995, against the backdrop of airstrikes made against the Bosnian Serb forces who were violating agreements, some 400 UN soldiers were taken hostage. In response the British and French Governments deployed additional forces to implement agreements more robustly. 24 Airmobile Brigade was deployed at short notice. Much to the annoyance of 1LI, only half the Brigade deployed to the Adriatic Coast under command of Brigadier Robin Brims and the Chief of Staff Major Richard Smith. This deployment itself, along with forces that deployed to Mount Igman overlooking Sarajevo, led to significant change. It represented a change in UN capability and determination to break the deadlock. The hostages were released unharmed; the siege of Sarajevo was lifted; the warring factions were forced into talking with the international community. Most important, the United States became militarily involved.

Thus at the end of 1995, 2LI under Lieutenant Colonel Ben Barry started an epic tour of Bosnia. Initially the Battalion was under a United Nations banner and then, when the Dayton Agreement was signed, under NATO auspices. This story is told in Ben Barry's book *A Cold War: British Army Operations in Bosnia 1995–1996*. The Dayton Agreement brought an end to a bloody civil war. It was implemented vigorously over the next several years. The British led a multinational divisional headquarters

Above: Maj Jan de Vos OCA Coy 2LI on Mt Igman.

Left: Alternate crossing points were commonplace.

Below: *UN Checkpoint.*

based in a metal factory in Banja Luka and provided the three-star Deputy Commander Operations in the Force Headquarters. In September 1998, Lieutenant General Jack Deverell took over as Deputy Commander (Operations) from Lieutenant General Sir Hew Pike in Headquarters SFOR in Sarajevo for six months. By this time, there was a well-established military structure of Multinational Divisions. The US were responsible for Multinational Division (North), the British for Multinational Division (South West) and the French for Multinational Division (South East). Each was presented with complex and often volatile political and inter-ethnic challenges. Equally, each reflected a plethora of national assumptions and prejudices, as well as political, legal and military constraints. This covered nearly every aspect of military operations and could be as diverse as some nations being unable to search civilians without direct evidence of wrongdoing because of their domestic law, whilst others scrutinized every order and instruction and sought clearance from their own capitals before complying. This made spontaneous and speedy military reaction difficult and emphasized the complex and demanding nature of coalition operations. The terms of the Dayton Agreement were well understood by the parties, if not always well observed, either in the letter or the spirit of the law. Such breaches of the military element of the Dayton Agreement by the armed forces of either

Right: Warriors advance on Banja Luka.

Below: The books of the tour.

Right: (L–R) Capt David Livingstone and Capt Steve Liddle RM, LCpl Reggie Mackenzie and Sjt Dean Portman on Mount Igman.

the Serb Republic or the Federation of Bosnian Moslems and Croats were more often a mixture of incompetence and bloody-mindedness than determination to undermine the agreement as an act of policy. Failure to comply normally resulted in NATO sanctions. Even though such sanctions were often no more than seizing (and sometimes destroying) equipment, they were seen by the parties as both painful and costly (mostly to their pride). However, in true Balkan style, there was much intrigue, conspiracy and manipulation of international organizations by the local community. Lessons learned under centuries of Ottoman rule were put to good use against their rather more gullible and substantially less ruthless modern-day 'occupiers'. In addition, there were different agendas in existence amongst the international organizations operating in Bosnia–Herzegovina which led to quite unnecessary tensions and in-fighting – to the frustration of many and the detriment of the operation, but without ever endangering the overall strategy. Indeed, as has been made clear by our experiences in Iraq and Afghanistan, the most difficult of all the challenges is to create a proper 'unity of purpose' within the international community in order to align military and civil operations so that they mutually support each other. Perhaps the most sensitive aspect of military operations was the responsibility for detaining alleged war criminals so that they could be brought before the International Criminal Tribunal Yugoslavia (ICTY). There was much speculation in the press that NATO was less inclined than it should have been to carry out this task. However, it was a national responsibility

to arrest such suspects and the task of Headquarters SFOR to coordinate and de-conflict these operations when they took place. Given the sensitive nature of special-force operations, this proved an interesting area on more than one occasion. The continued presence in communities of low-level war criminals who appeared immune from the national legal process and too lowly to interest the ICTY remained a barrier to the effective re-integration of communities, especially those in which there were large numbers of refugees. This period of slow but steady improvement was halted for a period in 1999 by the NATO air war against Serbia and the ground invasion of Kosovo. The people of the Serb Republic proved to be as appalled by the NATO offensive against Serbia as the Bosnian Croats and Muslims were delighted.

The military aspects of the Dayton Agreement were largely implemented in full by 2000. Major General Robin Brims led a reduction in force levels whilst commanding Multinational Division South West in that year. This was further developed by Brigadier Ben Barry when he returned to Bosnia to command the Banja Luka-based NATO formation in Bosnia. The political process, however, needed several more years of robust diplomatic activity, and once again the Army found itself holding the safety net whilst the Bosnian and international political community made slow progress across their high wire. The realities of peace agreements and their implementation as experienced in Bosnia, Kosovo and Northern Ireland were to provide invaluable comparisons as the Army's attention switched to Iraq and Afghanistan.

Kosovo

2LI's deployment to the Serbian Province of Kosovo-Metohija was based on a contingent requirement; and it soon became obvious that no planning had been carried out by HQ KFOR on what 2LI should do once they had deployed. A 'Mexican Stand-off' (between A Company and the Russians) at Priština Airport confirmed that few of the other contributing nations were aware of 2LI's presence.

Left: OC and CSM C Coy try out the Soviet equipment.

This lack of understanding and confusion was fully exploited by the Battalion Headquarters, who set about ensuring that 'fun' was to be had in what was potentially a volatile environment. Of note, joint exercises were planned with Russian Airborne forces (even though HQ KFOR thought it impossible) and the US Army – the latter resembling the famous helicopter scene from *Apocalypse Now*. Scores of American Blackhawks, Apaches and Russian Mi-8 Hips were made available for a 2LI and Greek 'airmobile deployment' – aviation resources which 1LI only dreamed of having in the days of 24 Airmobile Brigade!

'Metohija' means 'Monastic Land'. It thus allowed Major Nick Ilić (of Serbian extraction), the opportunity to plan a series of company- and battalion-level deployments around Kosovo – centred on each of the historic 11-/ 12th-century Orthodox monasteries that remained standing. In the process, priceless religious artefacts were moved to safety; and a delegation of monks were driven to meet the Serbian Patriarch in Peć. These humanitarian deeds were significant and reinforced the Serbs' faith in NATO's (albeit 2LI's) determination to preserve their way of life.

Below left: Nick Ilić and Radovan Karadžić.

Below: Nick Ilić and some Chetniks.

Sierra Leone

OPERATIONAL OVERVIEW

A former British colony, Sierra Leone lies squarely in West Africa. Along with Liberia, its neighbour to the east (itself with links to the USA), it is surrounded by the countries that formed what was known as French West Africa – the colonies seized for trade in the 17th and 18th centuries. Significant diamond, bauxite and rutile deposits means that the tale of Sierra Leone is a mirror-image of all the other recent conflicts in Africa, involving a country ranked as the poorest in the world yet at the same time unbelievably rich in resources but riddled with coups, power-hungry dictators and self-seeking governments.

The 1990s was a tumultuous decade for Sierra Leone as emerging groups vied for power and the diamonds. Ensuing instability led to the deployment of a West African stabilization force; a coup by disaffected ex-army officers who subsequently changed their allegiance; local peace agreements that were made and broken, an internationally brokered peace accord; a resurgence of violence; a faltering UN peacekeeping mission; and, finally, British armed intervention and the wholesale re-training of the Sierra Leone Army.

Right: Cpl Cox and a team from 2LI FSp Coy on patrol in WIMIK.

The emergence of the Revolutionary United Front

The Revolutionary United Front (RUF) was a rebel army that fought for control within Sierra Leone on and off for eleven years from 1991 to 2002.

The RUF was led by a man called Foday Sankoh and was created out of a number of Sierra Leonian political groups that had no clear ideology or claims; just that they were fed up with the military political elite in the capital Freetown exploiting and seizing almost all of the money being generated by Sierra Leone's vast mineral wealth – principally from the diamond fields in the east of the country.

Initially the RUF gathered itself and consolidated in the diamond fields of eastern Sierra Leone; they were funded for the most part by Charles Taylor, the president of Liberia – which borders Sierra Leone to its east. Taylor's interest, as with other regional actors, was to seize as much of the diamonds as possible for himself and the National Patriotic Front of Liberia, the organization that had carried him to power.

RUF operations started in early 1991 and any popular support they may have garnered amongst a public keen for more equitable investment of the country's wealth soon disintegrated. Villages were destroyed and thousands of people displaced, many fleeing into Guinea to the north. This being Africa – the winner takes the spoils – Sankoh did not honour previous undertakings but chose to use the funds generated by the diamonds to reinforce the coffers of the RUF and to buy arms in order to secure and consolidate his control of the country.

The President of Sierra Leone, Joseph Momoh, was himself ousted in 1992 by a group of military officers who were frustrated by the government's inability to contain the RUF. Led by Captain Valentine Strasser, the new administration called itself the National Provisional Ruling Council (NPRC).

In its area of control, the RUF regime was characterized for many by two things: the extreme brutality by which they ruled and their widespread use of child soldiers. For most the brutality was epitomized by machete-wielding fighters that would cut off the hands, arms or feet of anyone they suspected of opposing them. The RUF justified their atrocities by claiming that this prevented a person from bearing arms against them or, better still, from being able to work in the diamond mines that might in turn provide funds for the government. Thus it was that

when RUF raiding parties made punitive visits into a village they would often give their victims a choice: 'short sleeves or long sleeves?', giving the villager the choice of losing their arm above or below the elbow. By the end of 1995 the RUF controlled most of the country.

A Rogues' Gallery: ECOMOG, the Armed Forces Revolutionary Council (AFRC) and the Kamajors

Increasing concern within West Africa with the fragility of Sierra Leone led to the deployment of a Nigerian-led West African peacekeeping force entitled the Economic Community of West African States Monitoring Group – more commonly known as ECOMOG. A condition of the deployment was the establishment of a properly functioning civilian government; in April 1996 presidential and parliamentary elections were held and Ahmad Kabbah was duly elected as President, and the signing of the Abidjan peace accord took place in late 1996.

One of Kabbah's first decisions as president was to retain the services of Sandline International and Executive Outcomes, two private military companies contracted to train the Sierra Leone Army and the Kamajors.

In the face of ECOMOG stabilization activity within Sierra Leone, Foday Sankoh fled to Nigeria in March 1997 and was promptly placed under house arrest. In his absence Sam Bockarie took command of the RUF.

The peace was short-lived; disagreements over the terms of disarmament and disbandment set the conditions for the emergence of yet another group – the Armed Forces Revolutionary Council (AFRC). The AFRC was formed by Major Johnny Paul Koroma and seized power in a coup in May 1997.

A GREAT ESCAPE

Major Andrew Samsonoff of The Light Infantry was one of four UN military observers working with Kenyan peacekeepers in the West African state when their town was besieged by the Revolutionary United Front. 'Our camp, one of eight, was the first in the middle of rebel territory. We had opened it in mid-April and had very little take-up. Then ten rebels came on 1 May and handed over their weapons. The rebel movement, the Revolutionary United Front (RUF), saw the handover as desertion. Believing that the ten men were staying in the UN compound, although they had been sent back to their villages, 300 rebels launched an attack. There was an armed stand-off between them and 50 Kenyans which lasted four days. The rebels started looting the camp and burning it. Two Kenyans were taken hostage. The Makeni stand-off was probably the spark for the subsequent rebel offensive on Freetown. Once the rebels had killed a few peace-keepers, they were in their minds, at war. There had been a lot of anti-British remarks from the rebels so we felt there was a price on our heads. Some of the information we were getting from local civilians was that hostility was directed mainly at us, first of all for being British and secondly for being involved in the disarmament process That is why the four of us decided to escape.'

The four unarmed United Nations military observers decided at 3 in the morning to scale the back wall of their compound and disappear into the night. Acting on advice of a group of Kenyans, who had escaped from a different location, the men decided to head for the UN outpost at Magburaka, 40 miles away. They trekked through the jungle by night and hid in thickets by day to avoid being seen over a period of four days. One of them, Major Ashby RM, made one phone call to his wife Anna, who works for the Foreign Office in London, then all contact was lost until Monday. The four men carried only a shortwave radio, a satellite phone with a dying battery, a map, a global positioning system compass, one loaf of bread, half a tin of baked beans, army boil-in-the-bag rations and one litre of water each. 'Our main problem was lack of water. It's still the dry season here and although there were rivers marked on our maps, in practice they were in fact pools of stagnant water. We've been drinking some unusually coloured water.... We were so thirsty all the time that we did not really desire to eat. I had just recovered from a bout of dysentery and Phil had been down with malaria until two days before the gun battle'. The escapers met a farmer who took them to his village where the villagers treated them 'as though the Queen had come to visit', tending their cuts, feeding them their best food and helping them on arrival at the town of Magburaka to contact British forces following which they were airlifted to Freetown.

Staffed by a number of disaffected servicemen within the Sierra Leone Army and a number of associated rebel gangs, including the infamous West Side Boys, the essence of the AFRC was their dissatisfaction with the government of President Kabbah, non-implementation of the 1996 Peace Agreement with the RUF, and a growing concern that the country was dividing along tribal lines in reaction to perceived favouritism of the Kamajor Mende Tribe by Hinga Norman, the Defence Minister.

Throughout this period the Kamajors were the only large ethnic group that fought for the government as opposed to against it. Traditional hunters from the Mende tribe living in southern and eastern Sierra Leone, Kamajors earned a living contracting themselves to local elders known as Paramount

Above left: An SLA Patrol.

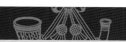

NEWTON BATTLE CAMP – SIERRA LEONE 2001

Newton Battle Camp trained SLA battalions from scratch. Route Clearance taught them how to counter ambushes: money ambushes with a large pile of currency in the middle of the road, followed closely by ensuing chaos; the three-mile ambush, with the killing area literally stretched over that distance and triggered by ripple fire; and the RPG ambush. Companies were also taught the two classic forms of attack: Deliberate, and Advance to Contact. For any of the readers who enjoy dangerous sports as a pasttime, may I thoroughly recommend a day on the range with the SLA. Capts Morgan and Faux now all suffer from very high blood pressure and a tendency to flinch at loud noises. The SLA Battalion's administration chain were not idle either. CSjt Stanley and Cpl Little set about the G4 world with gusto, ensuring that the daily rations of rice and fish heads were always on time and in the right place. Meanwhile WO2 Lewis was checking that Regimental Police performed their delegated tasks. The rate of escaping prisoners was cut down and the inspirational idea of providing helmets for the prisoners (red) and RP staff (white) ensured demi-god status and a place in SLA history. A rumour circulated that the RP staff would pray for his commission as an officer though no one was sure whether the CSM started this himself. The final stage was a five-day Final Test Exercise. Complete with purple chop-chop (food) pots attached to their webbing the battalions left NBC for a 12km insertion to Songo. Under the guidance of Major Evanson, a cunning and well-constructed position was created – the area was littered with pungi sticks, burning oil barrels and 'batsims' to raise the tempo of the attack. The experience of Newton Battle Camp was unforgettable. Jokes can be made about the SLA and its ability, but when the administration problems, the current lack of experienced and qualified junior commanders were taken into consideration, the ability of SLA was impressive. When we all next deploy to Wales or Scotland and it is raining one will always look back to the days on Hastings range and remember one of the oldest truths known to soldiers: Somewhere in the world a soldier is wetter and more miserable than you.

Chiefs. However their rise to ascendancy was secured when President Kabbah needed a reliable force to oppose the RUF when Sandline and Executive Outcomes were forced to cease their training and fighting mission in support of the government in 1996. Thus under the control of Hinga Norman the Kamajors were formalized as the Civil Defence Force that at its peak had 20,000 men under command.

Operations PALLISER and SILKMAN – building a new army from the RUF, AFRC and deserters from the Sierra Leone National Army (SLA)

Following the 1997 coup the AFRC demanded that ECOMOG release Foday Sankoh from incarceration in Nigeria. In doing so the AFRC set the conditions for an alliance with the RUF and as a joint force set about advancing on the capital of Freetown.

Driven back by ECOMOG, the AFRC and RUF force regrouped back in the east. President Kabbah was reinstated by ECOMOG and Johnny Paul Koroma was arrested, heralding a breakdown in AFRC and RUF relations. The AFRC attempted to seize the city for a second time in early 1999 and nearly succeeded in doing so before being evicted again by ECOMOG.

UK/US/UN intervention led to the agreement and signing of the Lomé Peace Accord on 7 July 1999 that set the conditions for the return of a stable government.

The Lomé peace deal took little time to deteriorate, resulting in a larger UN military intervention to enforce the peace before they too found themselves bogged down, virtually unable to operate and soon, in several places, UN units became wholly surrounded and taken hostage.

This set the conditions for a limited British deployment, Operation PALLISER in 2000, in order to restore peace and stability within the country.

With local forces routed, the fighting stopped almost immediately, leading to a larger and more sustained deployment of British battalions on Operation SILKMAN who set about the task of drawing together the disparate groups and administering a revamped Disarmament, Disbandment and Reintegration (DDR) amnesty for the former fighters so that they might form the basis of a wholly new and retrained Sierra Leone Army.

Foday Sankoh died in prison in 2003 prior to his attendance before the International War Crimes Tribunal. And now, in 2010, the Sierra Leone Army has sufficient confidence in its ability that it has just commenced its first international peacekeeping deployment to Darfur in the Sudan.

Below: Establishing radio communications with Freetown whilst escorting an IMATT advisor to a SLA RV.

Iraq

The invasion of Iraq in 2003 and the subsequent operation was the most controversial action in which the British Army has been involved for a generation. It is for others to determine the rights and wrongs of the Government's decisions: it was the soldiers' duty to achieve the mission in the best possible way. The British forces in southern Iraq around Basra were centred around a Brigade but one that was frequently reinforced. By 2006 the Shia rejectionists were very active in southern Iraq. But building up the Iraqi Army to the point where they were able to deal with the security challenge led to the eventual withdrawal of British forces. 1LI's involvement was continued by 5 Rifles which was the last Battalion of the British Army to leave Iraq as it handed over its role in Basra to US and Iraqi forces.

Operation TELIC was unpopular amongst the British public: but they retained their support for the Armed Forces through some very tough fighting and intense international scrutiny. The awards and battle honours that the Regiment gained in this campaign reflect the demands placed upon the most recent generation of soldiers and their ability to rise to the challenge with characteristic aplomb.

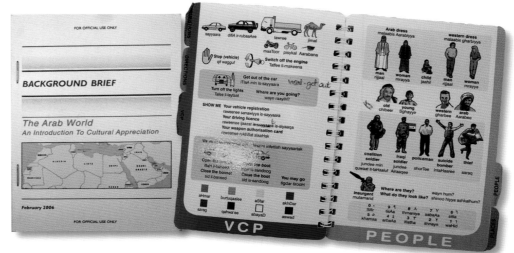

Operation TELIC

Operation TELIC was the UK contribution to the US-led Operation IRAQI FREEDOM. The political and legal background is covered elsewhere, not least in the exhaustive evidence presented to the Iraq Inquiry. Contingents of all three services were deployed in early 2003. 1 (UK) Armoured

Above: A wide variety of aide memoires were issued in Op TELIC.

Left: Op TELIC 8, B Coy on the move.

OPERATIONAL OVERVIEW

FIRST GULF WAR 1991–2 AND AFTERMATH

Britain had interests in Iraq during the days of Empire, and particularly in the period after the First World War until the 1950s. In August 1991, under the leadership of President Saddam Hussein and his Ba'ath regime, Iraq invaded and captured the adjoining city state of Kuwait, on the northern shore of the Persian Gulf. Operation GRANBY was the British contribution to 'Desert Storm', the US-led coalition campaign, which successfully liberated Kuwait in February 1992. Coalition forces, however, did not enter Iraqi territory, apart from setting up a safe haven for a few months in Kurdish territory. International diplomatic and political activity followed, with UN sanctions imposed against Iraq. The regime continued to suppress with extreme violence all internal opposition.

Throughout the 1990s there were very real fears that Iraq was re- arming, ready for further military action in the Gulf region, placing at risk its massive oil-producing capacity. There was some evidence that Iraq was gaining the technology to build weapons of mass destruction, including nuclear weapons, for use particularly against Israel and Iran, with whom it had fought an extremely costly war in the 1980s. In 2003 these fears provoked the invasion of Iraq by the US, supported by Britain and other nations.

ENEMY FORCES

The Iraqi Republican Guards Corps was formed in 1980 as an independent force charged with securing Saddam Hussein, the head of the Arab Socialist Ba'ath Party and President of Iraq. To many Iraqis the Republican Guards Corps (RGC) was the military elite. Initially just a brigade in size it was created to ensure the security of the president, but in 1986 it was expanded into a large division-sized force during the Iran–Iraq war (1980–8). At the Ba'ath party congress in 1986 the war was given precedence over all other effort; universities were closed and the government embarked upon mass mobilization which allowed the RGC to grow to 25 brigades.

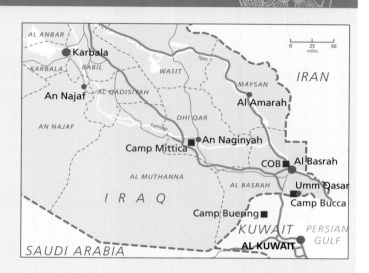

The newly constituted army retook the southern Al Faw peninsula from Iran. Four years later, the eight RGC divisions spearheaded Iraq's invasion of Kuwait and were charged with seizing the airports and airbases. In their subsequent retreat to Basra in the Gulf War of January 1991 one division was disbanded having suffered heavy losses. Thereafter the RGC played a key part in crushing the public uprisings within Iraq immediately after the war, notably of the Kurds in the north. By now split into two corps, the RGC did not fall under the command of the Ministry of Defence and was divided into two commands, one to the north and one in the south. Most visible were the four Baghdad, Medina, Nebuchadnezzar and Hammurabi Divisions arrayed around Baghdad to the south – as much to defend the city as to prevent the government running away. The capital of Baghdad was secured by the Special Republican Guard.

Further south hid the Fedayeen Saddam: paramilitary units of irregular forces which were not part of Iraq's regular armed forces. Neither elite nor well-trained, they were among the organizations most loyal to Saddam Hussein and were a reliable force against domestic opponents.

Division was allocated to southern Iraq. The formation, commanded by Major General Robin Brims, included two companies of 1LI as part of the 2 RTR battlegroup. But until March the main effort for the Armed Forces had been fire fighting, resulting in many units and individuals deploying at very short notice. Many considered that the name of the operation stood for 'Tell Everyone Leave Is Cancelled'. By 21 March, the UK had some 46,000 personnel in theatre, an impressive achievement, deploying twice as many vehicles as for Operation GRANBY in half the time. But logistics was extremely stretched and not all equipment, including body armour, reached the front line in time.

CENTCOM planned to attack the centre of gravity: the Saddam Hussein regime. US and UK planning for post-conflict operations envisaged a humanitarian emergency, large population movements, and major damage to infrastructure. It was assumed that the Iraqis would welcome the Coalition as liberators and that civil administration and Iraqi security forces would assist the occupying powers.

Regime change

On 19 March 2003, UKSF crossed into western Iraq to prevent Iraqi forces from launching ballistic missiles. LI officers filled key roles in the UKSF effort throughout the campaign, as they did in brigade and division HQs, in the many different organizations running the war, from the Green Zone in Baghdad to the permanent joint HQ in Northwood, the Ministry of Defence and the commitments and training staffs in land forces.

Land operations started on the night of 20 March. 3 Commando Brigade Royal Marines landed on the Al Faw peninsula and captured the extensive oil infrastructure in the Basra area. The main ground assault (G Day) followed on 21 March, with V (US) Corps launching at speed to by-pass west of An Nasiriyah, seizing crossings over the Euphrates. As part of the US Marine Expeditionary Force on the eastern flank 1 (UK) Armoured Division captured Al Zubayr and invested Basra, whilst the USMC raced up the eastern flank. US forces progressed rapidly towards Baghdad, culminating in Iraqi civilians and US Marines tying a noose around a statue of Saddam and tearing it from its pedestal on 9 April.

Concurrently 1 UK Armoured Division had deployed to protect the flank of US advance. 2 RTR battlegroup with its two companies of 1LI took part in the isolation of Az Zubayr. Armoured raids showed how the Iraq regime forces could be levered out of their urban positions without turning the town into rubble. Similar techniques were applied to Basra city, where Iraqi resistance collapsed on 6 April.

By 16 April the last pockets of organized resistance had crumbled. On 1 May President Bush announced the end of decisive combat operations from USS *Abraham Lincoln*. The two companies of 1LI were amongst the first UK troops to return home, as 20 Armoured Brigade had been warned for Operation TELIC 3.

Stability operations

The invasion did not lead to a major humanitarian crisis, no chemical or biological weapons were used, and no large-scale movement of people took place. But breakdown in law and order and widespread looting and vandalism caused massive damage to Iraq's already poor infrastructure and public services: health, education, water, sewerage, rubbish and electricity supply were all badly affected. On 23 May the Administrator of the Coalition Provisional Authority (CPA), Paul Bremer, dissolved existing ministries and branches of the armed forces and security services, and established new Iraqi Armed Forces, recruited and trained by Coalition forces. This 'de-Ba'athification' disempowered the Sunnis and many Iraqi officials. No single decision contributed more to the subsequent instability and war.

By July the US faced a growing and coordinated insurgency from former regime forces, particularly in Baghdad. And jihadists flocked to join Al Qaeda in Iraq (AQI). A car-bomb attack on the UN HQ in Baghdad caused the UN to withdraw from Iraq.

In southern Iraq, British troops were joined by an Italian brigade and contingents from the Czech Republic, Holland, Denmark, Romania, Australia and other nations to form

Multi National Division South East (MNDSE). But Iraqis were unwilling to put their faith in a force whose long-term commitment was unclear. Schools began to re-open, some of the electrical power returned and, although water remained in short supply, the newly established Umm Qasr water pipeline from Kuwait made a major difference. Joint patrols with the Basra Police commenced, aid was flowing into areas where it was most needed and there was a steady increase in activity by international agencies and aid organizations.

But contributions by other UK government departments were inadequate and reconstruction was too slow for the Baswaris. Unrest grew from impatience at the perceived lack of progress in the restoration of infrastructure and the handover of governance, reducing consent. On 16 June, 10,000 people forcibly demonstrated in Basra demanding Iraqi autonomy in the running of the city. The first post-war UK deaths from hostile action occurred on 24 June in Maysan Province when six members of the Royal Military Police were killed.

Shortly afterwards, the Iraqi Governing Council unveiled a timetable for the transfer of sovereignty, beginning in May 2004 with the formation of a transitional assembly. Iyad Allawi was appointed interim Prime Minister. Transfer of power from the CPA to the Interim Iraqi Government took place on 28 June. This focused on day-to-day administration including

Below: The FRG – the less-than-lethal answer to violent rioters.

providing security, promoting economic development and preparing for elections.

Saddam Hussein was captured in December. By then it was clear that no weapons of mass destruction had been discovered. Allegations of abuse of Iraqi prisoners by UK and US forces emerged in the media. The Sunni and AQI insurgencies grew as did Shia militias, including the Jaish al Mahdi (JAM) led by Muqtada al-Sadr. Coaltion casualties continued to rise. 1LI deployed as part of 20 Armoured Brigade in November 2003, responsible for Maysan province. The last weeks of their tour saw a steep escalation in violence as the first of two Shia uprisings took place. A second such uprising that summer saw widespread fighting throughout the country. In Basra a platoon of 2LI reinforcing 1 Cheshire was in the thick of the action. 2LI as a whole also reinforced Iraq from Cyprus.

Elections for the Iraqi National Assembly took place on 30 January 2005, although these were mostly boycotted by the

ON ATTACHMENT

Salamanca platoon of the Second Battalion was attached to the First Battalion The Cheshire Regiment in Iraq. Commanded by the relatively newly commissioned Second Lieutenant Will Follett, whose family had served in The Light Infantry for generations, their tour was extremely busy. Sadly one man, Lance Corporal Taff Thomas, was killed in action against the militia. The Commanding Officer of 1 Cheshire wrote:

'Your men have been a great credit to you and your Battalion. They have been highly professional and committed, courageous and well led. Furthermore, they have been in the thick of it throughout. I think it is worth giving you a feel for the tour as undoubtedly they will be too modest to do it themselves. As a battlegroup, we have endured 450 contacts, killing 193 militiamen and firing over 50,000 rounds of small arms ammunition. Our bases have been struck by over 100 mortars or rockets and we have encountered 43 improvised explosive devices. The courage and fortitude of all the Battle Group in this largely forgotten war has been astounding.'

Below: The 'Battalion Sniper' maintains a watchful eye.

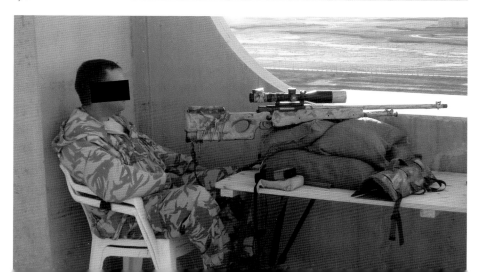

Sunni. The success of the elections and the role of the Iraqi Security Forces in supporting these gave the Coalition cause for a guarded optimism. Events showed that this optimism was misplaced. For example April saw an increased use by Sunni/AQI insurgents of suicide car bombs.

For MNDSE, the main effort in 2005 was to be Security Sector Reform (SSR), the mentoring and training of the Iraqi Army and police. In Maysan Province Shia militants moved from using simple roadside bombs to the more sophisticated explosively formed penetrator (EFP) devices. These were capable of penetrating Challenger and Warrior and considerably overmatched the Snatch Land Rover. Initially the only feasible countermeasure tactics were based on those used against IRA roadside bombs, but quickly physical countermeasures, including up-armouring Challenger and Warrior, came on line. But this made it much more difficult to conduct SSR. Some progress was made with the Iraqi Army, but the Foreign Office-led effort to train the Iraqi Police Service achieved little in either increasing effectiveness or rooting out corruption and the influence of the Shia militia. This was vividly demonstrated in September 2005, when two plain-clothes soldiers were detained and abused at the notorious Jameat police station, requiring forcible rescue by Challengers and Warriors. Responsibility for police training passed from the Foreign Office to the Army shortly afterwards.

The UK's decision to increase forces in Afghanistan in early 2006 increasingly placed Iraq as a lower priority than the increasing commitment to ISAF. This campaign with its unforeseen heavy fighting came to dominate media coverage, which paid less attention to the fighting in Iraq, which in 2006–7 was just as intense – albeit with fewer UK casualties. For the first time in public, the Chief of the General Staff commented publicly on the situation in Iraq on 13 October, describing the British Army as part of the problem in Basra.

A permanent Iraqi Government was formed under the leadership of Prime Minister Maliki on 20 May 2006, who shortly afterwards announced a state of emergency in Basra. 2LI deployed to Basra at this time, to be immediately faced with the aftermath of the shooting down of a Lynx helicopter, and a high intensity of attacks from the JAM. In September, PM Maliki blocked UK plans for major operations against militia influence in Basra; instead, Operation SINBAD was launched to improve security and set the conditions for the transition to Iraqi control of Basra Province. As the pulses of Operation SINBAD focused reconstruction and SSR effort on sections of the city, British troops were mounting intelligence-led raids on JAM leadership and supplies.

This 'war against the JAM' continued after 2LI was relieved in place by 2 RGJ in November 2006. They and the DDLI were part of 19 Light Brigade, commanded by Brigadier Tim Evans LI. This was possibly the hardest-fought part of the 'war against the JAM', with increasing attacks against UK forces causing significant casualties. Pitched battles resulted from

JAM efforts to contest resupply of bases and counterattack our raids against them. On 25 December, at PM Maliki's request, UK troops launched an operation to disband the Basra Serious Crimes Unit; the Provincial Council stopped contact with UK forces in protest.

The Rifles were formed in the middle of this tour – celebrated by the brigade commander and representatives of all the forming regiments going on patrol. Operation ZENITH, the repositioning of UK forces, began in January 2007 with the aim of consolidating forces on the Contingency Operating Base (COB) at Basra Airport. The Old State Building in Basra, Shaibah base, Provincial Joint Coordination Centre and Basra Palace were progressively handed over to the Iraqi Armed Forces throughout the year. Accordingly, the Prime Minister announced plans to reduce UK forces from 7,100 to approximately 5,500 – one month after President Bush unveiled his new strategy of the surge on 10 January.

An accommodation was reached under which JAM would cease attacks on the UK Army in return for the progressive release of 120 internees. This allowed 4 RIFLES to withdraw from Basra Palace out of contact, enabling the consolidation to the COB to take place. Moqtada al-Sadr subsequently froze activity of the JAM for six months on 29 August. All political parties in Basra, including those with militia links, signed an agreement to respect the rule of law on 4 December, allowing the transfer to PIC of Basra Province on 16 December. From that point UK forces supported operations only when requested to do so by the Iraqi authorities and worked with General Mohan, the Iraqi commander of Basra operations. By the end of the year, UK force levels had reduced to around 4,500.

However, one outcome of the departure of UK forces was that there was little restraint on JAM control of the city. As a result, on 23 March PM Maliki announced his intention to accelerate Iraqi-led plans to tackle criminality and militia influence in Basra. He launched Operation CHARGE OF THE KNIGHTS by deploying 40,000 more Iraqi troops and police. Initial Iraqi attacks were uncoordinated, the JAM resisted fiercely and the operation stalled. UK troops quickly reconfigured to form Military Transition teams (MiTTs) that fought alongside Iraqi commanders whilst advising them and calling for air strikes and artillery fire. This and the US surging attack helicopters and air power over Basra turned the corner and the Iraqi Army with UK and US support cleared the JAM from Basra and Maysan. On 10 May, the Iraqi Government and JAM signed a ten-point agreement on a ceasefire. For the remainder of the year, increased Iraqi assertiveness over national sovereignty prevailed, as they negotiated with the US and UK for a post-UNSCR legal framework.

20 Armoured Brigade and 5 Rifles (formerly 1LI) returned to Basra in November 2008. On 18 December, the Prime Minister confirmed that UK forces would complete their training and mentoring of the Iraqi Army by 31 May 2009 and withdraw from Basra by 31 July 2009.

Iraqi sovereignty

On the last day of 2008, UNSCR 1790 expired and all remaining provinces transferred to Iraqi control. On 1 January 2009, the US/Iraq Security Agreement and a new legal basis for UK forces entered into force and Iraqi airspace and Basra International Airport transferred to Iraqi civilian control. Iraqi provincial elections passed off peacefully on 31 January. The UK published its first comprehensive strategy for Iraq. On 31 March, the UK-led MND(SE) and US-led MND (Centre) merged to form MND (South) under US command. Formal completion of the UK military mission in southern Iraq was marked on 30 April, at which point the Iraqi Army's 14 Division was judged ready to plan, execute and sustain operations with minimal coalition support. On 31 May, MOU permissions allowing UK forces to conduct operations expired, and UK forces focused solely on the withdrawal of personnel and materiel, which was successfully completed under Operation BROCKDALE.

LAST POST

Private Michael Tench (18) of A Company, 2nd Battalion The Light Infantry, was the last Light Infantryman to be killed on operations. He died as a result of injuries sustained from an Improvised Explosive Device in Basra City, southern Iraq, on 21 January 2007. A talented boxer from Sunderland, 'Tenchy' joined 2LI in December 2005. Popular, fun, fit and professional to the core, he was buried with full military honours on 2 February 2007. Two thousand mourners lined the streets to pay their respects along the route of the cortege from Holy Trinity Church, Southwick, to the local cemetery, while 800 people attended the wake at the Roker Hotel. Tenchy's mother, Janice Murray, said, 'He was an inspiration to young men all over this country. I know he faced death with no fear in his heart. He believed in what he was doing.' Janice has been an inspiration to one and all since her son's death, selfless in raising well over £100,000 for a memorial in the North East for fallen service personnel and tireless in helping serving and ex-personnel.

Afghanistan

The Taliban and other Anti-Government Elements within Afghanistan

From 2001 until late 2003 the international community faced a wholly different enemy to that which confronts us now. Drawn predominantly from different ethnic tribes within the Pashtun population, the Taliban were devout Muslims with strong Deobandi-Salafi beliefs; many coming from the madrassas or religious schools. Additionally, the Taliban of 2001 also had a number of foreign volunteers, notably Uzbeks, Tajiks, Chechens and some Arabs. The Taliban were formally recognized by just three countries: the United Arab Emirates, Saudi Arabia and Pakistan.

Within much of Afghan rural society authority is wielded in a complex 'triangle' of power; laws are interpreted and enforced by a combination of inputs from the Khans or senior families within an area (the aristocratic 'lords'), the Maliks or elected local government officials, and the Mullahs – the parish priests. Historically the Khans and Maliks were the decision-makers who would sit at formal village or district meetings or shuras to dispense justice. Traditionally the Mullah was not a decision-maker but would lead the prayers prior to the outset of a shura as well as offering philosophical advice on the issues to be discussed.

The Taliban were the army of the Mullahs. The Mullahs were not used to decision-making or governance – the way to run a democratic nation. They had no experience of it at all and favoured the most severe and fundamental interpretation of the Koran. And so the Taliban set about dismantling the traditional

Right: Who let the rocket in? A Company 2LI at Kajuki Dam, February 2007.

OPERATIONAL OVERVIEW

There is a long history of Western politico-military involvement in Afghanistan, a mountainous country now of 22 million people, in which power has traditionally resided in tribal leaders, rather than central authority in Kabul. Britain fought three Afghan wars – in 1839–42, which was disastrous; in 1879–80, which was more successful; and in 1919. While the chief aims of these wars had been to dominate the Afghan tribal areas, thus denying the extension of Russian power into the region threatening British India, the North West Frontier region of India had always given the British trouble. The hill tribes are amongst the fiercest fighters on earth, fired by their Muslim faith and unwillingness to cede power to anyone. The Russians learnt the same lesson when Soviet forces invaded Afghanistan in 1979. They were forced to abandon the country some ten years later, having lost 15,000 soldiers dead and many thousands injured. In this struggle some Western nations had supported the Mujahidin, the Afghan freedom-fighters; but this fact is now a historical embarrassment to the West.

ENEMY FORCES

On Christmas Eve 1979 the Soviet Union invaded Afghanistan and proceeded to embark upon one of the most costly occupations in recent memory. By the time the Soviets withdrew in February 1989 they had lost 15,000 soldiers.

The departure of the Russians heralded an even more unstable period in Afghan history as regional and local warlords fought a civil war for territory or control in the vacuum of governance left by the withdrawal of the Russians and their subsequent replacement by an Islamic Jihad Council. In November 1994 local disaffection with the deteriorating state of internal security erupted in Kandahar when a man called Mullah Omar led a band of students on a mission to confront and hang two militiamen who had committed rape. The students promptly called themselves 'Taliban' or 'Students' and a popular uprising was born. The very essence of the Taliban at the outset was to create stability and order, but along sharia lines. Mullah Omar's tolerance for other Islamic hard-line groups allowed elements of a new group called Al Qaeda, many of whom had fought alongside the mujahidin during the Soviet occupation, but had recently been expelled from Sudan, to base themselves within Afghanistan. The attacks on the World Trade Center, New York and the Pentagon, Washington DC on 11 September 2001 were instantly traced to Al Qaeda leadership in Afghanistan and the US and other nations' troops occupied the country. The aim was, and remains, to bring security and democracy to the country, a daunting task amongst a mainly primitive but cunning population.

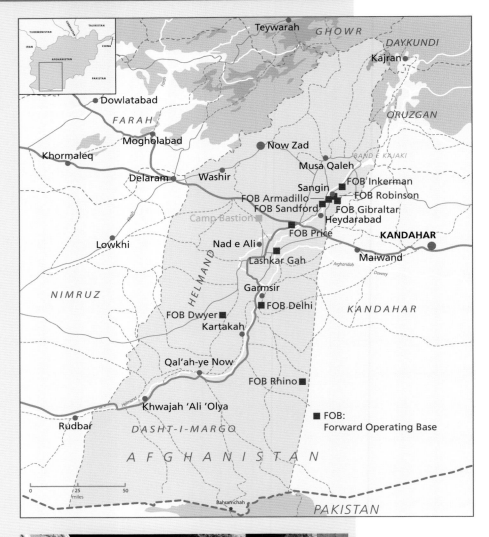

Left: Always time for a photo!

Above: On watch: Kajuki Dam, February 2007.

Right: Lt Tim Illingworth (standing, baseball cap and beard) and his team, who was later awarded the CGC for his actions.

CONSPICUOUS GALLANTRY CROSS

'On 10 September 2006, Lieutenant Timothy Illingworth deployed with a small team in support of a joint Afghan Police and Army operation to recapture Garmsir District Centre. During two days of heavy fighting, Lieutenant Illingworth and his team were constantly under fire whilst motivating, directing and advising their Afghan colleagues who successfully re-took Garmsir. Later that week an Afghan Police patrol supported by Illingworth's team, was ambushed. One British casualty resulted. In an effort to relieve the pressure on the Afghan Police, he led his Afghan company commander and a foot patrol to neutralize the enemy position. This inspired his Afghan Army colleagues who were reticent to advance on the heavily defended enemy position.

'The Afghani resolve to continue failed after three days of heavy fighting. Seeing this, Lieutenant Illingworth went to the front of the Afghan troops and moved alone to within 30 metres of the first enemy position under heavy fire. Soon after the company commander was killed. Lieutenant Illingworth took up the commander's rocket launcher, firing three rounds into the main enemy position in full view of them. He himself narrowly missed being killed. All but one of the Afghan force abandoned Illingworth, leaving him exposed and under withering fire. In spite of his isolation, he attempted to assault the enemy position expending seven magazines of ammunition. The enemy fire was unrelenting. He regrouped and rallied the remaining force to continue.

'Lieutenant Illingworth's bravery and example over seven days was well beyond the call of duty. His role was to mentor rather than fight. However, understanding the importance of Garmsir, he placed himself in a position of utmost danger to influence events. His outstanding courage, leadership and selflessness in pressing home his attack upset the enemy ambush and saved many lives. Such inspiring and raw courage from a relatively young and inexperienced officer was exemplary and justly merit the award of the Conspicuous Gallantry Cross.'

structures, intimidating or killing all of the Maliks and many of the Khans as they rigorously imposed an extreme form of sharia law. It is the destruction of these structures of local, tribal governance that is at the heart of the problems we face today. Such was their vigour to embrace this almost medieval code that they declared Shia Muslims to be non-Islamic and famously destroyed the Buddha statues in Bamyan in March 2001.

The Taliban's rout after 9/11 was almost but not quite total. Their front lines collapsed after a couple of weeks of intensive bombing and on 12 November 2001 they abandoned Kabul with most remaining fighters fleeing to the Pakistan tribal areas on the Afghan border.

The Taliban's leadership immediately went into hiding in the aftermath of 9/11 with its primary headquarters based in Quetta, known as 'the Quetta Shura', and other elements split between the Federally Administered Tribal Areas (FATA) along Afghanistan's eastern border and in Karachi, Pakistan's southernmost major city and main port of entry.

Since 2004 a new Taliban has emerged along with a number of other groups that have limited interest in the imposition of sharia but seek to secure the freedom of action to do as they wish be it narco-trafficking, armed criminality, contraband smuggling or local warlordism and are happy to do so under the Taliban 'brand'.

PART 5
The Way Ahead

Forming The Rifles

After many years of defending the practice of the Arms Plot, the system whereby units moved from station and role to new station and new role around the world every few years, the Army Board decided that the practice must stop. By 2004 the small size of the Infantry, the demand for battalions ready for deployment, and the desire for domestic stability were key factors that led to this decision. Most Arms and Services had ceased their Arms Plot when the Cold War ended.

The Army Board recognized that infantrymen would now need to move around battalions in order to enhance their professional development, for example to gain experience of different roles, and to suit their personal circumstances. To enable such movement and to preserve the integrity of the regimental system, the Army Board directed that the Infantry should reorganize itself into new groupings of large regiments of two regular battalions or more.

The Light Infantry could have ignored this reorganization, as it already met the requirement. But by early 2004 the Regimental Council determined that an even larger regiment would provide the best environment in which future generations could flourish. After consultation it was clear that the vast majority of the serving Regiment agreed with this proposal, despite some sadness at the prospect of change. It was further determined that we should build on the success of The Light Infantry in creating the new regiment. We recognized the value of our identity as an English regiment deeply rooted in its counties. In addition, our regimental structure, based on the four pillars of Regular and Territorial battalions, Cadets and Regimental Association, working to County Offices and a central Regimental Headquarters had served us well and was much admired by others. It had enabled us to sustain our reputation as one of the very best-manned regiments in the Army, a product of excellent recruiting and retention. It was gratifying that The Royal Green Jackets, The Devonshire and Dorset Regiment and The Royal Gloucestershire, Berkshire and Wiltshire Regiment had reached the same conclusion.

The Light Division Council, which represented the four regiments listed above, was also seized with the need to secure the best possible bases and roles for the five Regular Battalions, as many TA battalions, companies and platoons as could be afforded in all of our heartlands, the retention of our county offices to look after those heartlands, and the opportunity to encourage our Cadet organizations to join The Rifles. By placing ourselves at the vanguard of reorganization, the Light Division could secure a lion's share of the future Infantry – and this adaptability was recognized by the Army Board.

The enthusiasm of the serving element of the Regiment for change was understandably tempered amongst the retired community, who were more nervous of losing our identity and heritage in such a move. Nevertheless, with guidance sought and received from the former Colonels of The Light Infantry, lengthy and detailed discussions started with the other Forming Regiments of what was to become The Rifles. Since this was to be a new Regiment, created uniquely by the Forming Regiments coming together of their own free will, it was recognized that when announcing our decision we needed to promulgate its new name and cap badge.

In keeping with the traditions of our celebrated Light Division, it was agreed that name and cap badge would be the cornerstone of our

The Golden Threads of the past are carried through to The Rifles: publicity literature for the Durham Light Infantry Museum complements the publicity literature for The Rifles and (left) a Private of the 52nd, c.1850.

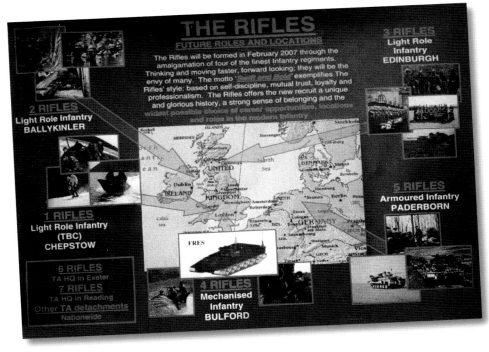

established protocol, guarded by the College of Arms, required some adaptation, so we added the Queen's crown to our bugle.

One key feature of The Rifles, a lesson learned by The Light Infantry and central to its success, is that it should have one clear identity and ethos throughout the regiment, rather than fragmenting into diverse battalions and units, each claiming a different heritage and displaying a different image. A Corporal and his family should be able to move from one battalion to another, Regular or TA, and feel at home, familiar with his uniform and shared tradition. This meant compromise on all sides, including the loss of several precious and unique Light Infantry customs, such as our Colour Serjeants wearing the red sash over the left shoulder, but with good will in equal proportions, decisions were reached by a series of committees representing all levels of each Forming Regiment. This was exemplified by the discussions surrounding the celebration of battle honours, which led to the decision to create a belt badge to be worn by all ranks. This is described separately by its designer, then Lieutenant Colonel Ted Shields, Commanding Officer of 2LI. The main thing is that if a Light Infantryman visits a battalion of The Rifles today, it will seem pretty familiar to him: apart from the familiar cap badge, it wears (Light Infantry) green, it marches at 140 paces to the minute, it responds to the Bugle and there is a relaxed informality between all ranks. General Sir John Moore would recognize the model.

identity and ethos. In the spirit of General Sir John Moore, we decided to keep things simple, clear and recognizable. Hence the name: The Rifles. Importantly this title does not lend itself to abbreviation or nickname. As for the cap badge, the bugle horn was accepted by all. The Light Infantry's bugle was chosen but

Right: A fireteam from 1 Rifles in a heavy firefight, Helmand Province, Afghanistan.

The work progressed satisfactorily, and by November 2005 all the regiments involved had agreed to form a new Regiment entitled The Rifles. It would be a regiment of five Regular Battalions (with 1LI becoming 5 Rifles and 2LI becoming 3 Rifles) and two Territorial Battalions. The Regiment's Charter was agreed in November 2005, and in June 2006 the Principles for The Rifles were also signed. These conformed to the conditions set by the former Colonels Commandant, and The Rifles were formed on 1 February 2007 as the first truly large infantry Regiment in the Army of the modern era with battalions deployed in a variety of roles providing the widest possible opportunity:

1 RIFLES at Chepstow to join 3 Commando Brigade.
2 RIFLES at Ballykinler in the light role.
3 RIFLES at Edinburgh in the light role.
4 RIFLES at Bulford in the mechanized role.
5 RIFLES at Paderborn, Germany in the armoured role.
6 RIFLES in the South West in the light role.
7 RIFLES in the North East in the light role.

The Light Infantry Legacy to The Rifles

The Rifles inherited from The Light Infantry the rich and unique legacy of the light infantry regiments of the British Army. This legacy can be divided broadly into three areas; its distinctive outward appearances and customs, its characteristics and its ethos.

Left: LCpl Pope calls 'All Officers'.

THE CHARTER OF THE RIFLES

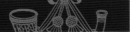

The Army Board has directed battalions to group into larger regiments to meet the operational and organisational demands of the future. In light of this, Her Majesty The Queen has graciously approved the formation of a new regiment. The Devonshire and Dorset Light Infantry, The Light Infantry, The Royal Gloucestershire, Berkshire and Wiltshire Light Infantry and The Royal Green Jackets recognise the profound impact of the Army Board's decision. They elect to join together to form a wholly new regiment called The Rifles; comprising seven battalions, five Regular and two Territorial, as well as other Territorial, Cadet and Association elements. They do this after thorough and careful consideration, of their own free will, to ensure the continued excellence of their service to The Crown. The four Founding Regiments will combine to form The Rifles from the Light Division.

The Rifles will take their inspiration from the Founding Regiments' Light Division ancestry, including their Line Regiment History. The Rifles will hold to the qualities advanced by General Sir John Moore and displayed by the finest of infantry regiments. They will demonstrate the values of independent thought and action, leadership, self-discipline, fortitude and steadfastness. The Rifles will strive for excellence and be known for their fighting spirit and strong sense of decency. They will be forward looking, at the forefront of military thought and determined to set the highest professional standards. The Regiment will give a place to all and anyone prepared to soldier loyally and effectively.

The Rifles will cherish and foster their links to the counties, cities and towns from which they come; and which underpin their strong sense of national identity. This new Regiment will be organised, operated and commanded so as to bring unity, professionalism and a sense of pride to all those who step forward with The Rifles.

Lieutenant General	Lieutenant General	General Sir Kevin	Major General NJ
Sir Cedric Delves KBE DSO	RV Brims CBE DSO	O'Donoghue KCB CBE	Cottam OBE
Col DDLI	Col Comdt Lt Div & Col LI	Col RGBW LI	Regt Col Comdt RGJ

25th November 2005

Light Infantry Customs

Rifle-Green Uniform

The Light Infantry rifle-green ceremonial uniform jackets, headdress and blazer continues forward into The Rifles with the addition of thin red piping at the base of No. 1 dress collars, black buttons and accessories and scarlet collar and sleeve cuffs overlaid with black braid on Mess Kit jackets and band parade uniforms. This is very similar to the uniform of the 60th, which retained scarlet in memory of their red-coat origins, but now represents as well the red-coat background of the other founding regiments of The Rifles.

The Bugle

In their original role light infantry adopted open-order tactics and skirmishing, fighting well forward of the main infantry formations. Individuals often found themselves beyond the range of the human voice and needed an efficient way of signalling to control battlefield manoeuvres and drill. The bugle provided the appropriate way of passing orders, and a complex system of calls was developed, many of them still in use today. For The Light Infantry the bugle remains the equivalent of the drums or bagpipes of other infantry regiments, hence 'Sounding Retreat' rather than 'Beating Retreat' will continue to be used by The Rifles.

Battle Honours

Whilst the playing field was not level (the DDLI came from two post-1881 regiments; the LI from five; the RGBWLI from three; and the RGJ from three), the DDLI can claim 44 per cent of the representational Battle Honours, the LI 70 per cent, the RGBWLI 67 per cent and the RGJ 65 per cent. The 34 representative Battle Honours are thus truly representative of the forming regiments (by quantity and iconography), history and geography. The belt badge design and its 34 representative Battle Honours were formally approved by Her Majesty The Queen in August 2006, in time to meet production timelines for the formation of The Rifles on 1 February 2007. The Rifles is, of course, forward looking. This explains the one blank scroll on the badge for the Regimental history which is yet to be written.

Cap badge

The bugle horn was the distinctive symbol used by all light troops and was incorporated into the badges of all former Light Infantry Regiments. It was also the cap badge of The Light Infantry. It was at the centre of the RGJ cap badge but was used 'alone' as the cap badge worn on a boss on the sidehats of officers and WOs and the collar dogs on No. 2 Dress for all ranks in the Light Division. Combined with a crown the bugle horn now forms the cap badge of The Rifles.

The Crossbelt

Adapted originally from light cavalry style, The Light Infantry officers' black crossbelt carried a whistle to pass on orders to dispersed riflemen in the same manner as the bugle, and a large version of the cap badge carrying representative battle honours. The Light Infantry adopted the black crossbelt on 10 July 1977, and the design is now being carried forward into The Rifles. Their new crossbelt will carry a large version of The Rifles belt badge and an 'Inkerman whistle' with chain on the front, and a pouch with The Rifles bugle horn cap badge on the back.

Light Infantry Drill

Light infantry drill descends from the original need for dispersed infantrymen to move rapidly and easily across the battlefield with the minimum of orders. Carrying rifles at

Top right: Officers at the Double.

Right: These two famous DLI Polo paintings by Lionel Edwards (1878– 1966) now hang in 3 RIFLES' Officers' Mess.

THE RIFLES' REPRESENTATIVE BATTLE HONOURS

'As a rifle regiment, battalions of The Rifles will not carry Colours. Instead, battle honours are entrusted to each Rifleman, who wears a representative selection of battle honours from all the forming regiments on the cross belt or belt badge.'

– The Principles of The Rifles, 11 July 2006

The British infantry of the line have borne their Battle Honours on their Colours since 1784 but, such has been the rifleman's role on the field of battle, no British (or Commonwealth) rifle regiment has ever carried Colours. A rifle regiment's Battle Honours – or a representative selection – have thus been displayed on cap and/or belt badges. But it was not just our rifle forebears who chose to display particular Battle Honours on their badges. The cap badge of the 13th Light Infantry (later the Somerset Light Infantry) included a mural crown and the title 'Jellalabad' following the award in 1842. The cap badge of Dorsetshire Regiment included the title 'Marabout' and the Egyptian Sphinx after that award in 1801. The 66th (Berkshire) Foot displayed their nine Peninsular War Battle Honours on their Officers' shoulder belt plate from 1829 to 1855.

It had previously been agreed that The Rifles' cap badge would be the bugle horn badge of The Light Infantry surmounted by St Edward's Crown. Representative Battle Honours would thus have to be selected for display on the belt badge only. The task of recommending to The Light Division Council which Battle Honours would best represent the new Regiment on the belt badge fell to the Working Group of Commanding Officers which met in late 2005 and early 2006. The Working Group's 'canvas' was:

> … a wreath of laurel intertwined with a scroll, bearing Battle Honours of the Regiment. Within the wreath, a Maltese Cross. On the divisions further Battle Honours of the Regiment. On the centre of the Cross, a circle inscribed 'The Rifles' and 'Swift and Bold'; within the circle a bugle with strings. Above the cross, a crown on a scroll, inscribed 'Peninsula'; below the cross, a further scroll.

It was universally agreed that 'Peninsula' – 'a campaign in which all the founding regiments served with distinction' (*The Principles of The Rifles*) – should take prime position above the Cross. This left space on the scrolls of the wreath and on the four divisions of the Cross for around 30 Battle Honours. The four forming regiments, themselves the product of 22 pre-Cardwell Reform (1881) regiments, had amassed a total of 913 Battle Honours of which 437 were shared between two or more. The Working Group finally produced a short list of 34 Battle Honours for consideration, recommending that three be 'paired' (Delhi and Lucknow; Ypres and Somme; and Korea and Imjin).

There were five selection criteria: general historical significance and public awareness but balanced by regimental iconography; exclusivity (in that the Battle Honour is exclusive to The Rifles); underpinning regimental ethos; chronological and geographical spread; and the opportunity to 'double hat' as, for example, the Royal Green Jackets had done for their cap badge where the 'Defence of Ladysmith' and the 'Relief of Ladysmith' were combined as 'Ladysmith.'

The nation's great battles are thus represented: *Plassey* (1757), exclusive to The Rifles, at which Clive of India took Bengal; *Minden* (1759) where the six Minden Regiments repelled the French cavalry; *Quebec* (1759) where Canada was secured for Britain; *Waterloo* (1815) where Napoleon was finally defeated; *Delhi* (1857) and *Lucknow* (1857–8) where the Indian Mutiny was crushed; *Inkerman* (1854), the Crimean battle where the British, outnumbered five to one, defeated the Russians; *Ypres* (1914–18) and the *Somme* (1916, 1918), the scenes of some of the heaviest fighting of the First World War; *El Alamein* (1942) which turned not just the war in North Africa but, arguably, the Second World War itself; *Italy* 1943–5 represents 58 Theatre Battle Honours awarded to antecedents of The Rifles although *Anzio* (1944) is accorded its own scroll; *Kohima* (1944), the turning point of the Burma Campaign; and *Normandy* (1944), actually awarded as the 'Normandy Landing,' but covering the Normandy campaign. *Vittorio Veneto* (1918) deserves greater public recognition for it was the Allied victory at this battle which led to the Austro-Hungarian surrender, the disintegration of that empire and pressure which led Germany to sign the Armistice.

The forming regiments each held particular Battle Honours dear. These Battle Honours may not have changed

Below: Exercising The Freedom of the City of Wells to mark The Tercentenary of The Light Infantry in the presence of HRH Princess Alexandra, 15 June 1985.

Below: Familiar Light Infantry imagery in a new context. The Rifles belt buckle incorporates the Maltese cross and battle honours of the antecedent regiments, with space for the future.

the course of history but represent courage, fighting spirit and determination to inspire all past, present and future Riflemen. They underpin the Regiment's ethos. Included are: *Copenhagen* (1801), exclusive to The Rifles, saw the destruction of the Danish Fleet and heralding The Rifles' commando role; *Marabout* (1801), exclusive to The Rifles, where the 54th (later the Dorsets) helped to secure victory against the French at Alexandria (where the 28th (later the Glosters) won the Back Badge); *Jellalabad* (1842), exclusive to The Rifles, where the 13th Light Infantry held out against Afghan forces for five months; *Ferozeshah* (1845) where the 62nd (later the Wiltshires) led the main attack against the Sikhs, suffering appalling casualties as a result; *Nonne Boschen* (1914) where five antecedent regiments prevented the Germans from breaking through the British line; *Calais* (1940) where the King's Royal Rifle Corps and the Rifle Brigade enabled Dunkirk to be kept open; *Pegasus Bridge* (1944), the first objective of D-Day seized by D Company 2nd Ox and Bucks Light Infantry; and the *Imjin* (1951), a battle of the Korean War where the Glosters' determination against extraordinary odds captured the imagination of the world.

The representative Battle Honours cover the span of post-Restoration (1660) British military history: the War of the Spanish Succession (The Rifles' oldest Battle Honour is *Gibraltar*, 1704–5); the War of the Austrian Succession including *Dettingen* (1743), the last time a British monarch commanded in battle; the Seven Years War; the Napoleonic Wars; the expansion of the British Empire; the Crimean War; the First and Second World Wars; the Korean War; and The Rifles' most recent Battle Honour, *Iraq* 2003. The geographic spread is equally comprehensive: from the West Indies (*Martinique*, covering three awards in 1762, 1794 and 1809) to Afghanistan (covering five awards from 1839 to 1919); from New Zealand (covering two awards in 1847 and 1866) to China (*Pekin*, 1860); from South Africa (covering five awards from 1846 to 1902) to the Middle East (*Megiddo* (1918), where General Allenby routed the Turkish Army); and from the Americas (*Quebec*, 1759) to the Far East (*Kohima*, 1944 and *Korea*, 1950–3).

Below: The Last Supper – 1LI Officers' Mess Final Dinner Night.

the trail rather than in the shoulder and all drill movements automatically starting and ending in the 'at ease' position typify light drill. Light pace, a quick march at 140 paces to the minute compared to the standard Army 120, and a double march at 180 paces to the minute rather than a slow march, are based on the original Light Infantry Regiments, which frequently on outpost duty, needed to move around the battlefield faster than other infantry units, and often at the 'double'.

Light Infantry Property
Light Infantry property is primarily to be found in the Officers' and Serjeants' Messes of the 3rd and 5th Battalions of The Rifles, being the old 2nd and 1st Battalions The Light Infantry. A few items of regimental property have been re-located to the other three battalions to ensure that The Light Infantry is represented across the Regiment. Current and future generations of The Rifles are able, therefore, to admire and reflect upon such magnificent trophies as the Askold Cup, the Lucknow Tureen, the 51st's coffin-shaped snuff box, 2KOYLI's Menin Gate and Lionel Edwards' two DLI polo oils (see p.177).

Light Infantry Mess Customs
Whilst Colours no longer reside in the Officers' Messes, there is much else that would be familiar to generations of Light Infantrymen. Officers of The Light Infantry neither drank the Loyal Toast nor suffered after-dinner speeches, a custom that properly – and thankfully – continues through into The Rifles. Nevertheless, the KOYLI custom of the silent toast to 'Dyas and the Stormers' is permitted when Commanding Officers of The Rifles seek to honour one of the Regiment's most distinguished forebears. Once observed in every Mess of Wellington's Army, the gallantry of the 'forlorn hope' led by Ensign Joseph Dyas of the 51st at Badajoz in June 1811 is not forgotten.

Light Infantry Characteristics

These are embodied by the very simple and clear **aims** which we set for the Regiment. These were to:

- *Foster an understanding and pride in our Regimental 'Culture'.*
- *Recruit, stimulate, encourage and, thus retain, a fully manned Regiment of thinking officers and soldiers, in order to foster pride, esprit de corps and a professionalism based on the 'Light Infantry Ethos'.*
- *Develop a cohesive, robust, adaptable, responsive and professional Regiment that is of High Morale by being fully manned, operationally effective, confident, successful, caring and enjoyable to serve in.*

The Light Infantry Ethos

Our legacy in this area is perhaps the most important as it is key to the way that The Light Infantry operated so successfully, and the basis we hope of the ethos of The Rifles. To quote from the regimental policy booklet *The Light Infantry Ethos.*:

We pride ourselves on being informal but professional. Our approach is one of relaxed efficiency and a lack of pomposity. We try to achieve the end result with a minimum of fuss but with flair and panache. We work hard at developing a close rapport with our soldiers and we look after them. We also pride ourselves on our adaptability and our ability to anticipate change – to be the trend and pace-setters – rather than merely reacting to the pressure of events. Our customs and traditions are, therefore, a reflection of our ethos: our drill is simple, swift and requires few orders; it sums up our approach and along with the Bugle it projects our image. Furthermore, our customs mark us apart and give us a distinctive and elite character. In short we believe that our approach enhances operational efficiency by developing a flexible, adaptable and original thinking corps of officers and NCOs who do not shy away from shouldering responsibilities and taking decisions at the correct level.

Extract from The Colonel Of the Regiment's Annual Report 2004

But what are our driving principles and our ethos that keep us in such good health? What is it that, despite the exceptional demands we are currently making, allows us to recruit and above all to retain our soldiers in this somewhat uncertain environment? At the risk of sounding rather old-fashioned, we do seem to have re-established over the past ten or so years some basic principles. My grandmother would probably have expressed these as: 'I don't mind what you do as long as you don't frighten the horses' and 'Remember your manners'. She would also have had some pithy but human comment on morality!

These do have an echo in modern military life. Perhaps the most significant is the reference to manners, because within these are the essence of the Regiment's attitude to leadership. The ability to say 'Good Morning' to your soldiers

Above: Exerting some personal influence on Op TELIC.

Below: The lighter side of life in The Light Infantry – Bryn Parry cartoons from Leading Light *and a reflection on the eternal burden of the Infantryman.*

The gate sentry is important: He is given a helmet, two flak jackets, a rifle, a pistol, Guard Orders, a stolen car list and an intercom. — Why can't he open the gate quickly? — LCpl Diamond.

Above: Overwatch of the Iranian border in Maysan Province.

Right: *Sjt Paul Kelly in a WMIK, Sierra Leone.*

to technological and organizational change in the British Army. When The Light Infantry found themselves once more at a point in history where change was required, the Regiment stood ready again to seize the opportunity in a proactive and forward-looking spirit. The birth of The Rifles inherits the best of all their founding regiments and brings to the Army a large body of men that will be trained to act, think and operate as Light Infantrymen always have been.

A mix of rifle regiment customs and an ethos that combines professional leadership, innovation, self-discipline, mutual trust and an empowering of the individual, a formula that proved so successful for The Light Infantry, is what we bequeath to The Rifles. We can take pride in what the Regiment achieved and also pride that our legacy will be carried on as the core foundation on which The Rifles will build and model their future. Perhaps our greatest legacy will be found in the years to come, when The Rifles, with strength in numbers, attitude and style, professionalism, ethos and reputation, will be at the forefront of the British Army in every way. It is perhaps unsurprising that with this legacy in place The Rifles are already forging a formidable reputation.

before they do so to you betokens care, an acknowledgement of friendship, courtesy and a wish to start the day with the good humour that is so important a part of comradeship. Far be it from us to echo the Hollywood film mogul who, when asked what he did first every morning, growled: 'Smile – and get it over with for the day'! Happy working environments breed good discipline, good local relations and thus greater freedom and fun for everyone.

I mentioned en passant the question of morality. Whilst we have to reflect modern standards and cannot be puritan, family values lie at the heart of much of our strength, particularly whilst Regiment or Battalion is deployed on operations. Support to them and by them is essential to strong morale and to war-fighting capability. We have made strenuous efforts to keep the wider families in our recruiting regions well-informed and your Royal Highness will have made your own judgements from your recent visits. All of these traits have been highlighted in the past year. Fighting a publicly unpopular campaign in a predominantly Muslim country, under a spotlight of publicity has required a mix of immense professionalism – judgement and courage are foremost in this – as well as military aplomb, coupled with the British soldier's greatest innate asset – his humanity. Your Regiment has shown all of these with style.

I have rather proudly written this 'state of the nation' introduction because it is the foundation on which we now have to absorb the changes announced on 16 December.

Conclusions

The lessons of past achievements, the example of illustrious predecessors and the many traditions based on them deserve to be remembered, but they are no substitute for an attitude of mind that always sees the future as an opportunity. For over 300 years Light Infantry have been at the forefront of adapting

Appendix
Key Regimental Appointments 1968–2007

COLONELS

Colonel-in-Chief
HM QUEEN ELIZABETH THE
  QUEEN MOTHER
HRH Princess Alexandra, the Hon
  Lady Ogilvy KG GCVO

Deputy Colonel-in-Chief
HRH Princess Alexandra, the Hon
  Lady Ogilvy KG GCVO

COLONELS OF THE
LIGHT INFANTRY
General Sir Geoffrey Musson GCB
  CBE DSO
Major General D N H Tyacke CB
  OBE
Major General P J Bush OBE
Major General B M Lane CB OBE
Major General J D G Pank CB
Major General A Makepeace-Warne
  CB MBE
Major General M D Regan CB OBE
General Sir John Deverell KCB OBE
Lieutenant General R V Brims CB
  CBE DSO
Brigadier T J Gregson MBE

Regimental Secretaries
Brigadier J F Snow CBE
Lieutenant Colonel ED
  Wardleworth MC
Lieutenant Colonel R W T Osborne
Colonel R E Waight OBE
Major R C H Berry MBE
Lieutenant Colonel P J Wykeham
Assistant Regimental
Secretaries
Lieutenant Colonel E N Thursby
Major A R Aird MBE
Major R C H Berry MBE
Major D H Lawrence

Major R S Cross
Major W J Spiers
Captain I I Foster

County Secretaries
Bodmin
Lieutenant Colonel J E E Fry MC
Lieutenant Colonel Salusbury-
  Trelawny MC DL
Major W H White DL
Major R Vyvyan-Robinson MBE
Major T W Stipling

Taunton
Lieutenant Col A C M Urwick
Lieutenant Colonel R G
  Woodhouse
Brigadier A H I Fyfe DL
Lieutenant Colonel D Eliot DL

Pontefract
Colonel N S Pope
Colonel F W Cook
Major J S Cowley
Major C M J Deedes

Shrewsbury
Colonel G M Thornycroft DL
Major C B Grundy MC
Major J H H York MBE
Major N A de C Jones

Durham
Colonel R B Humphreys DL
Colonel J A G Arnot MC
Major D A Bower
Major R S Cross DL
Major C Lawton MBE

1st Battalion
Commanding Officers
Lt Col C D C Frith OBE
Lt Col R E Waight OBE

Lt Col B M Lane MBE
Lt Col M J A Wilson MBE MC
Lt Col A Makepeace-Warne MBE
Lt Col A I H Fyfe
Lt Col B M Elliott MBE
Lt Col J G Williams
Lt Col M H Philp
Lt Col A A Gilbert MBE
Lt Col T F L Weeks
Lt Col T J Gregson MBE
Lt Col M C D Montagu
Lt Col R R Smith
Lt Col T P Evans MBE
Lt Col W J Pointing
Lt Col J H Bowron OBE DSO

Adjutant
Capt A I H Fyfe
Capt C F W Church
Capt A D Brown
Capt J F Deverell
Capt D A Wynne Davies
Capt R I Burns
Capt Mackain-Bremner
Capt T J Gregson
Capt S Laidler
Capt C H C Lynch-Staunton
Capt I M Jacob
Capt J P F R Bendall
Capt A E W Hamilton-Briscoe
Capt J C Hardy
Capt A S L Nash
Capt E J R Chamberlain
Capt N P S Thornton
Capt J A D De Labilliere MBE
Capt R A J Chisholm
Capt T J Knowles Jackson
Capt D N Graham
Capt I T Posgate

RSM
WO1 (RSM) R C B Cox
WO1 (RSM) C Frost

WO1 (RSM) C Harding
WO1 (RSM) H R Burnett
WO1 (RSM) S W A Pascoe
WO1 (RSM) B G Scott
WO1 (RSM) N Bassett
WO1 (RSM) W Stevenson
WO1 (RSM) G Walls
WO1 (RSM) S Taylor
WO1 (RSM) C C Matthews
WO1 (RSM) C G Bryant
WO1 (RSM) A Howarth BEM
WO1 (RSM) M Garner
WO1 (RSM) A Pickford
WO1 (RSM) R H Carter
WO1 (RSM) T Meggison
WO1 (RSM) P T Hill
WO1 (RSM) A A Wood
WO1 (RSM) M Gamblin
WO1 (RSM) R Humprhies
WO1 (RSM) J Macmillan

2nd Battalion
Commanding Officers
Lt Col A C Elcomb
Lt Col P F A Sibbald OBE
Lt Col R B Macgregor-Oakford OBE
  MC
Lt Col J A Hare MBE
Lt Col R St C Preston OBE
Lt Col T D V Bevan
Lt Col M H Dru-Drury MBE
Lt Col C M S Kaye OBE
Lt Col J W Parker
Lt Col R P Cousens
Lt Col C M J Elcomb
Lt Col M J W Grubb
Lt Col B W Barry
Lt Col T J Martin MBE
Lt Col D J Wood MBE MC
Lt Col E P Davies MBE
Lt Col H E Shields MBE
Lt Col R G Arundell

Adjutants

Capt C M J Deedes
Capt R G H Chetwynd Stapylton
Capt T Barker
Capt A H Penny
Capt J W Parker
Capt R P Cousens
Capt C M G Elcomb
Capt R V Brims
Capt A R Wright
Capt M C D Montagu
Capt J Malin-Smith
Capt R P Sartain
Capt E P Davies
Capt H E Shields
Capt G R T Bishop
Capt E G E Turner
Capt M R Goldsack
Capt J H Bowron
Capt A C P Norris
Capt P Gorman
Capt R N D Follett
Capt T N R Jackson
Capt M J D Lynch
Capt G T Sawyer

RSMs

WO1 (RSM) J Lee
WO1 (RSM) D W Wackett
WO1 (RSM) T G Jones
WO1 (RSM) R T Bevan
WO1 (RSM) J E Dudart-Aberdeen
WO1 (RSM) G A E Lloyd
WO1 (RSM) E Smith
WO1 (RSM) R Hockey
WO1 (RSM) D Wroe
WO1 (RSM) D G Jarrett
WO1 (RSM) C Lawton
WO1 (RSM) P J Evanson
WO1 (RSM) S Lyth
WO1 (RSM) N Measor
WO1 (RSM) D R Matthews
WO1 (RSM) G D Gilbert
WO1 (RSM) D W White
WO1 (RSM) G Wood
WO1 (RSM) S M Morte
WO1 (RSM) I D Cameron
WO1 (RSM) C Mcburney

3rd Battalion
Commanding Officers

Lt Col J P St C Ballenden OBE MC
Lt Col R B Robertson
Lt Col B J Lowe OBE
Lt Col J D G Pank

Lt Col J Hemsley
Lt Col S S Caney MBE
Lt Col M D Regan
Lt Col J F Deverell MBE
Lt Col R A Sale
Lt Col R V Brims MBE
Lt Col M J W Grubb

Adjutants

Capt T D Bevan
Capt J K Marsham
Capt M D Regan
Capt T Harris
Capt R A Sale
Capt N A De C Jones
Capt T F L Weeks
Capt P R Sharland
Capt R C Lloyd-Williams
Capt A C C Rose
Capt A C Homan
Capt S C D Mills
Capt R R Smith
Capt E G E Turner

RSMs

WO1 (RSM) T Mcwilliams
WO1 (RSM) J Breen
WO1 (RSM) R W Hall
WO1 (RSM) D W Rose
WO1 (RSM) T Marsh
WO1 (RSM) G B Watkins
WO1 (RSM) P Wharton MM
WO1 (RSM) G Blackburn
WO1 (RSM) R Jones
WO1 (RSM) M Mcgarrigle
WO1 (RSM) J D Harris
WO1 (RSM) H L Kennedy
WO1 (RSM) Bradley
WO1 (RSM) S Lyth

4th Battalion
Commanding Officer

Lt Col J H Jacob MC

Adjutant

Captain T B Vesey

RSM

WO1 (RSM) C E Darwin

5th Battalion
Commanding Officers

Lt Col P J Bush
Lt Col B V Houghton-Berry
Lt Col B M Lees

Lt Col D T L Beath
Lt Col S J Furness
Lt Col D L M Grover
Lt Col R D Nicholas
Lt Col R D Vellacott
Lt Col T Harris
Lt Col R N R Jenkins
Lt Col M J Rescorle
Lt Col P R Sharland
Lt Col A M W Mortimer MBE
Lt Col C C S Booth

Adjutants

Capt A Egremont-Lee
Capt K R V Harding
Capt M A G Watts MBE
Capt R A Draper
Capt R R J Hogg
Capt M J W Grubb
Capt C Burt
Capt A T D Lerwill
Capt J N L Spencer
Capt T J Daplyn
Capt C S S Booth
Capt R J Montagu
Capt R J Woollard
Capt J M Chapman MBE
Capt M M B Adams
Capt N J O'brien
Capt A A H Taylerson

RSMs

WO1 A R Love
WO1 E Darwin
WO1 J Lea
WO1 D E Jones
WO1 R C Iddison
WO1 T Marsh
WO1 A F Lyon
WO1 M R Grindley
WO1 C A Williams
WO1 R W Richardson
WO1 P J Rose
WO1 R Bradley Dcm
WO1 T K Jacobs
WO1 Hosking
WO1 R Wills
WO1 S Lyth Sep
WO1 S R Champion
WO1 B P Barkworth

6th Battalion
Commanding Officers

Lt Col K C R Gibson TD
Lt Col J R Lewes TD

Lt Col J F Hibbert
Lt Col H C Watson TD
Lt Col D K W Farrant
Lt Col A D Brown
Lt Col R M Estcourt
Lt Col D A Wynne-Davies
Lt Col T G French TD DL
Lt Col A A Amber MBE
Lt Col P J Pentreath

Adjutants

Capt R M R Hodson
Capt M S R Vincent
Capt I M C C Jacob
Capt G P Chambers
Capt A C Middleton
Capt E G E Turner
Capt I C Baker
Capt R G Davies
Capt T G Evans
Capt N Ilić QGM
Capt B J Dyer

RSMs

WO1 C Frost
W B Clough
WO1 P J Batey (RGJ)
WO1 R A Riglar (RGJ)
WO1 M D White
WO1 R A Crook (RGJ)
WO1 D B Holloway
WO1 R A Hanmer
WO1 T P Hodges
WO1 R J Smith
WO1 D V Gray (RGJ)
WO1 I K Barlow
WO1 K Lindon
WO1 T Meggison
WO1 E T Bell

7th Battalion
Commanding Officers

Lt Col M D C McBain DL
Lt Col J H F Spedding
Lt Col R S Flemming
Lt Col R G H Chetwynd Stapylton
Lt Col T M Barker OBE
Lt Col R J M Garrett
Lt Col I J Sawers
Lt Col P N Hinde
Lt Col R C Lloyd-Williams
Lt Col J N L Spencer
Lt Col C Lynch-Staunton

Adjutants

Capt R C Armstrong
Capt P G Garner
Capt G Whitmore
Capt R J Tolhurst
Capt C H S L Gwinn
Capt N J R Dougan
Capt R G Arundell
Capt B J H Tomkins
Capt A J Allport

RSMs

WO1 R V Raine
WO1 R B Millard
WO1 L Looby
WO1 D R Crook
WO1 D Wroe
WO1 C C Matthews
WO1 P E Bullock
WO1 Tregidgo
WO1 R A Noble
WO1 S C Eastley
WO1 J Hall May
WO1 D Wilson

8th Battalion

Commanding Officers

Lt Col C G Deedes
Lt Col D H R Stephenson
Lt Col C Burt
Lt Col R M J Rollo-Walker

Adjutants

Captain P A Kellett
Captain C M E Topham
Captain C R Humphreys
Captain A R Nicholl
Captain N C Corden-Lloyd
Captain J D Priestman
Captain R A Head
Captain M J Winston Davies

RSMs

WO1 J E Atkinson
WO1 P Barker
WO1 A Waites
WO1 M French Bem
WO1 G Haines
WO1 G M Dunkley
WO1 C W Mander

The LIght Infantry Depot

Unit Redesignated LIght Division
    Depot (Shrewsbury) Jan 1986
Depot Disestablished October 1986

Commanding Officers

Lt Col J F H P Johnson
Lt Col C W Huxley
Lt Col D Hancock MBE
Lt Col K Hitchcock
Lt Col R Holworthy
Lt Col J E Kendall MBE
Lt Col M A G Watts MBE
Lt Col J K Marsham

Adjutants

Captain M J A Bond
Captain C G Deedes
Captain R D Vellacott
Captain A A Gilbert
Captain D Eliot
Captain R O S Phayre
Captain D P Thomas
Captain A M W Mortimer
Captain A R Trelawny

Captain R G Williams

RSMs

WO1 (RSM) E W Herrington
WO1 (RSM) J G Brynolf
WO1 (RSM) I Hill
WO1 (RSM) C Harding
WO1 (RSM) A Fothergill MBE
WO1 (RSM) S W A Pascoe
WO1 (RSM) B Hassall
WO1 (RSM) M Kilburn
WO1 (RSM) P Luxton
WO1 (RSM) G A E Lloyd
WO1 (RSM) J Condon (RGJ)
WO1 (RSM) T Fairclough (RGJ)

List of Subscribers

This book has been made possible through the generosity of the following:

Corporal Moses Ackah
M M B Adams
Paul R Adamson
Mr G R Alexander
Major Philip Alexander
Corporal Paul 'Titch' Allen 1LI
Syd Allen 3LI
P J Allott
Patrick 'Paddy' D Almond TD CD
Mr Edward Alvey
Serjeant Slim Appleyard
Mr E A Arthur
Mr J D Ashley
J W Atkin
J E Atkinson
Lieutenant Colonel (Ret'd) Roger Attrill
Dr Brian Austin
Major C L'e Backhouse
Major Andy Bacon
John Badgery
Roger Bailey
WO2 Sean Baillie
Major Ian Baker
Brigadier Ben Barry OBE
Steve 'Baz' Bastian 3LI 2LI, Adj Chef
   2eme REP
Peter W Bayliss BA (Hons)
Tina Lesley Beamond
William 'Bill' Bearham 1LI
Captain Richard H W Beath
Colonel (Ret'd) Tim Beath
WO2 Mac Bell
Bobby Belshaw
Major James Bendall MBE
WO2 (Ret'd) Jimmy Benfold 1LI
J R Bentz
Lieutenant Colonel (Ret'd) R T Bevan MBE
Major G K G Blanchard TD
Ranald Blue
Colour Serjeant R 'Bob' Bogan BEM MSM
Major M J A Bond
Lieutenant Colonel Martyn Bonner MBE
Lieutenant Colonel (Ret'd) Christopher
   Booth
Private John Booth
WO2 Mick 'Louis' Booth

James Borbone
Colour Serjeant Alan Bosher
Colonel J H Bowron DSO OBE
John Bradford 8LI
Daniel and Scott, sons of John Bradford 8LI
Adrian David Thomas Bradley
G R Brimacombe
Robin Brims
Captain 'Baggy' Brown
Ian Brown
Mike Brown
Richard L Brudenell
Lieutenant Colonel Jos Brynolf MBE
Colour Serjeant Peter Buckley
Private Roy Bunt 1LI
Serjeant Mark Burge
Stuart Graham Burns
Mr Clive Burt
Thomas Cairncross
Iain Campbell
Denis 'Cav' Canavan
Colonel Stephen Caney
Major Andrew Carney
Captain D R Carroll
Major E J M Carson
Richard 'Shiner' H Carter
Andrew G Casewell
Captain Ben Casson
Lieutenant Colonel Guy Chambers
Mr B E Chance
Peter Chapman
Andrew Child
Nigel Chitticks
Robert 'Chad' Choudhury 2LI
Second Lieutenant Simon 'Bagpuss'
   Clarke LI
D Clements MM
Rifleman John Coates
WO1 (RSM) Tom Cobill 3LI
Mr C T Cockliff
Serjeant 'Coco' Cocoran 24433213
Rifleman Peter Colclough
Major Vic Collins
WO1 (RSM) Andrew Cook
Mr W Cook
Paul 'Coops' Cooper

John Corry
Corporal Chris Cousans
Major James S Cousen
Colonel R P Cousens OBE
Kenneth Cox
Lieutenant Colonel (Ret'd) R C B Cox
WO2 Taff Cox
Colour Serjeant Jason Credland LI(V)
Major (Ret'd) Dennis 'Denbo' Crook MBE
Tim Crowther
John Cummings
Major C D Dadd
Michael D Darby JP DL FCA
C E Darwin
Davidstow Airfield and Cornwall at
   War Museum
C F Davies94, C Company Clerk
Colonel Peter Davies
Robin Glyndwr Davies
Lance Corporal Norman 'Davo' Davison
   1DLI 3LI
WO2 G Dawson 24464222
Mr Anthony Deighton
Colonel Brian Denney TD DL
Michael John Devenish
Mick Dexter 3LI
Redvers Warren 'Dixie' Dixon
Tripp Donnelly
Private Gordon Doudie 2LI
James Downham
Brigadier R A Draper CVO OBE
Colonel (Ret'd) M H Dru Drury MBE
L Dunn, Signals KSLI
Jonathan Durrant
Ben Dyer
T E Edgar
John 'Titch/Eddie/J T' Edson KSLI 3LI
Lance Corporal Dave 'Dithery' Edwards
J A Edwards
Bob Elcock 3LI
Brigadier C M G Elcomb OBE
Mark 'Chalky' Ellis
Mr Mike Embleton
Lance Corporal Ross Evans 24839173
Major General T P Evans DSO MBE
Major (Ret'd) P J Evanson

Major James Faux, LI/Rifles
WO2 Kevin Fawcett 2LI
Captain Rupert Firbank 1LI
Major Damian Flanagan
Corporal Will Flintoff 24460581
Captain (Ret'd) Will Follett
Captain D N A Ford
Captain (Ret'd) I I Foster, RHQ
Richard Fullerton 2LI
Colonel S J Furness
Andy Furzer
Captain A A J Fyfe
Brigadier Alastair Fyfe
Alexander Fyshe
WO1 (Ret'd) Digger Gardiner
Colonel R J M Garrett
E J Gaut
Andrew Gavaghan (Senior)
Andrew 'Gav' Gavaghan
Major Graham 'Gilly' Gilbert
Simon Paul Gillum
Mr Colin Goodall
Private B Goodchild 1LI 24722014
D Goodwill
Mr P Goodwin
Corporal Raymond Green
Serjeant Tony 'Shed' Greenhouse
Brigadier Tim Gregson MBE
William Gribben
M J W Grubb
Ruth van der Gucht
G Guest
Colonel R J Guest TD
Yousef Haddun
Jim Hadfield
Major S H Hall
Major Anthony Hamilton-Briscoe
Major Crispin Harris
Lieutenant Colonel T Harris
Private Darren G Harvey
Frank E Harvey KSLI
James Hayward
Captain Matt Helsby
Lieutenant Colonel Jack Hemsley KSLI LI
Captain James A Hepworth
James Hereford
Lieutenant Colonel John R Heron
Lieutenant Colonel J F Hibbert
Major Ian Hill
Adie Hinks
Mrs Keith Hitchcock
Captain T P Hodges LI
Peter Hogg
William R J Hogg
Richard Holworthy
Andrew John Hones
Private D S Hook, 2nd Batt KSLI
E J Hooper Esq

Major R J Hooper
Captain Martin G Hopper
Captain Christopher Horsford
Captain M D Hosegood
Serjeant Roger Hosking 1LI
Colour Serjeant M J Howe MSM, KSLI 3LI
Humphrey Hubble
Major (Ret'd) Charlie Humphreys
Major (Ret'd) Bob Humphries
Captain Bob Humphries
David J K Humphrys
Lieutenant Colonel Nick Ilić MBE QGM
Peter Jackson
Steve 'Jacko' Jackson
Major T N R Jackson
Lieutenant Colonel John Jacob MC
John James 24291079
Philip James
Shaun James GM
Major Dave Jarratt
Private Jinx Jennings
Lance Corporal Anthony Johnson
Captain James Oscar Johnson
Kob Johnson
Phillip 'Johno' Johnson
Ian Jones (89)
Colour Serjeant Jim Jones 3LI/15 BDE RTC
    (Rifles)
Mike G Jones 3LI
Nigel Jones
Peter Jowitt
Peter Kavanagh
Guy Keeling
A J 'Ned' Kelley
Darren Kelly
Colonel John Kendall MBE
Andrew Kennedy 1LI
Major H L Kennedy
Lieutenant Colonel T D Kent-Jones TD
Lieutenant Colonel S R Keoghane
Captain Ollie King, TA 5LI/Reg 1LI
Lieutenant Colonel J A D de Labillière MBE,
    Rifles
Ben Lampard
Major General Barry Lane
Major (Ret'd) Chris 'Blondy' Lawton
Major Richard Le Fleming
Stuart Leah
Mark Leccia
Fred Leck BEM
Colonel Brian Lees LVO OBE
Serjeant Ernie Lethbridge
Captain D C C Lewis 3LI
M J Lewis
J LIddiard
Lieutenant Colonel John G T LIghtley
WO1 (RSM) Neil LIndley
Captain David LIvingston LI

Mrs C A Lloyd
Mr Graham Lloyd
Ifor Lloyd
Bryan Longman
Corporal (Ret'd) Michael Loveridge
Brigadier Brian Lowe
The Loyal Newport Volunteers
WO2 Mel Luke 1DLI 4LI 3LI
Charlie Lynch-Staunton
Major M J D Lynch
Captain Tony Lynn
Brigadier R B MacGregor-Oakford CBE MC
Gary J P H MacMahon
Mrs Antony Makepeace-Warne
Major Tony 'Spanner' Manley MBE
Captain Jasper Mann
WO2 Roy Mark 3LI
WO1 (RSM) J S Marriott
Major R E Marsden TD
WO2 Wilfy Marshall
Major (Ret'd) D R Matthews MBE
Corporal Wayne Mawston
Alistair 'Mac' McBride
Dougie McCarroll
Captain Ian McGregor
Ben McGuire
Tony 'Mac' Mclaughlin
Lieutenant Colonel T D McMurtrie OBE
Anthony Middleton
Peter Middleton
Mark Milford
Major S W Minton Beddoes TD
Mr A C Mitford-Slade
Richard Montagu
Lieutenant S W Moody
Captain Ben Morgan
Steve 'Mo' Morris
Andrew Mortimer
Mark Mortimer
John 'Mousy' Muers
Lieutenant Colonel (Ret'd) K G E Mulligan
    RLI
Colonel Rupert Nicholas
Major (Ret'd) David Nichols
John 'Niko' Nichols
WO2 Nik Nicholson
Major S J W Noble 3LI 2LI 528339
Major C J M Notley
Scott O'Brian
Captain Tim J O'Brien
Major Patrick O'Sullivan TD
Mark O'Hanlon
Major Christopher Ogden
Captain C M Oliver
Geoffrey Olley 2LI
Captain Martin E Orchard
Lieutenant Colonel R W T Osborne
Major Charles Ottowell TD

R A B Ouwens
Captain Charles Pack
Major General J D G Pank
Brigadier J W Parker CBE
Jim Parker 3LI
Mrs John Woodward Parker
John Parker DLI
Mr V Parker
Allan Parsons
Rifleman F Patrick
Lieutenant Colonel Mark Payne
Major James Peck
Captain Julian Penney
Serjeant Lee Pennington
Andrew Hugh Penny
J J Percy
Keith Petvin-Scudamore
Lieutenant Colonel Robin Phayre
Lance Corporal Terry Phillips 24531460
Mr A J D Pile
Chris 'Pilky' Pilkington
WO2 (Bugle Major) John 'Henry' Plumridge
Major Harley Pope
Serjeant Dean Portman
Bob 'Klon' Powell
Major R Prewitt
Lance Corporal Taf Pryce
Corporal Robin Pursey
Eddie Rabey
John Rafferty
Gary Ranu
Andrew 'Rory' Raw
Major General Michael Regan CB OBE
Corporal James Rennie
Lieutenant Colonel Mike Rescorle
Harry Richardson BEM, DLI 3LI
Mr A F B Ridgement
Serjeant M 'Riggs' Rigby, 5 Rifles
Ian M Robertson
Stephen Robson DLI 1LI
Captain Holmes Rogers
Private Tony Rothery
John Ruddy
Colonel Richard Sale
Rex Sartain
Captain Miles Savage

I J Sawers
Major Mike Sawyer
Mike Scarff
Major James Scott of Burnhead
Major S Sedman MBE
A H Sharp
Dr Pete Shepherd
Tony Shepherd
Captain Mark Shercliff
Brian 'Shaggy' Sheridan
Colonel Ted Shields MBE
Captain D A Shorter
Lance Corporal Philip Simmonds
Paul Simpson
N J Slade
Chris Smart
Major (Ret'd) Eric Smith
R A Smith
Major Richard Smith
John 'Snowy' Snowdon
Major Rob Spalton
Lieutenant Mark Speight
Lieutenant Colonel J N L Spencer
Lieutenant Colonel Phil Spencer
Mr W Spiers
Malcolm 'Mally' Spink
Captain Harry Spry-Leverton
Mike Spurrier
Lieutenant Colonel Shaun Staines
Private Mick Stallard
Captain Pete Stapleton 2LI
D H R Stephenson
Ross Stewart-Smith
Ray Stoker
Corporal Jonathan Leigh Sturgess
Corporal Kev Swindle
Corporal Tansley
Anthony 'Doo Dah' Tate
Captain (QM) Paul Taylor SCLI 1LI
Corporal Matt Teuton
The Commanding Officer and All Ranks of
    the 3rd Battalion The Rifles
Lieutenant James Thompson
Colonel M E Thornton OBE
Major R J Tolhurst
Lance Corporal 'Joffy' Tonge 2LI 24697697

WO2 Roy Tonge
WO2 Dale 'Sas' Towers
Serjeant Trebilcock MBE 1LI
Martin Tredwell
Captain Will Tricks
Mrs S M Triptree
Martin Trow
Captain Nicholas Robert Trowell
Major K M F Tuhey QVRM TD
Julian Tyndale
Richard Charles Vaughan
Colonel R D Vellacott OBE
Les Vickery
WO2 Jase Villiers
Mark S R Vincent
Major R Vyvyan-Robinson MBE
Mr Gordon Walls
Ian 'Wanny' Wanless
Revd E Ward, Padre 5LI
Patrick and Patsy Warren
Major A J P Watson TD
Major Michael H L Whistler MBE
WO1 'Chalky' White, Rifles
J M White
Iain Whittingham
Mr Keith Wickett
Major J C F Wilcocks
Lance Corporal Kevin Wilkins
Mr Geoffrey Wilkinson
Brigadier Gage Williams OBE
In memory of John Reginald Williams BEM
Lance Corporal Marcus Williams 24957800
Major Rod Williams
M Winwood BEM, KSLI 3LI
Stuart Wood
Thomas Wood
Major (Ret'd) Nick Wooldridge
Captain (Ret'd) Mark Wright
Peter I Wright
Major (Ret'd) D Wroe MBE DL
Mr P J Wykeham
Colonel D A Wynne Davies
Corporal 'Yeed' Yeadon
Major (Ret'd) Jeremy H H York MBE BA
    (Hons)
Major Robert K Yuill

Index

1LI 23, 28–49 *et passim*
2LI 23, 50–71 *et passim*
3LI 23, 72–91 *et passim*
4LI 23, 92–5 *et passim*
5LI see *LIght Infantry Volunteers*
6LI see *LIght Infantry Volunteers*
7LI see *LIght Infantry Volunteers*
8LI see *LIght Infantry Volunteers*

Abercorn Barracks, Ballykinler 28, 30, 52, 57–8
Adams, Gerry 55
Adams, Lieutenant Mark 38, 131
Afghan Wars 79, 170
Afghanistan 25, 45, 169–71
Airmobile Brigade 24, 42, 60, 61, 109, 154–6
al-Sadr, Muqtada 47, 167
Alanbrooke Barracks, Paderborn 30, 44, 49, 52, 62, 64, 65–7, 68, 74, 88–91, 134, 137
Albemarle Barracks, Ouston 120
Alderson, Private 60
Alexander Barracks, Dhekelia 52, 68–9
Alexander, General 82
Alexandra, HRH Princess 6, **7**, 22, 23, 24, 25, 78, *79*, 84, 94, 98, *100*, 119, 128, *128*, 131, 132, 133
Aliwal Barracks, Tidworth 74, 85, 156
Allawi, Iyad 166
Alma Barracks, Catterick 74, 80, 81–4, 108, 109, 118
Anderson, Captain Adam 132
Appleyard, Slim *85*
Archer, Peter 110
Argyll and Sutherland Highlanders, The 47, 85
Arkell, Second Lieutenant Andy 60
Armoured Brigade 44, 45, 48, 60, 61, 154
Armstrong, Bugle Major Alan 76
Army Foundation College 124
Army Training Regiment 123–4
Arundell, Lieutenant Colonel Ralph 70

Ashby, Major 162
Atkinson, Colour Serjeant 149
Ayton, Colour Serjeant 71

Badgery, Captain John 32
Baker, Captain Matt *112*
Baker, Ian 4, **64**
Balkans 157–60
Ballenden, Lieutenant Colonel J P StC 24
BAOR 34, 54, 57, 59, 61, 76, 97, 98, 154, 156
Barneby, Second Lieutenant Bill 145
Barringer, WO1 D 137
Barry, Brigadier Ben 4, 37, 65, 134, 157
Barwell, Private 55
Bath, Private K **33**
Beath, Colonel *100*
Beath, Richard **36**
Belize 24
Bell, Martin 63
Bendall, James 37
Bennet, Bandsman 138
Bennet, Private H 9
Benson, Major Michael 92
Berry, Major Ron 4, 94, 130, 137
Bessbrook Mill 59, 61, 63, *69*, 69
Bevan, Lieutenant Colonel Ron 133
Bevan, Lieutenant Colonel Tim 58, 131
Bevan, Penny 131
Bishop, Private B 9
Blackburn, Bugler 78
Blair, Prime Minister Tony 45
Bloody Sunday 30, 53
Blue, Lieutenant Ranald 57
Blyth, Chay 65
Blythe, Private N I 9
Bockarie, Sam 162
Bonaparte, Napoleon 12, 145
Bonner, RQMS Martyn 40
Bower, Major David 57
Bowes, Private P A 9
Bowron, Johnny 131
Boyne, Battle of 35, 80

Bradley, Corporal 79, 144
Brady, Lance Corporal Dennis 49
Brennan, Serjeant Derek 32
Brims, Lieutenant General Robin **8**, *8*, 42, 132, **133**, 156, 160, 165
Brooke Barracks, Berlin 30, 38, 41
Broome, Private Paul 80
Brown, Corporal 92
Brown, Lance Corporal 139
Buckingham Palace *86*
Bull, Major Chris 103
Buller Barracks, Munster 30, 34
Bullock, Private P L 9
Burfitt, Private J 9
Burkey, Neil 4
Burns, Private *30*
Burton, WO1 D 136, 137, 138
Bush, Major General Peter 126
Bush, President George 45, 166
Bushen, Private A P 9
Butler, Lady 110
Butler, Paul 57
Bygraves, Bugle Major 138

Cadwallader, WO1 M 136, 137
Caney, Lieutenant Colonel Stephen 84
Carlton, Tex 136
Carney, WO2 Andy 105
Carver, General Sir Michael 96
Catesby, Colonel Peter 108
Cay, Captain Andy 112
Chamberlain, Major Edward 44
Chand, Major General Prem 76
Chapman, Lieutenant Peter *64*
Cheshire Regiment, The 70
Child, Second Lieutenant 4, *161*
Chisholm, R A J 125
Churchill, Prime Minister Winston 82
Clark, General Mark 82
Clarke, Lieutenant Tim 52
Clarke, Private 30
Clifton Barracks, Minden 74, 78–81
Cocoran, Corporal 'Coco' *58*, 58
Colbeck, Colonel David 94

Cold War 8, 25, 34, 50, 66, 98, 174
Coldstream Guards 59, 136
Cornish, Corporal M 9, 49
Cosby, Corporal John Johnston 115
Cousens, Lieutenant Richard 4, 53, 58, 61, 62
Cox, Captain Robert 35
Craddock, Lance Corporal 112
Credland, Lance Corporal 63
Cresswell, Captain Ed 64
Cummings, Second Lieutenant *34*
Curtis, Private G M 9
Cyprus 23, 23, 25, 147–8
Czepukojc, Private 144

Davenport, Major Nigel 87
Davies, Lieutenant Colonel Peter 67
Davies, Private Paul 61
Davis, Captain Robin 62
de la Billière, General Sir Peter 42, 65, *123*, *130*
de Labillière, James 42, 131
de Labillière, J A D 125
de Labillière, Susie 131
de Vos, Major Jan *63*, *157*
Dee, Captain Doug **105**, 105
Dee, WO1 'Geordie' 76
Devenish, M J 125
Deverell, General Sir John (Jack) 140. 158
Devon and Dorset LIght Infantry 25, 113–15, 174
Dhekalia Garrison Church *50*
Dinwiddie, Major 55
Downward, Captain Christopher 78, 80
Dreghorn Barracks, Edinburgh 30, 43
Drury, Lieutenant Colonel Mike 59
Duke of Cornwall's LIght Infantry 12, 13, 14–21, 22, 23, 37
Duke of Edinburgh's Royal Regiment 109
Duke of Wellington's Regiment, The 59, 86
Duncan, Private 71
Durham Cathedral 23, *92*, 94

Durham LIght Infantry 13, 14–21, 22, 38
Dyas, Ensign 70, 179
Dyer, Ben 131
Dyer, Serjeant Bob 33

Earl of Huntingdon's Regiment 24
Eastaugh, Private P K 9, 77
Edward, HRH The Duke of Kent 76
Edwards, Corporal 78
Edwards, J A B 125
Elcomb, Lieutenant Colonel Tony 50, 63, 156
Eliot, Captain David 32
Elizabeth II, HM The Queen 22, 24, 57, 59, 80, 98, 119, 139, 177
Elizabeth, HM Queen, The Queen Mother 22, 22, 23, 25, 53, 62, 65, 77, 91, 98, 128, 132, 133
Elliott, Lieutenant B M 120
Engineer Regiment 45
Episkopi Barracks, Cyprus 30, 148
Episkopi, Battle of 149
Evans, Brigadier Tim 167
Evans, Captain Tim 90
Evans, Toby 4
Evanson, Major 163
Evanson, Major Paul 126–7
Exercise 'Crusader 80' 98
Exercise 'Eternal Triangle' 60
Exercise 'Fire Focus' 87
Exercise 'Forefront (North)' 56
Exercise 'Gaelic Holiday' 79
Exercise 'Grand Prix' 59, 66, 87, 90
Exercise 'Grim Reaper' 127
Exercise 'Iron Hammer' 61
Exercise 'Kauri Pine' 32
Exercise 'Key Flight' 87
Exercise 'Keystone' 87, 102
Exercise 'Lion Cub' 103
Exercise 'Lion Sun' 147
Exercise 'Lionheart' 59, 102, 106
Exercise 'Marble Tor IV' 102, 106
Exercise 'Mayan Sword' 40
Exercise 'Pond Jump West' 32, 33, 36, 61
Exercise 'Red Grouse' 59
Exercise 'Red Hand' 79
Exercise 'Sisyphus' 78
Exercise 'Spring Train' 59
Exercise 'Summer Sales' 61
Exercise 'Tristar' 84
Exercise 'Trumpet Dance' 38, 62
Exercise 'Wessex Warrior' 67
Exercise 'Wintex' 59
Exercise 'Yorkshire Canter' 58
Exeter Cathedral 113, 115
Fagg, Chris 4

Falkland Islands 25, 59, 89, 107
Falp, Corporal 76
Faux, Major James 8, 47, 163
Fenham Barracks, Newcastle upon Tyne 94
Fiennes, Ranulph 65
Firbank, Major Simon 41
Firbank, Rupert **41**
First Gulf War 45, 165
First World War 82, 94, 96, 126, 178
Fitzgeorge-Balfour, Lieutenant General Sir Victor 94
Fitzgerald, Lance Corporal 60
Flanagan, D J 125
Flavin, C/Serjeant 138, **139**
Follett, Lieutenant Will 167
Foot Guards 121
Fort George 55, 76
Fort Lewis 62
Fort St Angelo 85
Foster, Andy 4
Fox, James 78
Fox, Private S L 9
France, Private 82
Frith, Lieutenant Colonel Colin 28
Fullerton, Lieutenant Richard 58
Furness, Major 55, 100
Fyfe, A A J 125

Gadsden, Sir Peter 104
Garner, Captain Nick 134
Gaskell, Nick 131
Gaskell, Nikki 131
Gaskell, Private J 9, 55
George V, HM King 132
George VI, HM King 132
Gibbons, Professor John 60
Gibraltar 58–9
Gilbert, Major Graham **123**
Gloucestershire Regiment 109
Goldsack, Colonel Mark 8, 62, 133
Goodwin, C/Serjeant G 138
Gordon Highlanders, The 60
Gorman, Captain Piers 149
Graham, D N 125
Gray, Major C G 137
Green, Bugle Major C M 138, 139
Greener, Private R 9
Gregson, Brigadier 115
Grenadier Guards 61
Grenville, Hugo 66
Grubb, Lieutenant Colonel Martin 65, 90
Gun Club Hill Barracks, Kowloon 32
Gurkhas 72, 136
Guthrie, General Charles 109
Gutteridge, George 77
Hackett, General Sir John 96

Hague, Private 71
Hall, Private S R 9
Halliday, Doc 133
Hancock, Major David 28
Handel 65
Handy, Serjeant Peter 152
Harbottle, Brigadier Michael 93
Harding of Petherton, Field Marshall The Lord 28
Harding, Field Marshal 57
Harding, Lady 57
Hardy, Captain James 42
Hardy, James 4
Hare, Lieutenant Colonel Tony 56
Harris, Lieutenant Tim 94
Harris, Major Tim 105
Harris, Sean **62**
Harrison, CSM 'Harry' 49
Harrison, Private L J 9
Harrison, Private Lewis 82
Harrison, Private M E 9
Harrison, Private Michael 82
Hatton, Bob 136
Hawkins, Serjeant 167
Head, Dickie 4, 37
Heath, Janusz 53
Heaton, The Very Reverend, Dean of Durham 82
Hemsley, Brigadier 105
Henry the goat 80
Henry, Private 55
Hext, Captain Tom 37, 37, 131
Hiles, Private 58
HMS Bulwark 53
HMS Cornwall 129
HMS Invincible 24, 58, 129
HMS Vanguard 107
Hodge, Lance Corporal 78
Hodgson, Private 108
Hodson, Captain Richard 83, 84
Hogg, Lieutenant Will 63
Holloway, Corporal 'SAS' 105
Holman, Corporal Brian 123
Holman, WO2 B 138
Hooper, Edward 131
Hooper, Jeremy 131
Hopkins, Roger 34
Howard, Lieutenant Colonel John 41
Howard, Lieutenant Mike 35
Howarth, Corporal Alan 123
Humphries, Bob 57
Hussein, Saddam 25, 45, 62, 114, 165

Ilić, Major Nick 160, 160
Illingworth, Lieutenant Timothy 171
Imphal Barracks, York 59
infantry Battle School 126
Infantry Junior Leaders Battalion 121

Infantry Training Centre, Catterick 121, 124
Ingram, Bugle Major 136, 138
Iraq 25, 45, 164–8
Irish Guards 40

Jackson, General Mike 110
Jackson, Lance Corporal Peter **39**
Jackson, Peter 131
Jackson, Private Ian 30, 31
Jackson, WO2 Clive 96
Jacobs, Lieutenant Colonel John 92, 94
James II, HM King 35
James, Corporal 'Jesse' 79, 85
James, Private 144
James, WO1 Stuart 136, 137
Jarratt, Major Dave 57, **57**
Jewell, Jimmie 33
Johnstone, Venerable Archdeacon W E 87
Jones, Bugle Major 138
Jones, Bugle Major Bill 123
Jones, C/Serjeant Dave 105
Jones, Captain G O 137
Jones, Corporal 87
Jones, Major General Edward 61
Jones, Private R V 9
Junior Infantry Battalion 122
Junior Tradesman's Regiment 122

Kabbah, Ahmad 162
Kannan, Private B K 9
Karadžić, Radovan 160
Kaye, Lieutenant Colonel Colin 59, 155
Keeley, WO1 E 137
Kemp, Serjeant Mick 146
Kench, Second Lieutenant Nick 74
Kennington, Lance Corporal A 9, 78
Kent, Bugle Major Jock 138
King, Tom 25, 40
King's Own Scottish Borderers, The 45, 86, 87
King's Own Yorkshire LIght Infantry 13, 14–21, 22, 50, 58, 82, 84, 105, 132
King's Shropshire LIght Infantry 13, 14–21, 22, 82, 144
King's Shropshire LIght Infantry Museum, Shrewsbury 107
Kingston, WO1 A 137
Kipling, Rudyard 4
Kirkbride, Serjeant Corkie 95
Kitchener, Lord 93
Kiwi Barracks, Bulford 30, 40, 42, 52, 67–8, 108
Knox, WO1 A 137

Koroma, Johnny Paul 162
Kukri 57
Kunadomo, Lance Corporal Fred 77

Lack, Simon 39
Lambert, Dave 57
Lampard, Major Ben *70*, **71**
Lancers 45
Lane, Major General Barry 30, *32*, *104*
Lawson, Bandsman 138
Lawton, Private Blondie *93*
Leeming, WO1 A S 'Jack' 136, 137
Lever, WO1 M 137
Lewis, Private A S 9
Lewis, WO2 163
LI(V) *see LIght Infantry Volunteers*
Liddle, Captain Steve *159*
Life Guards 75
Light Dragoons 56
Light Infantry Depot, Shrewsbury 22, 121, 122–3, 124
Light Infantry Depot, Winchester 22, 24, 123
Light Infantry Museum, Bodmin 4, 80, 131, *133*
Light Infantry Museum, Winchester 41
Light Infantry Volunteers 23, 24, 96–109
Lisanelly Barracks, Omagh 30, 36, 74, 86–7
Little, Corporal 163
Littlejohn, Mr 33
Livingston, D G S 125
Livingstone, Captain David *159*
Logistic Brigade 45
Loring, Captain N C T 9
Loveridge, Corporal 55
Lowe, Major Brian 144, 145
LSL *Sir Lancelot* 84
Lucknow Barracks, Tidworth 30, 33, 34, 35, 42, 52, 62, 64, 91, *128*
Lynch, J J 87
Lynn, Serjeant *92*

MacCreedy, CSM 75
MacGregor-Oakford, Lieutenant Colonel Robert 53, 56
Mair, Bandsman 138
Makepeace-Warne, Antony 4, *32*, 53, 55
Maliki, Prime Minister 167
Marsh, Oliver 41
Marshall, David 136
Marsham, John 131
Martin, C B 125
Martin, Lieutenant Colonel Tim 65, 66

Martola, Major General A–E 92
Mason, Private 78
Mathews, WO1 J 137
Mauritius 23, 144–6
Mawston, Private 132
McAllister, Brigadier R W L 50
McBurney, WO2 132
McCaffrey, Bernard 144
McElwaine, Seamus 87
McGowan, Private 82
McLaughlin, Private R J F 9
McLaughlin, Serjeant Mac 123
McLeod, C/Serjeant V 138
McMurtrie, Second Lieutenant Tom 36
McVitty, Constable 87
Meadham, Greg 139
Meannee Barracks, Colchester 30, 31, 42, 50–6, 62, 77, 93, 94, 95, 156
Meehan, Martin 36
Meston, Private 77
Miller, Lance Corporal R 9
Milton Barracks, Gravesend 30
Minden, Battle of 10–11
Moffat, Corporal 58
Mohan, General 168
Momoh, Joseph 161
Montgomery Barracks, Berlin 50, 52
Moore, General Sir John 8, 12, 13, 54, 175
Morgan, Captain 163
Morrill, Corporal I R 9
Morris, C/Serjeant J 138
Morris, Private 80
Mortimer, Major Andrew 86
Mortimer, Mark **65**
Murray, Bonnie 4
Murray, Janice 168
Musson, General Sir Geoffrey 95, 144

Napier, WO1 K W 136, 137
Napoleonic Wars 13, 145
Neeves, Private 71
Nicholas, Corporal 53
Nicholas, Rupert 131
Nichols, Lieutenant David 35
Nicolas, Major 72
Nkomo, Joshua 83
Norley, WO1 P 137
Norman, Hinga 162
Norsworthy, Private M A 9
Northern Ireland 23, 150–3 *et passim*

O'Neill, Corporal 88
Offard, WO1 K 137
Offley, Tim 57
Omar, Mullah 170
Operation BANNER 33, 35, 54, 63, 67, 85, 153

Operation BROCKDALE 168
Operation BRONSKI 63
Operation CARA CARA 86
Operation COUNTERPOINT 86
Operation GRANBY 40, 138, *139*, 165
Operation GRAPPLE 42, 52, 66
Operation HERRICK 52, 111–12
Operation HIGHBROW 52, 70
Operation MOTORMAN 30, 36, 77, 151
Operation PALLISER 163
Operation ROGER *88*
Operation SILKMAN 44, 163
Operation TELIC 25, 45, 46, 47, 48, 52, 69, 108, 109, 113, 113–15, 139, 148, 164, 180
Operation ZENITH 168
Orchard, Captain Jonny *62*
Osborne, Lieutenant Colonel Richard 130, 131
Overton, Lance Corporal 80
Owen, Captain R 137
Owen, Major General David Lloyd 92
Owen, Serjeant Jap *63*
Oxfordshire and Buckinghamshire LIght Infantry 23

Pack, Charlie 36
Paisley, Ian *32*
Palace Barracks, Belfast 52, 65, 66–7, 74
Parachute Regiment, The 47, 61, 75, 85, 121, 122
Park-Weir, Major Ian 105
Parker, Brigadier Jim **54**, *54*, 60, 91
Parker, Corporal Jim **24**, **72**, **77**
Parr, The Reverend G 94
Parry, Bryn 180
Pattison, Corporal 88
Payne, M J C 125
Peninsula Barracks, Delinghofen 24, 52, 60–1
Peninsula Barracks, Winchester 118–19
Peninsular War 13, 56
Philip, HRH The Prince, Duke of Edinburgh 59, **110**, 132
Philp, Lieutenant Colonel Mitchell 37
Pickering, Lieutenant Graham 98
Pickering, Private 'Slug' *91*
Pickford, Lieutenant Colonel Bob *38*, 125–6
Pike, Lieutenant General Sir Hew 158
Pile, Captain Antony *76*
Platoon Commanders' Battle Course 127

Platoon Sergeants' Battle Course 126–7
Plumridge, WO2 J 138
Pope, Lance Corporal *176*
Portman, Corporal Dean *63*
Potter, Lee 57
Powell, Enoch 58
Power, Private 55
Preston, Lieutenant Colonel Roger 56
Prince of Wales's Own Regiment, The 80
Princess of Wales Royal Regiment, The 47, 110
Purvey, Captain M D 137

Queen's Dragoon Guards, The 65, 70, 75
Queen's Lancashire Regiment, The 60, 68, 84
Queen's Own Highlanders, The 85
Queen's Royal Hussars, The 45, 47, 48, 56, 84
Quinn, Major General 84

Radford, Lieutenant Colonel Tim *8*
Rann, Serjeant *83*
Regan, Major General Michael 42, 68, 85
Reah, Serjeant 36
Redford Barracks, Edinburgh 52, 69–71
Reilly, Thomas 35
Rennie, Sir John 144
RFA *Sir Bedivere 76*
Rice, Captain Rex 36
Rice, The Reverend D E 94
Richardson, Private A J 9
Ricketts, Major General Andy 94
Ridgement, Private 33
Ridings, WO1 R A 137
Rifles, The 4, 6, 13, 25, 49, 71, 110, 112, 119, 133, 174–81
Roberts, Private R B 9, 55
Robertson, Lieutenant Colonel Bruce 75, 76
Robson, Corporal Nev 55
Rooney, Kevin 144
Ross, Private K B 9
Rowe, Private R 9
Rowlands, David 48
Royal Air Force 119, 132
Royal Artillerty 61, 79, 96
Royal Corps of Transport 84
Royal Engineers 30, 84, 151
Royal Flying Corps 119
Royal Gloucester, Berkshire and Wiltshire Regiment 25, 110–12, 174

Royal Green Jackets 13, 22, 23, 37, 40, 88, 89, 97, 110, 118, 119, 131, 174, 178
Royal Horse Artillery Regiment 40, 96
Royal Irish Regiment 121
Royal Logistic Corps 120
Royal Marines 30, 33, 71, 77, 84, 89, 166
Royal Military Police 122
Royal Navy 24, 59, 119, 132
Royal Northumberland Fusiliers, The 94
Royal Pioneer Corps 122
Royal Regiment of Fusiliers 88
Royal Scots Dragoon Guards, The 80
Royal Scots, The 61, 64
Royal Signallers 83, 96
Royal Tank Regiment 45, 79, 96
Royal Welch Fusiliers, The 40, 57
Rudd, Private 60
Rudman, Private J R 9
Rudman, Private T 9, 53
Rutherfoord, Major Andrew 58

Salamanca Barracks, Dhekelia 84–5
Salamance, Battle of 22, 110
Sale, General 'Fighting Bob' 79
Sale, Richard **90**
Salthouse, Corporal D P 9, 85
Samsonoff, Major Andrew 162
Sandhurst, Royal Military Academy 118, 124–6
Sands, Bobby 151
Sandys, Duncan 95
Sankoh, Foday 161, 162, 163
SAS 42
Saville, Lord 30
Seaton Barracks, Plymouth 72, 74–7
Second World War 35, 41, 94, 126, 132
Section Commanders' Battle Course 127
Seven Years War 12
Shankill, Battle of 23, 74, 75
Shelley, Corporal 63

Shepherd, Philip 82
Sherwood, Lance Corporal Steven 111, 112
Shields, Lieutenant Colonel Ted 4, 43, 69, 131, 175
Shropshire LIght Infantry 136
Sibbald, Lieutenant Colonel Peter 50, 50, 53, 144
Sierra Leone 25, 161–3
Silver Bugle 4, 42, 131, 134
Simmonds, WO1 John 136, 137
Simpson, Corporal 108
Sinclair, John 131
Sir John Moor Barracks, Winchester 9, 12, 24, 131, 139
Sir John Moore Barracks, Shrewsbury 118, 119–20, 131
Skillen, Martin 79
Slater, WO1 E 137
Smart, Corporal Serjeant Chris 43
Smiley, Corporal Chuck 123
Smith, Major Richard 157
Smith, Martin 131
Smith, Private G 9
Smith, Private Wayne 80
Socks, Private 63
Somerset and Cornwall LIght Infantry 13, 14–21, 22, 23, 136
Somerset LIght Infantry (Prince Albert's) 13, 14–21, 22, 23, 79
Sore, Sas 57
Stafford, Private R 9
Stanley Barracks, Hong Kong 30
Stanley, C/Serjeant 163
Stephenson, Second Lieutenant Rex 94, **95**
Stesil, Corporal 45
Stiley, Corporal 111, 112
Stoker, Private T A 9
Stornoway Barracks, Lemgo 30, 52, 56–7
Strasser, Captain Valentine 161
Stripling, Trevor 4
Sulyok, Captain Paul 64

Sutton, Private 30
Swift, Lance Corporal 88

Taylor, Captain Paul 40
Taylor, Charles 161
Taylor, Corporal T P 9, 55
Taylor, JRSM 124
Taylor, WO1 M 137
Tchaikovsky 83
Teale, Serjeant 71
Tench, Private M A 9, 71, 168
Terendak Camp, Malacca 72–4
Terry the Cook 31
Thain, Private Iain 35
Thatcher, Prime Minister Margaret 58
Thomas, Lance Corporal P D T 9, 167
Thomas, Major David 87
Thompson, Corporal Michael 56
Thompson, JRSM 124
Thompson, Lance Corporal 132
Thompson, Private 88
Thorne, Brigadier David 58
Thornton, Mike 4
Thornton, Serjeant S 138
Tomkinson, Captain Ben 62
Tomlinson, LIsa 62
Tower of London 86
Trelawny, Second Lieutenant Andrew 33
Turnbull, Private R D 9, 64, 82
Turner, C/Serjeant Taff 105
Turner, Major Ewen 62
Turner, Tina 54
Tyacke, Major General David 57

UNFICYP 23, 33, 66, 76, 84, 92, 93, 94, 147, 148–9

Vickery, Lance Corporal 40
Victoria, HM Queen 13, 79, 110
Vigus, Corporal 36

Walker, Bugle Major 92
Walters, Lance Corporal 60

Ward, Sandy 144
Waterloo, Battle of 70
Waters, Roger 137
Watt, Serjeant Bill 30, 31
Watts, Mark 131
Weeks, Lieutenant Colonel Tim 40
Weeton Barracks, Blackpool 24, 30, 36, 52, 59–60, 74, 87
Wellington, Duke of 12, 13
Wells, C/Serjeant A 138
Wharton, Corporal Paul 38
Wheatley, JRSM 124
Whitelock, Sergeant A B 9, 55
Whitfield, Corporal 108
Whitmore, Major Graham 89, 89
Wilkinson, Bugle Major S 138
Wilkinson, Corporal Stan 123
Wilkinson, Private S J 9
Wilkinson, WO2 T 138
Willby, Private J J 9
William III, HM King 35
Williams, Captain Gage 30, 131
Williams, Private 88
Williams, Private T N 9
Wilson, Major Tony 53
Wilson, Matt 4
Wilson, Right Reverend John Leonard, Bishop of Birmingham 94
Wing, Captain Gill 87
Winston-Davis, Major Mark 118
Winter, Private J 9
Women's Royal Army Corps, The 106
Wood, Lieutenant Colonel David 67
Woodman, Private 82
Worcester and Sherwood Foresters Regiment 25, 136
Worsley, Lieutenant Colonel Henry 112
Wray, Corporal S 9
Wright, Corporal 180
Wykeham, John 4

York Minster 23
York, Captain Jeremy 145

Acknowledgements

Picture Credits

Every effort has been made to contact the copyright holders of all works reproducedin this book. If any acknowledgements have been omitted, please contact Third Millennium Publishing.

Alamy 18–19T; Matt Baker 111R, 112T and BR; via Matt Baker 142–3; Ben Barry 37Tl and B, 63 others, 64 all, 66T, 157, 158, 159TR and BR; Jonny Bowron 45; Bridgeman pp10–11, 14, 17; Andy Child 24, 53T, 66B, 67, 69BL, 161, 162, 163; Nick Cole 8; 'Coco' Corcoran 58; Courtesy Infantry Battle School 125L, 126–7; Courtesy Julian Platt 20; Courtesy MoD 141; James Cousen 25, 44, 49, 68TL, 164; Variously James Cousen/LI Photographic Archive/Jonny Bowron 47; Crown Copyright 175; Durham Record Office 23, 92, 93, 95; Toby Evans 101TR, 106B, 108, 109; Paul Evanson 55BR; Via WO2 Steve Flavin 9, 12, 39T; Green Light 91BL and BR; Aubrey Hamilton Brisco 177T; Nick Ilić 160; Tim Illingworth 170, 171B; Imperial War Museum 19B, 21B; David Jarratt 57all; Ben Lampard and Colin Oliver 69T; Ben Lampard and Colin Oliver 70 all, 169, 171T, 172–3; LI Archive, Bodmin (Regimental property) 14–21 (except Alamy 18–19; IWM 19, 21; Topfoto 16, 18), 29, 32 all, 39B, 51 all, 80T, 84, 7; LI Photographic Archive 22, 26–7, 28, 30, 31 all, 33T, C, 37BR, 38 all, 40–1 all, 42–3, 43R, 50 all, 53BL and BR, 54 all, 55T, BL and C, 60T and B, 68R, 72, 74, 75, 76, 77, 78, 79, 80B, 81T, 85, 86BL, 87, 88 all, 91T, 96, 97, 98, 99, 100, 102, 103, 104, 106T, 107, 118B, 119, 120BL and BR, 122, 123, 124, 125R, 128T, 130, 132TL and TR, 133L, 134B, 137, 139, 140, 144, 145, 146, 150B, 152, 154, 155, 156, 166, 167, 174BL, 176; LI Photographic Archive ©the artist's estate 56; LI Photographic Archive/Tim Illingworth 69BR; LI Regimental property ©David Rowlands 48; Light Infantry Archive from *The Story of the Bugle Horn* (Regimental Property) 13; Mark Mortimer 65; Janice Murray via Ted Shields 168; Rupert Nicholas 131; Mark O'Hanlon 149; Bryn Parry 4; Dean Portman 63T; Private collection 147; Richard Reed 37TR; RHQ The Rifles 174T, 175T, 177BL and BR; The Rifles Exeter Office (ex RHQ DDLI) 113–5; Richard Sale 81C, BL and BR, 86TL and BR, 90 all; RichardSale/Dave Jarratt/LI Photographic Archive 134; Ian Sawers 52; Ian Sawers/LI Archive, Bodmin (Regimental property) 73; Brian Sheridan 33L, B and R, 36 all, 153; Ted Shields 43T; via Ted Shields 82; *The Silver Bugle* 38BR, 83, 89 all, 129T, 136; Andy Solars 9, 12; Mike Thornton 120T, 121; via Mike Thornton 150T; Topfoto 16T, 18B, 132B; Dawn Turner 134T; Ewen Turner 62; The Wardrobe, Rifles Office, Salisbury 110, 111T; Jake White 2, 118T; Matthew Wilson 71; Mark Winston Davis 116–7; P J Wykeham 133R

'Second to None': A Portrait of The LIght Infantry 1968–2007
2011 © Authors and Third Millennium Publishing LImited

First published in 2011 by Third Millennium Publishing LImited, a subsidiary of Third Millennium Information LImited.

2–5 Benjamin Street
London
United Kingdom
EC1M 5QL
www.tmiltd.com

ISBN 978 1 906507 41 1

All rights reserved. No part of this publication may be reproduced ortransmitted in any form or by any means, electronic or mechanical, including photocopying, recording, or any storage or retrieval system, without permission in writing from the publisher.

British Library Cataloguing in Publication Data
A CIP catalogue record for this book is available from the British LIbrary.

General Editor Colonel Mark Goldsack
Design Matthew Wilson
Production Bonnie Murray
Reprographics Studio Fasoli, Verona, Italy
Printed by Gorenjski Tisk, Slovenia

On Ilkla Mooar baht 'at

Wheear 'ast tha bin sin' ah saw thee, ah saw thee?

On Ilkla Mooar baht 'at

Wheear 'ast tha bin sin' ah saw thee, ah saw thee?

Wheear 'ast tha bin sin' ah saw thee?
  On Ilkla Mooar baht 'at
  On Ilkla Mooar baht 'at
  On Ilkla Mooar baht 'at

Tha's been a cooartin' Mary Jane

Tha's bahn' to catch thy deeath o` cowd

Then us'll ha' to bury thee

Then t'worms'll come an` eyt thee up

Then t'ducks'll come an` eyt up t'worms

Then us'll go an` eyt up t'ducks

Then us'll all ha' etten thee

That's wheear we get us ooan back

The Farmers Boy

The sun had set beyond yon hill,
Across the dreary moor,
When weary and lame, a boy there came,
Up to the farmer's door,
"Can you tell me whe'ere I be,
And one that will me employ,"

To plough and sow, to reap and mow,
And be a farmer's boy,
And be a farmer's boy?

The farmer's wife cried "Try the lad,
Let him no longer seek".
"Yes Father do" the Daughter cried,
While the tears rolled down her cheek:
"For those who would work, 'tis hard to want
And wander for employ".

Don't let him go, but let him stay,
And be a farmer's boy,
And be a farmer's boy?

The Farmer's Boy grew up a man,
And the good old couple died,
They left the lad the farm they had,
And the daughter for his bride;
Now the lad that was, the farm now has,
Oft he thinks and smiles with joy.

Oh, happy day he came that way,
To be a Farmer's Boy,
To be a Farmer's Boy.

Blaydon Races

Aw went to Blaydon Races, 'twas on the ninth of Joon,
Eiteen hundred an' sixty-two, on a summer's efternoon;
Aw tyuk the 'bus frae Balmbra's, an' she wis heavy laden,
Away we went alang Collingwood Street, that's on the road to Blaydon.

Ah me lads, ye shud only seen us gannin',
We pass'd the foaks upon the road just as they wor stannin';
Thor wes lots o' lads an' lasses there, all wi' smiling faces,
Gawn alang the Scotswood Road, to see the Blaydon Races.

We flew past Airmstrang's factory, and up to the "Robin Adair",
Just gannin' doon te the railway bridge, the 'bus wheel flew off there.
The lasses lost their crinolines off, an' the veils that hide their faces,
An' aw got two black eyes an' a broken nose in gan te Blaydon Races.

(chorus)

When we gat the wheel put on away we went agyen,
But them that had their noses broke they cam back ower hyem;
Sum went to the Dispensary an' uthers to Doctor Gibbs,
An' sum sought out the Infirmary to mend their broken ribs.

(chorus)

Noo when we gat to Paradise thor wes bonny gam begun;
Thor was fower-an-twenty on the 'bus, man, hoo they danced an' sung;
They called on me to sing a sang, aw sung them "Paddy Fagan",
Aw danced a jig an' swung my twig that day aw went to Blaydon.

(chorus)

We flew across the Chain Bridge reet into Blaydon toon,
The bellman he was callin' there, they call him Jackie Broon;
Aw saw him talkin' to sum cheps, an' them he was pursuadin'
To gan an' see Geordy Ridley's concert in the Mechanics' Hall at Blaydon.

(chorus)

The rain it poor'd aw the day an' myed the groons quite muddy,
Coffy Johnny had a white hat on - they war shootin' "Whe stole the cuddy."
There wes spice stalls an' munkey shows an' aud wives selling ciders,
An' a chep wiv a hapenny roond aboot, shootin' "Noo, me lads, for riders."

(chorus)